McGRAW-HILL SERIES IN POLITICAL SCIENCE

Joseph P. Harris, CONSULTING EDITOR

A Short History of
International Organization

McGraw-Hill Series in Political Science

JOSEPH P. HARRIS, *Consulting Editor*

BONE · American Politics and the Party System

CHASE · The United Nations in Action

FERGUSON AND McHENRY · The American Federal Government

FERGUSON AND McHENRY · The American System of Government

FERGUSON AND McHENRY · Elements of American Government

FIELD · Governments in Modern Society

FRANK · Cases on the Constitution

GOSNELL, LANCASTER, AND RANKIN · Fundamentals of American National Government

GROSS · The Legislative Struggle

HARTMANN · Basic Documents of International Relations

HARTMANN · Readings in International Relations

HOLLOWAY · State and Local Government in the United States

LEONARD · Elements of American Foreign Policy

LEONARD · International Organization

MANGONE · A Short History of International Organization

MILLETT · Management in the Public Service

NEUMANN · European and Comparative Government

REED · Municipal Management

RIEMER · Problems of American Government

STRAUSZ-HUPÉ AND POSSONY · International Relations

TURNER · Politics in the United States: Readings in Political Parties and Pressure Groups

VANDENBOSCH AND HOGAN · The United Nations—Background, Organization, Functions, Activities

WALDO · Ideas and Issues in Public Administration: A Book of Readings

WILSON · The American Political Mind

WILSON · Police Administration

A Short History of

International Organization

GERARD J. MANGONE

Associate Professor of Political Science

Swarthmore College

McGraw-Hill Book Company, Inc.

NEW YORK   TORONTO   LONDON

1954

A SHORT HISTORY OF
INTERNATIONAL ORGANIZATION

Preface

Change is both a blessing and a curse. In a world of tempest and sweeping change any book on international affairs must lack the latest treaty, the latest government declaration, or the latest plan for an international organization. But what really counts, I think, is that the student of world politics appreciates the direction of change and the courses of decision which have been opened for our generation by the long pull of history.

This book, therefore, does not try to be a seed catalogue of international organizations, copying in dull detail every charter, meeting, or diplomatic delegation, for such a work would obscure the true objective of the study of international law and organization by mistaking events for movement, by emphasizing items rather than composition. I have, instead, attempted to portray the development of international organization along constitutional lines with attention to procedure and law, hoping to indicate a potential, though by no means inevitable, growth toward world order.

Important as the UN may be, for example, it is here regarded as a part of a more vital process which has been going on for centuries. Therefore, the Concert of Europe, the League of Nations, the international administrative agencies of the nineteenth and twentieth centuries, and the regional international organizations share the space of the text so as to impart a sense of the real achievements as well as the frustrations of international society. To secure peace under international law, we ought to know in which directions international organization can move; I sincerely hope that this short history will contribute to that understanding.

To my good friends who have generously given their comradeship during the very lonely, painful days of writing, I wish to express my heartfelt thanks.

GERARD J. MANGONE

THIS BOOK IS DEDICATED TO

The earnest men and women of the United Nations, the specialized agencies, and other international organizations, who are helping statesmen develop international law so that the peoples of the world, of all tongues, creeds, and colors, may find cooperation the key to fortune, dignity, and peace with justice.

Contents

Foreword

Why is it that, when Humpty-Dumpty fell from the wall, all the king's
horses and all the king's men could not put him together again? Did they
lack glue? Or the patience to gather the fragments and fit the ragged
edges together? How ridiculous it must seem to the Perfect Brain that a
single species called man inhabiting a single planet called earth shatters
his world with a political mallet and recklessly drives the national pieces
hither and yon. Yet this species called man has occasionally demonstrated
good sense and sometimes a brilliant imagination.

Although the issues of international organization are today clouded
under the glowering power struggle between the United States of America
and the Union of Soviet Socialist Republics, the need for peacefully ac-
commodating threescore and ten governments to the harried resources of
the earth remains obvious. Cooperation among them is imperative to fulfill their own needs peacefully; the institution of agencies, well conceived
and well managed, whether to facilitate the delivery of the mails or the
arbitration of backbiting controversies, steps up the pace toward civilization. Sad it is to enumerate the failures of many international organizations, some the wishful thinking of idealists, some aborted for want of
proper nutrition, and some sabotaged by misplaced national ambitions.
But why confine ourselves to failures when real achievement is written
so large upon the annals of history?

When one plunges into the study of international relations he is apt
to emerge quite soaked with ideas of universal peace. He may even pick
up some plans for freeing world trade or integrating social services or, indeed, a striking blueprint for the political unification of the nation-states
which now occupy the surface of the globe. But somehow, always, the
barnacles of "sovereignty" (maligned word!) weigh down his thoughts,
and he begins to see through the cloud of his own naïveté that international
organization must be a patient, painful, perilous task.

International organization has a history distinguished by the trials, errors, and achievements of men in their perseverance toward a new world
order. At a time when deep and awesome shifts of power are shaking the

1

crust of world politics, the lessons of the past and the issues of the present for international law and organization need careful study. All governments, supported by their earnest citizens, day after day are making vital decisions upon their participation in, cooperation with, and contribution to international agencies. Errors cannot easily be redeemed, and the world is too poor, too excited to permit delays. Now is the time to profit by history and advance the clock to a new hour of international cooperation and peace.

STATES AND SOVEREIGNTY

Any study of international politics and organization has to begin with the states of the world. Who are they? How are they? When are they willing to do what? The United States of America sends some fifty-eight ambassadors and twenty-five ministers abroad to represent its national interests. Seventy-six states from Afghanistan to Yugoslavia are members of the International Telecommunication Union. Sixty states belong to the United Nations. This curious arrangement of the world into a large number of independent parts is a relatively new phenomenon of civilization. Religions, economies, languages, and historical associations have been split by the formation of modern nation-states during the past four centuries; today this social unit is the key to international politics and international organization. Although every improvement in man's technique of living—in communications, transportation, and production—strives to knock down boundaries, the division of the world into national compartments vigorously continues. Only within the last fifty years, Albania, Bulgaria, Burma, Ceylon, China, Cuba, Czechoslovakia, Egypt, India, Indonesia, Iran, Iraq, Ireland, Israel, Jordan, Lebanon, Libya, Norway, Pakistan, Panama, the Philippines, Poland, Saudi Arabia, and Syria have appeared or reappeared as independent states.

The disparities in size, population, and resources among the many states of the world affect the power which any one of them can exercise in imposing its designs—peaceful or warlike—upon the society of nations. Vatican City, which is master over its territory, occupies only 109 acres of land, while the Soviet Union extends across one-sixth of the earth's 51,271,000 square miles. Continental Australia has fewer inhabitants than tiny Belgium. With a mere 7 per cent of the world's population, the United States makes use of almost twice as much oil and rubber as all the other states on the globe combined; it consumes as much iron, zinc, copper, and lead as the entire 2 billion people who live outside its borders [1]. *

* The notes to which bracketed numbers refer will be found at the end of each chapter.

Another important aspect of the modern state system is the idea of sovereignty. In the words of Jean Bodin, famous sixteenth-century French lawyer, sovereignty is "the supreme power, not bound by laws, over citizens and subjects," and he is sovereign "who, after God, acknowledges no one greater than himself [2]." The complicated contractual relationships of the medieval age and the overlapping of the Christian commonwealth with the local political orders are left behind. It is sovereignty in the Western tradition which marks off the state from all other corporate bodies, for the state, unlike churches, universities, guilds, unions, or various clubs, acts as a final authority for all persons living within its territory. Centuries ago the European national dynasties denied their subordination to either the universal Church or the Holy Roman Emperor, and states have since insisted upon their absolute legal independence. As the Eastern peoples came under the political sway of the West they found in the European idea of nationalism a rationale for their claim to independent governments and sovereignty.

Contemporary governments under the management of popular bodies have exploited this dogma of sovereignty to its last full measure of usefulness. While the idea has often served liberal independence movements with distinction, its excessive form of impassioned nationalism has time and again choked sensible plans for international cooperation. Even in such a seemingly minor matter as hoisting a United Nations flag above a national standard, puffed-up pride in sovereignty forbids the rite. And where more momentous issues of international organization are involved, the largest and the smallest state can take equal umbrage in the supposed sanctity of sovereignty as they flout their responsibilities to the community.

The eighteenth-century Swiss diplomat, Emmerich de Vattel, publicized the idea that the nations of the world, not having established a civil society, lived in a state of nature and were, therefore, free and equal. "A dwarf," he wrote, "is as much a man as a giant; a small republic is no less a sovereign state than the most powerful kingdom [3]." The modern nation-state system has studiously maintained the legal independence of its members and specifically exempted from international organization a very wide range of activities which come under "domestic jurisdiction." Equality for states, however, has not only meant equal *access* to the law but has served as a claim to *judge* the law—even when the state itself is involved in the controversy. To remove this claim is one of the major tasks of international organization.

Lawyers have spilled much ink on the question of sovereignty and its compatibility with a system of international law which states *seem* to obey. Perhaps it will be enough at this point to say that although governments firmly maintain the doctrine of sovereignty, by custom and by treaty arrangement they have often abided by rules which they themselves did not make. The development of international organization in the nineteenth and twentieth centuries, moreover, has slowly modified the doctrine of the equality of states, a corollary of sovereignty [4]. Most international organizations have now accepted the principle of qualified or majority voting where formerly the rule of unanimity prevailed; a few, like the International Bank for Reconstruction and Development, have found a formula for weighted voting which reflects the monetary contribution of the member state. Although Article 2 of the United Nations Charter stridently announces that the UN is based upon the principle of "the sovereign equality of all its members," it has painstakingly elaborated the prerogatives of five nations and, indeed, granted them a veto power hitherto unknown to international organizations.

Partly because every institution from the International Telecommunication Union to the UN is voluntary and partly because states vary considerably in their power, the whole development of international organization necessarily proceeds with catlike tread upon a most slippery surface. Perhaps nothing can indicate the true course of international organization better than the subtle encroachments recently made upon the hallowed ground of state sovereignty. To watch the emerging international institutions and their effect upon international legal patterns should be one of the most profitable occupations of the student of world affairs. Only a stickler for protocol would argue that any state of today's constellation, whether a member of an international organization or not, is independent, for the life of a nation overflows its frontiers, but every state worthy of the name is independent in some way and may embarrass or frustrate the best-laid plans for international cooperation.

THE DYNAMISM OF INTERNATIONAL SOCIETY

The most vexing problem of international organization is to accommodate the rivalries of nation-states [5] within a legal procedure, a task made doubly difficult by the inherent dynamism of international society. Consider for a moment the strain placed upon international rules by the rapid, shifting power relationships of states. At the end of the First World War, for instance, Austria-Hungary, pivot of central European politics for centuries, simply disappeared as a great state. As the mighty British Empire of the nineteenth century has gone down the ladder of influence, the callow United States of America has gone up. Regardless of ideology, the intensive mobilization of national resources by the Soviet Union in two decades has jarred all the scales of international power. Within the brief span of a dozen years Italy, Japan, and Germany, sworn enemies of the democracies, were vanquished, emasculated, and then joined to the West in alliances. Diplomats must calculate as never before the weight of India and China in international affairs.

Nothing is static in international politics. Nation-states are unruly. Populations expand, new resources are discovered, and technologies improve. The nub of the problem for international organization is how to accommodate these continuous changes within the community to a system of law. Between 1860 and 1910, to take one historical example, the French population increased by a mere 3 million while the German population was registering a phenomenal gain of 26 million. International politics quickly felt the pressure of German diplomacy. When Great Britain shifted from coal to oil for fuel to move its Navy during the First World War, it signaled the vital importance of the Persian Gulf region for future world politics. Just within the last decade, Russia has climbed from seventh to third place in surface naval power [6]. It is virtually impossible to measure accurately the recent discoveries or improvements in bombs, missiles, or other destructive techniques on the scale of power, but these are additional dynamic factors which keep international politics in a constant state of flux.

Meanwhile, the inspiration or corruption of morale within nations also goes on, making new prints of the power picture. Peoples have been splendidly stirred to action by fresh leaders or a fervent doctrine [7]. The stiffening of the British backbone by the bold address of Winston Churchill during the Second World War has become a classic illustration of the power of morale. Hundreds of times, in the past and present, zealots have rallied the poor and the weak to the blazing standard of national unity and independence, continually demonstrating the latent and unpredictable power of group emotion. Just as often, a country may be sapped by cynicism and despair. Whether inspired or depressed, the state must have its power position reevaluated—and again there may be troublesome demands to be met or dangerous vacuums to be filled by international diplomacy.

The dramatic rise and fall of states strains the ethics, customs, and treaties which may prescribe the best norms for international society. By 1870, for instance, not only had Russia recovered from her defeat in the Crimean War, but France, a victor, was now herself gnashed by Germany. Russia coldly denounced [8] the treaty stipulations (neutralization of the Black Sea) forced upon her in 1856. One could also cite the Hague conventions of 1899 and 1907 on warfare so carefully drawn as standards of international law by the assembled states. At the opening of the First World War, however, they were already out of date in respect to airplane bombing. Every schoolboy knows that the "scrap of paper" neutralizing Belgium did not bar Germany from her best approach to her enemy France in 1914. Despite the Covenant, Japan fortified the islands placed under her mandate by the League of Nations. When an act of the United States Congress in 1912 exempted American coastwise shipping from paying tolls in the Panama Canal, it violated the Hay-Pauncefote Treaty with Britain. Walter Hines Page, Wilson's ambassador in London, wrote, "We made a bargain—a solemn compact—and we have broken it [9]." Only Wilson's personal plea before Congress for honorable conduct brought repeal of the Act by a nation newly awakened to its role as a world power. Young nations, too, supposedly free from the taint of imperialism, have shown a lack of regard for legal principles when they grow strong enough to enforce their national interests. The Republic of Indonesia found the federal form of government, to which it had agreed as a condition of independence from the Dutch on 2 November 1949, rather "unwieldy [10]." Within a year the nationalists had changed Indonesia into a unitary state. India accepted British legislation granting her independence and providing that the princely states could opt for either India or Pakistan, but in September 1948 compelled Hyderabad at gun point to join the state of India. In 1951 Iran made a blind grab for British properties and seemed to shriek as loudly as any other state of the past that the national interest condoned all arbitrary conduct.

International organization cannot escape such elements of power and such tempers as nations have traditionally displayed. Without an appreciation of the international environment, sentimental students of world affairs can become the prisoners of their own ideals. Too often men have blissfully closed their eyes to the dirty aspects of politics only to be startled, if not frightened, by the apparent incorrigibility of society. In the field of international politics sheer disaster may be concordant with such egregious folly.

To hold the springs of national power within the paper box of international organization requires the utmost delicacy; to train peoples and governments to a sense of world responsibility when their economy or pride is bursting at the seams calls for bravery. Yet no other attitude will suffice to bring the nations of the world into cooperative endeavors, and the wonder remains that so much has been accomplished by international organization under such trying conditions. On all levels of political organization man is relentlessly faced with the crude dilemma of an intrinsically dynamic society to be hemmed in by the spindling fences of the law. International society, however, compounds its own problems, for it still tolerates the use of force by its individual members, the states.

NATIONAL VERSUS INTERNATIONAL LAW ENFORCEMENT

Normally the government of a nation-state monopolizes the force of the community and sternly prevents any violence among the conflicting groups of its society [11]. But international society clearly lacks such order; indeed, it has long recognized extended violence, or war, as a legitimate end of the state for welfare and security. International organization was compelled to begin in the shadow of this acknowledgment, keep itself within the short perimeter of peaceful cooperation, and avoid any direct challenge to the traditional war powers of nations. The Hague Peace Conferences of the early twentieth century tried to regulate the *practices* of international war; the League of Nations from 1920 on sought to regulate *international war itself*. During the Second World War the United Nations, under the benign guardianship of the five Great Powers, was designed to *eliminate all aggressive wars*. Although the success of each of these three endeavors to block the arbitrary practice of violence by nations against each other may be sincerely questioned, the objective of international organization in this respect remains clear.

Another drawback of international agencies compared to the nation-state comes from their incapacity to reach the individual. Even in federal states the national government may tax, apprehend, or punish the individual citizen without the intercession of a local or regional government. But an international organization has no claim upon the citizens of a nation-state; it cannot levy taxes upon individuals or seize, try, or punish them for violations of international law. On the other hand, it is only fair to say that these conditions do not keep the government of a state from effectively discharging its international obligations. For example, although states have frequently opposed an increased rate of contributions fixed for them by an international organization, they have dutifully taxed their citizens for the extra expense. Someone caught in international-copyright poaching, submarine-cable cutting, abusing a foreign diplomat, or disobeying the international law of the high seas will ordinarily not escape condign punishment by his own government.

International organization has not tried to touch individual citizens directly, for such an invasion of state sovereignty is premature. Rather have new treaties and conventions among states attempted to pin down the responsibilities of governments toward individuals under their jurisdiction. For instance, the International Labor Organization may require a working-hour rule to be considered by a national parliament for its citizens although the delegation of the state concerned may have voted against the proposal. In 1951, an international convention prohibiting acts of government which destroy a religious, racial, or ethnic group (geno-cide) went into effect. On 7 December 1948, moreover, the General Assembly of the UN adopted the Universal Declaration of Human Rights, enunciating what it deemed the basic rights of men against government everywhere. Only intended as a forceful statement of what national laws ought to provide, the declaration has been followed by a draft covenant on human rights which would bind states to a recognition of such rights as free speech, equal access to the law, security of person, and freedom of movement for persons under their jurisdiction. Were such a convention ratified, however, the following words written by a scholar of human rights would be quite correct:

The person derives his rights from international law; the state rests under international obligations. The international community may provide procedures to protect those rights and to enforce those obligations, yet no human rights relationship between the individual and the international community arises. It remains in all cases the state and the individual who together form the two parties to the relationship [12].

In sum, international organization must first labor in the direction of trapping the arbitrary, warmaking power of sovereign states; second, it must impress national governments with international obligations which will control individuals under their jurisdiction. To be sure, this is a circuitous route toward a specific legal goal. Yet we must live with the world as it is in order to make it what we would like. A true cognizance of the power rivalries among states and the aims of international organization is indispensable to the construction of peace.

No issue can be taken here with those who point out that international organization cannot succeed in duplicating the law and order of the nation-state; little fire is kindled by admitting that only a world government can give the kind of security guaranteed by a single sovereign. But the rub of the question arises from the obvious unwillingness of the nation-states, small or large, to yield the ultimate control of their armed forces to any single authority. They have a very just suspicion that the premium for insurance against international warfare may require a sacrifice of too many other national values. After all, security is but one need of the individual or the state. Absolute security can be a prison entombing creativity, repressing enterprise, and closing out all the adventure which makes life zestful. Before citizens transfer their allegiance to a world state they have a right to know how and what it will command. In the meantime, nations will take their chances upon international war.

International organizations as they are presently constituted must take these basic propositions into account. It would be foolish to overestimate their power, but it scarcely serves the hope of mankind to deprecate their achievements. The follower of the hard-boiled school of politics who is completely "realistic" about power misses the truth just as badly as the idealist who constructs the new world solely by reference to the figments of his mind. It should never be forgotten that the agencies which tie the states of the world to common enterprises are attempting to create a climate of opinion rather than dictation, a climate of cooperation rather than coercion.

THE PROMISE OF INTERNATIONAL ORGANIZATION

So many agreements have been made among states that international transactions generally go without a hitch and without special comment. Trains chug across borders, ships land foreign cargoes, and mails fly around the world—while dollars, pounds, francs, kroner, rupees, pesos, and yen trickle into banks over the globe. By international regulations men and women of different continents are protected against unsafe air navigation, exorbitant narcotic trade, patent and copyright pirates, and noxious labor standards. The United States participates in no less than sixty international agencies [13]. In the political arena, the most powerful states of the world are joined in daily discussions on the salient issues of war and peace. All this has been made possible by a long series of international conferences stretching back for hundreds of years, sometimes precipitated by the vision of wise men and only successful when animated by a spirit of cooperation.

The history of international organization, nevertheless, is virtually an infant compared to the long, gnarled development of the nation-state. All governments need their myths and techniques, their ideas and institutions which realize the desires of a society. The modern state has been fired by the idea of nationalism and maintained by the old institutions of kings, councils, and courts which have reinforced the national traditions. By contrast, the "government" of states toddles along with inchoate ideals and rudimentary institutions. Clearly a single faith in world society has not yet coalesced; the vines of international organization are rooted in very shallow soil.

History shows that states have been hammered into one piece. A peaceful amalgamation of villages, cities, and provinces has been exceedingly rare. Only after the state had been made secure against both internal and external upset did those freedoms appear which mark off the constitutional polity from tyranny. Is one justified, therefore, in expecting international organizations to grow in peaceful, evolutionary fashion until the government of the world becomes a reality? Parallels with the organic process of nature may lead into pitfalls of illogic. Furthermore, it is hardly necessary at this instant of history for international organization to emulate the integration of the nation-state. Instead, a sincere concentration of statesmen and students upon the urgent demands of the greatest community—the halt of international aggression and the promotion of human welfare—will at least further the bonds of sympathy among states and encourage the growth of international lawmaking, law-judging, and law-enforcing institutions.

Without wearing rose-colored glasses, the observer of international affairs can discern in the history of international organization a fascinating trend in world society. In number and in function, international organizations have rapidly multiplied during the last century. International law, first, looks more and more toward treaty agreements rather than toward foggy custom. But many treaties are now prompted by the discussions and the resolutions of international organizations which, in this sense, crystallize opinion and provide a foundation for international compacts. Precision and flexibility, two sound characteristics of legislation, are thus entering the door of the international lawmaking process. It can also be shown that member states have allowed to international organizations more and more power for making rules to which the states do not directly consent but regularly obey. Such obligations, while not under the rubric of international law, do contribute to a more articulate legal community. Second, although the national courts in their hearings of international cases have generally been fair, constant pressure is exerted today upon states to bring their legal issues to an international tribunal and their political issues to an international council. By no means has the practice become universal, but the direction in which states ought to proceed has been marked, institutions are available, and the history of international organization has drawn a logical pattern for the future. Finally, there is the practice of delegating special tasks and special responsibilities to standing councils of international organizations. Except in rare cases, such councils do not pretend to use physical coercion to enforce the principles or resolutions of the international organization. But they can galvanize world opinion against the arbitrary actions of states in a way hitherto impossible. It is much too early to draw conclusions, but there is the possibility that such councils may be gradually empowered with sanctions—diplomatic, economic, or military—against lawbreakers.

The limited achievements of international organization may be disappointing to some. With a wry smile of cynicism they may turn to more abrupt ways of attaining world order and world peace. At least an investigation of the history of international organization may put into perspective the long struggle to formulate basic rules of international conduct and the enormous difficulty of constructing effective international agencies. To realize our debt to the past and our obligation to the future is the surest way of understanding what needs to be done now.

NOTES

1. The study of political geography is essential to an appreciation of international politics and organization. See G. E. Pearcy and R. H. Fifield, *World Political Geography*, New York, Crowell, 1947; D. Whittlesey, *Environmental Foundations of European History*, New York, Appleton-Century-Crofts, 1949; J. Gottman, *The Geography of Europe*, New York, Holt, 1950; G. B. Cressey, *Asia's Lands and Peoples*, 2d ed., New York, McGraw-Hill, 1951; and H. W. Weigert (ed.), *New Compass of the World*, New York, Macmillan, 1949.

2. J. Bodin, *Six Books of the Republic*, 1576. Of special interest here are J. W. Allen, *Political Thought of the Sixteenth Century*, New York, Dial Press, 1928; H. E. Cohen, *Recent Theories of Sovereignty*, Chicago, University of Chicago Press, 1937; and E. Cassirer, *The Myth of the State*, New Haven, Conn., Yale University Press, 1946.

3. E. Vattel, *Le droit des gens*, 1758, Préliminaires, 18.

4. See H. Weinschel, "Doctrine of Equality of States," *American Journal of International Law*, Vol. 45, No. 3 (July 1951), pp. 417–442. Also H. Kelsen, "The Principle of Sovereign Equality of States as a Basis for International Organization," *Yale Law Review*, Vol. 53 (1943–1944), pp. 207–220.

5. For recent books which broadly demonstrate the struggle for power among nations, see H. Morgenthau, *Politics among Nations*, New York, Knopf, 1948; F. L. Schuman, *International Politics*, 5th ed., New York, McGraw-Hill, 1953; R. Strausz-Hupé and S. Possony, *International Relations*, New York, McGraw-Hill, 1950; and G. Schwarzenberger, *Power Politics*, New York, F. Praeger, 1951. Still valuable is W. Sharp and G. Kirk, *Contemporary International Politics*, New York, Rinehart, 1938.

6. F. Uhlig, Jr., "The Threat of the So-

viet Navy," *Foreign Affairs*, Vol. 30, No. 3 (April 1952), pp. 444–454.

7. For studies in "psychological" power see such works as E. H. Carr, *The Twenty Years Crisis*, New York, Macmillan, 1942, and J. T. MacCurdy, *The Structure of Morale*, New York, Macmillan, 1944, as well as B. Russell, *Power*, New York, Norton, 1938, and B. de Jouvenal, *On Power*, New York, Viking, 1939.

8. The Tsar's Foreign Office announced through its ambassadors in Vienna, London, Paris, and Berlin: "His Imperial Majesty is convinced that Peace and that Balance of Power will receive a fresh Guarantee if they are based upon a more just and solid foundation than one resulting from a situation which no Great Power can accept as a normal condition of its existence."

9. B. J. Hendrick, *The Life and Letters of Walter H. Page*, New York, Doubleday, 1924, 3 vols., Vol. I, p. 249.

10. Republic of Indonesia Information Office, *Seven Years of Independence*, New York, 1952, pp. 17ff.

11. N. J. Spykman, *America's Strategy in World Politics*, New York, Harcourt, Brace, 1942, has good introductory remarks on international society as contrasted with national societies.

12. P. N. Drost, *Human Rights as Legal Rights*, Leiden, A. W. Sijthoff's Uitgeversmij, N.V., 1951, p. 56. *Cf.* A. N. Holcombe, *Human Rights in the Modern World*, New York, New York University Press, 1948; H. Lauterpacht, *International Law and Human Rights*, New York, F. Praeger, 1950; and G. Manner, "The Object Theory of the Individual in International Law," *American Journal of International Law*, Vol. 46, No. 3 (July 1952), pp. 428–429.

13. Compiled from *International Organizations in Which the United States Participates*, U.S. Department of State Publication 3655, February 1950.

CHAPTER 1 *International Organization before Napoleon*

I plundered the city of Shinuhtu, Samirina [Samaria] and the whole land of Bit-Humria [Israel]. I drew the Iamanean [Ionian, Cyprian] from out the sea of the setting sun, like a fish. I deported [the people] of the lands of Kasku, Tabalu and Hilakku. I drove out Mita [Midas], king of the land of Muski. By the city of Rapihu I defeated Egypt. Hanunu [Hanno], king of Gaza, I counted as booty. I subdued seven kings of the land of Ia', a district of the land of Iatnana, whose abodes were situated seven days' journey in the midst of the sea of the setting sun. And Merodach-baladan, king of Chaldea, who dwelt on the shore of the Bitter Sea, who exercised the kingship over Babylon against the will of the gods, my mighty hand conquered. All of his wide land I divided from end to end, totally, and put it under my officials, the governor of Babylon and the governor of the land of Gambulu. The yoke of Assur I imposed [1].

Thus were the exploits of the terrible Sargon of Assyria (724–705 B.C.) chronicled by his royal scribe. International organization for the early kingdoms of the Near East, thriving on the muddy riverbanks of the Tigris, Euphrates, and Nile, was incomprehensible. Almost constantly at war with their neighbors or recalcitrant vassals, the dynasties of Sumer-Akkad, Elam, the Hittites, and Egypt demanded two things from those whom they conquered: humble subservience and regular tribute.

The word "state" or "nation," as used today, can hardly be applied to these ancient kingdoms. Elam, for example, merely comprised several tribes which had settled in the walled towns along the Uknu River in Mesopotamia and had been yoked together by one monarch. The Babylonian Empire held its sway over subject peoples only by repeated conquests. In the Egypt of Thutmose III (1500 B.C.), homage to the Pharaoh's gods and annual tribute to the tax collector could not be escaped by client provinces, but the local populace retained its own laws, dynasties, and frontiers [2]. In such an unsettled world under the iron rule of force, international agencies could not exist. Indeed, the refinement of imperial administration was a major interest of the rulers of Egypt, Persia, and Rome. To drain the wealth of the subjugated provinces adequately and to quell the sporadic revolts against imperial authority required a decentralized government by satraps or proconsuls appointed by the court and speedy communications through an official postal system. The Persian king, for instance, either personally visited or sent magistrates to all parts of his realm to inspect the local administrations. He particularly checked on the encouragement of agriculture. The Roman governor of Bithynia, Pliny the Younger, raised with the Emperor Trajan in his correspondence such problems as the need for new public baths, adequate fire protection, corruption in aqueduct contracts, and the law to be applied against Christians [3]. For their security and foreign trade, however, the ancient capitals depended upon strict military alliances with friendly princes and the swift destruction of all potential enemies. Nowhere was a permanent international agency among such empires established.

The experience of the Yellow River Valley was the same. Chinese history dawned upon petty, warring states, feudal in character, until the Ch'in and Han Dynasties (221 B.C.–A.D. 220) united them into a mighty empire of 12,233,062 households of 59,594,978 individuals. Here, too, the most important task for the ruler was the effective administration of such enormous territories in an age of primitive communication. Excluding the military commands, the chancellor of the Empire at the height of the Hans' power required more than 300 aides and a clerical staff of 282 men; the imperial secretary, who checked on the conduct of the bureaucracy itself, employed over 500 assistants. Through a court conference domestic and foreign policy was discussed and recommended, by majority vote, to the Emperor—including the making of peace or war [4]—but the notion of international organization with the kingdoms which pressed upon the northern and western borders never fitted into the ancient political patterns.

SEEDS OF INTERNATIONAL ORGANIZATION

The practices of the ancient world, though lacking international organization in the modern sense, indicate some of the relationships among peoples which eventually called for international conferences and international regulation. Ancient Egypt imposed a tariff upon imports from foreign states while conceding to aliens the right to work and even acquire property without molestation. The sovereigns of Babylon and Assyria sometimes asked for redress of wrongs suffered by one of their subjects while traveling through the land of the Pharaohs. The Arthasastras, an-

cient writings of India, mention the right of trading with foreign countries and the privileges to be accorded to alien commerce as well as the
general hospitality to be offered to ships in distress. The immunity of
diplomats from arrest and violence was clearly recognized, and an elaborate chivalric code regulated warfare among the Aryan peoples [5]. Such
practices were rather regularly observed in the eastern Mediterranean
world, especially among the Greek peoples.

But one must turn to the treaty or contract between two rulers for an
enduring record of interstate practices. The treaties of the past are the
first steps toward international organization.

The idea of a contract between individuals and between states is one of
the oldest ideas of human history. It is an important basis for both civil
and international law. Tablets recording the sale of private property
date back to the third millennium before Christ. According to the famous
clay cone of Entemena (2850 B.C.), a treaty between the cities of Lagash
and Umma in Sumeria had, through arbitration, amicably fixed an "international" boundary line. An elaborate peace treaty (1280 B.C.) between
Rameses II of Egypt and Hattusili, King of the Hittites, has a typical
diplomatic preamble and provides for the renewal of peaceful relations,
mutual guarantees against invasion, and the extradition of fugitives [6].

Although the Greek people were politically divided into city-states, the
homogeneity of their religion and culture encouraged a multiplication of
interstate agreements beyond all other ancient experience. Well over 200
inter-Aegean treaties have been reckoned prior to 338 B.C. Frequent warfare among the Greek cities called for numerous articles of peace, but
these terms often went further than the settlement of current claims by
providing for arbitral tribunals composed of both the litigants and a neutral to smooth out any new frictions arising between the signatory states.
In both the One Year Armistice (423 B.C.) and the Peace of Nicias (421
B.C.), the Athenians and Spartans agreed in the event of future disputes
to "have recourse to law . . . as may be agreed upon between the parties."
Not only were treaties of alliance abundant in Greece, but several pacts
included an exchange of citizenship and reciprocal trading privileges
for the contracting parties [7].

International organization is hardly compatible with rampant imperialism by one state which seeks hegemony over the world. A prerequisite
for international organization is the mere existence of several states which
can treat with each other on equal terms. Theoretically, Rome recognized
three types of treaties with other peoples: one with equals; one with subordinates, but not vassals; and one with prostrate states. The early treaties
with Carthage, as an instance of the first type, pledged Rome not to sail

beyond a certain promontory of the North African shore while extending reciprocal trading privileges and a military alliance. At the other extreme, the treaty between Rome and Aetolia in 189 B.C. forced the Aetolians "to maintain the empire and majesty of the people of Rome" through money payments, military support, and the guarantee of hostages [8]. After the destruction of Carthage (146 B.C.) and the defeat of Mithradates, King of Pontus, by Pompey (62 B.C.), the total subjection of the Mediterranean world to Rome contradicted any idea of international organization.

In the infancy of the Tiber River republic, a court of recuperators had sometimes been established by treaty to adjudicate private commercial disputes between the citizens of Rome and foreigners. With two or three judges representing each of the states involved and a single third party, the court acted as a kind of international tribunal for private controversies, but Rome herself never recognized interstate arbitration except in those cases where Rome played the part of mediator or referee in the disputes of other states [9]. Other ancient customs such as the immunity of envoys from violence, privileges granted to aliens, asylum, and arbitration were adapted to the preeminent political position of the Empire. The most significant contribution of Rome for the future of international organization was the court for foreigners. A praetor who administered law in cases involving an alien (*i.e.*, non-Roman citizen) resided in Rome and traveled throughout the provinces, endeavoring to do justice to men with different principles and backgrounds by drawing together the strands of law which seemed "common" to all peoples. Thus a variety of international standards and practices was assimilated into the main stream of Roman jurisprudence under the title of *jus gentium,* and this heritage of a common law of nations remained with Europe after the community had broken up into separate political entities.

After the collapse of Roman authority in the West, the history of the Mediterranean-European world is a mixture of rising tribal kingdoms and the spread of two great world religions. In the ninth century, four powers dominate the scene: the Franks, the Byzantines, the Abbasid Empire with its capital in Baghdad, and the Umayyads in Spain. While the Byzantines held off the encroachments of the Abbasid caliphate upon the eastern Roman domain, the Franks contained the Umayyad Moslems on the Iberian Peninsula. Diplomatic relations between Harun al-Rashid and Charlemagne were maintained, primarily with the idea of alliance against Byzantines and Umayyads, but such an unsettled world with its anxious struggles for life and death, with the sharp-sword zeal of the Arabs urging a universal Islam [10], left little for the development of international organization. The most international institution just emerging into a role

which would place its emissaries in every Christian capital, call great
international councils, and truly transcend political sovereignties was the
Roman Catholic Church.

In the Orient, the future of international organization was even less
promising. The great Mongol Empire fashioned by Genghis Khan in the
thirteenth century reached from the Yellow Sea to the Black Sea. Its amazing expansion was based upon ruthless terror, which broke all will to
resist, and a swift communications system. At the very time when the
feudal West was looking back nostalgically to Pax Romana, the East ex-
perienced Pax Tatarica. Trade flourished between the Italian communes
and the Mongol provinces which linked the Far East and Europe. Merchants were granted trading privileges and safe-conduct passes by the
ruling Khans. The immunities of ambassadors, the sacredness of religious
places, and the trading rights of aliens were often acknowledged as they
had been in the Mediterranean empires, but the only "international" institution was the great imperial council of the vassals of the Khan called together on rare occasions [11]. By the end of the fourteenth century, however, the disintegration of the Mongol Empire closed the possibility of
more stable international relations with the West.

The ninth-century consolidation of Charlemagne's empire, the constant
threading of Europe by Christianity, and the steady settlement of the wan-
dering tribes from the north and east on the riverbanks and in the fertile
valleys of Europe gradually gave rise to a group of peoples with a common faith and a shared tradition—although politically fragmented. Instead of regarding neighboring kingdoms as naturally hostile, fit only to
conquer or resist by force, medieval Europe, through Christianity and the
feudal hierarchy under the revived Roman Empire in 962, began to find
a rude but basic association which over the course of centuries prepared
the way for modern international organization. From the eleventh century onward, there was a steady increase in the number of written treaties,
not only those bringing war to a close but also conventions providing for
truce, mediation, extradition, marriages, exchanges, or sales of dominions, commerce, and leagues of alliance. The practice of extradition, for
example, is illustrated in the treaty between William of Scotland and
Henry II of England in 1174 as they agreed to the trial, or rendition for
trial, of felons who had fled across the state boundaries. The Treaty of
Paris (1303) between Philip IV of France and Edward I of England, in
which each pledged not to protect any outlaw fleeing from the realm of
the other, is also a modern extradition treaty [12]. From the twelfth century onward, moreover, a sense of public international opinion and responsibility among the ruling Christian princes was slowly fostered by
various arbitrations and declarations. In 1176, for example, the ambassa-

dors of Navarre and Aragon were sent to neutral Henry II of England to receive judgment in a dispute between the two kingdoms, and both parties deposited four castles as surety that they would abide by the judgment. In the controversy between the Roman Emperor Frederick II and the Pope, long arguments for the cause of each were sent to all the chiefs of Christendom. In 1356, Edward III of England addressed notes to the Pope, the Emperor, "and all the princes, lords, and people of Christendom" which set forth the villainy of John of France and justified Edward's course of action—the declaration of war.

Especially in Renaissance Italy, living in the memory of the endless international relations of Rome and united by a common Christian faith, did international customs harden and international agreements multiply. Energized by trade with northern Europe and the Levant, the maritime cities concluded numerous treaties with the sovereigns ruling the shores of the Black Sea and the Mediterranean. Pisan, Genoese, and Venetian barks sailed to the Crimea, Greece, Syria, Cyprus, Egypt, and Tunis. Colonies of Italians clustered within the cities of Constantinople, Tyre, Caesarea, and Jaffa. Conventions between the Italian and other Mediterranean states provided for trading privileges, reciprocal suppression of piracy, succor for shipwrecks, and the elimination of reprisals on innocent individuals for the acts of another citizen. The protection of religion, language, and customs in the Italian colony was secured by the appointment of a consul who not only maintained political connections with the sovereign but also administered estates, acted as a notary, and judged civil cases involving Italian nationals. Thus, important new foundations for international "law" were laid, although nothing approximating international organization yet appeared to bind the interests of the several states.

In Italy itself, the independent cities traded intensively with each other. Treaties of extradition, guarantees of protection for land and river trade, and agreements on the mutual recognition of court judgments multiplied. The increase of Italian intercity political and economic relations after the thirteenth century encouraged the establishment of permanent diplomatic legations for the first time in history. Furthermore, the practice of mediation and arbitration thrived. St. Louis, King of France, in 1270 obtained a five-year truce among Genoa, Pisa, and Venice; in 1428 the successful mediation of the Pope brought peace to Venice, Florence, and Milan. Genoa and Venice agreed to a general arbitration of any disputes between them in 1235; through peace treaties which Milan signed with various other communes—in 1353, 1377, 1379, and 1454—arbitration was provided for disputes arising from interpretation of the terms of the treaty [13].

Before the solidification of the nation-state in Europe, therefore, in the sixteenth century, many customs and an impressive number of treaties existed which were molding international relations. While political centralization had not fully advanced the claim of sovereignty, the mark of the modern state system, the princes had at hand commonly accepted international procedures and made contracts with each other backed by the faith of their common religion. No permanent international agencies of administration were established during the ancient or medieval period of history, but a variety of leagues, some for defense, some for religious worship, and some for trade, had been formed. Limited by their historical epoch, they are nevertheless of interest as primitive forms of international organization.

LEAGUES AND ASSEMBLIES

As early as 681 B.C., the small states of China, threatened by the Ch'u Kingdom, had formed a league for mutual defense. Irregularly over a period of two hundred years, assemblies were held to discuss cooperation in waging war against common enemies. But most important from the point of view of early international organization were the several amphictyonic councils and political confederations which marked the unique pattern of Greek history. The amphictyonic councils, of which the Delphic council was the most illustrious, were composed of representatives of those tribes devoted to the same temple. Bound by the same religion, some city-states would agree upon the joint maintenance and security of holy places and provide for a council to discuss or manage such matters. The council members swore to observe the inviolability of shrines and the safety of pilgrims, and they pledged themselves to moderate rules of warfare: for example, the interruption of water supplies and the razing of cities were forbidden. The Delphic Amphictyony, however, touched political regulation only as an incident to its function as a religious cooperative. Invaluable as an assembly of Greek opinion on matters of common concern, such as setting a price on the heads of citizens who had assisted the Persians or launching a crusade against some sacrilegious city, nevertheless the Amphictyony had no force beyond the willingness of each member tribe to follow its resolutions. The most glaring weakness of the council lay in its voting arrangements, for as an ancient tribal institution it did not reflect the fifth-century-B.C. locus of power in cities like Athens, Corinth, and Thebes but rather granted two equal votes to each of its twelve tribes, some of which included great cities, some of which were exhausted and insignificant. Only in the last centuries before Christ were the voting arrangements reformed, but by that time the shadow of Macedon and Rome had passed over the Greek peninsula.

Out of amphictyonic councils it may be presumed that such Greek political confederations as the Phocian League, the Akarnian League, and the Boeotian League emerged. The Lycian confederation presents the first historical evidence of weighted voting in an intersovereign assembly, for each of the large cities had three votes compared to two votes for middle-sized cities and one vote for each of the tiny settlements in Lycia. In the Achaean League there were genuine foundations for a Greek federal state: an assembly of the cities met twice annually to vote on "national" affairs; a senate, equivalent to a standing committee, an executive council, a secretary, and a general were elected. Continuous joint action in foreign affairs and federal tax levies on each of the member cities were distinctive attributes of the confederation [14]. All these leagues, however, had the advantage of linking peoples with the same racial-cultural background in a political union, and in this respect they were very different from modern international organizations.

Some leagues, mostly for defensive purposes, were formed on the Italian peninsula in ancient times—the Etrurian, the Samnium, and the Latin being the most important—but the might of Rome relentlessly crushed and amalgamated these allied cities. In the medieval period, transitory alliances of one group of Italian city-states against another frequently occurred, but no permanent league fostered further international organization. Perhaps the most famous confederation of medieval times was the treaty among the Swiss cantons of Uri, Schwyz, and Unterwalden in 1315. It was followed by pacts with Lucerne (1332), Zurich (1351), Glarus and Zug (1352), and Berne (1353) primarily for cooperation in repelling attacks. This league became the nucleus of the modern state of Switzerland.

A singular illustration of a combination of city-states for the promotion of trade was the Hanseatic League. The League originated as a society of commercial towns on or near the Danish isthmus for the protection of trade through the equalization of tolls and the suppression of piracy. Gradually obtaining mastery of the North and Baltic Seas, the Hanse, including upwards of fifty cities, defeated both Denmark and Norway in 1370, thereby securing a virtual monopoly of sea trade and many other strategic economic concessions. As a political organization, the Hanse prescribed rules for the admission of new members, forbade any member city to make war without the approval of its four closest neighbors, and permitted only the Diet to commit the whole League to war. Between 1363 and 1550 the Hanse convoked fifty-three general assemblies. Administrative expenses were shared by the members, an agenda was circulated prior to the Diet's meeting, and resolutions were passed by a majority vote of cities represented. Such resolutions were binding upon the entire League; failure to comply on the part of one town might lead to expulsion from the Hanse, the loss of all trading privileges, the arrest of visiting merchants, and the confiscation of the town's property in all the cities of the League. Because the Hanseatic League was an international corporation with an administrative center in Lübeck and self-governing "factories" in foreign ports from London to Novgorod, it ran counter to the rising tide of nationalism and the dynastic state of the fifteenth and sixteenth centuries. In 1478 the Hanses were expelled from Russia; in 1579 England abolished all their privileges [15].

EMERGENCE OF MODERN INTERNATIONAL RELATIONS

The magnificence of the Roman Empire dazzled the medieval princes looking backward. German princes again and again tried to reestablish the ancient realm and recover the ancient glory. Not until the sixteenth century did the division of Christendom by Protestantism and the strengthening of national dynasties finally loosen the last weak grip of the Empire upon the mind of Europe and give rise to the modern state system. Through a series of peace conferences, moreover, between the Emperor and the kings during the seventeenth and eighteenth centuries, statesmen were brought together to settle terms and provide for future relations. Peace terms required conferences and conferences opened the way to international organization.

One of the early key arrangements of the modern state system was the Treaty of Cateau-Cambrésis (1559) negotiated during a truce among the armies of France, Spain, and England. By the Religious Peace of Augsburg in 1555, the Holy Roman Emperor had conceded toleration to Lutheran princes and cities, but any further "secularization" of Catholic Church property was deemed unlawful. The dissatisfied Lutheran princes enlisted the aid of France in their military struggles against Emperor Charles V. When he abdicated, his son, Philip II, King of Spain, continued the war with France. It happened, however, that Mary Tudor was the wife of Philip II and England was allied to Spain. In consequence, France at last turned from the perennial medieval dream of building an Italian empire and drove the English from the Continent while taking the three key positions of Verdun, Metz, and Toul on the eastern frontier.

The most important arrangement, however, of the new state system was the epoch-making Peace of Westphalia in 1648. Forty years earlier France, England, Brandenburg, Ansbach, Hesse, and the Palatinate had successfully extended their good offices to the Dutch and Spaniards, terminating the bitter, protracted struggle for independence of the Netherlands' provinces. For ten years Europe was at peace, and for ten years Europe paused on the rim of a holocaust. The appointment of Ferdinand of Styria, a militant Catholic, as king-designate of Bohemia in 1617 set off a rebellion by the Protestant nobles against the Holy Roman Emperor. Alliances between the Protestant states and France were vigorously thrown against the Empire and Spain. Then, over the next thirty years, the heart of Europe was lacerated by German, Austrian, Bohemian, Spanish, Danish, Swedish, and French soldiers in an exhausting and ferocious conflict finally ended by peace negotiations at Münster and Osnabrück in Westphalia.

No international organization was established by the Peace of Westphalia in 1648. Indeed, no real consideration was given to the economic and social distress left in the territories wasted by the havoc of warfare. But the joining of practically every European state in a diplomatic conference signaled the opening of a new era in international relations. Of all the many European sovereigns only the Sultan of Turkey was not mentioned in the Articles of Peace, and delegates from every state except Muscovy, Turkey, Poland, and England attended the conferences, which extended over three years.

By the terms of peace the impotence of the Holy Roman Empire was confirmed, for the German princes secured virtual political independence in their domains. Henceforth Protestants were to meet Catholics on equal terms in the Imperial Diet. At the expense of the Austrian Hapsburgs, the dynasty which monopolized the imperial throne, France (by the Treaty of Münster) and Sweden (by the Treaty of Osnabrück) received territorial compensation. The independence of the United Provinces of the Netherlands and Switzerland was acknowledged by all the signatories of the peace treaties.

As the image of Rome faded from view, Europe entered the age of nation-states. Neither the Emperor nor the Pope, twin guardians of the medieval system, was to provide the guarantees of future international covenants. Not even a common Catholic faith could now provide a pledge, but states alone were to assure their agreements. Article XVII of the Treaty of Osnabrück, for example, read as follows: "All and each of the contracting parties of this treaty shall be held to defend and maintain all and each of the dispositions of this peace against whomsoever it may be without distinction of religion."

Rudimentary acts of international regulation which were to serve as important precedents lay in the treaty provisions for the abolition of many tolls upon commerce among the states of the Empire and the declaration that the navigation of the Rhine was to be free. Finally, each principality of the Empire pledged that, if injured, it would first seek to bring its cause to a "friendly composition of the ordinary procedures of justice." Should the dispute not be terminated in three years, the other parties, being notified that "gentle means" had not succeeded, were obliged to aid the injured party by counsel or force.

As an international assembly, the Congress of Westphalia bore little resemblance to the intricate organization of twentieth-century peace conferences. No officer presided, no committees were formed, no votes were taken. But the cities of negotiation, including the route between Münster and Osnabrück, were neutralized from the war while both Papal Nuncio Chigi and Ambassador Contarini of Venice acted as mediators for the plenipotentiaries in Münster. Of the greatest importance to international organization, however, were the gathering of hundreds of envoys in a diplomatic conference which represented practically every political interest in Europe and the achievement by negotiation, rather than by dictation, of two great multilateral treaties which legalized the new order of European international relations [16].

The second great peace treaty in the foundation of modern international relations was the Peace of Utrecht in 1713. Louis XIV of France had dominated the latter part of the seventeenth century in Europe, and his wars were fought to make France mistress of the Continent. Austria, as the Roman Empire, had been defeated in its pretensions of control over Europe, and the Grand Monarch of France then made his bid for the paramount position. Between the Treaty of the Pyrenees (1659), which stabilized the southern boundary of France with Spain in a formidable mountain range, and the Peace of Utrecht, Louis XIV engaged his armies in four major wars whose net effect was to extend and integrate the French realm along its northeastern frontier but to deny once and for all the French ambition to unite the vast Spanish possessions with France. The War of the Spanish Succession (1701–1713) ended in the Peace of Utrecht.

Like Westphalia, the Peace of Utrecht was a fundamental arrangement of the state system in so far as it shattered imperial aspirations and furthered the creation of several independent sovereignties. The United Provinces of the Netherlands and Switzerland had gained international recognition at Westphalia in 1648. By the terms of the seven treaties signed at Utrecht on 11 April 1713 between France and Great Britain, the United Provinces of the Netherlands, Prussia, Portugal, and the Duke of Savoy, and the one treaty signed at Rastadt on 6 March 1714 between France and the Holy Roman Empire, three new dynasties received international sanction. First, the Protestant succession to the British throne was recognized by France; second, the Elector of Brandenburg took the title of King of Prussia, the nucleus of modern Germany; finally, Nice was restored to Victor Amadeus, Duke of Savoy, and he was proclaimed King of Sicily. Six years later Sicily was exchanged for Sardinia, thus bringing

Piedmont and Sardinia under the House of Savoy, which forged modern Italy [17].

Hostilities were still in progress between France and the coalition led by England when the plenipotentiaries assembled in Utrecht during January 1712 to confer on a general peace. Indeed, no suspension of fighting between France and England occurred until six months after the peace negotiations had begun. Portugal did not arrive at a truce with France until ten months after the conference had opened, while the Empire maintained an active state of war with France all through the negotiations at Utrecht. Before the formal opening of the congress, the plenipotentiaries met to discuss and agree upon procedure. Among other things, it was resolved that the conference should meet regularly on Wednesdays and Saturdays without special ceremony. The first meeting, attended by eight plenipotentiaries from the allies and three from France, met, therefore, at 10 A.M. January 29, "wherein nothing happened but Compliments, and Mutual Assurances and Exhortations to avoid all Disputes, and everything that might retard the Conclusion of the Great and Good Work. . . ."

Within two months the conference at Utrecht was virtually suspended over the method of negotiating. The British insisted upon specific answers in writing to their specific demands upon the French, but the diplomats of Louis XIV did not wish to be bound by written answers; instead, they proposed to treat with the allies "by conference." Although the general conference came to a standstill, vigorous negotiation went on between the plenipotentiaries in private, especially on the part of England who acted as a mediator for her allies against France. On 13 March 1713 the Lord Bishop of Bristol, chief plenipotentiary for England, reminded the allies that the Congress had been opened fourteen months, "and therefore, it was high Time to bring the Great Work to a Conclusion." On April 11, at two o'clock in the afternoon, the plenipotentiaries of France came to the Lord Bishop of Bristol's house in Utrecht and signed the treaties of peace and commerce; at four the ministers of the Duke of Savoy appeared to sign; about eight o'clock in the evening Prussia initialed the treaty, followed by the Portuguese who arrived at midnight; finally, the Dutch plenipotentiaries concluded the signing of the Peace of Utrecht at a little past one in the morning [18].

During the seventeenth and eighteenth centuries, modern plans for international organization appeared. The Duke of Sully, minister of Henry IV of France, suggested in his memoirs a European confederation of fifteen states; William Penn in 1693 proposed a diet of states, including Muscovy and Turkey, wherein voting would be weighted according to the foreign trade of the states. Fénelon had commented on the congress at Utrecht: "Neighboring states are not only under obligation to treat one another according to the rules of justice and good faith; they ought in addition, for their own safety, as well as for the common interest, to form a kind of general society and republic [19]." At Utrecht itself, the project of the Abbé de Saint-Pierre for perpetual peace called upon the sovereigns to submit their differences to judicial decision. In the event that any sovereign should refuse to cooperate in the judgment, the other states would unite their military forces against him.

Such schemes, humanitarian in outlook and containing the germs of future international organization, gained no acceptance within the seventeenth- and eighteenth-century state system—not quite free from its feudal origins nor yet pressed by rapid interstate communications. Clinging to personal sovereignty as a norm of political life, the princes established no practical international agencies.

The treaties signed at Westphalia and at Utrecht stabilized the western European state system, but two other powers, destined to play major roles in future international affairs, had not been included: Russia and Turkey. Not until 1606 did Turkey maintain regular diplomatic relations with Europe on the basis of equality. In the negotiations for peace between Austria and Turkey at Sitvatorok, the Turks for the first time in history had given their representatives full powers while admitting the title of "Emperor" to the Austrian ruler. Tribute and truce, the mark of vassalage and subordination, yielded to diplomatic amenities and a definitive peace, the mark of equality among Western state sovereigns. But the most significant international conference of the seventeenth century, after Westphalia, was the peacemaking at Carlowitz in 1698. Turkey and Russia, for the first time, were parties to a general European congress whose purpose was to conclude the wars between the Ottomans and Venice, Poland, Austria (Empire), and Russia. Permitting England and Holland to act as mediators at this assembly, Russia and Turkey implicitly recognized the modern practice of the Western state system to negotiate settlements among sovereigns and the rightful interest of other powers in such international agreements [20].

In northern Europe, Russia joined the coalition of Brandenburg, Denmark, and Poland against Sweden, and by 1721 Tsar Peter had taken possession of Livonia, Ingria, Esthonia, and Karelia, all on the eastern bay of the Baltic, thereby opening Russia's window to the horizon of Europe. By driving Sweden back across the sea and then crushing Poland between them, Russia and Prussia won their key places in the new European state system where international organization was to begin.

EIGHTEENTH-CENTURY INTERNATIONAL CONFERENCES AND CONVENTIONS

With the major dominions of Europe staked out by dynastic sovereigns, the eighteenth century reflected the contending desires of the dynasties, through marriage, inheritance, intimidation, or war, to secure or enlarge their possessions. Alliances and coalitions speckled the history of the greater powers as they sought to play one rival off against another: negotiations between princes multiplied and diplomats traveled throughout the Continent in almost constant occupation.

To adjust the quarrels among states, quarrels which now affected every other member of the European state system, "congresses," emulating the meetings at Westphalia, Carlowitz, and Utrecht, became an accepted mode of international diplomacy. Thus, at Cambrai in 1722 representatives from Britain, Austria, Spain, France, the united Netherlands, and several German states met for a period of three years to discuss, though not settle, a dispute between Spain and Austria; at Soissons in 1728 another gathering was called on the British-Spanish controversy over Gibraltar. In the War of the Austrian Succession (1740–1748), every European state except Denmark, Switzerland, and Turkey was involved, and the congress at Aix-la-Chapelle worked out the final peace treaties among six European states [21]. Again in the Seven Years' War (1756–1763), coalitions of Austrians, French, and Russians faced British and Prussians. At one point in this prolonged struggle, Austria offered to send plenipotentiaries to a peace congress, but because of the designs of the belligerents to improve their diplomatic leverage in bilateral negotiation the proposal was rejected, and peace was reached eventually through separate treaties at Paris and Hubertusburg. Similarly the Congresses of Focşani and Bucharest (1772–1773) between the Russians and Turks, with Prussia and Austria offering mediation, and the Congress of Rastadt (1797–1799) between France and Austria, with many of the German states in attendance, continued the idea of collective international settlements although they failed to make peace among the belligerents. At the Congress of Teschen in May 1779, France and Russia not only mediated three treaties among Austria, Prussia, the Elector Palatine, and Saxony, but also guaranteed the terms [22].

By the eighteenth century, Europe had come a long way from the crude conquests of the ancient empires. Rivalry among states was undiminished, but the development of several kingdoms, none of which could subdue all the others, engendered coalitions; these coalitions, unstable in themselves, made general settlements of peace by combining war with diplomacy.

The integration and pacification of single kingdoms had encouraged intrastate and interstate commerce—with a growing recognition by states that friendly international trade was a surer index to prosperity than the booty of military subjugation. Treaties of commerce between sovereigns were rare in the Middle Ages, for political alliances monopolized the attention of petty princes and feudalism itself denied the major condition of modern commerce—a mass market. Trade conventions, indeed, were often signed between towns rather than between kings [23]. Beginning with the seventeenth century, however, the increase of trade among the European states and with their colonies all over the world contributed to the development of a common interest which served as a basis for international organization. By the turn of the seventeenth century, for example, the British had organized trading companies for the Levant, the Baltic, and Russia as well as the famous East India Company. France chartered twenty-two different trading companies between 1599 and 1642, and the commercial fleets of the Dutch were unparalleled, ranging from Java in Asia to Brazil and New Amsterdam in America and to Archangel in Russia.

In Russia, pursuing the reform policies of Nastchokin and Prince Golitsyn, Peter the Great vigorously pushed foreign trade. Although Austria and Germany lagged behind the commercial developments of western Europe, Prussia welcomed foreign artisans and agriculturists. Many strangling internal tolls in Germany were gradually abolished and several new canals were built. Hamburg, Bremen, and Lübeck prospered with the foreign trade of northern Europe; the Rhine River, through Holland, became an international commercial highway for southern Germany.

The chief symbol of national and international monetary exchange, banks, got their start in the seventeenth and eighteenth centuries: in 1609 the Bank of Amsterdam was organized, in 1619 the Bank of Hamburg, in 1688 the Bank of Stockholm, in 1694 the Bank of England, in 1703 the Bank of Vienna, in 1765 the Banks of Berlin and Breslau, and in 1772 the Loan Bank of St. Petersburg [24]. The rapid multiplication of commercial relations among states of eighteenth-century Europe led to innumerable conventions dealing with tariffs, trade specifications, navigation rules, licensing, etc. Whereas the Treaties of Münster and Osnabrück had treated commercial clauses, such as the removal of tolls imposed during the war and the guarantee of free navigation of the Rhine, only parenthetically to the general political-religious settlement at Westphalia, France and Britain in 1713 at Utrecht signed a separate Treaty of Navigation and Commerce containing no less than forty-one articles, and on the same day France concluded commercial agreements with Holland and Portugal.

One of the most important matters of commerce at this time which became a standing item of international conferences was "freedom of the seas." Out of the controversy emerged the Armed Neutrality of 1780, a highly interesting step in the direction of international organization.

ARMED NEUTRALITY OF 1780

Controversy over freedom of the seas, especially the right of a neutral shipowner to carry a belligerent's goods without liability to capture and confiscation, smoldered during this era of mercantilism. In the Utrecht conventions, all parties agreed that free or neutral ships were to make all goods aboard free from capture—excepting only contraband of war. Indeed, between 1654 and 1780, only fifteen treaties sanctioned the confiscation of enemy goods on neutral ships, while thirty-six treaties mentioned the new principle, "free ships—free goods."

During the war between Great Britain and France, Spain, and the United States, Catherine of Russia declared (March 1780) that the non-contraband goods of subjects of belligerent powers were free from capture when aboard neutral ships and, furthermore, that ports could be regarded as blockaded only when the attacking power had so stationed its vessels as to make the approach to the port "clearly dangerous." Russia proposed to guarantee this treatment to her own neutral ships by armed convoy. Of special interest to the development of international organization, however, was the communication of this declaration to the high and mighty lords of the States-General of the Netherlands and the courts of Copenhagen, Stockholm, and Lisbon in April 1780, inviting them "to make common cause with her, as such a union may serve to protect the trade and navigation, and at the same time observe a strict neutrality [25]."

Between 9 July 1780 and 21 February 1783 Denmark-Norway, Sweden, Prussia, the Netherlands, Austria (Empire), Portugal, and the Kingdom of the Two Sicilies each acceded to a convention by which they pledged to enforce their neutral rights on the sea, not only by convoying their own ships but also by giving aid and protection to the commerce of their fellow signatories against arbitrary action by a belligerent. The system of "armed neutrality" therefore hinged on the cooperative action of sovereign states in a common interest. Neutral rights under international law were asserted by a multilateral convention binding upon all members [26].

While it is true that each state of the armed neutrality acted in its own interests (indeed, when belligerents themselves they accorded scant "rights" to other neutrals), nevertheless, the balance of power in Europe forced continuous diplomatic negotiation to tip the scales one way or another. By the same process, the common interests of states were discussed and defined. The transitory military alliance to repel an aggressor, so common to all history, now found itself elbowed by agreements to respect religions, treaties of navigation and commerce, and, in the instance of armed neutrality, a convention to protect a crudely sketched international "law."

The demand for territorial-commercial adjustments among the vying dynasties of the period before Napoleon found its expression in warfare, partly because the sovereign ultimately justified violence as in the interest of the state and partly because no international agencies existed through which a state's grievance might be channeled for settlement or, at least, discussed. But at the end of war, when the claims of the belligerents had been proved only by their strength of arms, diplomats attempted to legalize and thereby stabilize such changes by treaties. This procedure forced new consultations and new congresses, the very backbone of modern international organization. The Napoleonic Wars overwhelmed Europe, but no revolutionary break in the process of international organization occurred. Instead, statesmen turned back to the achievements of the eighteenth century for guidance and tried to pick up, continue, and develop the international-congress system so auspiciously inaugurated.

As a development of the nation-state system of Europe, with its dynastic centralization at home and its diplomatic construction of a balance of power abroad, modern international organization differs from the past in three major respects. Its foundation is still the treaty or interstate contract, but, first, the stress is on a *multilateral agreement* rather than a bilateral accord; second, treaties under modern international organization attempt to harmonize *continuity and self-perpetuation* of the basic document *with modification* of the terms; third, and most characteristically, modern international organization is *institutionalized* by periodic councils and permanent secretariats. In the succeeding chapters, each of these aspects of international organization is explicit. The hypothesis is posed, therefore, that these innovations reveal a remarkable and, with qualifications, still hopeful evolution of international politics toward a more prosperous and peaceful world since the decades of the Napoleonic Wars.

NOTES

1. Daniel D. Luckenbill, *Ancient Records of Assyria and Babylonia*, Chicago, University of Chicago Press, 1927, 2 vols., Vol. II, p. 41.

2. G. Maspero, *The Struggle of the Nations*, New York, Appleton-Century-Crofts, 1897, pp. 271ff. See M. I. Rostovtzeff, *A History of the Ancient World*, New York, Oxford, 1927; H. R. Hall, *The Ancient History of the Near East*, London, Methuen, 1927; M. L. W. Laistner, *Survey of Ancient History*, Boston, Heath, 1929; W. E. Caldwell, *The Ancient World*, New York, Rinehart, 1937; and Ralph Turner, *The Great Cultural Traditions*, New York, McGraw-Hill, 1941, 2 vols.

3. A. H. L. Heeren, *Historical Re-*

searches into the Politics, Intercourse, and Trade of the Principal Nations of Antiquity, London, Henry G. Bohn, 1846, Vol. 1, pp. 261ff. See also F. C. T. Bosanquet, *Letters of Caius Plinius Caecilius Secundus,* trans. by Melmoth, London, G. Bell, 1892, Book X.

4. Wang Yu-chuan, "An Outline of the Central Government of the Former Han Dynasty," *Harvard Journal of Asiatic Studies,* Vol. 12, Nos. 1, 2 (June 1949), pp. 134–187.

5. See S. V. Viswantha, *International Law in Ancient India,* London, Longmans, 1925, Chaps. III–V, and Pramathanath Bandyopadhay, *International Law and Custom in Ancient India,* Calcutta University Press, 1920.

6. L. W. King, *A History of Sumer and Akkad,* London, Chatto & Windus, 1923, p. 101; S. Langdon and A. H. Gardiner, "The Treaty of Alliance between Hattusili, King of the Hittites, and the Pharaoh, Rameses II of Egypt," *The Journal of Egyptian Archeology,* London, Vol. 6 (1920), pp. 179–205. See also A. Nussbaum, *A Concise History of the Law of Nations,* New York, Macmillan, 1947.

7. Thucydides, *Books iv and v.* For original treaty texts, see M. N. Tod, *A Selection of Greek Historical Inscriptions,* London, Oxford, 1933, 1948, Vols. I, II. For Greek arbitral practices, see C. Phillipson, *The International Law and Custom of Ancient Greece and Rome,* London, Macmillan, 1911, 2 vols., Vol. II, Chap. 20, and M. N. Tod, *Sidelights on Greek History,* Oxford, Blackwell, 1932, Lecture 2.

8. Polybius, *III, xxiv, xxv.*

9. Phillipson, *op. cit.,* pp. 45–89.

10. M. Khadduri, *The Law of War and Peace in Islam,* London, Luzac, 1940; see also A. A. Vasiliev, *History of the Byzantine Empire,* trans. by S. Ragozino, Madison, Wis., University of Wisconsin Press, 1928, 2 vols.

11. For an original account of Kublai Khan's communications system, see H. Wright (ed.), *Travels of Marco Polo,* London, Henry G. Bohn, 1854, Book II, Chap. 20, and H. Yule (ed.), *The Book of Ser Marco Polo,* London, J. Murray, 1926, Book II, Chap. 26. A semi-fictionalized history of the Mongols may be found

in M. Prawdin, *The Mongol Empire,* New York, Macmillan, 1940.

12. R. Ward, *An Enquiry into the Foundation and History of the Law of Nations in Europe,* Dublin, P. Wagan *et al.,* 1795, is very valuable as an early collection and record of medieval international relations.

13. A. P. Sereni, *The Italian Conception of International Law,* New York, Columbia University Press, 1943, Part I.

14. See E. A. Freeman, *History of Federal Government,* London, Macmillan, 1893.

15. J. W. Thompson, *Economic and Social History of Europe in the Later Middle Ages,* New York, Appleton-Century-Crofts, 1931, Chap. 5; see also H. Zimmern, *The Hansa Towns,* New York, Putnam, 1907, and E. Daenell, "The Policy of the German Hanseatic League Respecting the Mercantile Marine," *American Historical Review,* Vol. 15, No. 1 (October 1909), pp. 47–53.

16. For the texts of the Treaties of Münster and Osnabrück as well as the original language of hundreds of treaties between A.D. 800 and 1730, consult Jean Dumont, *Corps universel diplomatique du droit des gens,* Amsterdam and The Hague, 1726–1731, 8 vols. See also G. H. Bougeant, *Histoire des guerres et des négociations qui précédèrent le Traité de Westphalie,* Paris, 1751. See also Henry Wheaton, *History of the Law of Nations,* New York, Gould Banks, 1845; Anton Gindley, *History of the Thirty Years War,* New York, Putnam, 1884; James Bryce, *The Holy Roman Empire,* New York, Macmillan, 1892; David J. Hill, *A History of European Diplomacy,* New York, Longmans, 1906, 3 vols.; R. B. Mowat, *A History of European Diplomacy, 1451–1789,* New York, Longmans, 1928; C. V. Wedgwood, *The Thirty Years War,* London, Henderson and Spaulding, 1947; and L. Gross, "The Peace of Westphalia," *American Journal of International Law,* Vol. 42 (January 1948), pp. 20–41. For a concise survey of diplomatic relations of the fifteenth to eighteenth centuries, see C. Petrie, *Earlier Diplomatic History, 1492–1713,* London, Hollis and Carter, 1949.

17. For this period, see Le Comte de Garden, *Histoire général des traités de paix,* Paris, Amyot, 1848–1887, 3 vols.;

Earl Stanhope, *History of England Comprising the Reign of Queen Anne 1701–1713*, London, J. Murray, 1870; J. W. Gerard, *The Peace of Utrecht*, New York, Putnam, 1885; and G. M. Trevelyan, *England under Queen Anne—The Peace and the Protestant Succession*, London, Longmans, 1934.

18. Procedure at the Utrecht peace conference is based upon T. Broderick, *A Compleat History of the Late War in the Netherlands*, London, Thomas Ward, 1713, 2 vols., especially Vol. I.

19. *Oeuvres de Fénelon*, Paris, 1872, Vol. IV, p. 360, quoted in Hill, *op. cit.*, Vol. III, p. 338.

20. Edward S. Creasy, *History of the Ottoman Turks*, New York, Holt, 1877; see also A. H. Lybyer, *The Government of the Ottoman Empire*, Cambridge, Mass., Harvard University Press, 1913.

21. For a general diplomatic history of this period, see Hill, *op. cit.*, Vol. III; for special studies, consult Richard Lodge, *Great Britain and Prussia in the Eighteenth Century*, Oxford, Clarendon Press, 1923, and *Studies in Eighteenth Century Diplomacy*, London, J. Murray, 1930; Arthur M. Wilson, *French Foreign Policy during the Administration of Cardinal Fleury, 1726–1743*, Cambridge, Mass., Harvard University Press, 1936. For texts of treaties between 1761 and 1790, see G. F. de Martens, *Recueil des principaux traités de l'Europe*, Göttingen, Dietrich, 1791, Vols. I–III, and *Supplément au recueil des principaux traités de l'Europe*, Göttingen, Dietrich, 1802.

22. See Ernest Satow, *A Guide to Diplomatic Practice*, New York, Longmans, 1917, Chap. XXV, for an account of European peace congresses.

23. Martens, *Supplément*, Vol. I, Discours préliminaire.

24. For seventeenth- and eighteenth-century commercial developments, see C. Day, *A History of Commerce*, New York, Longmans, 1907, and C. A. Herrick, *History of Commerce and Industry*, New York, Macmillan, 1920; for a discussion of banks, see H. de B. Gibbins, *History of Commerce in Europe*, London, Macmillan, 1915, Chap. 4.

25. Russian Memorandum Containing a Project for an Armed Neutrality, presented to the States-General of the Netherlands, 3 April 1780, *Annual Register*, London, J. Dodsley, 1781, pp. 346–347.

26. A history of the main principles involved in the practice of visit, search, and capture of neutral ships and property on the seas, as well as an account of the armed neutralities of 1613, 1691, 1693, and 1756, may be found in C. J. Kulsrud, *Maritime Neutrality to 1780*, Boston, Little, Brown, 1936. These treaties, however, were bilateral, concerning mostly Denmark and Sweden, and without a common formula. A comprehensive treatment of the armed neutrality of 1780, with all the documents, is in J. B. Scott (ed.), *The Armed Neutralities of 1780 and 1800*, New York, Oxford, 1918.

APPENDIX 1

I. *Abstract from the Treaty of Münster, 24 October 1648, which, with the Treaty of Osnabrück, Made the Peace of Westphalia* (an original translation from the Latin text)

Be it known to each and every one who is concerned or howsoever he may be concerned: that after the conflicts and the civil commotions which had their origin in the Roman Empire many years ago had increased to a point where not only all Germany, but also several neighboring kingdoms, especially most powerful France, were so embroiled that a long and bitter war was started, first, between the most exalted and most powerful prince and lord, FERDINAND II, Elected Emperor of the Romans . . . with his allies and partisans on the one part, and the most exalted and most powerful prince and lord, LOUIS XIII, Most Christian King of France and Navarre . . . and his allies and partisans on the other part, then after their death . . . FERDINAND III . . . and . . . LOUIS XIV . . . it finally came to pass, by Divine Goodness, that through the efforts of the most exalted Republic of Venice (whose concern for public peace and welfare during the most troublesome times of the Christian world was never lacking) both sides were open to the thought of universal peace, and toward that end, through a convention of both parties held at Hamburg on the 25th of December, new style, or the 15th, old style, in the year of Christ, 1641, the 11th day of July, new style, or the 1st day, old style, in the year of Christ, 1643, was agreed upon for the beginning of a congress of plenipotentiaries at Münster and Osnabrück in Westphalia. . . .

Let there be a universal, perpetual, Christian peace and a true and honest friendship between His Most Holy Majesty, Caesar, and His Most Christian Holy Majesty, likewise between each and every ally and partisan. . . .

Let both sides forget and let there be an amnesty of all things which have been done from the beginning of these troubled times in whatever place or in whatever manner by one party or another during hostilities . . .

Those of the Augsburg Confession who had been in possession of churches . . . are to be restored to their ecclesiastic state in 1624; others desiring the practice of the Augsburg Confession are free to do so either publicly in churches at stated hours, or privately in their own homes, or . . .

Moreover it is provided that differences in the political status no longer exist and that all electors, princes, and states of the Roman Empire are confirmed in and guaranteed their ancient laws, prerogatives, liberties, privileges, free exercise of local law, either spiritual or temporal . . . that they enjoy without contradiction the right of suffrage in all imperial deliberations, especially in the making or the interpretation of laws, the declaration of war. . . .

It being to the public interest that with peace established trade should revive everywhere, for that purpose it is agreed that levies and tolls . . . without the approval of the Emperor and imperial electors . . . shall be removed . . .

Henceforth let trade and travel be free to those who dwell on either bank of the Rhine, or in nearby provinces; above all let the navigation of the Rhine be free, and no party shall be allowed to impede, detain, arrest, or harm . . . ships . . . and each and every party of this transaction shall be held to guard and protect each and all the terms and laws of this peace against anyone whomsoever regardless of religion, and if it happen that some clause be violated, the offended first of all shall urge the aggressor from the path of his action by submitting the cause to either a friendly composition or the processes of law, and if in the space of three years these differences are not ended by one or the other of these means, then each and every one of the parties to this transaction are bound to join themselves to the wounded party and to help him with all their advice and arms to redress the injury. . . .

II. *Abstract from the Treaty of Peace and Commerce Concluded at Utrecht, 11 April 1713, between Great Britain and France* (eighteenth-century English text)

Whereas it has pleased Almighty God, for the Glory of His Name, and for the Universal Welfare, so to Direct the Minds of Kings, for the Healing, now in His own Time, the Miseries of the Wasted World, that they are disposed towards one another with a Mutual Desire of making Peace: Be it therefore known to All and Singular, whom it may Concern, That under this Divine Guidance, the Most Serene and Most Potent Princess and Lady Anne, by the Grace of God, Queen of Great-Britain, France, and Ireland; and the Most Serene and Most Potent Prince and Lord Lewis XIV, by the Grace of God, the Most Christian King; Consulting, as well the Advantage of their Subjects, as Providing (as far as Mortals are able to do) for the Perpetual Tranquillity of the whole Christian World, have resolved at last to put an End to the War, which was unhappily Kindled, and has been obstinately carried on above these Ten Years. . . .

That there be an Universal, Perpetual Peace, and a True and Sincere Friendship between . . . Anne . . . and . . . Lewis XIV; and their Heirs and Successors. . . .

All Offences, Injuries, Harms, and Damages, which the aforesaid Queen of Great-Britain, and Her Subjects, or the aforesaid Most Christian King, and His Subjects, have suffered . . . during the War, shall be Buried in Oblivion . . . the Most Christian King promises, that no One besides the Queen Her Self and Her Successors . . . shall ever by Him or by His Heirs or Successors, be Acknowledged, or Reputed to be King or Queen of Great-Britain. . . .

Whereas the most Destructive Flame of War, which is to be extinguished by the Peace, arose chiefly from thence, that the Security and Liberties of Europe could by no means bear the Union of the Kingdoms of France and Spain under one and the same King . . . it is Provided and Settled that . . . the Crowns of France and Spain are so Divided and Separated from each other . . . they can never be joined in One.

That there be free use of Navigation and Commerce between the Subjects of both their Royal Majesties, as it was formerly in time of Peace. . . .

The said most Christian King shall restore to the Kingdom and Queen of Great-Britain . . . the Bay and Streights of Hudson . . . the Island of St. Christopher . . . all Nova Scotia or Acadia . . . the Island called Newfoundland, with the adjacent islands. . . .

However, in case (which God Almighty forbid) the Dissensions which have been laid asleep, should at any time be renewed . . . the Ships, Merchandizes, and all the effects, both Moveable and Immoveable, on both sides, which shall be found to be in the Ports . . . Dominions of the Adverse Party, shall not be Confiscated or any wise Endamaged: But the intire Space of Six Months shall be allowed to the Said Subjects of each of Their Royal Majesties, in which they may Sell . . . or carry or remove them from thence . . . without any Molestation.

Lastly, solemn Ratification of this present Treaty, and made in due Form, shall be exhibited on both Sides at Utrecht, and mutually and duly exchanged within the Space of Four Weeks. . . .

CHAPTER 2 *The Age of Consultation*

The havoc of international war has compelled statesmen to turn their attention to the positive construction of peace by international organization. The peace congresses of the seventeenth and eighteenth centuries endeavored to conclude general contracts which would define the possessions and the privileges of all the sovereigns in the European community, although the kings and queens and princes, chafing from restraint or restless in ambition, denied any international power save God and broke their oaths again and again. Nothing pricked their conscience, nothing bridled their power. The search for an enduring peace after widespread international war, nevertheless, has continued from Vienna in 1815 to San Francisco in 1945, and the states of the world, incapable of achieving security by themselves, have looked about and consulted with each other.

THE TREATY OF CHAUMONT AND THE CONGRESS OF VIENNA

At the height of his power, Napoleon Bonaparte was master of France, Italy, Spain, Switzerland, Sweden, Poland (Duchy of Warsaw), and the German Confederation of the Rhine. Prussia lay prostrate before his infantry and cannon. Austria joined his camp. Great Britain, alone, resisted, while Russia engaged in war with Turkey. Eleven states of Europe had combined at different times into three military coalitions against France between 1792 and 1806, and each coalition had disintegrated before the triumphant armies of Napoleon. When the Treaty of Chaumont was published on 9 March 1814, Europe had been racked by war for almost twenty years.

The Treaty of Chaumont, concluded by the Fourth Coalition, bound Austria, Prussia, Russia, and Great Britain to make a common cause in the defeat of Napoleon. Toward this end each of the three Continental

34

states pledged to maintain 150,000 soldiers in the field while Great Britain agreed to pay subsidies to each ally totaling 5 million pounds. This Quadruple Alliance, moreover, bound the partners for a period of twenty years beyond the fall of Napoleon. Each state promised to supply 60,000 men, if necessary, to maintain the peace terms against any future violation of peace by France. By their determination to oust Napoleon, pacify France, and fix a stable political order for the Continent, Russia, Prussia, Austria, and Great Britain had agreed "to concert together" on the measures required to ensure peace for themselves and Europe [1]. Twenty-one days later the Allied armies, led by Tsar Alexander, entered Paris. A new era of international organization had imperceptibly edged its way into the stream of international politics.

The Congress of Vienna, which met between September 1814 and June 1815, was not a peacemaking body, for peace had already been reached with France by the Treaty of Paris on 30 May 1814. The plenipotentiaries of all the Allied Powers and France assembled in Vienna "for the purpose of regulating in General Congress, the Arrangements" which would complete the provisions of the Paris treaty. By intention, therefore, the Congress gathered to liquidate the unsettled political problems which the years of warfare had raised for Europe, for the armies of France had toppled kings, smashed boundaries, abolished old governments, and created new states. It is important to note, moreover, in tracing the development of international organization, that a state of war had existed all during the negotiations at Westphalia and Utrecht, but the deputies to Vienna met in time of peace to answer the claims of nearly every state of Europe.

With their families and retinues, the delegations sent to the Congress swelled Vienna to a bursting point. Never had modern Europe witnessed the collection of so many crowned heads and their distinguished diplomats in one place. Tsar Alexander I of Russia, Emperor Francis I of Austria, and King Frederick William III of Prussia were surrounded by such statesmen as Count Nesselrode, Count Capo d'Istria, Prince von Metternich, Prince Hardenberg, Prince von Humboldt, and many other diplomats, experts, and clerks. France was represented by the wily Talleyrand and three other plenipotentiaries. Great Britain sent its great foreign secretary, Lord Castlereagh, three additional plenipotentiaries, and a small staff of a dozen. In addition to the five major powers and Spain, Portugal, and Sweden, seven other sovereigns as well as thirty-six German states were represented at the Congress. Both the Pope and the Sultan dispatched emissaries to Vienna. Indeed, counting minor principalities and special-interest groups, there were 216 different delegations at the Congress, and it has been estimated that 100,000 people visited Vienna during the colorful assembly [2].

By comparison with the pre-Napoleonic international gatherings, the Congress of Vienna made some remarkable advances toward international organization in the extent of (a) its political settlement, (b) the diversity of economic-social problems treated, and (c) the procedure of the Congress itself. Not only were there 121 articles in the body of the Treaty of Vienna, but the Final Act of the Congress also legalized by unanimous international consent 17 other acts, declarations, regulations, and protocols to which different states had previously adhered during 1815 [3].

Political Settlements. France, the defeated power, had already disgorged its conquests by the Treaty of Paris and had, rather generously, been confined to its boundaries of 1792. The main work of the Congress was to restore or dispose of those territories in Poland, Italy, Germany, the Netherlands, and Switzerland which Napoleon had overrun. The Treaty of Vienna united Poland with Russia but established the free, neutral, and independent town of Cracow under the protection of Austria, Prussia, and Russia. Prussia received a large cession of Saxon territory as well as many other cities, counties, and principalities. While the King of Sardinia added Genoa to his possessions, Austria obtained Illyria on the east side of the Adriatic Sea and the rich Italian states of Lombardy-Venetia. Tuscany, Modena, and Parma became Austrian satellites. In southern Italy, the Kingdom of the Two Sicilies was restored to the Bourbon King Ferdinand.

In addition to the free town of Cracow three other states received international sanction by the Congress of Vienna. Articles 53 to 64 outlined the basic structure of the German Confederation, while the new Kingdom of the Netherlands, uniting the Netherlands and the Belgian provinces under the Prince of Orange-Nassau, was acknowledged by all plenipotentiaries. Finally, the Declaration of the Eight Powers on the affairs of the Helvetic Confederacy (20 March 1815) was ratified, thereby affirming the integrity, independence, and neutrality of Switzerland.

Economic-Social Problems. Characteristic of the new epoch of international organization unfolding itself at the beginning of the nineteenth century was the scope of the economic and social problems discussed and acted upon at Vienna. Entirely through the pressure of Great Britain, France had agreed, by an additional article to the First Peace of Paris, to abandon her own slave trade within five years and to support Britain at the Vienna Congress in a resolution calling upon all states to decree the end of a "traffic repugnant to the principles of natural justice and of the enlightened age." On 8 February 1815, therefore, the great powers at Vienna solemnly declared that they looked forward to the universal abolition of the slave trade—although no specific time could be assigned to the execution of this noble project. This resolution became an integral part of the Treaty of Vienna and was to be the starting point of a long struggle to end the slave trade in the nineteenth century. Since that struggle forms an integral part of the development of international law after the Congress of Vienna, it is treated rather extensively in Chapter 4.

The navigation of rivers was dealt with more comprehensively at Vienna than in all preceding European congresses, for not only was every international river bounding or traversing the signatory states declared open to commerce, but, in particular, the states pledged "to regulate, by common consent, all that regards their navigation." In the case of the Rhine, provisions for an elaborate international central commission of control were drafted. This was the first statute of its kind in the history of modern international organization. The development of international river commissions in the nineteenth century, which forms such an important part of the growth of international agencies, is treated more extensively in a later chapter.

A forerunner of the modern attempts at achieving international protection of minorities and human rights lay in the approval of the Constitution of Germany by the Congress of Vienna. Unofficial delegations from German Jews had pleaded against the discriminations imposed upon their brethren. Part of the new Constitution, therefore, *required* the Diet to consider means for ameliorating the civil status of Jews in Germany and to pay particular attention to measures by which the civil rights of this sect might be secured in the confederated states.

Not less noteworthy in the history of international organization was the standardization of diplomatic rank reached in the Congress of 1814–1815. For centuries the etiquette of precedence had plagued the courts of Europe, frequently leading to fatuous conduct on the part of ambassadors and ministers who vied for positions of honor. Quarrels often ended in street brawls among the diplomats' retainers and sometimes provoked the threat of international war. Until 1806 the precedence of the Pope and the Emperor of the Romans over all other princes was acknowledged. The remaining princes, however, struggled for precedence, some asserting that the rights of antiquity entitled them to special place, others claiming an absolute equality of all crowns. In Westphalia, for example, Sweden had refused to yield to any state. Queen Anne, in issuing the invitations to the congress at Utrecht, felt it necessary to say, "We, with the Lords-States-General, have unanimously agreed to send our Ministers to the Congress, in the Quality only of Plenipotentiaries, and that they shall not take on them the Character of Ambassadors . . . thereby to avoid . . . Disputes about the Ceremonial, and the Delays that the same might occasion." But the frictions over rank at the courts, especially where many foreign legations were present, wore down the patience of diplomacy. To complicate matters, the distinction between ambassadors, ministers, envoys, nuncios, etc., was fuzzy.

By a *règlement* signed 19 March 1815, the Eight Powers divided diplomatic characters into three main classes: (*a*) ambassadors, legates, and nuncios; (*b*) envoys, ministers, and other persons accredited to sovereigns; (*c*) chargés d'affaires accredited only to ministers of foreign affairs. Furthermore, precedence within these classes would henceforth depend upon the date of the agent's arrival at his mission, seniority always prevailing except in the case of papal representatives. Although the accomplishment of these rules seems insignificant in light of the central problems of international organization today, nevertheless, it represented a considerable achievement in having the European states admit a basic equality in their negotiations with one another, not simply at a peace conference, but on a day-to-day basis at all the courts and foreign offices of the world.

Procedure. At Münster in 1648 and at Carlowitz in 1699, the assembled states had availed themselves of mediators through whose hands the various proposals and counterproposals of terms had passed. At Münster the plenipotentiaries never met in general session; at Osnabrück only the French, Swedish, and imperial ambassadors had negotiated directly. At Carlowitz, after four doors had been built into the conference room (one for the imperial ambassador, one for the Ottoman ambassador, and the other two for the other representatives), plenipotentiaries and mediators had sat down and made terms. The congress of Utrecht had been opened with a speech by the chief *British* plenipotentiary, had elected no presiding officer, and had appointed no committees. Oral versus written negotiation had been a major issue of the conference. Fighting continued during a good part of the peace negotiations and, in fact, except for nine general meetings, most of the bargaining went on outside the conference on a bilateral basis.

The Peace of Paris had terminated hostilities, and Article XXXII clearly provided that a congress should be held in Vienna to settle accounts. The Emperor of Austria, therefore, issued the invitations and Prince von Metternich, foreign minister of Austria, was designated President of the Congress, a practice standardized in the nineteenth century. Furthermore, Friedrich von Gentz, Metternich's secretary, was appointed secretary-general of the Congress. Invitations were issued to all countries, enemies or allies, and the neutrals also sent delegations to Vienna. Prussia, Russia, Austria, and Great Britain had secretly agreed in the Paris treaty to make all final decisions, but when Talleyrand arrived at Vienna he skillfully maneuvered the Allies out of absolute control of the Congress and insinuated France into the inner councils. Talleyrand's dexterity upset the awkward plans of the Allies for the Congress, and the work fell sometimes into the hands of the Four, sometimes into the hands of the Four with France, Spain, Sweden, and Portugal, the other signatories of the Paris peace treaty. Special committees, by necessity rather than by careful planning, were selected to deal with German affairs, the slave trade, Switzerland, Italian affairs, diplomatic precedence, and international rivers. Some were chosen by the Four and some by the Eight Powers. Of special importance was the Statistical Commission, which made a complete census of territories in dispute among the powers, thereby providing a reasonable basis for negotiation and heralding the modern practice of international organization with its fact-finding commissions and valuable statistical agencies [4].

To meet the shrewd diplomatic challenge of Talleyrand, who had argued that legally the eight signatory powers of the Paris peace treaty should direct the Congress and, furthermore, such direction ought to be confirmed by the whole Congress, the four major Allies postponed the plenary session scheduled for October 1. In truth, the Congress of Vienna never met except in a final plenary session to sign the Final Act, after eight months of negotiation. While the Eight Powers sat together nine times, the vital work of the conferences was shaped and decided by Prussia, Russia, Austria, and Great Britain—with France admitted to their councils after January 1815—who met as a group forty-one times during the Congress.

CONSULTATIONS OF THE QUADRUPLE ALLIANCE AND FRANCE

During the Congress of Vienna, Napoleon had left the island of Elba and landed in France, again calling the nation to arms, but his new career ended in quick defeat as the eight Allies drew together and declared that Napoleon "had placed himself outside the law . . . cut himself off from civil and social relations . . . and, as an Enemy and Disruptor of the World, he has exposed himself to public prosecution." The Final Act of the Congress was signed on 9 June 1815, and a few days later Napoleon, the first modern international war criminal, fought the Battle of Waterloo. On 20 November 1815, the Second Peace of Paris was concluded, and, on the same day, the major states of Europe opened a completely original avenue of international organization. By a new Quadruple Alliance, Russia, Prussia, Austria, and Great Britain were now determined to guarantee the peace terms and thwart any revival of French aggression. Therefore, they agreed "to renew their Meetings at fixed periods . . . for the purpose of consulting upon their common interests, and for the consideration of the measures which at each of these periods shall be considered the most salutary for the repose and prosperity of Nations and for the maintenance of the Peace of Europe [5]." The age of consultation in international organization had begun.

Liquidation of the Napoleonic Wars continued long after the Second Peace of Paris; in consequence, the ambassadors representing the Great Powers in London, Frankfurt, and Paris met in formal conferences in the years following 1815. Nothing comparable had followed Westphalia or Utrecht. The London ambassadorial conference dealt unsuccessfully with methods to abolish the slave trade, the menace of Barbary pirates, and the execution of the Treaty of Kiel between Denmark and Sweden; the Frankfurt committee also accomplished little in discussing the disputes of Bavaria, Baden, and Austria; but the Paris conference met with greater success. France, broken in defeat, had been occupied by an inter-Allied army of 150,000 men under the supreme command of Wellington. Each of the major powers supplied 50,000 troops, while the smaller powers made up the balance. Each contingent had its own commander, but Wellington was responsible for the army of occupation as a whole, and the means of international coordination was the ambassadorial conference at Paris. Thus, the notion of a supreme military chief commanding various national armies while reporting to an international organization was introduced between 1815 and 1818.

THE CONFERENCE OF AIX-LA-CHAPELLE

Article V of the Second Peace of Paris had stated that the utmost extent of the duration of the military occupation of France was to be five years, and that the period might be reduced to three years by the Allied sovereigns if they felt that order and tranquillity had been restored earlier. Ostensibly, the Four Great Powers met at Aix-la-Chapelle on 27 September 1818 only to consider further their relations with France in respect to the military occupation, the satisfaction of war claims, and future diplomatic relations. Through careful maneuvering, British Foreign Minister Castlereagh and Austrian Foreign Minister Metternich managed to prevent the invitation of Spain and other secondary states to the meeting, thereby placing the superintendence of European affairs in the hands of Russia, Prussia, Austria, and Britain. To avoid affronting the lesser sovereigns, the decision to call the Conference was based upon Article V and the military occupation of France, although Castlereagh wanted to justify the Conference by Article VI of the Quadruple Alliance in which the Big Four had agreed to periodic reunions. More than any man, Castlereagh looked forward to a new age of consultation in international politics by means of round-table discussion among the Great Powers [6].

Never before 1818 had the Great Powers met in time of peace to settle

European problems by consultation. In truth, the meeting was forecast by the Paris peace treaty and was a part of the liquidation of the war troubles, but the idea of an international diplomatic center scanning and discussing the controversies of the Continent was novel. It was also fundamental to the growth of international organization.

Once the immediate problems of the French occupation and indemnities had been eliminated at Aix-la-Chapelle, the very nature of the Great Power conference and its future use became an issue. Castlereagh envisaged a permanent system of reunions, as indicated in Article VI of the Quadruple Alliance, not only to work out by consultation the difficulties raised by the Napoleonic Wars but also to soothe any future political irritations of the Continent. Toward this end France was now invited to participate in the consultative system of the other Four Powers. But the British Cabinet, admonished by George Canning, was in no mood to commit itself in 1818 to the unprecedented idea of *regular* international meetings, and so informed Castlereagh.

Meanwhile, Tsar Alexander advanced the startling proposition that the Great Powers ought to guarantee to each other their existing forms of government and territory. Three years earlier the devout and romantically unbalanced Russian Emperor had gotten the Prussian and Austrian monarchs to sign a Treaty of Holy Alliance in which they declared that they would regulate their public acts according to the benign principles of the Christian religion. Except to reinforce public opinion that the sovereigns were leagued against any liberal reform, the "Alliance" had no practical operation; but at Aix-la-Chapelle, Alexander looked forward to a league of nations, open to all states, which would by concerted action suppress any threat—including domestic revolutions—to the stability of Europe. Curiously enough, the Tsar's proposal looked back one hundred and five years to the Peace of Utrecht and looked forward one hundred and one years to the Treaty of Versailles; it was at Utrecht that the Abbé de Saint-Pierre had offered a project which would guarantee to each of the sovereigns perpetual peace both within and outside their kingdoms, and it was at Versailles that the Covenant of the League of Nations declared that "the Members . . . undertake to respect and preserve as against external aggression the territorial integrity and existing political independence of all Members." Ironically the Tsar's plan appalled the British in 1818 as the League appalled many Americans in 1919, for both treaties seemed to expect each member to support the status quo—in both foreign and domestic affairs—without reservation. Gradually, therefore, the more limited but more feasible view of the British prevailed at Aix-la-Chapelle—that the powers, for the peace and security of Europe, "judged it necessary to hold *particular* reunions, whether between the august sovereigns themselves or their respective ministers and plenipotentiaries, in order to deal with their special interests jointly . . . the period and limit of these reunions will each time be arranged in advance through Diplomatic Communications [7]."

In those instances where the interests of other states might be involved, the Great Powers agreed that no meeting would be held until a formal invitation to participate in the discussion had been extended to the states concerned. The international conference open to all states in time of peace was not formally recognized.

Although the Aix-la-Chapelle reunion originated in the need for discussing further the relations of the Great Powers with France, ample time had been set aside for a number of other questions affecting Europe, namely, the revolt of the Spanish-American colonies; the international slave trade; the depredations of the Barbary pirates; the treatment of Napoleon on St. Helena; the emancipation of Jews; the quarrels between Spain and Portugal, Denmark and Sweden, Bavaria and Baden, etc. The Conference had neither the power nor the inclination to decide and settle all these questions, but the net achievement of clarifying the issues and adjusting a number of them by friendly discussion among the assembled Great Powers indicated the utility of international consultation.

Some disputes among the German states, a cession of territory to the Netherlands, and minor Italian claims emanating from the Napoleonic Wars were not settled at Aix-la-Chapelle, but these were relegated to a conference of ministers at Frankfurt in 1819. Having once disposed of these questions, the Conference ended, and the consultative system was left without a central organ or a fixed day of reunion.

Aix-la-Chapelle in 1818 marked the high tide of early European consultation. In the three succeeding conferences at Troppau in 1820, Laibach in 1821, and Verona in 1822, the concerted opinion and action which had characterized the Great Powers in their common struggle against a revolutionary France rapidly disintegrated. Although Britain had been as concerned as Russia, Prussia, and Austria in restoring stability to the Continent of Europe by stamping out Bonapartism, she did not feel that the Quadruple Alliance should be interpreted as a subscription to repression and reaction everywhere. In that respect Britain's policy diverged from that of the three eastern European sovereigns and foreshadowed the early collapse of the consultative system established in 1815.

THE CONFERENCES OF TROPPAU AND LAIBACH

The effect of France's revolutionary armies marching through Europe under the banners of republicanism and constitutionalism, no matter how perverted by Napoleon, was not quickly spent in the Italian states or Spain. In January 1820 a revolution of the troops forced Ferdinand VII to accept the liberal Spanish Constitution of 1812; on 18 April 1820 the Russian government circulated a memorandum to its ministers in the courts of the other four powers which pointed out that the Allies had joined to wipe out revolution in France but that revolution had now shifted its ground to Spain. Should not the five ministers at Madrid speak with the one voice of the Alliance which would indicate its dismay at the means used to secure a new kind of government?

Austria, however, was not interested in either joint diplomacy or a conference, for the likely result, in case of Spanish intransigence, would be an Allied intervention and the march of Russian troops westward. As for Britain, she could not accept the view that the consultative system should operate in every disturbance of Europe, regardless of the gravity of the situation or the states concerned, and she flatly pursued a course of nonintervention in Spain. The Tsar's proposal for consultation on Spain, another aspect of his long-run scheme for a confederation which would guarantee all existing governments, was refused.

In the case of Naples, however, the situation was different. There the revolution of July 1820, by forcing the liberal Spanish Constitution of 1812 upon Ferdinand IV, King of the Two Sicilies, affected Austria's interests in northern Italy, already seething with conspiracies against the clumsy foreign rule. Metternich, aware of the British distaste for collective intervention, merely attempted to gain Russian support before taking action. But the Tsar, annoyed at the coolness of Austria to his suggestions on Spain, again called for a conference of the Great Powers. From this predicament the peacetime conferences of Troppau and Laibach originated.

Castlereagh would not take part in a league of the Great Powers against revolution in Spain or Naples. Indeed, no doubt of Austria's special interest and justification for taking action in Naples troubled the British policy, but with the opposition in the House of Commons attacking the government on every front, the foreign minister adamantly turned from any association of Britain, even verbal, with the acts of Austria in Italy. As for France, the more moderate constitutional leaders of the government were persuaded by the British view to refuse the sanction of the Great Powers to Austrian intervention. It happened, therefore, that the Troppau meeting in Austrian Silesia opened 23 October 1820, with British and French representatives, not plenipotentiaries, empowered only to report the proceedings of the Conference back to their governments. Inevitably the Crown Prince of Prussia and the Emperors of Austria and Russia, with their respective ministers, drew together and privately agreed to a protocol which would have automatically condemned any revolutionary government and bound the powers, if such a revolution "threatened" other states, "to bring back the guilty state into the bosom of the Great Alliance" by peaceful means or, if necessary, by arms [8]. Such a document was completely unacceptable to Britain and did not receive the endorsement of France, but even as the unofficial view of the "Holy Alliance" it brought to the surface the rock of disagreement upon which the consultative system of the five sovereigns was split.

Meanwhile, on 20 November 1820, Austria, Prussia, and Russia, later joined by France, invited the King of the Two Sicilies to meet them in Laibach in order to consider further the best means of "maintaining peace, delivering Europe from the flame of revolution, and setting aside or annulling . . . the evils which result from the violation of all principles of decency and morality [9]." The Troppau Conference then adjourned to Laibach, where the representatives of all the Italian states assembled with the Great Powers between 8 January and 12 March 1821. Time and again Metternich and the Russian representatives, Pozzo di Borgo and Capo d'Istria, tried to bring forth declarations from the Conference which would have indicated to Europe the unanimity of the Five Powers against revolution and the communal support of Austrian intervention in Italy. But Britain would not adhere to any statement premised on the right of the Great Powers to intervene *as a body* when domestic revolution in one state seemed to threaten other states. As a result, Austrian troops were dispatched to Naples and then to Turin, to stamp out revolutions and restore autocrats by an agreement among the three eastern sovereigns only. The final declaration of the Conference of Laibach, signed by Prussia, Austria, and Russia, read: "Expressly intended to combat and repress rebellion, the Allied Forces, far from serving any exclusive interest, have come to the aid of subjugated peoples . . . as a support for their liberty, not as an attack upon their independence." To their ministers at foreign courts they wrote: "To conserve that which is lawfully established, such must be the invariable principle of their policy, the starting point and final goal of all their resolutions," and that another reunion would be held during the next year to review the military occupation of Naples and Turin [10].

The Conference at Troppau met in eight plenary sessions; another fifteen meetings were called at Laibach. Without full powers, however, the British and French delegates did not participate in the many informal and intimate conversations of the Holy Alliance powers where policy was really formulated. No protocol was signed by all the powers; instead, Gentz, who had acted as secretary-general at Vienna, Aix-la-Chapelle, Troppau, and Laibach, merely recorded the proceedings in a journal. At Troppau and Laibach the Quadruple Alliance consultative system stumbled, yet the Allies still tried to speak as an international organization acting collectively —or, in the case of Britain, not acting collectively—for the peace and security of Europe.

THE CONFERENCE OF VERONA

During the course of the Troppau-Laibach assemblies, France had pursued an equivocal foreign policy reflecting the struggle between the constitutional monarchists and the ultra-Royalists within her own government. Though France could not endorse the collective-intervention doctrine formally, she had been passive to the Russian-Prussian-Austrian declarations, had joined in the invitation of the King of the Two Sicilies to Laibach, and, at one point, had offered to mediate between the revolutionary Piedmontese and the Allied Powers. As Louis XVIII's ministers moved to the right after 1820, the revolutionary government of Spain just across the Pyrenees troubled France as much as the Italian insurrection had threatened the patronizing rule of Austria. The fear of the French conservatives was further exacerbated when a new success of the Spanish liberals against their faithless King, Ferdinand VII, led to the establishment of a regency on 14 September 1822, the virtual imprisonment of the sovereign, and the annulling of all official acts signed by him since 7 March 1820.

Following the lead of Austria, therefore, France began to seek a mandate from the Allied Powers to intervene in Spain and restore the "legitimate" government of the Bourbons.

The Conference of Verona, the third and last of the conferences under the system of reunions established by the Quadruple Alliance in 1815, was the meeting promised at Laibach for further discussion of Italian affairs. A preliminary gathering at Vienna in the summer of 1822 had diverted Alexander from his purpose of invoking the Alliance against Turkey on behalf of the rebellious Christian Greeks. To assist the Greeks against their legal government was a contradiction of the Tsar's own logic: namely, wherever revolution occurred Europe ought to take every measure to repress it. The uppermost question, therefore, in the Tsar's mind—and in the French policy—was the remedy necessary to purge Spain of revolution. For Britain the issue of the Spanish American colonies, now in various stages of revolt, assumed paramount significance, especially should

France dominate the Spanish government and thereby attempt an American expedition to reconquer the colonies.

At Verona, the conferences began 20 October 1822. Short shrift was given to Italian affairs: the withdrawal of Austrian troops (called Force Allié in the original circular) from Piedmont was to be completed by 30 September 1823, while the army of occupation in the Two Sicilies was to be reduced to 17,000 men [11]. But the action to be taken on Spain again splintered Britain from the Allies. With his customary zeal, Tsar Alexander at first offered to put 150,000 Russians into an international army for action in Spain. This plan terrified Metternich, who briefly closed ranks with Britain against collective intervention and then set out to persuade the French of the folly of such a course. Once the specter of the Tsar's armies crossing Austria had vanished, Metternich was not averse to concerting with France, Prussia, and Russia in a common policy against the Spanish Cortes. The three eastern courts then issued identical advice to their representatives in Madrid to press for changes in the Spanish government and, should this request be refused, to break off diplomatic relations.

From the beginning, the British policy was plain. Castlereagh had died on 1 August 1822, just before the Verona Conference which he had planned to attend. The Duke of Wellington, the British plenipotentiary, faithfully followed Castlereagh's basic policy, as he wrote from Verona to London that he would object to everything except that France should explain herself and that if there should be any defensive treaty or even declaration against Spain, he would decline to become a party to it [12].

The French ministers were by no means unanimous in their attitude toward Spain, but as the ultra-Royalists grew stronger the mediation of Britain was refused and the moral support of Prussia, Austria, and Russia at Verona encouraged military action. In April 1823 the French attacked Spain; on May 23 Madrid fell without a shot being fired.

THE END OF CONSULTATION UNDER THE QUADRUPLE ALLIANCE

The Conference of Verona marked the last consultation of the Five Great Powers under the system inaugurated at Chaumont on 9 March 1814 and renewed by the Quadruple Alliance on 20 November 1815. With only a weak provision for regular reunions, without any secretariat save Metternich's servant, Gentz, and without even encompassing all the states of Europe, the system nevertheless envisioned the stability and security of the Continent by international cooperation. To call it an international "organization" by twentieth-century standards may seem inept, yet considering the ruthless actions of the dynastic states and the lack of any semblance of

"European" responsibility up to the nineteenth century, only the most cynical could deny the intrinsic value of such a concert of powers who might talk before acting, listen before demanding, and, perhaps, labor to justify their ardent policies before the cool opinion of their fellow sovereigns.

It was to be expected that the Alliance would serve the national interests of the participating states. Castlereagh had no illusions about it:

In this Alliance, as in all other human Arrangements, nothing is more likely to impair, or even to destroy its real utility, than any attempt to push its duties and its obligations beyond the Sphere which its original conception and understood Principles will warrant. It was an Union for the re-conquest and liberation of a great proportion of the Continent of Europe from the military dominion of France; and having subdued the Conqueror, it took the States of Possession, as established by the Peace, under the protection of the Alliance. It never was, however, intended as an Union for the Government of the World, or for the Superintendence of the Internal Affairs of other States [13].

On Italy, consultation had served Austrian interests; on Spain, consultation had served French interests. The key to the Quadruple and Holy Alliance system, however, was Alexander I, for, in truth, although Russia never obtained any special advantage from the Conferences of Aix-la-Chapelle, Troppau-Laibach, or Verona, the Tsar was the prime ideological mover of the system as a bulwark against revolution. In a confused way Alexander sought a permanent international organization for the government of Europe; in practice his plans meant dictation by the Great Powers and the suppression of all popular movements endangering the established order.

The rebellion of the Greeks against their Turkish rulers, however, beginning in 1821, threw the Tsar into a quandary, for here the Russian national interests called for support of the Greeks and the weakening of Turkish power. At Vienna in 1822 Metternich had dissuaded the Tsar from intervention in Greece. Still wrestling with his conscience and Russian national policy, Alexander proposed in June 1824 a division of Greece into three parts, to be vassals of Turkey, and collective mediation on the part of the Allies between Greece and Turkey—with enforcement if necessary. To consider his plan he invited the Four Allies to another reunion at St. Petersburg. Unalterably opposed to any action which might lead to a war between Russia and Turkey, neither Britain, France, nor Austria was willing to give Russia an excuse for intervening in Greece on behalf of the Alliance. In fact, Britain refused to attend the meetings held between February and April 1825, while Austria, at St. Petersburg, shied away from any forthright statement of policy. On 7 April 1825, therefore, the conference issued an innocuous protocol asking the Sublime Porte of Turkey to grant of his own free will satisfaction to his subjects in revolt and offered the good offices of the assembled powers. No reference was made to armistice, intervention, or enforcement. Eight months later Tsar Alexander was dead and so was the international organization of the Quadruple Alliance [14].

THE CONCERT OF EUROPE CONTINUES

The legal mechanism for consultation among the Five Great Powers failed in 1825, but the practice of international conferences, in time of peace, among the states of Europe to regulate their political views and interests had been firmly established. No permanent machinery existed, but a series of conferences from 1826 to 1913 served to inculcate the habit of multilateral consultation and testified to the genesis of international organization.

Greek Independence. Alexander had not been able to obtain a mandate for Russia from the Quadruple Alliance system. Nevertheless, as early as 1827 Britain and France had agreed by treaty to work with Tsar Nicholas on mediating between Greece and Turkey with the understanding that Greece would be semiautonomous, paying tribute to the Porte. Should mediation be refused, the Allies *in concert* would appoint consular agents to Greece; should an armistice be refused, the Allies would use every means, short of declaring war themselves, to prevent conflict.

Between 12 July 1827 and 25 July 1832, fifty-one meetings took place in London among the representatives of Britain, France, and Russia on the Greek independence movement. During the course of the conversations, an Allied fleet routed the Turks at Navarino while a French expeditionary force and a Russian army compelled the Porte to accept the terms for Greece laid down by the Allies. The military debacle of Turkey, however, led the Allies not only to declare Greece independent but to guarantee it in a protocol of 3 February 1830. Furthermore, each of the Allies promised not to send troops into Greece without the consent of the others. In 1832, as final evidence of international cooperation, Russia, France, and Britain not only selected a sovereign for the new state, King Otho of Bavaria, but also mutually guaranteed a loan to be contracted by Greece up to 60 million francs. Sixteen more meetings of the Allies were held in the summer of 1837 to clear up boundary lines, military service, and conditions of the internationally guaranteed loan.

Belgian Independence. At the same time as the Greek independence movement was under the consideration of an international conference, the Belgians revolted against their Dutch government. The French upset of the Bourbons in 1830 had touched off the fires of nationalism in Brussels on August 25, and on October 4 the Belgians declared their independence.

By the terms of the Vienna Congress Treaty, the Great Powers had established a Kingdom of the Netherlands which joined the Belgic provinces to
the United Provinces of the Netherlands. After one defeat in suppressing
the revolution, King William of the Netherlands called upon Britain,
France, Prussia, Austria, and Russia to help maintain the integrity of the
state which they had created. Conferences, therefore, "by means of their
Ambassadors and Ministers accredited to the Court of London" began 4
November 1830. An armistice was invoked immediately. After six meetings, the Five Powers collectively recognized the independence of Belgium
on 20 December 1830. Negotiations then continued on the basis of a treaty
of eighteen articles which carved out the limits of a new Belgian state
whose neutrality would be guaranteed by the Five Powers. In return, the
Belgians would share just about half the total state debts of the Netherlands.

The King of the Netherlands, loath to accept the dissection of his realm,
dispatched an army of 36,000 men to Belgium and within ten days had
the country at his mercy. On the threat of Britain's fleet and the actual
entry of a French army into Belgium, the Dutch forces withdrew. This
demonstration of Dutch strength, however, put the Netherlands in a better
bargaining position at the London Conference. Shortly thereafter, on
14 October 1831, a new treaty of twenty-four articles, more favorable to the
Netherlands' territorial claims, was presented to the contesting governments. King William, however, remained obstinate in the face of this over-
ture and refused to evacuate Antwerp.

Always favorable to the Belgian cause, Britain and France now proposed
intervention to the Conference. Russia, Austria, and especially Prussia, on
the other hand, had sympathized with the Dutch against their rebellious
subjects. Russia, however, was distracted by a violent Polish insurrection
and neither Austria nor Prussia was willing to countenance the general
warfare which might ensue if they thwarted Britain and France. On 1
October 1832, therefore, after seventy meetings, the three eastern sovereigns dissociated themselves from any coercion of the Netherlands, and
the Conference virtually ended.

The western powers proceeded to blockade the Dutch coast, and a
French army besieged Antwerp. After prolonged diplomatic wrangling,
the British and French promised to raise their embargo of Dutch goods
and ships on 21 May 1833, while the Netherlands pledged not to take any
further military action against the Belgians. Not until 1838 did King William grudgingly accept the principles of the 1831 treaty of twenty-four
articles. The Conference of the Five Powers then reassembled at London
in April 1839 and consummated two treaties: one between the Five Powers
and the Netherlands, another of identical wording between the Five

Powers and Belgium, while the German Confederation acceded to the provisions concerning the Grand Duchy of Luxembourg [15].

Although all states had not been parties to the negotiation and although the final terms suited chiefly the aims of Britain and France, nevertheless a general war had been avoided in an area appropriately described as "the cockpit of Europe," and the legal position of Belgium, independent and neutral, had been ratified amicably by a collective international agreement. Another experience with international consultation, moreover, had been recorded, and statesmen had been given another opportunity to work out their problems by peaceful parleys. Far from perfection, far from offering a panacea to all political ills, the technique of consultation at least offered patience and understanding in diplomacy.

Europe slumbered uneasily between 1815 and 1853. Revolutions struck practically every state, some bloodless, some violent, some the cracking of decrepit empires and crusty governments. But no European international war interrupted the beginnings of industrialization, the grasp of the middle classes for power, and the throb of nationalism. When a dire international crisis developed between Russia and the Ottoman Empire in 1853, the European powers fell back upon their experience with consultation and called a conference.

The Eastern Question. From the middle of the eighteenth century onward, Russia had steadily advanced her influence south at the expense of the enfeebled Turkish Empire. By the Treaty of Kuchuk Kainarji in 1774, Russia secured the northern coast of the Black Sea, established a permanent embassy at Constantinople, and gained the right of protecting all Orthodox Christians in Turkey. Russia annexed the Crimea in 1783 and extended her boundaries to the Dniester River in 1792. The terms of the Treaty of Bucharest in 1812 advanced the Russian border to the Pruth River, and in 1826 Russia became a protector of Serbia, nominally within the Ottoman Empire. When the allied fleet intervened on behalf of the Greek independence movement, the Russian armies attacked Turkey by land. In consequence, the Treaty of Adrianople in 1829 not only stipulated that Greece would be independent but granted special interests to Russia in the provinces of Wallachia and Moldavia (Rumania). Finally, Russia lent aid to the Sublime Porte in repressing a revolt of Mehemet Ali of Egypt; in return, Turkey signed a secret convention at Unkiar-Skelessi in 1833 which would have closed the straits of the Dardanelles to the warships of all nations—except Russia.

A new revolt of Mehemet Ali moved with such swiftness that the ambassadors of the Five Great Powers in Constantinople cautioned the Sultan to "abstain from all definitive negotiation without their cooperation."

Both France and Britain, fearful of a Russian thrust through the Dardanelles into the Mediterranean should Turkey be further weakened, obtained the agreement of the Great Powers and Turkey that so long as the Porte was at peace no foreign warship would be admitted into the straits. In effect, this declaration canceled the privileges granted to Russia by the Treaty of Unkiar-Skelessi.

THE CONFERENCES OF VIENNA AND THE CRIMEAN WAR

Russian pressure on Turkey was not to be relaxed by paper conventions. In 1853 the Tsar prodded the Sultan by offering a permanent alliance in exchange for recognition of Russia as the protector of the Greek Church throughout the Turkish Empire. Since the Orthodox Christian subjects numbered 12 to 15 million people and the Greek Church exercised extensive temporal as well as spiritual power over them, the Sultan, encouraged by France and Britain, demurred. In June the Tsar's troops occupied the provinces of Moldavia and Wallachia. Immediately the British and French dispatched a fleet to the mouth of the Dardanelles. At the same time the French foreign minister, following the diplomatic methods of the century, proposed another international conference to discuss the crisis.

The Tsar would not recognize the right of the other powers to halt his enterprise, but through the skillful diplomacy of Count Buol, Austrian foreign minister since 1852, a conference began in Vienna 24 July 1853, to "mediate" between Turkey and Russia. Though Russia did not attend, she offered no remonstrances to the meeting and, at one point, an equivocal project for conciliation set forth by the Conference almost won acceptance by both sides.

The intention of Russia, nevertheless, to humble Turkey, even to dismember "the sick man of Europe," was patent; the Turks themselves, increasingly resentful and belligerent, declared war on 4 October 1853. For the first time in the history of modern international organization, however, a nonbelligerent international conference continued to meet and to use its joint influence to end hostilities between two major states. On December 5 the Conference of Vienna called upon Turkey to submit the bases upon which she would negotiate peace; on January 13 Turkey replied to the Conference that Wallachia and Moldavia must be evacuated first, that the Porte would grant religious privileges to all states, and that Turkey recognized the obligations of the Treaty of 1841 on the straits. On February 2 the Russian reply to these points discounted the 1841 convention entirely, called for peace negotiations between Turkey and

Russia *only,* with a separate article on religious liberty and protection, and agreed to evacuate the Danubian provinces *after* peace was made. By this time the British-French fleet had entered the Black Sea.

On March 5 the Vienna Conference considered a draft of preliminaries for a peace treaty submitted by Russia, but neither France nor Britain would admit the modifications to the Turkish proposals made by Russia, especially the point that the British-French fleet should be withdrawn as Moldavia and Wallachia were evacuated. Thus, the Crimean War began 27 and 28 March 1854. Two final conferences at Vienna, on April 9 and May 23, reaffirmed the principles upon which Austria, Prussia, Britain, and France were united. Although the German states did not join the war, they agreed that

. . . their governments remain united in the double aim of maintaining the territorial integrity of the Ottoman Empire, for which the evacuation of the Danubian provinces is and will continue to be one of the essential conditions, and of strengthening in a manner according with the feelings of the Sultan and by all means compatible with his independence and sovereignty, the civil and religious rights of the Christian subjects of the Porte [16].

Austria greatly feared the establishment of Russia in Moldavia and Wallachia. With Prussia seconding her actions, she prevailed upon the Tsar to leave the provinces without relinquishing his claims; by an agreement with the Sultan, Austria herself occupied the area. Meanwhile, four points were submitted by Austria to all the interested courts as a basis for negotiation: (*a*) the Danubian provinces were to be placed under a collective guarantee of the Great Powers; (*b*) the navigation of the Danube was to be free; (*c*) Russia was to abandon her claim to exclusive tutelage over Turkish Orthodox Christian subjects; and (*d*) the Treaty of 1841 was to be revised in order to attach more completely the existence of the Ottoman Empire to the European equilibrium and "put an end to the prepondance of Russia in the Black Sea."

On 7 January 1855 Russia accepted the four points as a basis for negotiation and another conference opened in Vienna on March 15 with the Five Powers and Turkey in attendance. In a sense, the second Vienna Conference was a continuation of the meetings abandoned just twelve months previously for, by consultation, the Great Powers were still groping for a settlement of their differences on the Eastern question. Unfortunately, however, they had forgotten the experience of pre-Napoleonic conferences which attempted to draft peace terms during a state of war. Russia had not been decisively defeated, troop movements and fighting continued, and, therefore, Prince Gortchakov balked at penning the Russian fleet in the Black Sea. This conference met fourteen times before its end, 4 June 1855.

Peace, nevertheless, was not far off. The Russians abandoned Sevastopol on 8 September 1855, in good order, but with frightful losses in personnel (12,913 officers and men in a single day) and the gutting of the Black Sea fleet. Not only did the ministers of Saxony and Bavaria attempt to mediate between St. Petersburg and Paris, but Austria, now gravely concerned about the benevolence of Napoleon III toward Sardinia, which had joined the coalition against Russia, sought to end the Crimean War. On 16 December 1855, Austria sent an ultimatum to Russia asking the Tsar to adhere within thirty days to five points, not very different from the basic four points discussed at the latter Vienna conference, or else Austria would make a common cause with Britain and France. Appealing as a last resort to Prussia for an opinion, Tsar Alexander II was advised by his uncle Frederick William IV to yield. Exactly thirty days after the ultimatum Russia notified Austria that she would accept the specified points as the basis of negotiation.

THE CONGRESS OF PARIS IN 1856

The Congress of Paris assembled 25 February 1856 to finish the aborted work of the two Vienna conferences. Invited to this European assembly were not only the great belligerent powers but also Sardinia, which had supported the British-French cause by sending 18,000 men to the Crimea. The Prussian delegates and Austria which had drafted the terms of negotiation did not arrive until March 18, but thereafter they participated in all meetings. After electing Count Walewski, foreign minister of the host government, President of the Congress, "a custom consecrated by precedents and recently observed at Vienna," the Congress at its first sitting agreed to an immediate and general armistice.

During the course of twenty-four meetings between 25 February and 16 April 1856, the plenipotentiaries of the great states of Europe hammered out one general treaty of peace, on the lines of the four points, and three conventions: (a) closing the straits to all warships, (b) neutralizing the Black Sea, and (c) nonfortification of the Aaland Islands. Finally, an important declaration on international maritime law was made.

Although the Crimean War as a whole was a localized affair propping up the sagging Turkish Empire against the ambition of Russia, the preliminary negotiations and peace settlement followed and developed the earlier experiences of international organization. The powers at Paris, for example, agreed to respect the territorial integrity of the Ottoman Empire and "consider any act aimed at its violation as a question of general interest," thereby admitting Turkey to the advantages "of the public law and concert of Europe." Citing the Congress of Vienna (1815) declaration on international rivers, the Congress of Paris declared that the Danube was also free for navigation and established an international commission to clear out the mouth of the river in order to facilitate such navigation. Furthermore, the governments of the signatory powers agreed to bring their Declaration on Maritime Law "to the attention of all states which had not been called to participate in the Congress of Paris and invite them to accede to it [17]."

Gradually European foreign offices were accepting international conferences as a normal way of managing international politics even in time of peace. Nothing comparable to this experience had existed before Napoleon. As the conference method was used it acquired precedents, ceremonies, style, and fuller exposition. One has only to compare the terse protocols published by the Congress of Vienna, the meetings at Aix-la-Chapelle, Troppau-Laibach, and Verona with the more complete descriptions of the conferences on Belgium held in London or the proceedings at the Congress of Paris in order to catch the trend of international organization in the nineteenth century.

THE FRUITION OF INTERNATIONAL CONSULTATION

It is virtually impossible to trace the rapid multiplication of international conferences during the latter half of the nineteenth century. Some, like the conference between Great Britain, Austria, Denmark, France, the German Confederation, Prussia, Russia, and Sweden-Norway in 1864, grew out of common effort to stop a war in progress (Austria-Prussia versus Denmark); others met to find agreements which would prevent the outbreak of hostilities. The conference in London, 1867, over the status of Luxembourg, for example, brought together all the great states of Europe, including the new Kingdom of Italy, and pledged them to respect the perpetual neutrality of Luxembourg, thereby easing for a few years a point of tension between France and Prussia [18].

The significance of this multiplication of conferences lies in the adaptability of the device of consultation to late-nineteenth-century diplomacy in both peace and war and the willingness of states to submit their propositions, pleas, and arguments to the hearing of other states. The new system of consultation among states, however, did not and could not fashion instantaneously an international community. Respect for the law and the swift punishment of criminals as typified by the national community loomed upon a horizon very distant from the first simple steps toward international organization.

THE LONDON CONFERENCE OF 1871

In 1870, with France pinned down by Bismarck, the Russian Chancellor Gortchakov repudiated the Paris Treaty of 1856 which had limited the size of the Tsar's naval forces in the Black Sea. He commented acridly that written law, founded on treaties, no longer retained the same moral sanction as it had in other times. Austria and France were dismayed; Britain was incensed. Europe turned to Bismarck for judgment. With astuteness, the great German leader proposed the convenient device of a conference —in London.

Perforce Europe yielded in 1871 to the Tsar's unilateral denunciation of the Black Seas clause, yet Russia had been maneuvered into placing its cause before a conference of fellow sovereigns. The other clauses of the 1856 Paris treaty, moreover, remained intact and the Conference restated the ultimate rationale of international organization: that treaties must be observed and changes in a compact should obtain the consent of the contracting parties [19].

During the nineteenth century Prussia won its struggle with Austria for leadership of the Germanic peoples. Nothing pointed to this shift in power more accurately than the fact that Berlin had initiated the 1871 Conference in London and that Berlin, rather than Vienna, was the site of two of the most important European meetings of the latter part of the century. Both in 1878 and in 1884 to 1885 imperial Germany was the host government to the major states of Europe in consultation with each other.

THE CONGRESS OF BERLIN IN 1878

The Congress of Berlin in 1878, like the Paris meeting of 1856 and the London meeting of 1871, centered upon the relative position of Turkey and Russia. In truth, almost every decade of the nineteenth century witnessed some new concession wrung from enfeebled Turkey by the Christian states of Europe, particularly by the expanding Russian Empire. Serbia and Montenegro began a new thrust into Turkey by declaring war upon the Porte in 1876. The alarmed diplomats of the major powers drew together in Constantinople and advised Turkey to reform her imperial administration; Turkey refused this recommendation, and the meeting disbanded only to reassemble in London on 31 March 1877. Again Turkey was exhorted to reform her government and demobilize her armies, and again Turkey refused. Thirty days later Russian troops marched into the Balkans.

On 3 March 1878 Russia dictated twenty-nine articles of peace to the

Turks at San Stefano which would have virtually given the Tsar control
of the entire Balkan area. Great Britain, however, could not bear the continuous liquidation of the Turkish Empire by Russia, for the Bosporus,
the Suez Canal, and the Persian Gulf, all vital to the British national interest, lay in the path of the Russian movement southward. Seconded by
France, Austria, and Italy, therefore, Britain insisted that no revision of
the 1856 and 1871 conventions could take place without the consent of
the signatory powers and that the Treaty of San Stefano must be reviewed.
Russia acquiesced, and Berlin extended an invitation to still another international conference.

"In the outward unanimity and technical precision of the Berlin Congress the European Concert achieved its masterpiece [20]." This was
the judgment of Henry F. Munro in a confidential document prepared
for the United States government during the First World War. Within
fourteen months a new era of international collaboration was to begin,
but looking backward from 1918 the historian could perceive the fruition
of international consultation. At Berlin in 1878 the chief states of Europe
solidified the conference system by respecting precedents, improving
procedure, and solving international problems by collective negotiation.

Personnel and Political Achievements. The Congress of Berlin met in
time of peace to consider fundamental changes of two multilateral treaties.
In an inchoate way the great states of Europe were "legislating," revamping
international law. Invited by Prince von Bismarck, chancellor of Germany,
Great Britain sent its prime minister, Disraeli, two additional plenipotentiaries, and a staff of approximately forty officials from the British Foreign
Office plus other military and technical advisers; Russia appointed its
chancellor, Prince Gortchakov, as its first plenipotentiary; Austria, France,
Italy, and Turkey dispatched their leading statesmen to Berlin. Each
mission included a staff of diplomats, secretaries, and experts to advise the
plenipotentiaries. Between 13 June and 13 July 1878 the delegates assembled twenty times in plenary session and concluded the Treaty of
Berlin which, in effect, created Bulgaria and increased the power of Austria, Russia, Serbia, and Montenegro at Turkey's expense. Yet the enormous claims of the Treaty of San Stefano were so reduced in Berlin that
Turkey remained a European power, stretching from the Adriatic to the
Black Sea, blocking the southward thrust of the Germans and the Slavs.
Consultation of the Great Powers on Turkey, moreover, had averted war
between Russia and Great Britain [21].

Procedure: Secretariat and Committees. Scarcely noticed at the time,
yet a marked development in the course of international organization,
was the appointment of a secretariat representing two states rather than
the host government alone. At Vienna, Aix-la-Chapelle, Troppau, and

Laibach the Austrian Friedrich von Gentz had acted as Secretary-General; at Paris in 1856 a French diplomat had recorded the discussions; at London in 1867 and 1871 a British diplomat had acted as secretary to the conferences. But in Berlin, Bismarck, as President of the Conference, nominated not only Radowitz, German minister at Athens, as secretary, with three other German aides, but also de Moüy, first secretary of the French Embassy at Berlin, as an assistant secretary. For the first time in the history of international organization the secretariat of a conference comprised more than one nationality. Six years later at another Berlin conference a Frenchman and two Germans served as secretaries; since 1878 the practice of mixed secretariats has been continuous.

Up to the Berlin Congress of 1878, only two other international assemblies of the powers had used formal committees for work preliminary to the final agreement of the plenipotentiaries—the monumental Congress of Vienna, which had employed ten different committees, and the Paris Congress of 1856 following the Crimean War, which had used a frontier committee and a drafting committee. Beginning with the Berlin Congress of 1878, however, the employment of committees and commissions at international conferences became standard procedure. The eight sessions of the Berlin Congress resolved in the establishment of a boundary committee which worked almost continuously until the end of the conference on the complicated border lines of the Balkans. In its work the committee called upon several military commissions for technical information. At the same time a drafting committee was elected to put into treaty form the articles debated and approved by the entire Congress.

The Treaty of Berlin formulated a relationship of the nations in the Balkans which endured for a generation, but the zeal of nationalism in the small states and the impotence of Turkey meant constant subterranean tremors for the foundations of peace. While custom and procedural developments were strengthening the practice of international consultation throughout the nineteenth century, no continuous international organization yet provided the channels through which the energy for change might be funneled, controlled, and spent.

WEAKNESS AND BREAKDOWN OF THE CONSULTATIVE SYSTEM

The Greeks, at the ninth session of the Congress of Berlin, had presented their complaints of Turkish administration and made claims to territory. Crete, in particular, aspired to union with Greece. By Articles 23 and 24 of the Treaty of Berlin, however, the Sublime Porte promised to reform the administration of Crete while the Great Powers offered to mediate any further territorial disputes between the two states. The international system of consultation moved awkwardly. Insurrection in Crete flared within a generation; infatuated by nationalism, the Greeks sent a military expedition to the restless island. Great Britain, France, Austria, Russia, Germany, and Italy staved off violent change, nevertheless, by concerted action in landing detachments of marines during February 1897. The language of a contemporary dispatch from the Russian government to the Prime Minister of Great Britain is strikingly indicative of a modern approach to political change in the international community: ". . . all the Naval Commanders should decide upon landing detachments . . . for restoring tranquillity to the island, which would thus be held, so to speak, in trust by European forces until such time as the Cretan question had been settled by the Concert of European Powers [22]." But the consultative system did not move with enough alacrity to prevent Greece from declaring war upon Turkey two months later. Only when the rash Greeks met a rough defeat did the Great Powers mediate peace between the contending states.

In its clumsy handling of crises lay the fundamental weakness of the consultative system: without a continuous organization the Great Powers convened sporadically and acted only by unanimous consent. The opinion of the small disinterested states during the nineteenth century was not regarded as relevant to the solution of international political conflicts. As the six powers of the European concert arrogated to themselves, therefore, general control over the peoples of the world—in Europe, in Asia, in Africa—the twentieth century opened upon an array of two giant nation-state combinations: the British-French bloc favored by Russia and the German-Austrian bloc favored by Italy. Because the consultative system was restricted to a few states, because the relationship of the members was defined only in bilateral agreements or joint pronouncements on specific situations, because the Concert of Europe did not provide the opportunity for continuous consultation and continuous organization to mitigate conflict, it failed to meet the pressing needs of international society.

THE ALGECIRAS CONFERENCE OF 1906

In 1906 Europe faced a new political crisis. During the latter part of the nineteenth century Morocco had been pressed by several states of Europe and the United States of America to grant special status to their diplomatic missions for the protection of their nationals and property. In 1880 an international conference of all the interested states held sixteen meetings in Madrid and signed a convention regulating the rights and obligations of foreigners in Morocco [23]. But the balance between the German-Austrian bloc and British-French bloc had become so delicate that when France asserted a protectorate over Morocco in 1905, it raised an international crisis verging upon war. Again the powers fell back upon a conference which opened in Algeciras on 16 January 1906.

The United States had not attended any significant European international conference until after the Civil War; at Algeciras she made her first bow in an arena open to immediate political repercussions. Also in attendance, in addition to the Six Great Powers of Europe, were Belgium, Spain, Morocco, the Netherlands, Portugal, and Sweden who had signed the Madrid Convention of 1880.

The salient issue of the Conference was the degree of control France should obtain over Morocco. Germany, of course, resisted every proposal which would place France, with her interested partner Spain, in a commanding position over the police, the trade, the finances, and the foreign nationals in Morocco. Through long parleys and grudging concessions the powerful states of Europe managed to devise very complicated—and very unworkable—devices of an international character. Thus, the police for the eight ports of Morocco open to foreign commerce were to be the Sultan's police, but French and Spanish instructors were to assist in the organization and the training of this force. Rules on the recruitment, discipline, training, and administration of the police were to be jointly formulated by the Moroccan war minister, the chief French and Spanish instructor, and an inspector-general of Swiss nationality. Finally, the police rules had to be submitted to the diplomatic corps at Tangier for advice and consent.

The international police arrangements for Morocco were paralleled in complexity by the agreement upon a state bank. The administrators of the bank were to be selected by the several states which signed the Algeciras Convention if they also subscribed to the bank's capital fund. The examiners of the bank were to be nominated by the banks of Germany, England, Spain, and France. A Moroccan high commissioner was to supervise the emission of bank notes and act as liaison between the bank and the imperial treasury. Lawsuits brought against the bank by Morocco were to be tried before a special tribunal selected by the diplomatic corps, with French commercial legislation applicable to such suits; as a last appeal, the case might be taken to the Swiss federal tribunal in Lausanne [24].

The accord reached at Algeciras after eighteen plenary sessions and ten committee meetings did not endure. Within five years France had won an outright protectorate over Morocco by appeasing Germany with land in the Cameroons of Africa. Nevertheless, the meeting did postpone violence for a few years and thereby offer the world a last breath and hope for peace. When consultation and the European conference system finally failed to cope with the rabid ambitions of the nation-states, the scourge of war flailed Europe.

International consultation in the early twentieth century proved inadequate to contain the turbulence of the Balkans. In 1908 Austria-Hungary violated the multilateral Treaty of Berlin (1878) by occupying Bosnia and Herzegovina while refusing to heed any international conference which would not accept this annexation as a premise for negotiation. Italy stabbed Turkey in 1911 and took Tripoli as loot. Next, Montenegro, Serbia, Bulgaria, and Greece assaulted Turkey and whipped her out of Europe. As they divided the spoils among themselves they fell to brutal fighting. The Treaty of Bucharest of 10 August 1913 brought a shallow peace, for the great states of the world had watched the ruthless scrapping of the Treaty of Berlin but had failed to provide any organization which could relieve the tensions of international society and thereby allow political change without recourse to war.

The rudimentary mechanism of the *ad hoc* conference was only a beginning to more apt international organization, but it had gradually won respect and sometimes postponed disaster. At the final crisis of the age of consultation, the British made a last appeal to this device in order to avoid the calamity of war between Austria and Serbia which would drag into its vortex the lives and treasure of peoples around the world.

THE END OF THE AGE OF CONSULTATION

On 23 July 1914, twenty-five days after the assassination of the Archduke Ferdinand at Sarajevo by Serbian nationalists, Austria demanded, among other things, that Serbia remove from its military service and government administration all those guilty of propaganda against Austria-Hungary and that all movements directed against the territorial integrity of the Dual Monarchy be suppressed. These clauses, however, also reserved to Austria the right to provide the names of the culpable officers and insisted that Serbia accept the collaboration of Austria in uprooting subversive movements. To this impairment of her sovereignty Serbia was given forty-eight hours to reply.

Russia could not stand by and see her ally Serbia humiliated. Tension mounted. On July 25, Sir Edward Grey, British Foreign Minister, telegraphed Sir Horace Rumbold at Berlin that the only chance for peace would be for the Four Powers, Italy, France, Germany, and Britain, "to keep together" and ask Russia and Austria not to cross frontiers until there was time "to endeavor to arrange matters between them." On the same day the Russian Foreign Minister said that he would like to see the question placed in the hands of England, France, Italy, and Germany. This prompted Sir Arthur Nicolson, British Permanent Undersecretary for Foreign Affairs, to recommend to Grey an immediate conference of ambassadors to explore means of preventing an outbreak of hostilities.

During the next tense day, both Italy and France welcomed the opportunity to consult. By then Austria was grimly determined to punish Serbia. Russia, having compelled the Serbians to yield on some points and having made several proposals for further negotiation, began mobilizing its army. All diplomatic eyes turned to Germany, for Austrian policy was anchored firmly to Berlin. A conference of the powers, including Germany, might once again have surmounted a crisis without war. But the will was lacking. On July 27 the British ambassador to Germany wired Grey [25]:

Secretary of State for Foreign Affairs says that conference you suggest would practically amount to a court of arbitration and could not, in his opinion, be called together except at the request of Austria and Russia. He could not therefore, desirous though he was to co-operate for the maintenance of peace, fall in with your suggestion. I said that I was sure that your idea had nothing to do with arbitration, but meant that representatives of the four nations not directly interested should discuss and suggest means for avoiding a dangerous situation. He maintained, however, that such a conference as you proposed was not practicable.

The age of consultation ended as it had begun—with an earth-shattering war which tore at the roots of civilization. Men still heeded their extravagant ambitions and neglected their everyday needs. Neighbor still turned violently upon neighbor and with the cloak of sovereignty the states of the world continued to conceal their crimes in the inherent right of war. But consultation among the great states had introduced a principle of community interest quite different from the roughshod interstate tactics of the centuries preceding Napoleon. An interest of the Great Powers, at least, in the political stability of Europe had been postulated, and a mechanism for adjusting the most serious grievances had been demonstrated.

Consultation, however crudely, gave states their first opportunity to work together on community problems. Consultation, again and again, suggested techniques of organization and procedure which gradually became a normal part of diplomacy. From Westphalia in 1648 to Berlin in 1878 there was a slow but perceptible development of the conference method which offered the first hope of an international constitutional order by substituting paper arguments for sheer violence. Modern international organization, with its wide array of institutions, evolved from the conferences of the preceding centuries. The events of 1914 proved that sporadic consultations would not suit the rapidly mounting international pressures of the twentieth century, and when the peacemaking states assembled in 1919 after the great purge of war they built a new system upon the old foundations.

NOTES

1. For the French text of the Treaty of Chaumont, see G. F. de Martens, *Nouveau recueil de traités*, Göttingen, Dietrich, 1817, Vol. I, p. 683.
2. Comte A. de la Garde-Chambonas, *Anecdotal Recollections of the Congress of Vienna*, London, Chapman & Hall, 1902.
3. *The British and Foreign State Papers* (hereafter abbreviated *B.F.S.P.*), London, James Ridgway and Sons, 1839, Vol. II, has most of the relevant documents on the Congress of Vienna and subsequent conferences in the official French language. E. Hertslet, *The Map of Europe by Treaty*, London, Butterworths & Harrison, 1875, 4 vols., Vol. 1, contains English translations of the important instruments. See also C. K. Webster, *The Congress of Vienna*, London, Oxford, 1919; for personalities and a description of the conferences, see H. Nicolson, *The Congress of Vienna*, New York, Harcourt, Brace, 1946, which contains a highly useful bibliography.
4. For descriptions of procedure, see Ernest Satow, *A Guide to Diplomatic Practice*, New York, Longmans, 1917, as well as *International Affairs*, London, H.M. Stationery Office, 1920, Vol. 23, No. 151.
5. Treaty of Alliance and Friendship between Great Britain, Austria, Russia, and Prussia, 20 November 1815, Art. VI.
6. C. K. Webster, *The Foreign Policy of Castlereagh, 1815–1822*, London, G. Bell, 1931, 2 vols., is a comprehensive study of the international diplomacy of the period from the British point of view; M. Capefigue, *Le Congrès de Vienne*, Paris, 1847, is an account of the 1814–1846 international meetings from personal observation.
7. Protocole de la conférence, Aix-la-Chapelle, 15 November 1818, *B.F.S.P.*, Vol. VI, p. 15.
8. Walter A. Phillips, *The Confedera-*

tion of Europe, London, Longmans, 1920, pp. 208–209.
9. Circular to the Austrian, Prussian, and Russian Ministers at Foreign Courts, Troppau, 8 December 1820, *B.F.S.P.*, Vol. VIII, p. 1150. For Castlereagh's rejoinder to the claims of the eastern European princes to intervene in domestic affairs, see his circular to the British ministers, 19 January 1821, *B.F.S.P.*, Vol. VIII, p. 1160.
10. *Ibid.*, pp. 1199–1205.
11. *Ibid.*, Vol. X, p. 921.
12. Dispatch from Wellington to Canning, Verona, 29 October 1822. For French policies and diplomacy during the Verona Conference as well as a report on the military campaign in Spain, see *Mémoires du Chancelier Pasquier*, Paris, E. Plon, Nourrit, 1894, Vol. V, Part II.
13. Confidential Minute of Viscount Castlereagh on the Affairs of Spain, communicated to the courts of Austria, France, Prussia, and Russia in May 1820, *B.F.S.P.*, Vol. X, p. 73.
14. A. Debidour, *Histoire diplomatique de l'Europe*, Paris, Librairie Felix Alcan, 1916, Vol. 1, pp. 211–226.
15. For documents on the London conferences on Greece, see *B.F.S.P.*, Vol. XVI, pp. 1083–1099; Vol. XIV, pp. 629–639; Vol. XVII, pp. 6–220, 373–527; Vol. XIX, pp. 4–54; Vol. XXII, pp. 931–964; Vol. XXV, p. 747. For conferences on Greece held in Constantinople, see Vol. XVII, pp. 220–370; for those at Poros, see Vol. XVII, pp. 405–431. Documents on the London conference on Belgium will be found in Vol. XVIII, pp. 723–921; Vol. XIX, pp. 55–184. The treaties of 1839 are in Vol. XXVII, pp. 990–1003. See also "The Netherlands," *Peace Handbooks*, London, H.M. Stationery Office, 1920, Vol. V.
16. Protocole d'une conférence tenue au Ministère des Affaires Estrangères à Vienne, le 9 avril 1854. See G. F. de Mar-

tens, *Nouveau recueil général de traités,* Göttingen, Dietrich, 1857, Vol. XV, p. 543. For an extensive history of the Near Eastern question including pertinent treaties of the eighteenth, nineteenth, and twentieth centuries, see "The Balkan States," *Peace Handbooks,* Vol. III, Part One, 1920.

17. Documents and protocols of the Paris Congress of 1856 may be found in Ministère des Affaires Estrangères, "Congrès de Paris," *Documents diplomatiques,* Paris, Imprimerie Nationale, April 1856.

18. Text of the treaty neutralizing Luxembourg is in *B.F.S.P.,* Vol. LVII, p. 32.

19. The protocols of the six meetings of the London Conference of 1871 may be found in *B.F.S.P.,* Vol. LXI, pp. 1193–1226; the final treaty is on pp. 7–10.

20. Henry F. Munro, *The Berlin Congress,* Washington, Government Printing Office, 1918, p. 36. This study is confined to the technique, procedure, and general conduct of the Congress.

21. A single collection of the correspondence, memoranda, protocols, and treaties of the Congress is contained in Ministère des Affaires Estrangères, *Documents diplomatiques, affaires d'Orient,* Congrès de Berlin, Paris, Imprimerie Nationale, 1878.

22. Dispatch from the Marquess of Salisbury to Sir N. O'Conor, Foreign Office, 14 February 1897, in *B.F.S.P.,* Vol. XC, p. 1310.

23. Protocols and text of Madrid convention are in *B.F.S.P.,* Vol. LXXI, pp. 639–644, 814–896.

24. See Ministère des Affaires Etrangères, *Documents diplomatiques, affaires du Maroc, protocoles et comptes rendus de la conférence d'Algésiras,* Paris, Imprimerie Nationale, 1906.

25. Telegram from Sir E. Goschen to Sir Edward Grey, Berlin, 27 July 1914. For this and other British Foreign Office documents of the period, see G. P. Gooch and Harold Temperley (eds.), *British Documents on the Origins of the War, 1898–1914,* London, H.M. Stationery Office, 1926, Vol. XI, especially pp. 88–128. See also John S. Ewart, *The Roots and Causes of the Wars, 1914–1918,* New York, Doubleday, 1925, 2 vols.; S. B. Fay, *The Origins of the War,* rev. ed., New York, Macmillan, 1930, 2 vols.; and K. Foster, *The Failures of Peace: The Search for a Negotiated Peace during the First World War,* Washington, American Council on Public Affairs, 1941.

APPENDIX 2

I. *Treaty of Alliance between Austria, Russia, Great Britain, and Prussia* (concluded at Chaumont 1 March 1814)

Art. V. The High Contracting Parties, reserving to themselves to concert together, at the time when peace is concluded, upon the most proper means of guaranteeing to Europe and to themselves reciprocally the maintenance of that peace, are no less agreed to enter without delay into defensive arrangements for the protection of their respective States in Europe against every attempt of France which might change the results of this pacification.

Art. XVI. The present treaty of defensive alliance, having for its goal the maintenance of a balance in Europe, of assuring the peace and the independence of the powers, and of preventing the invasions which for so many years have desolated the world, the High Contracting Parties have agreed to extend it for twenty years. . . .

II. *Treaty of Alliance and Friendship between Great Britain, Austria, Russia, and Prussia* (signed at Paris 20 November 1815)

Art. VI. To facilitate and to secure the execution of the present Treaty, and to consolidate the connections which at the present moment so closely unite the Four Sovereigns for the happiness of the world, the High Contracting Parties have agreed to renew their meetings at fixed periods, whether under the immediate auspices of the Sovereigns themselves, or by the respective Ministers, for the purpose of consulting upon their common interests, and for the consideration of the measures which at each of those periods shall be considered the most salutary for the repose and prosperity of Nations and for the maintenance of the Peace of Europe.

III. *A Record of the First Meeting of the Congress of Berlin in 1878*

The Plenipotentiaries were called together today Thursday, 13 June, at two o'clock.

Count Andrássy spoke as follows:

"Gentlemen, I have the honor to propose that you entrust the Presidency of the work of the Congress to His Serene Highness, Prince Bismarck. This is not only a custom consecrated by precedent, but at the same time homage to the Sovereign whose hospitality the representatives of Europe are now enjoying. . . ."

These words having been received by the enthusiastic agreement of all the Plenipotentiaries, Prince Bismarck thanked his Colleagues . . . and finally accepted the Presidency.

The President proceeded to set up the secretariat as follows:

"I propose to you M. de Radowitz, Minister of Germany to Athens, as Secretary of the Congress and, as assistant-secretary, Count de Moüy, first secretary of the French Embassy at Berlin. . . ."

The President wished to add to that which he had just read some observations upon procedure. He thought that in order to facilitate the work of the Congress it would be fitting to agree that every proposal and document intended to form a part of the Protocols be presented in writing and be read by the initiating Member. It seemed that rather than follow in order the paragraphs of the Treaty under discussion, it would be preferable to arrange the questions in order of their importance . . .

All the members of the Congress agreed with these proposals of Prince Bismarck.

The Earl of Beaconsfield took the floor. . . .

Prince Gortchakov declared . . .

M. D'Oubril agreed completely . . .

Sadoullah Bey declared that he could not accept . . .

Prince Bismarck proposed finally that the Assembly meet again on next Monday, the 17th, at two o'clock. This date was accepted unanimously. . . . The meeting adjourned at 3:15.

Signed: V. Bismarck, B. Bülow, C. F. v. Hohenlohe, Andrássy, etc.

Certified as conforming to the original:

Radowitz, Count de Moüy

IV. *The Last Appeal to Consultation before World War I* (British Foreign Office documents)

Berlin, July 25, 1914—Sir H. Rumbold to Sir Edward Grey

Secretary of State says . . . he immediately instructed German Ambassador at Vienna to pass on to Austrian Minister for Foreign Affairs your suggestion for an extension of time limit, and to "speak to" his Excellency about it . . . he admitted quite freely that Austro-Hungarian Government wished to give the Servians a lesson, and that they meant to take military action. He also admitted that Servian Government could not swallow certain of the Austro-Hungarian demands.

St. Petersburg, July 25, 1914—Sir G. Buchanan to Sir Edward Grey

. . . From a conversation he had with Servian Minister yesterday, Minister for Foreign Affairs thought that, in event of Austrian attack, Servian Government would abandon Belgrade and withdraw their forces to interior, while they would at the same time appeal to Powers to help them. His Excellency was in favor of such an appeal. Obligations taken by Servia in 1908 to which reference is made in Austrian ultimatum were given to Powers and not to Austria . . . Were Servia to appeal to Powers, Russia would be quite ready to stand aside and leave question in hands of England, France, Italy, and Germany. . . .

July 26, 1914—Sir A. Nicolson to Sir Edward Grey

I think the only hope of avoiding a general conflict would be for us to take advantage at once of suggestion thrown out by [Russian Minister for Foreign

Affairs] in Buchanan's telegram . . . that you should telegraph to Berlin, Paris, Rome, asking that they shall authorize their Ambassadors here to join you in a Conference . . . If you approve will you telegraph to Resident Clerk to whom I am giving draft telegrams in above sense.

July 26, 1914—Sir Edward Grey to Resident Clerk, Foreign Office, London

I approve Nicolson's draft telegrams and they should be sent off at once.

July 26, 1914—Sir Edward Grey to Sir F. Bertie, British Ambassador at Paris. Repeated to Vienna, St. Petersburg, Nish, and Berlin

Ask Minister for Foreign Affairs if he would be disposed to instruct Ambassador here to join with representatives of Italy, Germany, France, and myself in a conference to be held here at once in order to endeavour to find an issue to prevent complications. . . .

CHAPTER 3 *Nineteenth-century Society and
International Administration*

The full impact of the industrial revolution struck Europe in the nineteenth century; the world of time and space shrank more rapidly in one
hundred years than it had during all the ages since the birth of Christ.
Caesar's nimble couriers had traveled from Rome to Britain as quickly
as the dry dispatches from the English ambassador in Naples to Lord
Castlereagh in London. But two of the many astounding devices of the
nineteenth century, the steam engine and the electric telegraph, tele-
scoped weeks into days, days into hours, and hours into seconds.

After the shock waves of Bonapartism had subsided, states formerly
isolated from each other by time found themselves in touch with new
neighbors. While the acceleration of trade through improved communications and cheaper transportation meant a gain in the living standard of
Europe, it also raised the irritating problem of transcending national
boundary lines. No less did proximity expose all states to a new contagion
with old diseases.

International economic and social problems always require political
activity for their ultimate solution, but some economic and social needs
affect power relationships less than others. Consultations by the Great
Powers during the nineteenth century, for example, on the status of
Spain, Belgium, Turkey, or Serbia instantly challenged the European balance of power itself and thus proceeded with a nervous and hesitant pace
toward a comprehensive international organization. During the nineteenth
century, however, a spate of international problems offered to statesmen
and specialists alike the opportunity to confer without rousing too roughly
the delicate sentiments of national pride; indeed, without loss of treasure
or prestige the states of Europe fell upon their twin enemies—poverty
and disease. To utilize the steamboat, the railroad, and the telegraph
efficiently required international cooperation, while these communica-

tions, in turn, opened the dark door of envy and ignorance to let in the hope of organized international work.

INTERNATIONAL RIVER COMMISSIONS

Rivers since ancient times have borne the heaviest traffic of communities linked by trade. The Yangtze, the Ganges, the Tigris, the Volga, the Nile, and the Thames have all nourished narrow, crowded cities of commerce. Without paved roads or rails, the waters of the five continents were the highways of nations throughout the history of mankind until the nineteenth century. When a long peace came to Europe and men contemplated the rich rewards of barter, rivers came first under international observation.

The Rhine River, flowing from western Switzerland and either bordering or traversing Austria, Germany, France, and the Netherlands, drains fertile valleys, great forests, and both coal and iron territories. The course of the river cuts through one of the most densely populated areas of Europe. By Roman and German law as well as the agreements in the Treaties of Münster (1648), Ryswick (1697), and Baden (1714), the principle that international rivers in Europe ought to be free to public navigation had long been asserted. But the arbitrary tolls imposed by local princes and the right of cities to compel the transfer of cargo to local ships clogged the avenues of trade. As early as the sixteenth century a council of princes holding land along the banks of the Rhine had been established to consult on joint problems of navigation and security from attack upon the river and its towpaths. Despite some elimination of the shipping hazards, traditional monopolies and special privileges clung like barnacles to the transfer of merchandise by water. At the end of the eighteenth century there were no less than thirty-two toll stations from Strasbourg to Holland [1].

The French Revolution cracked the shell of privilege everywhere it turned. On 20 November 1792 the Executive Council of France affirmed that no nation could claim to occupy exclusively the channel of a river and prevent the neighboring peoples who touch the upper banks from enjoying the same advantages of navigation upon the river. By treaty with Holland in 1795, navigation of the Rhine, Meuse, and Scheldt was declared free for the contracting states. But the first international administration of a river, a decisive step in the history of international organization, was the Octroi of the Rhine signed by France and the (Holy Roman) German Empire on 15 August 1804, for it provided that "there shall be a director-general empowered to direct and supervise the establishment and the collection of navigation tolls; . . . to administer everything in respect to the tolls and to watch over the execution of the present agreement (Art. XLII). . . . The director-general shall be named jointly by the high contracting parties . . . (Art. XLVII) [2]."

By this agreement the director-general of the Rhine became a prototype of the international civil servant, responsible not to his government but to the governments as a collective organization signatory to the treaty. To this day the leading officials of many international organizations bear the title "director-general." The Octroi of the Rhine furthermore provided for assistant inspectors and collectors at the toll stations, to be appointed by individual governments, and an international commission to determine finally all appeals on questions of tolls and police regulations on the Rhine. The basic structure of modern international administrative agencies —an international conference or commission whose members are appointed by their governments and a director "appointed jointly"—was clearly foreshadowed.

After the Napoleonic Wars the Congress of Vienna reasserted the principle of free navigation of international rivers and engaged all parties to consult on regulations for navigable streams traversing or bordering their states [3]. Because of disputes between Prussia and Holland a new definitive treaty for the administration of the Rhine could not be concluded until 1831, at Mayence. The riparian states vested both legislative and judicial powers in an enlarged international commission. Litigation on matters concerning navigation, duties, collision, and so forth could be taken on appeal from the courts established by the states for such cases *either* to the appellate national court *or* to the international commission. The appointment of a chief inspector, moreover, like the former director-general, was made by the commission. Not only was he paid from a common treasury and sworn to obey the rules of the central commission, but he was elected jointly—with Prussia casting one-third of the total number of votes, France casting one-sixth, Holland casting one-sixth, and the other German states (Baden, Hesse, Bavaria, and Nassau) casting the remaining third.

With the shift in the German balance of power after Prussia defeated Austria in 1866, a new treaty for the administration of the Rhine River had to be signed in 1868. The international commission, representing each riparian state and meeting annually, continued to pass resolutions for the improvement of navigation and to hear appeals from the Rhine courts until 1914. The success of appeals from local jurisdiction to the commission is indicated by the fact that whereas 61 cases were taken from the Rhine courts to the commission between 1832 and 1868, 216 cases were appealed between 1869 and 1911. Since all tolls had been abolished in 1868 the chief inspector, the only international appointee, was eliminated, but the commission favorably demonstrated in the succeeding years the advantages of international administration.

Not less than 32 million dollars had been spent on improving the Rhine River between 1831 and 1870; traffic between the Swiss and Dutch borders during this period more than quadrupled itself. By 1912 almost 1 million tons of coal, coke, iron ore, cereals, machinery, fruits, textiles, and other merchandise were passing through the Rhine and its estuaries. In a typical year prior to the First World War, the central commission spent at least 3 million dollars on improving channels and harbors. Commerce had evoked international administration on the Rhine, and success had crowned its efforts—especially in permitting an appeal from national sovereignty to an international body. To be sure, the decisions of the commission had to be enforced by the individual state and resolutions passed by the commission could not be implemented without the consent of the states directly involved; to be sure, the internationally appointed director-general or chief inspector lost his job in 1868; nevertheless, as a monument to nineteenth-century international administration, the Rhine Commission marked a path of promise [4].

Other international river commissions, attuned to the spirit of the Congress of Vienna, were established for the Elbe in 1821, the Douro in 1835, the Po in 1849, and the Pruth in 1866. None reached the success of the Rhine Commission, yet each mirrored the trend toward international administration. An outstanding example of international cooperation, however, was initiated by the European Commission for the Danube in 1856.

The Danube mouths to the Black Sea had been seized by the Russians from the Turks under the Treaty of Adrianople in 1829. Having no commercial interests in the Danubian hinterland, Russia allowed the channels of the river to silt. Furthermore, by the practice of clumsy quarantine regulations, the government added bungling administrative delays to the perils of navigation. The steamships of the 1820's, especially encouraged by the Hapsburgs, accelerated Danubian trade and impelled the Austrians to blast the Iron Gates, a series of rapids connecting the fluvial transit of the German states and Austria with the maritime Danube coursing through the Turkish principalities. Shortly thereafter Great Britain took an interest in the Danube, as her traffic in wheat from the Balkans increased a dozen times after 1840. The obstruction to British trade on the Danube by the Russians reinforced London's contemporary view that Turkey must not become a puppet state of the Tsar and was a secondary cause of the Crimean War.

By Articles XVI and XVII of the Treaty of Paris (1856) two Danubian commissions were to be established: one, as a directing and supervising agency, would comprise Great Britain, Austria, France, Russia, Sardinia, and Turkey; the other would include only riparian states for the actual execution of navigation rules and necessary river improvements [5]. In fact, the riparian commission never came into existence and the European Commission gradually arrogated to itself the task of dredging the river, building quays, formulating regulations, and supervising the police. Although appointed and paid by the Sultan of Turkey, the inspector-general and the captain of the Port of Sulina were considered as "acting under the direction of the European Commission, and as invested with an international character." These agents could be removed on the request of the commission, but the Sublime Porte could not relieve them from duty without the agreement of the commission [6].

Political changes following the Congress of Berlin (1878) compelled a new regulation for the Danube in so far as Rumania became an independent state controlling the whole of the Danubian delta except for one arm possessed by Russia. Turkey lost her riparian interests save for her nominal control over Bulgaria. In consequence, Rumania was admitted as a member of the commission, and the inspector-general of navigation, the captain of the port, and other employees were appointed and paid by the European Commission alone. Further stress was placed upon the "international" character of the employees, a fundamental aspect of international administration today, by the provision for electing the chief officials "by a simple majority vote and without distinction of nationality." The European Commission assumed its own flag for the buildings and ships under its control while it authorized its employees to wear special brassards. It then extended its authority upriver, first to Galatz and five years later to Brăila [7].

For the first time in history a commission of both riparian and non-riparian states cooperated upon the improvement of an international artery of trade; though each state had its selfish interest, the whole fraternity of nations profited. Fifteen feet of mud was scooped up along the river mouth near Sulina between 1857 and 1905; jetties, buoys, a lighthouse, a seaman's hospital, and a lifeboat service were provided through the auspices of the commission. Such aids to navigation on the Danube reduced the number of wrecks by 90 per cent and cut the navigation charges in half. Rumania jealously guarded her right of jurisdiction over ordinary civil and criminal cases, but with its power to levy and collect tolls, license ships and pilots, and impose fines for violations of the navigation rules, the European Commission marked a clear course through the shoals of early international administration [8].

With modifications due to the political changes wrought by two world wars, the Central Rhine Commission was reorganized in 1949 to include not only the riparian states but also the United Kingdom and the United

States as occupying powers of Germany. The commission is still charged with ensuring the freedom of navigability on the river to the commerce of all nations, supervising the technical needs for navigation, preparing ordinances on navigation itself, and acting as a high court of appeal in litigation involving navigation of the river. The Danube fell into more troublesome times after the Treaty of Versailles than the Rhine. Although a new statute of 1921 reaffirmed the authority of the European Commission, Rumania attempted to limit its jurisdiction to the navigable channel, and as Hitler cast his shadow over the Balkans in the 1930's Rumania gave poor cooperation to the commission. After the Second World War Russia dominated every riparian state of the Danube except Germany and Austria—both divided by military occupation. At Belgrade in 1948 the seven Danubian states and the United States, the United Kingdom, and France met to consider a new statute for the Danube commission. Russia and her satellites refused to recognize equal treatment for riparian and nonriparian states and denied to the United Kingdom, France, Greece, Italy, and Belgium, all former members, a place on the new Danube commission. Within the framework of Soviet control the work of the commission continues, but Yugoslavia, having broken its ties with Moscow, asked for a revision of the commission's procedure late in 1952.

Not only natural waterways, such as the St. Lawrence, the Congo, and the Yangtze, received international attention prior to 1914, but artificial canals of trade fell under the scrutiny of nations. As early as 1850 the United States and Great Britain promised that they would protect "from interruption, seizure or unjust confiscation" and "guarantee the neutrality" of an interocean canal built through Central America [9]. At the opening of the Suez Canal the Sultan of Turkey had declared that the waterway would always be open to the commerce of all nations, and in 1873 a conference of states at Constantinople widened this principle to include warships. Having bought 176,602 shares in the Egyptian Canal Company in 1875, Great Britain addressed a circular letter to its representatives at Paris, Berlin, Vienna, Rome, and St. Petersburg which set forth the general principle of the freedom of transit and neutrality for the Suez Canal. In 1885 the Great Powers—with the Netherlands, Spain, and Egypt (in a consultative capacity)—assembled in Paris to draft a treaty for the international regulation of this important commercial connection between the Mediterranean and Red Seas. To the dismay of Great Britain the conference proposed an international commission, modeled upon the European Commission for the Danube, to supervise and safeguard the terms of the treaty [10]. Since Britain occupied Egypt and accounted for 75 per cent of the canal's tonnage, her national point of view prevailed. The Treaty of Constantinople (1888) so emasculated the Suez International

Commission that its only feeble task in the event that anything menaced the safety or blocked the passage of the canal was to "acquaint the Khedivial Government with the danger they shall have observed in order that [the Government] may take measures necessary to insure the security and free use of the Canal [11]." The International Commission for the Suez, because of the objection of Great Britain, was never given any real authority, so that it merely paid lip service to the idea of international administration. It quietly died in 1904.

RAILWAYS

While the nineteenth century witnessed a boom in canal building, both oceanic and fluvial, the railroad quickly surpassed all other means of transportation for speed. Seeking a way to cart coal from the mines more easily, men had devised wooden rails for a little truck hauled by oxen or horses as early as the seventeenth century. The steam engine and iron rails, however, revolutionized land transportation. The first English railroad was opened to the public in 1825, and the Americans began their era of railroad building in 1829. The French government in 1842 ordered the construction of a far-flung railway system with Paris as the hub; Belgium, Switzerland, and the Netherlands joined the movement, and the Tsar peremptorily connected St. Petersburg with Moscow. Only 90 miles of railroad operated through Austria in 1839, but within sixty-five years 13,000 miles of track spanned the Empire from Salzburg to Budapest, from Prague to Trieste [12].

Because of the dependence upon England for locomotives and railway equipment, a standard track gauge was generally adopted in Europe, except Russia and the Iberian Peninsula, for all main lines. This good start toward a unified transport system at once ran into the problem of political frontiers; where passengers and goods had to cross a border, cooperation between railroad companies became essential. A common ticket or bill of lading, a consistent law of liability for the carrier, and a standard procedure in administration were essential to efficient international transportation. Mergers within the United States could provide giant interstate systems, but in Europe cooperation among the political sovereignties remained basic to a full use of the railroad's potentiality.

The Association of German Railroads (Verein Deutscher Eisenbahn Verwaltungen) began in 1847 as a private organization of independent companies intent upon standardizing their relations with the public and with each other in respect to passenger and freight traffic. Acting within the framework of the German Confederation which, as yet, exercised little jurisdiction over such railroad matters, the association made great progress in formulating uniform rules on transport contracts, division of freight receipts, determination of loss or damages, and track gauges, crossings, switches, safety devices, and so forth. In 1864 several non-German railroads joined the association, and even where railroads were nationalized (a definite trend of the nineteenth century) delegates from the government-owned railroads continued to attend general conferences, heed the recommendations of an expert committee, elect a managing railroad for the association, and share the cost of a permanent secretariat. All members settled their disputes with each other by arbitration [13].

The Association of German Railroads remained a private international organization to promote the efficient operation of international railways, but in formulating laws applicable to interstate traffic the approval of states themselves could not be escaped. Switzerland, therefore, in 1878 invited the interested European states to participate in discussions looking toward a comprehensive legal convention. Twelve years later Germany, Austria, Hungary, Belgium, France, Italy, Luxembourg, the Netherlands, Russia, and Switzerland signed a treaty establishing a uniform law for the transport of goods by rail between their countries. Responsibility for delay, damage, or loss was defined, the evaluation of claims standardized, and judicial remedies made available. A new step toward international administration was taken when the delegates agreed upon a central office for international rail transport. This office acted as a clearinghouse of information and accounts for the member states and their railroads; furthermore, upon request, the central office could arbitrate controversies among members. Appointed by the Swiss Federal Council, the director of the central office and his subordinates performed an unsung but invaluable service for the rattling-iron and hissing-steam age of the nineteenth century. Without coercion, states consented to work together on a common problem and solved their difficulties through a common office. This was the root of international administration which proliferated [14].

TELEGRAPH

From its inception the electric telegraph was virtually inseparable from the railway. The slender wires stretched beside the tracks across endless spaces tied cities together with a sensitive nerve system. The first trial of an electric telegraph took place on the London and Northeastern Railway in 1837, and the first line opened to the public went from Paddington to Slough on the Great Western Railway in 1843. Although the American Samuel Morse also demonstrated the telegraph in 1837 and established a public line in 1844, the United States did not immediately face the problem of having a speedy means of communication thwarted by a dozen national frontiers [15].

The telegraph had been in use for only a few years when the first bilateral treaty regulating wire service was signed by Austria and Prussia in 1849, and as early as 1853 the French agreed to share an office with the Swiss to facilitate the transmission of telegraphic messages across their respective borders. But the chief development in international communications during this period stemmed from three regional treaties of 1850, 1852, and 1855 which gradually linked the German states with the Latin states in common telegraphic procedures and the agreeable exchange of useful information: messages were assured of secrecy and rapid dispatch according to classification, while the various national administrations promised to circulate documents describing the operation of their services. Little progress was made toward eliminating the innumerable and illogical taxes which foiled the advantages of the telegraph. France took the initiative by concluding a series of bilateral adjustments on tariffs with her immediate neighbors, but on 17 May 1865 twenty European states gathered in Paris to work out a comprehensive international convention. Each state reaffirmed the principles of prompt and secure telegraphic service to all patrons and acknowledged a common system of priorities and records for messages. Six sections of the Convention, moreover, regulated taxes upon telegraphic messages; all the contracting states thus gained one orderly, consistent scheme of costs for transmitting information by wire.

The Convention, furthermore, was unique in so far as it was open to all states of the world and subject to periodic revisions at conferences to be held at each of the capital cities of the contracting nations. From bilateral and *ad hoc* agreements the family of European states steadily moved toward multilateral conventions with machinery for amendment and revision. This nineteenth-century phenomenon opened the vista of permanent international organizations. At the very least the International Telegraphic Convention chronicled a new universality for international organization, as practically every European state and Persia and India adhered to the agreement [16].

Having agreed to principles of telegraphic communication, the states next faced the task of implementing their accord. Clumsily, at first, there was merely a haphazard exchange of information, but by the time of the second conference in Vienna (1868) the delegates seized their courage and created the first international administrative office, at once a model and beacon for international organization. An International Bureau of Telegraphic Administrations was organized to take such measures, in the common interest, as would facilitate the execution and application of the Convention. While the Swiss telegraphic administration actually operated the Bureau, all the members of the Convention bore the costs on a weighted scale of contributions [17].

In 1872 another of those vital steps forward in the history of international organization took place. It raised neither acclamation nor furor at the time, yet it was a fundamental change in the procedure and function of an international agency which was to influence many organizations not yet born. By amendment to the basic telegraphic Convention, the delegates to the third conference in Rome, first, provided: "In questions to be resolved by the consent of the contracting administrations, those to which no reply has been received within a maximum of four months will be considered as accepted." States agreed to be bound, therefore, by technical regulations to which they did not specifically consent but from which they merely abstained. While the limitations on an international agency's power are still set by the basic Convention, the rule-making power within those limits has greater flexibility and less obstruction by the formal consent of states.

Second, the Rome conference declared that "the International Bureau prepares the work of the Telegraphic Conferences. It provides the papers and necessary copies for editing and the distribution of amendments, *procès-verbaux,* and other information."

Finally, the director of the Bureau was given the right to assist at conference meetings and even to take part in the discussions, without a vote [18]. By the Rome Convention of 1872, therefore, the states of Europe redefined and strengthened the role of an international secretariat, an integral part of all modern international organizations. To a permanent bureau the nations gave money and information so that it might coordinate their interests and promote their prosperity; to a permanent bureau they entrusted the day-to-day relationships of their telegraphic administrations and the preparation of new agreements for the modification of their telegraphic conventions. Not until this time had states consented to follow amendments to rules on which they had given no explicit view.

With ten years of experience behind them, the nation-states in 1875 launched an international administration of telegraphic services destined to endure and benefit the entire world. Up until the St. Petersburg conference of 1865, the telegraphic conferences, like all other government conferences, had been diplomatic in character: that is, individuals represented their governments directly. But at St. Petersburg it was agreed that periodic conferences of the telegraphic administrations would be held, the time and place to be determined by the *administrative confer-*

ence itself, and that these conferences could propose tariff or other changes in telegraphic administrations. While such recommendations lacked force without the actual consent of the governments, nevertheless the unanimous judgment of a conference including all interested telegraphic administrations rarely admitted opposition by an individual state.

Six telegraphic administrative conferences were held between 1875 and 1905, each elaborating ways and means for improving service, each opening the advantages of its membership to other states. At the Lisbon conference of 1908 no less than fifty administrations from all parts of the world were represented. Unknown and unsuspected a century before, the international administration of telegraphs thrived in the late nineteenth century, preparing the world for new developments in international organization [19].

POSTAL UNIONS

Coincident and almost parallel with the formation of the International Telegraphic Bureau, the Universal Postal Union shared the spotlight of international administration after 1874. Its work, continuous now for three-quarters of a century, reinforced the notion that states one day might solve all their differences most practically and expeditiously through international organization.

In 1840, a New Yorker would pay 12½ cents to send a letter to Philadelphia, but 18¾ cents to send a letter to Baltimore, Providence, or Boston [20]. This differential was nothing compared to the difficulties attendant upon international mail. Those who wrote letters to foreign countries often paid postage to their own state, to a sea transport, to the country or countries of transit, and to the delivering administration. A wide diversity of rates, errors of delivery, and awkward delays ill suited an age which depended upon speedy communication and bustling commerce. Not only were routes and rates complicated, but each state had its own regulations on the acceptable size and weight of letters; meanwhile, balancing accounts by determining the portion of postage due to each agency on each letter hopelessly muddled the situation.

During Lincoln's administration, the Postmaster General of the United States addressed to the states maintaining diplomatic relations with America a note suggesting that international adjustment was the only sensible means for avoiding the many embarrassments to foreign commerce. In reply fifteen states met in Paris to talk about their common postal problems. After a full and frank discussion thirty-one articles met the approval of the delegates as "principles" for international postal administration; these principles not only guided all bilateral postal agreements between 1864 and 1873 but formed a basis for the multilateral convention finally achieved in 1874. Charges for weight, rather than distance, simplified international accounting, and greater responsibility for losses of mail marked the progress toward international postal administration.

The Austro-German Postal Union of 1850 had proved the advantages of a unified postal administration. Proud of this experience, the director-general of posts in the North German Confederation in 1868 called for a universal congress to consider a postal union for all states of the world [21]. This imaginative first plan to link all nations in a single postal territory broke fresh ground for the burgeoning of international organization. No previous international scheme had sought such universality; no previous proposal had dared hope for such unity of purpose and action. Slowed by the arrogance of France, thwarted by the Franco-Prussian War, and postponed for one year by Russia, the brazen idea (there were many skeptics!) waited painfully until 1874 for consideration. To Berne twenty-two states sent their high-ranking postal officials, who fashioned within twenty-four days one of the most significant international organizations in the history of nations.

John Sly wrote, "Viewed as an experiment in a new postal relation, the work of the Congress was revolutionary [22]." The hodgepodge of administrations instantly fused into one single postal territory; freedom of transit was guaranteed; for all prepaid letters a single rate of 25 centimes was fixed; the unit of weight, 15 grams, was chosen as the basis for letter fees; and a single charge was levied upon all commercial papers, books, newspapers, and so forth. But these immediate effects were surpassed by the progressive international structure of the General Postal Union which the congress organized.

Borrowing heavily from the international telegraphic conventions, the General Postal Union won the honor of first setting up a complete, permanent international administrative union which separated the diplomatic agreement from the administrative regulations of the agency. The convention specified that every three years the plenipotentiaries of the participating states would assemble in order to "perfect the system of the Union, to introduce necessary improvements, and to discuss common business." In 1878 the name of the General Postal Union was changed to the Universal Postal Union with thirty-one member states, and provision was made for both diplomatic congresses and conferences of postal administrations. Of special note for the history of international organization, however, was the provision that some articles of the convention might be amended by a two-thirds vote or a simple majority. In truth, even in those agreements where unanimity was required, experience quickly demonstrated that no modern state could afford to isolate itself from the international postal system by refusing to accede to the decisions of the Union. Thus, a modern international organization, acting upon a majority principle within a limited sphere of international affairs, began.

The 1874 convention entrusted a central office, the International Bureau of the General Postal Union, with the collection, publication, and distribution of information of all kinds useful to international postal service. The Bureau, moreover, was entitled to give opinions, upon request, to parties in a dispute, to introduce any proposals made for amendment of the administrative rules, and to facilitate the handling of accounts among states. In 1891 the International Bureau was given authority to balance and liquidate the postal accounts for international service among the members of the Union. The Bureau itself was placed under the supervision of the Swiss postal administration and the director-general, aided by a staff of six employees (all Swiss appointees), was directed to assist at conferences, where he might participate in discussions without a vote, and to make an annual report to the members of the Union. The expenses of this office were apportioned among the states according to their rank and importance in postal trade [23].

The membership of the Universal Postal Union steadily increased until virtually every state and its colonies in the world joined the organization. United States Postmaster General Jewell [24] correctly predicted in 1875 that

. . . the period is not distant when a cheap and uniform postage, with total abolition of international postage accounts, will obtain universal application in all countries of the world in which postal service is regularly organized. Such a unification of the conditions of postal intercourse throughout the world must prove a most efficient means of advancing the general prosperity and of promoting the peace and fraternity of nations.

The International Telegraphic Bureau and the Universal Postal Union were forerunners of a remarkable multiplication of international agencies designed to answer the emergent economic and social needs of the late nineteenth century.

HEALTH

The annihilation of time and space by modern communications, while beneficial to commerce and impelling states toward economic cooperation, also facilitated the spread of contagious diseases. The first quarantine (derived from the Italian word for "forty," the number of days Biblically attested to purify the soul) in America, for example, occurred at New York in 1758 to prevent the importation of yellow fever; vessels were detained in the harbor for at least thirty days [25]. Cholera since ancient times had found its breeding ground in India and in 1830 struck Europe heavily, even crossing the Atlantic Ocean a few years later and ravaging New York State in 1854. The outbreak of the disease in Mecca, which thousands of Indian, Persian, and Turkish pilgrims visited annually, raised a new and dreadful threat for Europe in the nineteenth century. Purely national precautions failed to stop the deadly advance of the Oriental scourge, and six times between 1830 and 1892 the disease became epidemic in Europe.

The first international sanitary council stemmed from the anxiety of European powers to awaken Turkey to her responsibility for the international menace of cholera. Pressed by Britain and France, the Sublime Porte permitted an international council, including four Turkish representatives, to function in Constantinople after 1838; another council appeared at Tangier in 1840 upon the insistence of the diplomatic corps to the Sultan of Morocco; a third international health agency, composed exclusively of doctors, was organized in 1881 at Alexandria, with eighteen representatives, four of them Egyptian; a fourth sanitary council was instituted at Teheran. Despite these auspicious starts toward a single, coordinated international health organization, the first international health conference at Paris in 1851 failed to win the unanimous support of the twelve states present, and it was not until 1881 in the New World that significant international cooperation on health was achieved.

Empowered by a joint resolution of Congress on 14 May 1880, the President of the United States convened an international sanitary conference to consider how a reliable and satisfactory international system of notification of diseases, especially cholera and yellow fever, might be established. Hand in hand with the implementation of such a system rose such problems as what officer should certify the health of a port or vessels therein, what kinds of inspection ought to be made of a ship liable to carry disease, and what penalties might be imposed for offenses arising under an international system [26]. The international conference of 1881 not only answered these questions agreeably by adopting a detailed convention but also provided two international health offices—one in Havana, one in Vienna—and miniature commissions of doctors in twenty-two other cities. Free, standardized health bills, the inspection of ships by local port authorities and certification by resident consuls, the publication of health statistics, and the channeling of all available public-health information to the two central offices carried the nineteenth-century states to a new level of international understanding and assistance.

Since 1851 each onslaught of cholera in Europe had provoked another diplomatic conference, but not until 1892 when a virulent attack resulted in the death of 15,000 Germans, French, and Belgians—not to mention hundreds of thousands of Russian and Turkish subjects—did the national interests yield to vigorous international health reforms. Thirteen states then formally acknowledged at Venice the Egyptian khedivial decree of 1881 which had instituted the Conseil Sanitaire, Maritime, et Quarantenaire at Alexandria to prevent the introduction of disease to Egypt or its transmission abroad. The sanitary conference permitted a more strict control over ships passing through the Suez Canal. The convention set forth detailed regulations for handling pilgrims to Arabia, prescribed the necessary sanitary equipment of ships, required doctors to be aboard, and enumerated the health measures to be taken in the transit of vessels. Ten sanitary guards selected by the Council from both European and Egyptian noncommissioned officers acted as an international health police under the director of the Suez health office. The Council, moreover, elected a disciplinary committee to hear complaints against officials concerned with the quarantine service and a finance committee to bring fees and costs into balance [27].

One year after the Venice convention of 1892, the states of Europe closed two more gaps in the international system of health. The notification of an outbreak of disease became mandatory upon each party to a new sanitary convention at Dresden. To answer both the advocates of strong prophylactic measures and the stalwarts of noninterference with shipping, the states also agreed upon a *maximum* permissible quarantine, the first international accord ever reached upon this vehemently disputed subject.

But the European sanitary conferences still lacked a permanent, central international health office. Again the New World moved more quickly. The American states meeting in Mexico City in 1901 and 1902 recommended that a general conference of the representatives of the health organizations of the different American republics be held regularly. Such representatives, the American states agreed, should be empowered to conclude sanitary regulations and conventions. Again international organization passed from the hands of diplomats to specialists and experts. To facilitate the work of these sanitary conferences an executive board of five members was elected in 1902 at the First International Sanitary Convention. It was called the International Sanitary Office and had permanent headquarters at Washington, D.C. [28].

One year later, at Paris, eighteen nations, including the United States, finally "created an International Office of Health according to the principles which guided the formation and the function of the International Bureau of Weights and Measures [29]." Receiving all available information on the status of infectious diseases within the contracting states, the Office was charged with making regular public reports to all the members. In this work its expense was shared by the parties to the Convention, and, after another delay, the Bureau finally came into existence in 1907.

Impressed by the success of international administrative agencies in first overcoming the stubborn resistance of nations to anything smacking of international supervision, sanguine observers of the political scene have often been charmed into thinking that the coordinating process was quick and natural. Yet in transport, in communications, and in health, years dragged on with nothing but pompous talk. Conference labored after conference to wrest a modicum of international control or, at least, guidance from the cold detachment of the nation-state. For every visionary of a new world order in which nations walked in a fraternity dedicated to smoother transport, faster communications, and better health, at least one skeptic could mutter sarcastically, what would the Danube commission have been except for the political interest of England? Why should it have taken generations to form a simple, efficient telegraphic or postal union? How many frightful deaths in a century were needed to gain standard health bills, quarantines, and international statistics?

Nevertheless the achievement of even these minor concessions from the sovereignty of states signaled a striking advance for international organization. Placed in the perspective of history before Napoleon and after the First World War, these multipartite conventions first gave states an opportunity to discover what harvests they might reap from cooperation, and second provided a trial arena in which nations could duel over procedure and protocol with foils rather than cutlasses. Solving technical problems never eliminated war, but it reduced some friction either within or among nations; bringing experts together in administrative conferences could not deter the rabid ambition of kings, but it provided experience for further meetings and formalized some international responsibility.

Step by step, moreover, always looking backward as well as forward, nineteenth-century states began to select personnel dedicated to the community welfare rather than to any single national interest. These men, engineers of the European Commission for the Danube, accountants of the Postal Union, or sanitary police of the Alexandria Health Council, afforded an early nucleus of international administration. They augured an entirely new concept of world politics: a corps of administrators and technicians, staffed and paid by the pooled resources of the nation-states, owing first allegiance to an international organization.

SCIENTIFIC ORGANIZATIONS

Nineteenth-century commerce owed all its great advances to modern science nurtured by free inquiry. Newton, Boyle, and Volta had to precede Stephenson, Fulton, and Morse. Cooperation upon scientific matters did not lag in the trend toward international organization. As early as 1861 the eminent mathematician, General Baeyer of Prussia, suggested a conference of geodetic scholars to bring together and compare results on the measurement of the earth. Fourteen states sent delegates to Berlin in 1864. A permanent commission of seven members to superintend the work of the International Geodetic Association was established with a central office attached to the Prussian Institute of Geodetics. Not until 1886, however, did the central office achieve an administrative and financial independence typical of international public unions.

The Geodetic Convention of 1864 had also provided for triennial convocations of the members of the Association. At the first reunion of 1867 the delegates, then representing nineteen states, recommended the universal use of the metric system and the creation of a bureau of weights and measures. This view had already been anticipated by the International Statistical Conference at Paris in 1855, when it argued the logic of the decimal system for weights, measures, and moneys. Pressure for an international bureau of weights and measures, however, was due to the inaccessibility of the standard meter and kilogram constructed between 1790 and 1798 and located in the French archives. Copies of the models, moreover, which had been distributed to various countries had gradually lost their absolutely exact identity with the original because of temperature and expansion differences.

France herself set up a commission on the meter with foreign members as advisers in 1869; following the Franco-Prussian War, twenty-nine governments sent forty-seven delegates to Paris to work out means for devising standards both agreeable and available to all states of the Metric Union. A preliminary study gained rapid acceptance. In 1875 a final conference of plenipotentiaries brought the International Office of Weights and Measures into existence. By the convention a bureau was established (at Sèvres) "in a special building offering all the guarantees necessary for quiet and stability." Here new standards of the meter and kilogram were placed and exact reproductions distributed to the states of the Metric Union.

The organization of the Metric Union typified the structure of those international agencies which developed in the course of the nineteenth century. Their trace upon twentieth-century international organizations has been indelible. First, the *règlement* of the Metric Union prescribed general conferences of member states at least once every six years. Second, an executive board of fourteen members, entitled the International Committee, was to be elected by the general conference and responsible to it. This committee actually would govern the work of the organization, call general conferences, determine costs, and maintain direct contact with the member states. Third, the Metric Union required an international office supervised by the International Committee. The regulations of this office provided that the director and his two chief assistants be chosen by secret majority vote by the International Committee. The director, of his own right, was to recruit seven other employees. Finally, the founders of the Metric Union agreed to prorate expenses on the basis of population [30].

PATENTS AND COPYRIGHTS

As early as 1531 the King of France had bestowed royal privileges to persons introducing new manufactures, but the notion that the individual had a "right" to his invention was first enunciated by the revolutionary National Assembly in 1791. That such a right should be protected by international cooperation, moreover, was the idea behind the origin of the Bureau for the Protection of Industrial Property.

The Parliament of Great Britain in 1623 had forbidden the granting of royal letters patent "beyond a term of fourteen years for the sole working or making of any manner of new manufactures within this realm to the true and first inventor and inventors of such manufactures." But not until the nineteenth century did the increasing application and distribution of inventions require new patent laws—in 1839, 1844, 1849, 1853, and 1883. Similarly in other countries of the world new legislation had to cope with such problems as the mode of applying for patents, the term of protection for exclusive ownership or use, the accreditation of the originality of the invention, and the penalties for violation of patents. As might be expected, different regulations evolved in different countries. Even conforming to national law and gaining the sanction of his own government, the inventor might find his device or manufacture quickly copied in another country, thereby despoiling him of the profits due his ingenuity and labor. Some nations negotiated bilaterally and signed reciprocal protection treaties, but the scope of the problem clearly indicated the need for a multilateral convention.

Although a private group of industrialists, meeting in Vienna in 1873 and Paris in 1878, first urged the creation of an international organization for safeguarding the ownership of industrial inventions, their governments proceeded slowly. Not until 1883 did eleven states reach the agreement which established the Union for the Protection of Industrial Property. Under this convention the subjects and citizens of each of the contracting states began to enjoy the same advantages of the law regarding patents, industrial designs, and trade-marks which had been or would be extended by any member of the Union to its own nationals. At one blow, therefore, a protection against violation of patent rights by equal recourse to the national law was guaranteed to the inventor by eleven states. In the next decade four more states joined the Union, and gradually the circle widened to encompass most states of the world [31].

To gather the wealth of information about the protection of industrial property from copying, to prepare statistical information, and to improve the Union, an international office was opened at Berne with its expenses prorated among the member states. Once again the chief administrative officer, the director, was empowered to assist at the plenary conferences of the Union and to deliver an annual report on the work of the organization. A new convention at Madrid in 1891 enlarged the service of the international office to include the registration of trade-marks for those states desiring it. Between 1893 and 1914 the Bureau for the International Protection of Industrial Property registered over 11,000 trade-marks. Another tie thus joined the states of the world, not creating permanent bonds but teaching nations the value of cooperation and international organization.

Concurrent with the demand for the protection of inventions the plea of artists and authors for just recognition and reward for their creations inspired another international organization. This movement for the protection of literary and artistic works also originated with an unofficial gathering, the Congress of Authors and Artists at Brussels in 1858. Although copyright had been known as long as the printing press (the first recorded copyright to an author having been granted in 1486 by Venice to Antonio Sabellico, the Republic's historian), much of its history was related to the privilege or monopoly of printing or reprinting certain works—as the word "copyright" suggests. Not until the famous statute of 1709 in Great Britain did a government legally recognize:

Whereas printers, booksellers, and other persons have of late frequently taken the liberty of printing, reprinting, and publishing books without the consent of the authors . . . too often to the ruin of them and their families . . . the author of any book . . . shall have the sole right and liberty of printing such book or books for a term of one and twenty years. . . .

Denmark recognized the rights of authors in 1741, Saxony in 1773; the United States passed its first Federal Copyright Act in 1790; republican France legislated on the rights of authors in 1793, and Napoleon extended this law to Belgium, Holland, Italy, and Switzerland.

The fabulous rise of literacy in the nineteenth century and the rapidity of communications across national borders posed new threats for authors. The protection of British law could not prevent the flagrant piracy of a literary or artistic work in Holland or Italy. As late as 1831 in England or the United States anyone had the right to publish a book which had first appeared in a foreign country.

Reciprocity of copyright protection began about this time between Prussia and other states of the German Confederation. A convention of 1840 between Sardinia and Austria for the security of authors' rights was joined by five Italian states; another such treaty between Britain and Prussia won the acceptance of ten German states. No single comprehensive treaty, however, governed the protection of literary and artistic property prior to the formation of the International Copyright Union in 1886. In fact, thirty-three bipartite conventions governed fifteen states on this subject up to the inception of the international organization.

Following the Congress of Authors and Artists in 1858, various representative assemblies of authors, artists, scholars, journalists, and librarians in 1861, 1877, 1878, and 1883 pressed for an international union to guarantee the universal protection of literary and artistic property as well as dramatic and musical works. Finally, in 1883, the Swiss government communicated to various other governments a draft of ten articles for the Union which had been prepared by the International Literary and Artistic Association, and Berne invited these governments to a diplomatic conference to consider the proposal. Fourteen nations responded to this call in 1884. Yet another diplomatic conference was necessary in 1885 and still another in 1886 before nine states ratified the first International Copyright Union. By this convention foreign authors immediately enjoyed the same protection of the laws governing copyright as the nationals in nine states. Within a generation the number spurted to fifteen. More than that, an international "law" was passed that translation rights in every contracting state would be guaranteed to an author for a period of ten years. Other regulations, stressing neither more nor less privilege than a state accorded its own citizens in matters of copyright, covered periodicals, dramatic productions, and musical arrangements. Pursuant to a well-defined formula, the Union organized an international office under the supervision of the Swiss government to gather and publish information pertaining to the protection of literary and artistic property. Again a director, able to assist at conferences and participate without vote, headed the international agency; again expenses were prorated among the members. Practice had proved the role and organization of international administrative agencies within a dozen years, and nineteenth-century states slowly became accustomed to them [32].

COMMERCE

To elaborate each of the international unions which evolved from the dramatic interdependence of states in the nineteenth century would be futile. In the period preceding the First World War nations reached out in every direction for congresses, conventions, and conferences to weld the chains of commerce to the body politic. Between 1900 and 1905 not less than eighteen official international conferences were held with anywhere from four to forty-one states in attendance. What a far cry from international organization before Napoleon!

Even in such a delicate matter as tariffs, Europe broke tradition. A sugar union was organized with enough power to modify the import levies upon sugar by member states. Various nations had been subsidizing their beet-sugar industry up to the turn of the century in order to stimulate exports. Such a policy threatened the economy of the British West Indies and exposed the chief importer, Great Britain, to severe price hazards. On the other hand, the subsidizing governments worried about increasing expenditures but feared international competition. Only an agreement by all states could restrain the unreasonable stimulus to the sugar industry, mitigate ruinous price wars, and prevent the dumping of excess production.

Early international conventions in 1864 and 1877 utterly failed to halt the practice of sugar bounties. But in 1902 seven nations granted to a Permanent International Sugar Commission the unprecedented power of determining whether any sugars being imported by the signatory states had the benefit of a national bounty. In such cases the Commission could then decide, *by majority vote,* the amount of duty to be applied by each signatory state to offset this price advantage. When Russia, with ten other states, acceded to the 1907 Sugar Convention she pledged not to export more than approximately 200,000 tons of tax-exempt sugar per year. Revision of this figure also lay within the province of the International Commission. Russia, therefore, clearly shared the hitherto sacrosanct control over exports with an international organization [33].

That this early commodity control achieved its basic intent needs little demonstration: subsidies by national governments to their beet industry had cut the proportion of cane to world sugar production from 85 to 34 per cent within half a century; after the Brussels Convention of 1902, cane steadily climbed to 75 per cent of the total world sugar output [34]. More remarkable from the point of view of international organization was the acceptance of a commission composed of nine representatives from each state, seated at Brussels, assisted by a permanent bureau and forceful enough to require changes in tariffs and exports.

AGRICULTURE

The problems of agriculture now called for international recognition. A union of eleven states had worked to prevent the dissemination of phylloxera since 1878, and another international convention in 1902 had protected wild birds, but no official organization devoted itself to the general interests of agriculture throughout the world until 1905.

The vision of an International Institute of Agriculture, oddly enough, came from a merchant who, by pluck and integrity, headed the largest department store and mail-order house on the Pacific coast in the 1880's. David Lubin, son of a Polish immigrant, based his business career on fearless honesty. After a rich success he never lost interest in his community. Among several campaigns for justice he saw the problems of agriculture as paramount. His many enthusiastic arguments distilled into a single plea: landowning farmers, like the minions of commerce or industry, must organize if agriculture is to share in the modern economy fairly. This organization, balanced against trusts and cartels, must be international.

The bold Sacramento merchant first presented his ideas to the unofficial International Agricultural Congress at Budapest in 1896. In succeeding years he sketched his plans to fifteen crowned heads or rulers of national governments. The Department of Agriculture in Washington regarded Lubin as a crank, and while the Grange listened with interest to his urgings for cooperative farm credit, nothing came of it. With characteristic vigor he finally secured an audience with the King of Italy in 1904 and singlehanded persuaded the monarch and the Italian government to call an international diplomatic conference to consider his idea [35].

In the view of David Lubin and other farsighted individuals, the people badly needed an institution, unpolitical in its aims, world-wide in its scope, competent to furnish reliable information on the quantity of crops, the availability of farm labor, and the threat of agricultural pests or disease. Such an organization would also strengthen the interests of farmers through rural cooperation, agricultural insurance, and agrarian credit. On 25 May 1905 forty nations met in Rome to discuss the formation of the International Institute of Agriculture.

The diplomatists proceeded cautiously and, as often happens, the initiative passed from the pioneers of the movement to the more seasoned hands of the career officials. Shorn of some of its bolder ambitions, the International Institute of Agriculture was formed, with thirty-eight nations ratifying its charter. The Institute was entrusted with the collection and dissemination of world-wide information on agricultural production, rural wages, and plant diseases, while it was urged to "study" questions of cooperatives, insurance, and agricultural credit.

The convention of 1905 provided for two houses, both composed of representatives from each member state of the Institute, and a general assembly to be convened from time to time by agreement. Executive functions were vested in a permanent committee. Each of these agencies was permitted to nominate its own officers, but one secretary-general served them all. The International Institute of Agriculture slipped a new, liberalizing wedge into the log jam of international action by providing that a quorum for voting purposes would be two-thirds of the membership. Furthermore, the Institute left it up to the states themselves to decide what share of the expenses they wished to carry, but those states which paid more obtained more votes in the organization [36].

Inspired by David Lubin, the International Institute for Agriculture first devoted itself to gaining information and stamping out speculation on the farm areas under production, probable yields, and actual harvests. Just before the First World War, approximately 6,000 copies of three different bulletins of the Institute were issued monthly. Even Russia, which traditionally had been reluctant to supply information, began to cooperate with statistics. Still ahead of these hard-won, essential methods of disseminating information on agricultural production were the sharper international challenges of tariffs, freight charges, credit, and stock-piling. But the first international organization for agriculture had helped, by its emphasis on cooperation, its use of a general assembly, executive committee, and secretary-general, and its liberalizing voting arrangements, in the further development of international agencies.

Other international organizations crowded the late nineteenth century: the International Penitentiary Commission (1880), the International Seismological Union (1903), and such permanent offices as the International Bureau for the Publication of Customs Tariff (1890) and the Opium Commission (1909), not to mention such organizations as the Permanent Council for the Exploration of the Sea (1899) and the International Committee of the Map of the World (1909).

The striking growth of public international unions in the late nineteenth century aroused the optimistic hopes of many citizens and statesmen for world peace. The ability of states to cooperate through standing institutions on problems of communications, health, commerce, and agriculture suggested that political tension was being reduced. Sarajevo clouded that illusion. Yet what had been won by men of courage and faith was not lost in the wake of the international devastation of 1914 to 1918. Indeed, the early international agencies were only harbingers of a day in which hundreds of international organizations, employing thousands of people, should span the earth, touching in one guise or another the purse and prayer of every national citizen and prompting, pushing, or threatening every state toward some new task.

From the first hesitant, politically hedged attempts to create an international agency to improve navigation on rivers, states had grudgingly recognized the advantages of international cooperation on matters which spanned political frontiers. Every one of the organizations created, despite the generous praise given them in later years, had been severely criticized by some individuals and regarded with coldness by some governments; every one of the organizations had to wait through dreary arguments and often many years before its basic convention was signed and ratified. Only looking back from the twentieth century, with its multitude of international offices, does the procession of organizations seem so steady in its gait, so certain of its future.

Because they were rooted in genuine needs, most of the international administrative agencies nurtured before the peace of Versailles not only survived the war but flourished in a new array. Those which failed to perform useful functions for the national governments which supported them withered away. Other economic and social needs soon bubbled to the surface of international attention, and the reconstruction of peace in the twentieth century compelled nations to consult and collaborate on new economic and social problems. The nineteenth century had supplied the precedents, the procedures, and some good proofs of the efficacy of international organization.

NOTES

1. J. P. Chamberlain, "The Regime of International Rivers: Danube and Rhine," *Studies in History, Economics, and Public Law,* Vol. 105, No. 1 (1923), New York, Columbia University Press, p. 156. This is a comprehensive study prepared in large part for the inquiry of President Wilson on questions affecting the peace after the First World War. It contains an extensive bibliography on the regulation of the Rhine and Danube Rivers.

2. G. F. de Martens, *Recueil des principaux traités,* Göttingen, Dietrich, 1835, Vol. VIII, Arts. XLII, XLVII, pp. 261, 292.

3. "Règlement pour la libre navigation des rivières" and "Articles concernant la navigation du Rhin," Annex XVI, *B.F.S.P.,* Vol. II, p. 162.

4. For texts of the Treaties of Mayence,

31 March 1831, and Mannheim, 17 October 1868, see *B.F.S.P.,* Vol. XVIII, p. 1076; Vol. LIX, p. 470. See also F. B. Sayre, *Experiments in International Administration,* New York and London, Harper, 1919, pp. 131–141, for a commentary on the powers of the Rhine Commission.

5. Ministère des Affaires Estrangères, "Congrès de Paris," *Documents diplomatiques,* Paris, Imprimerie Nationale, April 1856, p. 11.

6. Final Protocol, Conferences relating to Navigation of the Mouth of the Danube, October, November 1865, and Public Act of the European Commission of the Danube signed at Galatz, 2 November 1865, Art. VIII, *B.F.S.P.,* Vol. LV, pp. 89, 96.

7. Additional Act to the Public Act of the European Commission of the Danube,

signed at Galatz, 28 May 1881, *B.F.S.P.*, Vol. LXXII, p. 7.

8. For a documented report on Danubian navigation in the period immediately following the First World War, see W. D. Hines, "Report on Danube Navigation," Advisory and Technical Committee for Communications and Transit of the League of Nations, 1925.

9. Convention between Great Britain and the United States of America signed at Washington, D.C., 19 April 1850, Art. V, *B.F.S.P.*, Vol. XXXVIII, p. 4.

10. Ministère des Affaires Estrangères, *Documents diplomatiques*, Commission Internationale pour le Libre Usage du Canal de Suez, avril–novembre, procès-verbaux Nos. 11, 13, 1885, Paris, Imprimerie Nationale, 1885. See also Sir Travers Twist, "Le canal maritime de Suez et la commission internationale de Paris," *Revue de droit international*, Vol. 17, Paris, pp. 615–630.

11. Convention between Great Britain, Austria-Hungary, France, Germany, Italy, the Netherlands, Russia, Spain, and Turkey, Constantinople, 29 October 1888, Art. VIII, *B.F.S.P.*, Vol. LXXIX. See also the complete study by Charles W. Hallberg, *The Suez Canal*, New York, Columbia University Press, 1931; also H. J. Schonfield, *The Suez Canal in World Affairs*, New York, Philosophical Library, 1953.

12. L. G. McPherson, *Transportation in Europe*, New York, Holt, 1910; also C. Day, *A History of Commerce*, London, Longmans, 1907.

13. Ruth Masters, "International Organization of European Rail Transport," *International Conciliation*, No. 330 (May 1937), New York, Carnegie Endowment, pp. 493–500.

14. For origins of the movement to establish international law for railroads, see Bulmerincq, "Règlement international des transports par chemin de fer," *Revue de droit international*, Vol. 10 (1878), pp. 83–99. Text of the Bern convention, 1890, is in *B.F.S.P.*, Vol. LXXII, p. 771.

15. Major William F. Friedman, "Report on the History of the Use of Codes and Code Language," *International Radiotelegraphic Conference of Washington, 1927*, Washington, Government Printing Office, 1928, Chap. II.

16. For the first bilateral treaty on telegraphs, see G. F. de Martens, *Nouveau recueil général*, Göttingen, Dietrich, 1856, Vol. I, p. 591; the 1865 telegraphic convention is in *B.F.S.P.*, Vol. LVI, p. 294; see also M. de Kirchenheim, "Les congrès internationaux de la poste et du télégraphe," *Revue de droit international*, Vol. 13, pp. 342–348. Three valuable studies of international administrative agencies of the nineteenth century are G. Moynier, *Les bureaux internationaux des unions universelles*, Paris, Fischbacher, 1892; P. Reinsch, *Public International Unions*, Boston and London, Ginn, 1911; and L. Woolf, *International Government*, New York, Brentano, 1916.

17. International Telegraphic Convention signed at Vienna, 21 July 1868, Art. LXI, *B.F.S.P.*, Vol. LIX, p. 335.

18. International Telegraphic Convention signed at Rome, 14 January 1872, "Règlement de service international destiné à complèter les dispositions de la convention télégraphique," XXXIV, *B.F.S.P.*, Vol. LXVI, p. 1027.

19. For the Lisbon conference participants, see *B.F.S.P.*, Vol. CII, p. 291; an incisive study of the International Telegraph Union is contained in K. Clark, *International Communications*, New York, Columbia University Press, 1931, pp. 90–122.

20. *The Merchants Magazine*, New York, Freeman Hunt, Vol. 2 (March 1840), p. 256.

21. See H. Weithase, *Geschichte des Weltpostvereins*, Strasbourg, Hertz, 1893.

22. John Sly, "Genesis of the Universal Postal Union," *International Conciliation*, No. 233 (October 1927), p. 419.

23. See Treaty between Great Britain, Austria-Hungary, and others relative to the formation of a General Postal Union, signed at Berne, 9 October 1874, especially Art. XVIII and Detailed Regulations, XXVII, *B.F.S.P.*, Vol. LXV, p. 13. Also Convention between Austria-Hungary and others, for the formation of a Universal Postal Union, signed at Paris, 1 June 1878, *B.F.S.P.*, Vol. LXIX, p. 210, and Règlement de détail et d'ordre pour l'exécution de la convention de l'Union Postale Universelle, conclue à Vienne, le 4 juillet, 1891, XXXVI, *B.F.S.P.*, Vol. LXXXII, p. 762.

24. *Annual Report of the Postmaster-General of the United States for the Fiscal Year Ended June 30, 1875,* p. xvi.

25. J. M. Woodworth, "The General Subject of Quarantine with Particular Reference to Yellow Fever and Cholera," in J. Ashhurst, Jr. (ed.), *Transactions of the International Medical Congress,* Philadelphia, 1877, p. 1059.

26. See *Foreign Relations of the United States,* Washington, Government Printing Office, 1880, pp. 5–7.

27. International Sanitary Convention between Great Britain and others, signed at Venice, 30 January 1892, *B.F.S.P.,* Vol. LXXXIV, p. 12. "Here we have an international administrative organ with a technical staff of eighty-seven international health officers, etc., with an expenditure annually of £80,000 derived from an international tax levied upon ships and pilgrims."·Woolf, *op. cit.,* p. 236.

28. See "Resolution on International Sanitary Police, Second International Conference of American States, Mexico City, 22 October 1901–31 January 1902," in J. B. Scott (ed.), *The International Conferences of the American States, 1889–1928,* New York, Oxford, 1931, p. 94. The first sanitary convention pursuant to this resolution was held in 1902, the second in 1905, and others regularly since then.

29. Sanitary Convention between Great Britain, Austria-Hungary, and others, signed at Paris, 3 December 1903, Annex III, *B.F.S.P.,* Vol. XCVII, p. 1085.

30. Convention between the Argentine Republic, Austria-Hungary, and others, respecting the creation of an International Office of Weights and Measures, signed at Paris, 20 May 1875, *B.F.S.P.,* Vol. LXVI, p. 562. See also Moynier, *op. cit.,* pp. 57–73.

31. The most significant work in this field is S. Ladas, *The International Pro-tection of Industrial Property,* Cambridge, Mass., Harvard University Press, 1930. See also J. Vojáček, *A Survey of the Principal National Patent Systems,* New York, Prentice-Hall, 1936. For the convention between Belgium, Brazil, and others, see *B.F.S.P.,* Vol. LXXIV, p. 44.

32. The excellent companion work to *The International Protection of Industrial Property* is S. Ladas, *The International Protection of Literary and Artistic Property,* New York, Macmillan, 1938. See also R. R. Bowker, *Copyright, Its History and Law,* Boston, Houghton Mifflin, 1912. Text of the Convention between Great Britain, Belgium, and others for the Creation of an International Union for the Protection of Literary and Artistic Works, signed at Berne, 9 September 1886, is in *B.F.S.P.,* Vol. LXXVII, p. 22.

33. See International Convention relative to Bounties on Sugar (Great Britain, Austria-Hungary, and others) signed at Brussels, 5 March 1902, *B.F.S.P.,* Vol. XCV, p. 6; also Protocol recording the Accession of Russia to the International Sugar Convention of 8 March 1902, signed at Brussels, 19 December 1907, *B.F.S.P.,* Vol. C, p. 487.

34. Noted by B. C. Serling, *International Control of Sugar, 1918–1941,* Stanford, Calif., Stanford University Press, 1949, from H. C. P. Geerligs, *The World's Cane Sugar Industry, Past and Present,* Manchester, 1912, p. 21.

35. See O. R. Agresti, *David Lubin, A Study of Practical Idealism,* Boston, Little, Brown, 1922, for a vivid biography of a man who crusaded for an international organization.

36. Convention between Great Britain and other Powers for the creation of an International Agricultural Institute signed at Rome, 7 June 1905, *B.F.S.P.,* Vol. C, p. 595.

APPENDIX 3

Selected List of International Conferences 1850 to 1905 *

1851   First International Sanitary Conference, held at Paris. Twelve powers represented. A convention affecting the navigation of the Mediterranean executed by five powers. Later conferences held in Paris in 1859; Florence, 1867; Vienna, 1874; Washington, 1881; Rome, 1885; Venice, 1892; Paris, 1893 and 1897.

1853   General Conference as to Statistics, held at Brussels, on the initiative of Belgium. Twenty-six powers were represented. A permanent international bureau set up, at Rome, since 1885 (Institut international de Statistique). Publishes a bulletin. Meets biennially.

1853   Maritime Conference for the Adoption of a Uniform System of Meteorological Observations at Sea. Held at Brussels, August 23 to September 8, on the initiative of the United States.

1857   Conference of Copenhagen to capitalize the Sound Dues claimed by Denmark. Sixteen powers represented. Agreement with Denmark reached, to which most of the maritime powers acceded, she receiving 35,000,000 rix-dollars.

1861   Conference at Hanover to secure the Abolition of the Tax by Hanover on the Navigation of the Elbe. Seventeen powers represented. Convention signed commuting Hanoverian right for about 2,800,000 thalers.

1863   Conference of Brussels, July 15, to compound with the Netherlands for the Free Navigation of the Scheldt. Convention signed by twenty-one powers, for composition of about 17,000,000 florins.

1863   Conference of Paris on a Postal Union. Led to that of Berne in 1874.

1863   Conference of four powers on Sugar Duties.

1864   First International Conference on Weights and Measures. Held at Berlin. Fourteen powers attended. An international central bureau established at Berlin under charge of a permanent commission, meeting annually. Twenty-seven powers now adhere to it.

1864   Conference of London as to Marine Signalling.

1864   Conference of Paris as to Marine Signalling.

1865   Monetary Conference of Paris, resulting, December 23, in the Latin Monetary Union, between four powers, lasting till 1886. Conference of Paris in 1885 of four powers substituted (November 6) another convention.

1865   Conference of Paris on Telegraphic Correspondence. Twenty powers were represented. A convention was agreed on, and afterwards ratified, constituting "L'Union télégraphique universelle." Similar confer-

* Reprinted from *American Journal of International Law*, Vol. 1, Part II (July and October 1907), pp. 808–829, with the permission of the American Society of International Law.

ences followed, in 1865 at Vienna, in 1871 at Berne, in 1875 at St. Petersburg, in 1879 at London, in 1882 at Paris, in 1883 at Berlin. A permanent bureau was set up at Berne in 1869, and is still maintained. It is in correspondence with forty bureaus of as many different states, and over twenty private corporations. It issues an official Gazette, *Le Journal Télégraphique.*

1866   Conference of Paris as to the Navigation of the Danube. Confirmed the work as to neutralization by the European commission (see art. 108 *et seq.* of the Final Act of the Congress of Vienna of 1815).

1867   Monetary Conference of Paris. Twenty-two powers represented. The five franc piece recommended as the monetary unit.

1870   International Commission on the Metric System, first met at Paris. Thirty powers represented. At a subsequent meeting in 1875, a convention agreed to, May 20, setting up at Paris an International Bureau of Weights and Measures (Le Bureau du Metre) to be maintained by *pro rata* contributions from the contracting powers, and managed by a permanent international committee of one from each power, meeting annually.

1872   Conference of the International Telegraphic Commission at Rome. Convention signed January 14 by twenty-one powers.

1873   Monetary Conference at Copenhagen. Three powers represented. The Scandinavian Monetary Union formed May 27.

1874   Conference of Berne, September 15, on a Postal Union. Resulted in a convention forming one (October 9). Permanent international bureau maintained at Berne since 1875, which is in correspondence with about fifty postal administrations of different powers. Congresses of delegates from the powers adhering to the convention met quinquennially to perfect and improve the union, but in case of need special international conferences may be called with the consent of two-thirds of the powers adhering. That of 1891, at Vienna, acted on the subject of international telephony. An official journal published monthly in three languages, *L'Union Postale.*

1874   Monetary Conference of Paris between five powers.

1875   Congress of International Telegraphy, at St. Petersburg. International convention agreed on, December 21, between sixteen powers.

1876   Conférence Géographique Internationale of Brussels. Seven powers participated. Created the "Association internationale Africaine."

1876   Monetary Conference at Paris between five powers.

1877

1878   Conference at Berne to provide against the Phylloxera. Convention signed by seven powers, September 17, *ad referendum,* setting up a permanent bureau at Berne. Five ratified it.

1878   Le Congrès International de la Propriété Industrielle. Met at Paris, and again, by adjournment, in 1880. Reconvened in 1883, when ten powers were represented, and formed an International Union for the Protection of Industrial Property, with a permanent bureau at Berne.

A convention for this purpose was confirmed at Berne in 1886, and ratified by many of the powers, going into effect in 1887.

1878   Monetary Diplomatic Conference at Paris, held on the initiative of the United States. Twelve powers represented. It set up a permanent international bureau in Berne.

1879   Conference of London as to International Telegraphy. Convention signed by nineteen powers, July 28.

1881   Conference of Berne to regulate railroad transportation. Convention agreed on at a later conference at Berne in 1890, and ratified by ten powers. Central bureau at Berne. Publishes a "Zeitschrift für den internationalen Eisenbahntransport."

1883   Conference of London (February 2 to March 10) on the Navigation of the Danube. Convention agreed to, March 10, approving rules established by the permanent European Commission on the Danube.

1883   Conference of Brussels as to the Exchange of Official and Scientific Documents. Met again in 1886 and framed a convention, establishing a bureau of international exchanges, which eleven powers have ratified.

1884   Conference of Washington on a Prime Meridian. Adopted that of Greenwich.

1885   Conference of Paris as to the Freedom of Trade through the Suez Canal. Eight powers represented. A permanent international commission has been established with its seat at Paris.

1886   Conference of Berne, between ten powers, on Literary and Artistic Property. It constituted a "Union internationale pour la protection des oeuvres littéraires et artistiques," with a permanent international bureau at Berne, consolidated in 1892 with that for the protection of industrial property. Hungary acceded to the union in 1906. Publishes a monthly journal, *Le Droit d'Auteur.*

1887   Conference of London as to abolition of Sugar Duties. Convention signed in 1888.

1887   Conference as to the Liquor Traffic on the North Sea. Convention adopted November 16, 1887.

1888   Congress of Constantinople to regulate the use of the Suez Canal. Thirteen powers represented. Treaty concluded, in October, between six powers.

1888   Congress of Paris as to Sugar Bounties, April, May, and August.

1888   Union Internationale pour la Publication des Tarifs Douaniers; formed
1890   at Brussels. Most of the civilized powers adhere. A permanent bureau at Brussels publishes bulletins in five languages.

1889   Conference of St. Petersburg as to International Telegraphy.

1889   Conference of London on Sugar Duties. Eight Powers represented. Nothing accomplished.

1889   Conference of Berne, in September, to promote the well-being of the Working Classes.

1889   International Marine Congress as to Uniform Rules to Secure Life and Property at Sea, or "International Maritime Congress," held at Washington, on the call of the United States, October 16 to December 31. Twenty-seven nations represented. Considered co-operative plans for destroying floating derelicts and for preventing collisions. Rules adopted which went into effect July 1, 1897. Pronounced against a permanent international maritime commission.

1890   Conference of Brussels formed L'Union pour le Publication des Tarifs Douaniers. Has a permanent seat at Berne. Publishes a bulletin.

1890   Conference at Berne as to Railroad Transportation. Nine powers represented. Convention agreed to, October 14, establishing a permanent bureau at Berne, publishing a monthly journal. Went into effect January 1, 1893.

1890   Conference at Stockholm as to Fisheries in the North Sea. Second meeting at Christiania in 1901. Central council established at Copenhagen. Nine powers represented.

1892   Monetary Congress of Brussels on the initiative of the United States. Nothing accomplished.

1893   International Sanitary Conference at Dresden, March 11 to April 15, for the Repression of Epidemic Diseases. Twenty powers represented. Convention signed, *ad referendum.*

1893   Monetary Conference of the five powers of the Latin Union at Paris, October 15 to November 15.

1894   International Sanitary Conference at Paris, February 7 to April 3. Sixteen powers attended. Regulations adopted to prevent spread of cholera, with special reference to pilgrimages to Mecca. Portugal adhered to them in 1898.

1894   Conference of Berne, September 25 to October 3, as to the Publication of Treaties by a governmental union created for that purpose. Eighteen powers represented. Fourteen others expressed sympathy. Nothing accomplished.

1895   Monetary Conference of Paris.

1896   The International Maritime Committee formed. Fifth meeting at Hamburg in 1902.

1896   Conference of Paris on the Protection of Artistic and Literary Property. Most of the powers attended. Convention of Berne revised.

1897   Conference of Paris as to Ocean Telegraphy.

1897   Sanitary Conference at Venice, February 16 to March 19, to take measures against the Plague. Convention adopted March 19. Signed by seventeen powers. Switzerland adhered in 1898.

1898   Conference on Sugar Taxes at Brussels, June 7 to 25. Nine powers represented. Adjourned to December 16, 1901, and again to January 20, 1902. Convention signed.

1900   Conference of St. Petersburg as to International Telephony.

1900   Conference of Brussels as to Abolition of Sugar Duties.

1902   International Conference at Brussels as to the Regulation and Production of Sugar. A convention adopted, and a standing International Sugar

Commission created, meeting semi-annually. Permanent bureau at Brussels.

1903   Conference of Berlin on Wireless Telegraphy, August 4–13. Eight powers represented. Convention signed by seven powers.

1903   International Sanitary Convention of Paris. Convention signed December 3.

1905   International Congress of Agriculture at Rome (May 28). Forty-one powers represented. Agreed to a convention for the formation of an International Institute of Agriculture, with seat at Rome.

CHAPTER 4   *The Development of International Law*

Every modern state, with rare and perhaps diabolical exceptions, carries on its manifold relations with other nations of the world according to honored custom, accepted rules, and specific agreements. These practices of states are collected under the rather shallow title of international law.

International organization and international law depend upon each other. Without the overwhelming evidence of centuries that governments ordinarily do fulfill pledges made in the name of the state, no minister would have signed a treaty; without treaties based upon this "law," the history of international organization could not have begun. Reciprocally, however, international organizations have clarified, extended, and reinforced international law, for until the eighteenth century moral speculation and hazy custom provided the chief rationale for those international acts judged to be legally correct.

WESTERN CIVILIZATION AND THE UNITY OF LAW

Socratic and Stoic philosophers gave an early and distinct stamp to Western civilization by their insistence upon the unity of nature and man's singular faculty of perceiving the true and universal law of nature through the use of his reason [1]. From theorizing upon individual ethics it was a short, civilized step to apothegms on the right behavior of nation toward nation. Thus, Cicero instructed his son that men ought to observe duties to both enemies and slaves, that wars should be undertaken to secure peace, and that the vanquished deserved the mercy of the victors [2]. Such deductions from reason with a humanitarian outlook formed the background of international law.

As Christianity moved westward from Judea, moreover, it assimilated or paralleled the high moral teachings of the Greek philosophers. Justin the Martyr, for example, wrote in 150: "We are taught that Christ is the first born of God, and we have shown that he is the reason of whom the whole human race partake, and those who live according to reason are Christians, even though they are accounted atheists. Such were Socrates and Heraclitus [3]." St. Augustine carefully demonstrated that there was one light of wisdom common to all wise men [4]. The historical mission of the Catholic Church, meanwhile, was to unite all the world in Christianity by instructing men in the universally true prescriptions of God. These dicta recognized no boundary line of city, province, or state but applied equally to all creatures of the Deity.

The Middle Ages of Europe through the Church and the faith rested upon a literal international society and international law. Not until the eleventh century was the final cleft between the Greek and Latin churches hewn. In 1414 the most spectacular international congress of history assembled at Constance to settle the vital affairs of a religious Europe shredded by three rivals, Benedict XIII, Gregory XII, and John XXIII, for the Holy See. About 100,000 foreigners visited the city. The retinues of the three popes and the cardinals exceeded 1,800; there were 19 archbishops, about 130 bishops, 100 abbots, 1,800 priests, and their entourage totaled another 5,000 persons; not less than 1,800 scribes were reckoned. The Emperor with the princes, electors, dukes, and marquises from all parts of Europe had guards approximating 5,000 men; envoys, deputies, and gentlemen with soldiers and servants brought the list up to a few thousand more. Between 700 and 1,500 common whores were also counted [5]!

As indicated by the representation at the Council of Constance, no genuine dissociation of the Church from political life could be made during the age of faith. The settlement of the Papacy and the organization of the hierarchy affected the wealth and dominion of virtually every secular lord. In time the Church breathed the fire, if not the form, of its religious tenets into the emerging national dynasties. Not only did the callow states of Europe inherit the *jus gentium* of the Romans, law which had once transcended different peoples by bringing Roman and non-Roman citizens to a common process and judgment before a Roman praetor, but Christianity also grafted the teachings of reason and natural law upon the law courts of the new dynasties. Some Roman lawyers, indeed, had insisted that those practices of peoples which were universally observed could be identified with reason and natural law. Because of the philosophic background of natural law and because of the perennial inquiry into what natural law required and what men (or nations) *actually* did, it comes as no surprise that the first exponents of international law in its modern sense were theologians with the conviction that an immutable law (divine and/or reasonable) governed the universe.

The question of international law was sharply framed for inquisitive minds in the sixteenth century, when Europe was suddenly placed in contact with entirely different peoples of entirely different cultures in the New World. Francisco Vitoria, professor of theology at the University of Salamanca, denied the right of his Spanish compatriots to enslave the Indians recently discovered in America or to confiscate their property, for "the Indian aborigines are not barred . . . from the exercise of true dominion. This is proved from the fact . . . that they are not of unsound mind, but have according to their kind, the use of reason [6]." Backing his scholastic deductions were Scripture, the words of the saints, and the doctors of the Church. Francisco Suárez, another Spanish theologian, further advanced speculation on international law by drawing an important distinction between the governance of natural reason over the universal community and, where natural reason lacked details, the law *customarily* followed among states. This fundamental dichotomy between what is acknowledged law by the actual conduct and agreement of states and what is legally right by the honest use of man's reason has since persisted in Western society. The Nürnberg war-crimes trial again dramatized it in 1946.

Two other men of the sixteenth century, both devoted to the mighty Philip II of Spain, attempted a separate formulation of the rules of warfare; each contributed a little in weaning the proofs of his argument away from the Catholic Church authorities. Pierino Belli in 1558 wrote the rambling treatise *On Military Matters and War,* which grappled with the age-old problem of defining a just war and also encompassed such affairs as truces, booty, contracts in war, privileges of soldiers, and the treatment of prisoners. Balthazar Ayala in 1582 covered much the same ground in his book *On the Law and Duties of War and Military Discipline,* in which he cited Ovid, Virgil, Horace, Aristotle, Euripides, Tacitus, Xenophon, the Plinys, and contemporaries like Froissart, Bodin, and Hotman, in addition to the usual host of sacred writings, Church fathers, and Roman law glossators [7]. But Vitoria, Suárez, Belli, and Ayala were stanch Catholics. It remained for Protestants to systematize international law for the modern world. Why?

THE SECULARIZATION OF INTERNATIONAL LAW

The Peace of Westphalia marked the emergence of the modern state system, for it admitted not merely the coexistence but the equality of Protestant states within the orbit of western Christendom. The sixteenth and seventeenth centuries had watched the steady division of the old Catholic community into unorthodox sects. New states, like the Netherlands and

Switzerland, growing states, like Great Britain and Sweden, and autonomous German states, like Brandenburg and Saxony, all clamored now for an equal place in the galaxy of sovereigns. Permanent legations, the heart of international intercourse, were established; commercial treaties multiplied to pierce the rising national frontiers; and the enigma of neutrality puzzled the statesmen of a new two, three, or four-sided Europe. In this international system where the religion of the state was the religion of the ruler, not one Catholic faith, theologians and lawyers were hard pressed to prove that there was in the ever-increasing international relations of war and peace a single law which governed the several states. Protestants addressed themselves to this task, for they had divided the trunk of Christianity, and the shoots of their reasoning sprouted in England, the Netherlands, and Germany.

Alberico Gentili, an Italian lawyer turned Protestant, fled his native land for England where he lectured on law at Oxford. His magnum opus *On the Law of War*, published in 1598, veered the course of international law sharply from theological principles into the avenue of the existential: namely, the usage, customs, and consent of nations in their relations with each other. He bluntly opened his first chapter by writing that "it does not appear to be a function either of the moral or of the political philosopher to give an account of the laws which we have in common with our enemies and with foreigners [8]." Furthermore, Gentili said without equivocation that as the rule of a state and the making of its laws are in the hands of the majority of the citizens, so is international law confirmed by the habit of the greater part of the world. This, indeed, broke the trail of the past and shifted the evidence of legality, for where Gentili did call upon natural law and reason to witness the validity of international law, these abstractions merely added their majesty to the common practices of states.

The citations by Gentili from Scripture and the Church fathers, moreover, paled by comparison with his long list of notations from poets, playwrights, and, especially, historians of all ages, but his reasoning on the central problems of just war, the rights of ambassadors, or the law of treaties was tortured and obscure, if not contradictory. Liberated from pure religious-philosophic doctrine, international law still awaited a systematic and comprehensive analysis. This was the work of Hugo Grotius of Holland.

Writing at the time of the barbarous Thirty Years' War, Grotius held "it to be most clearly proved that there are laws for the community valid both in respect to war, and during war [9]." The central proposition of *On the Law of War and Peace*, composed in 1623 to 1624, was that human nature itself fosters natural law, for human nature itself impels man to live in society, and where there is society there is law. The acceptance of obligations, which is inherent in all man-made law, is also the rule of nature; otherwise there could be no society. The obligations of states to each other—whether through custom or through treaty—derive from the natural law of the universal society, as true and as binding in war as in peace.

The reasoning of Grotius followed the line of the Spanish theologians, Vitoria and Suárez, rather than Gentili, but as a Protestant theologian, philosopher, jurist, and statesman, the Dutchman was not encumbered by their religious motives nor constrained by their Church authorities. Also, for the Schoolmen, international law remained peripheral to their main inquiry into the eternal laws of truth and justice under God; Grotius advanced international law to a science by a cogent organization of the subject (even though the law of peace was ill treated) which he integrated with a complete and ennobling philosophical scheme.

Where Gentili realistically stressed overriding custom in the making of a legal system among states, Grotius adhered to the paramountcy of the natural law. Yet the Dutch virtuoso did not lose sight of the accretions to international law due to international practice: for instance, when discussing treaties, he wrote that "some treaties establish that which is conformable to Natural Law; others add something to it." In a new secular spirit of seventeenth-century religious tolerance he did not castigate Catholics nor did he entertain any doubt that treaties could be made with non-Christian states, for natural law "is so far common to all men that it recognizes no distinction of religion [10]." It cannot be forgotten that during the lifetime of Grotius the Turks perched on the threshold of Europe, extensive colonization of the Americas began, and the Portuguese, the Dutch, the English, and the Spanish arrived in China, Japan, and the Philippines for trade.

Two years after the great Peace of Westphalia had laid the foundations of modern Europe, Richard Zouche, the successor to Gentili as professor of Roman law at Oxford, treated "law between nations" as the "law which has been accepted among most nations by customs in harmony with reason." Furthermore, he said, "anything upon which single nations agree with other single nations, for example by compacts, conventions, and treaties, must also be deemed to be law between nations." Virtually no trace of Scripture or Church authorities or the metaphysics of natural law remained in Zouche's 195-page inquiry on the obligations of states to each other in time of peace and war [11]. Custom and actual practice as related by the historians or cited by Ayala, Gentili, and Grotius clearly supported his brief examination of such modern problems as whether a naturalized citizen is bound by the laws of his native land, whether new possession may be awarded on the strength of an ancient title, whether an ambassador may be sued, whether neutral flags protect enemy goods on the sea, and whether armed women who do the work of men should be spared in war.

FROM NATURAL LAW TO A POSITIVE LAW OF NATIONS

More and more international lawyers pointed to the positive acts of states, tacitly recognized by custom or definitely sealed by treaties, to prove that the world was governed by universal obligations and, therefore, a legal system. A diminishing few, like Samuel von Pufendorf of Saxony, still clung to the notion that natural law furnished the only set of norms for states [12]. Yet the tide of contrary opinion grew irresistible as the evidence of international acts mounted. Important documents of international relations had been printed in the fifteenth and sixteenth centuries, notably the various papal bulls, the Peace of Arras (1483) between Louis XI of France and Maximilian of Austria, the Agreement of Picquigny (1475) between Louis XI and Edward IV of England, and the capitulations between France and the Ottoman Porte (1570), but no general practice of printing treaties by public authority can be found prior to the seventeenth century. Not until the eighteenth century, moreover, did the collection and publication of treaties enable statesmen and jurists to have at hand a ready reference to acts of international intercourse.

In 1683 Frédéric Léonard published *A Collection of All the Modern Treaties Concluded among the Sovereigns of Europe* which, in truth, included only documents from 1672 to 1681. So successful was the venture, however, that Léonard later published a six-volume collection covering the period from 1435 to 1690 [13]. In 1693 Leibniz issued his *Diplomatic Code of the Law of Nations,* and Thomas Rymer in England began the first national collection of treaties at public expense. But the outstanding pioneer of treaty compilation was Jean Dumont, for he envisaged nothing less than the publication of all the documents of international law since the beginning of records. Dumont divided international law quite simply into natural law, or doing nothing to others which you would consider unreasonable and unjust if done to you, and contractual law, or treaties, contracts, arbitrations, agreements, capitulations, donations, and renunciations among peoples and princes [14]. With painstaking care he collected and organized the documents wherever available to substantiate "positive" international law.

Between 1791 and 1801 the first seven books of a collection of treaties destined to be a continuing series appeared under the editorship of Georg Friedrich von Martens, and in 1825 Lewis Hertslet began his duly celebrated volumes of *British and Foreign State Papers,* which annually included all the principal treaties and related documents made public by the states of the world.

This profusion of written instruments of international behavior dethroned natural law. Neither Vitoria nor Gentili nor Grotius had read such articulate testimony to the conduct of nations. When the most widely quoted international-law publicist of the eighteenth century, Emmerich de Vattel, turned to his chapter on treaties in *The Law of Nations*, he wrote that the subject of treaties was doubtless one of the most important in the mutual relations and affairs of nations. Vattel, a Swiss Protestant, cosmopolitan and enlightened, innocently heralded the French Revolution for the natural rights of man; to the society of nations he boldly transferred the myth of individual liberty and equality in the state of nature. ". . . the Nations, composed of men, and considered also as free persons who live together in the state of nature, are naturally equal, and possess by nature the same duties and the same rights. Strength or weakness make no difference in this respect [15]."

The doctrine of the equality and independence of sovereigns has since bewitched international law. From a democratic standpoint it meant equal access to the imperial judgment of the law while it stressed freedom to regulate domestic matters. But in a community of states, fearful of a common legislature or executive power, the dogma has frequently served anarchy. Equality and independence have been pretexts for the denial of international practices to which a state has not given express consent. Equality and independence have been used sometimes to deny the judgment of one state by others in international affairs. Most critically, however, because states have considered themselves independent, they have insisted that all matters of domestic jurisdiction cannot be judged by an international agency—whether a council or a tribunal—and they have gone so far as to claim that they themselves are the judges of what constitutes "domestic jurisdiction."

The eighteenth century, nevertheless, prepared statesmen and jurists to regard treaties as a flexible means for shaping a rigid legal system. Natural law, however rationalized as God's will or the innate character of man or the *civitas maxima*, still flitted like a precious filigree across the text and pronouncements of jurists. Venerable custom still gained a respectful hearing. But compacts, from ancient to enlightened times, compacts among French, British, and Dutch or Chinese, Indian, and African, pointed to the sworn obligations and responsibilities of nations. When, in the nineteenth century, several nations joined in a single pledge, the jurists could properly say: "But, of all the achievements of the past hundred years, the thing that is most remarkable, in the domain of international relations, has been the modification and improvement of international law by what may be called acts of international legislation [16]."

THE ABOLITION OF THE SLAVE TRADE

Few subjects allow a more hopeful interpretation of the development of international law by multipartite treaty than the suppression of the slave trade. Negroes had been chained and shipped to the Spanish colonies soon after Columbus reached Cuba, and the English began importing slaves to America during the reign of Elizabeth. In 1631 Charles I chartered a British company to engage in slave trading; this outfit was followed by the exclusive Royal African Company of 1672. The Treaty of Utrecht (1713) secured a monopoly for the British in the Spanish colonies for thirty years. Approximately 15,000 slaves every year were dragged from the forests of Africa, bludgeoned and jammed into foul holds, and painfully carried across the ocean.

This noxious practice of trading in the bodies of Negroes persisted without organized protest in western Europe for more than two centuries. Such flagrant evils of a cruel system of human exploitation finally whipped up a storm of indignation in eighteenth-century Europe. In 1794 the French radicals abolished slavery throughout French possessions. Denmark condemned the trade in 1802. In England, moreover, the nation which had profited most from the slave trade, public opinion, under the steady pounding of the Quakers and men like Anthony Benezet, Granville Sharp, and Thomas Clarkson, bristled against the vicious trade of human cargoes. Twelve high-minded men formed a committee in June 1787 and resolved to collect evidence demonstrating the rapine and bloodshed of slave selling. Mr. Clarkson alone, traveling from shire to shire, sometimes welcomed, sometimes venomously abused, obtained the names of more than 20,000 seamen who had been aboard slave ships [17].

The British Parliament, meanwhile, was pelted with petitions against the noisome trade. Between 1789 and 1791 the House of Commons heard evidence on the subject [18]. For thirteen querulous years thereafter, the advocates of abolition led by William Wilberforce struggled to win the House of Lords and the House of Commons to their side. On 25 March 1807 Parliament yielded. Slave trading was banned throughout the British realm. Henceforth Great Britain led the movement for international regulation of the slave trade.

Prohibition of the slave trade to Britain or Danish or American subjects (after 1806) did not prevent other flags from protecting slave traders. The institution of Negro slavery endured in the Western Hemisphere until almost the last decade of the nineteenth century. Where a market existed, captains hauled their black, beaten captives for sale.

By customary international law no vessel registered by one state can be stopped and searched by another on the high seas unless in the exercise of belligerent rights or in the pursuit of a pirate [19]. Only the reciprocal right, conferred by treaty, to visit and arrest foreign ships engaged in the slave trade promised to throttle such commerce. The path to this reasonable accommodation of sovereign rights at sea, however, was choked with difficulties. By additional articles to the Paris peace treaty of 1814, Great Britain got France to declare the slave trade "repugnant to the principles of natural justice," to end the practice by French subjects within five years [20], and to support Great Britain at the Congress of Vienna in calling for universal abolition of the wicked traffic. In consequence, the Eight Power Declaration of 8 February 1815, later appended to the Definitive Treaty between the Powers at Vienna, acknowledged the duty and need for suppressing the slave trade. While the European states righteously condemned this odious commerce and promised to consider cooperation in extirpating it, they failed to authorize any international capture of their vessels at this time.

Some international jurists during the first part of the nineteenth century maintained that the slave trade repelled universal morality, brooked natural law, and was therefore illegal; others wagged their gray heads and asserted that opinion alone did not alter the customary international law of the high seas.

Without express permission to visit and search suspected slave ships, no state could legally intercept the pernicious trade. Portugal and Spain first consented to search by conventions with Great Britain in 1817; other treaties were signed with Sweden in 1824 and Brazil in 1826. Although Castlereagh had tirelessly proffered a pact to the Great Powers at Aix-la-Chapelle in 1818 and the Foreign Office pursued the matter at Verona in 1822, neither Russia, Prussia, Austria, nor France contemplated with equanimity the search of their vessels upon the high seas. John Quincy Adams, American Secretary of State, replied to similar propositions of the British that the admission of a right to search ships of the United States by foreign officers "would meet universal repugnance in the public opinion of the country [21]."

By treaties with France in 1831 and 1833, however, Great Britain at last gained the consent of one great power to stop vessels engaged in slave trading. To these conventions Denmark and Sardinia adhered in 1834, the Hanse towns and Tuscany in 1837, Naples in 1838, and Haiti in 1839. Still the pacts were carefully circumscribed: only barks cruising along the west coast of Africa, around Madagascar, Cuba, Puerto Rico, or Brazil could be halted and, if alleged slave ships, would be handed over to their own national authorities [22].

The epitome of the British endeavors to outlaw slave trading was reached by international consultation at London in 1841. Austria, Prussia, and Russia each granted to the others and to Great Britain the right of visit and search over a wide belt of the tropical oceans [23]. Belgium accepted this limitation of sovereignty in 1848. Of the important marine powers, only the United States still thwarted the quick demise of the Negro traffic. Jealous of her independence from Europe and ever suspicious of the British Navy, the United States refused to permit any interference with ships flying the Stars and Stripes.

Although forbidden by statute in 1807, the slave trade flourished among Americans until 1860. National responsibility for enforcing antislave statutes shifted from the Department of the Treasury to Navy, to State, to War, to Interior. Light penalties for offenders, an apathetic government, and the thriving market of the Southern states further vitiated the law. In 1842 the United States grudgingly agreed to patrol the west coast of Africa to catch slave vessels lurking under her flag, but even this chore was done haphazardly. Not until Lincoln's administration did the United States grant by treaty the mutual right of visit and search to Great Britain while providing for mixed courts at New York, Sierra Leone, and the Cape of Good Hope for the instant trial of slave traders [24].

Customary international law had tolerated the slave trade, but step by step, treaty by treaty, the leading nations of the world condemned and sentenced it. First, at sea, they had permitted other states to board, search, and arrest suspected ships; next, they resolved in 1885 at the Conference of Berlin that territories in the Congo basin under their sovereignty or influence "should not serve either as a market or passageway for the trade in slaves of any race whatsoever [25]." To these views thirteen states subscribed.

The most decisive international action against the slave trade, however, was the General Act of the Brussels Conference of 1890. Attended by sixteen states, including the United States, Turkey, and Persia, the Conference was presented with the problem by Lord Vivian of Great Britain [26] at the second session:

. . . in recent years the growing strength and extension of operations of the Arab slave traders, whose terrible ravages have been so forcefully pictured by Cardinal Lavigerie and by African explorers, have given a new boost to this traffic. It is by the ports of the Zanzibar coast that the slaves are sent partly to Arabia and the Persian Gulf, but principally to Madagascar and other islands.

From the coast of Mozambique towards these islands there is constantly a certain exportation which is particularly difficult to halt because of the configurations of the coast . . .

After thirty-three sessions the states settled on a comprehensive treaty of exactly 100 articles: military, economic, and social reforms to check the trade were pledged by each power; within one year of ratifying the treaty, each state promised to declare (or propose to its legislature) laws making slave hunting or capture by violence a criminal offense; a limited right of visit and search of ships was extended multilaterally, and to facilitate the control of vessels an international bureau was established at Zanzibar to which each power would submit statistics, names of authorities, ship lists, copies of trials of condemnation, and so forth. Finally, regulations for the control of liquor and firearms in Africa were provided [27]. While international law, therefore, had not provided for the search of ships by public vessels of another flag in time of peace and under suspicion of slave trading, a large number of states, by treaty, agreed to this practice, thereby imposing new international obligations upon themselves.

THE REGULATION OF FISHERIES

The sovereignty of ships on the high seas constantly put states in a quandary. Slave trading had been practically eliminated on water by international treaties, but meanwhile the abuse of fisheries situated beyond territorial waters went without penalty: some vessels used drift nets and others trawled, dragging or ripping the lines in their wake. Cruisers had no authority to verify the papers or arrest foreign ships suspected of uprooting or cutting nets.

The first bilateral agreement on the regulation of fisheries which permitted a modicum of international control came in 1839 after bitter protests by English and Scotch fishermen against the encroachments of the French in the Channel fisheries. A convention between the two states provided for an international commission which, in 1843, issued detailed regulations on the marking of ships and agreed that the cruisers of one nation might check the identity of the vessels of the other in waters lying between France and Britain. Any suspicion of abuse of nets, fishing out of season, and so forth could be reported to a police ship of the other state. Where the parties were congenial and the damages slight, the commandant of any cruiser might arbitrate, but the treaty stoutly upheld the national monopoly of fisheries within territorial waters and bays [28].

In the North Sea, however, not two but six European states vied for the shimmering catch of halibut, herring, plaice, and cod. The British government, therefore, explored the possibility of international regulation with France, Belgium, Holland, Denmark, and Norway-Sweden; on 8 October 1881 these states, with Germany, met at The Hague. Within seven months an international convention (which all but Norway-Sweden ratified) was completed along the principles enunciated by the Anglo-French fisheries treaty. Although the multilateral accord shunned the subject of conservation and failed to go beyond the indirect international police control of the 1843 regulations, nevertheless the states of the world had again in concert "legislated," had again overridden customary law and manufactured a precedent for the future regulation of international fisheries [29].

At the conference on policing the North Sea fisheries, the delegates had also unanimously protested against the evil of floating cabarets which, immune to prosecution, hovered near fishing fleets, selling cheap tobacco and liquor to men. Morale weakened and discipline failed with serious consequences to the individual and the fishing enterprise. The representatives had also called attention to the importance of safeguarding submarine cables from the claws of fishing smacks [30]. The upshot of these prudent remarks was two more international conferences which placed further obligations upon the contracting states beyond general international law.

By 16 April 1885 twenty-four states had ratified a convention providing for the protection of international cables; within a year seventeen of these states had passed laws penalizing willful or malicious damage. Almost simultaneously delegates from Germany, Belgium, Denmark, France, Great Britain, and the Netherlands met nineteen times in 1886 and hammered out a multilateral document which proscribed the sale of alcohol to fishing smacks on the North Sea. Both treaties, like the fisheries convention, permitted visits to a suspected vessel by the officers of any one of the contracting parties, but the prosecution of an alleged criminal was confined to his own nation [31].

Out in the Bering Sea, beyond the marginal waters of the United States, meanwhile, American cruisers began seizing British Columbian vessels for violation of American laws designed to protect seals which annually returned to breed in the Alaskan islands. Eventually the dispute between Great Britain and the United States came before arbitrators; the American claim to jurisdiction over foreign vessels on the Bering Sea was denied. In 1911, after ineffective national regulations by the interested states, the United States called the Pelagic Sealing Conference in Washington. Russia, Japan, Great Britain, and the United States then agreed by treaty "that their subjects and citizens . . . shall be prohibited . . . from engaging in pelagic sealing in [certain waters] . . . and that every such person and vessel offending against such prohibition may be seized . . .

and detained by the naval or other commissioned officers of any of the Parties to this Convention [32]."

In the last forty years, moreover, a number of conventions for the protection of halibut, salmon, and whales have been signed by various maritime states, again placing obligations upon the contracting states far beyond the requirements of general international law. Through treaties, especially multilateral treaties, therefore, states have supplemented the traditional body of international law to some degree in this field; over the long run it is not unreasonable to maintain that they have "legislated"— at least for themselves.

SAFETY OF LIFE AT SEA

When Benjamin Harrison was President of the United States, James G. Blaine, Secretary of State, welcomed twenty foreign nations to the International Maritime Conference in Washington in these words: "The already existing and the rapidly increasing intercourse between continent and continent, between nation and nation, demands that every protection against the dangers of the sea and every guard for the safety of human life be provided [33]." Common law for peaceful maritime commerce had existed for centuries. Some fundamental rules of the sea on collision, on jettison, on salvage, and so forth dated back to the ancient Rhodian sea laws, or the medieval judgments of the island of Oléron in the Bay of Biscay, or the fourteenth-century Consolato del Mare of Barcelona, or the code of Wisby Island in the Baltic. Louis XIV had embodied many of these dicta in the comprehensive French Marine Ordinance of 1681. Nevertheless, the gaps in this customary international law, further widened by the diverse interpretations of national tribunals, left doubt and danger for mariners, risk and hardship for merchants [34]. The International Maritime Conference of 1889 worked generously to achieve universal acceptance of rules for the prevention of collisions, the determination of seaworthiness of vessels, the saving of life and property in shipwrecks, the removal of obstructions to navigation, and the standard marking of buoys throughout the world. Again the effectiveness of the principles upon which the assembled admirals, captains, and other naval officers agreed hung upon the national legislatures, yet the consensus and collateral action of the leading maritime powers in practice made international law. Where polite inquiries for a permanent international maritime commission or an international tribunal to try questions of collisions between subjects of different nationalities arose, the delegates paused and refused to go further. In 1889 diplomats still squirmed at the whisper of international courts. But the unification of maritime laws in peace by multilateral convention progressed: in 1910 nine powers acknowledged identical rules governing collisions at sea; at the same time ten states, including the United States, agreed on the law of salvage [35]. After the frightful loss of the S.S. "Titanic" in 1912, world-wide sentiment supported the first International Conference on Safety of Life at Sea, at which thirteen states suggested minimum standards of subdividing ships, boatage, and lifesaving equipment, as well as the use of radio and fixed routes across the North Atlantic guarded by an iceberg patrol [36]. Unfortunately the First World War truncated this bold thrust at international lawmaking, but subsequently, in 1929 and 1948, the initial endeavor received full endorsement by multilateral conventions.

International law, throughout history, has owed its fame to the laws of war rather than to the laws of peace, for the control, if not the elimination, of violence has been the hope of civilized man. During the nineteenth century, states began a valuable adjustment of national law to international purpose in the slave trade, liquor traffic, ocean fisheries, maritime navigation, and other areas of mutual interest. But the surprising climax of this international legislation was the brazen grip by which humanists, businessmen, and politicians seized the dilemma of regulating warfare itself. An epoch of international consultation closed on this optimistic note.

THE REGULATION OF MARITIME WARFARE

One vicious tactic of maritime warfare which plagued the commerce of neutrals was privateering. States licensed private individuals, not necessarily citizens, to capture enemy vessels. Frequently the discipline of a vagabond crew failed and, with plunder the prime motive, outrages were heaped on belligerent and neutral alike. Commissioned by a letter of marque, privateers were often little more than legal pirates. Sweden and Holland wrote an ineffective agreement disavowing privateers as early as 1675; Prussia and the United States rejected the use of private armed vessels against each other in 1785. Despite various fits of restraint, however, privateering was almost universal in the seventeenth and eighteenth centuries.

The wanton excesses of corsairs during the Napoleonic Wars shocked a liberal bourgeois age, for the depredations of private property sailing the seas far exceeded the abuses of land warfare. Great Britain, in particular, humiliated by the American privateers from 1812 to 1814 which captured no less than 1,300 prizes and sacked countless others, and ever dependent upon marine commerce for livelihood, moved against the international practice. Partly because of changing international sentiment, partly because of the dearth of Russian cargoes, both the British and

French renounced the use of letters of marque during the Crimean War [37]. Europe now poised on the edge of a new era in international law.

The armed neutralities led by Russia in 1780 and 1801 against the British claim to seize enemy goods aboard neutral ships had eventually collapsed. As a concerted effort to stipulate the international law of war on the high seas, the declaration had been premature, chiefly lacking the consent of the greatest of maritime powers. Yet, the doctrine vigorously persisted that free (neutral) ships make free goods while neutral goods aboard enemy ships were not liable to capture unless contraband of war. Having taken up arms against Russia in the Crimea, Britain declared on 28 March 1854 that she would "waive the right of seizing the enemy's property laden aboard a neutral vessel" and that it was "not Her Majesty's intention to claim the confiscation of neutral property . . . found on board enemy ships [38]." After a half century of indecision, the major powers of the earth and sea were ready to choose the direction of international law.

Another principle of maritime warfare, advocated for decades by traders and supported by the armed neutralities of 1780 and 1800, was that blockades had to be effectively maintained by a belligerent—by a string of ships in communication with each other—to secure the right of capturing blockade runners. Mere declaration or "paper" blockades should obtain no legal validity. The Napoleonic Wars had witnessed this latter pretense carried to ludicrous extremes: in May 1806 the British declared a blockade of the Continent from the Elbe River to the port of Brest; in November France retaliated by announcing that all the British isles were blockaded. Although the hysteria of war had induced such wild presumptions, the relatively tranquil years following 1815 confirmed the abiding international opinion that only effective blockades deserved the recognition of neutrals.

In 1856 the psychological moment arrived to pronounce the convictions of international society on privateering, neutral ships and neutral property in time of war, and blockades. The end of the Crimean War had brought the Great Powers and Sardinia together at Paris to draft terms of peace. With dispatch and grace they concluded this task. Then, at the twenty-second meeting, Count Walewski, Foreign Minister of France, said that although the delegates had gathered specifically to consider the Eastern question, he would be sorry not to use the occasion for clarifying certain other questions and declaring certain principles which might further assure the peace of the world. After citing the problems of occupied Greece and Rome, the disturbances of the Two Sicilies, and the insinuations of the Belgian press against the French government, Count Walewski added that whereas the Congress of Westphalia had established liberty of conscience and the Congress of Vienna had promoted abolition of the slave trade and the free navigation of rivers, it would be worthy of the Congress of Paris to lay the foundation for a uniform maritime law during war. For the delegates, therefore, France adroitly sketched four principles which quickly won the approbation of the conference:

1. Privateering is and remains abolished.
2. The neutral flag protects the enemy's goods, except contraband of war.
3. Neutral goods, except contraband of war, are not subject to seizure under the enemy's flag.
4. Blockades to be binding must be effective, that is to say, maintained by a force actually sufficient to interdict the approaches to the enemy's coast [39].

The Declaration of Paris went beyond a staid affirmation of policy by seven powers; it sensed the emergent mood of international legislation based upon the consent of the community of states; without precedent, therefore, each signatory promised to acquaint states not present at the conference with the declaration and invite them to accede to it. At least thirty-five states ultimately agreed that the Declaration of Paris had cogently stated modern international maritime law. Only the United States, Spain, and Mexico, with long coast lines and skimpy navies, hesitated, for swarms of privateers might still be needed to rattle the spars of enemy commerce. Although the South commissioned privateers against the North in the American Civil War and in 1865 Chile licensed armed vessels against Spain, neither the Franco-Prussian War nor the Spanish-American War contravened the resolutions taken at Paris. Thus, by proclamation and practice, the states of the world had collectively inscribed new rules upon the tablets of international law.

THE REGULATION OF LAND WARFARE

The spoliation of maritime attacks has scarcely compared with the ravages and horror of land warfare. Grotius had been repelled by the barbarity of the Thirty Years' War, and all Europe had gasped at the enormities of the Napoleonic bloodletting campaigns. But not until the liberal awakening of the nineteenth century with its respect for the individual and its sentiment for humanity did the states of the world attempt to prescribe by treaty the international rules of war. Relief for the wounded led the cause, for if statesmen would not heed the admonitions of the Abbé de Saint-Pierre or Immanuel Kant or Jeremy Bentham to construct a new international society which condemned war itself, at least human suffering in battle might be mitigated.

No more haunting description of the ghastly butchery of war has been written than *Un souvenir de Solferino,* by Henri Dunant. This Swiss gentleman witnessed the harrowing struggle between the Austrians and the Franco-Sardinian forces on 24 June 1859 in which 3 field marshals, 9 generals, 1,566 officers, and about 40,000 soldiers fell in a ferocious battle lasting sixteen hours. Another 40,000 casualties resulted from exhaustion and disease. At Solferino, magnanimous men and women with pitiful resources had unselfishly tended sick and wounded soldiers cast like wreckage off the bloody tides of battle. Most noteworthy aid in the past had been rendered by religious orders and sisters of mercy; during the Crimean War, the Grand Duchess Helen-Pavlovna left St. Petersburg with 300 women for the Russian hospitals at the front, while Florence Nightingale enlisted 37 English nurses and embarked for Constantinople in November 1854. But Henri Dunant argued that these single efforts, no matter how generous, had remained unfruitful without organized support. Would it be too much to hope that an international congress could "formulate some international principle, consecrated by treaty which, once agreed upon and ratified, would serve as the constitution for *Sociétés de secours pour les blessés* in the various countries of Europe [40]?"

Dunant next appeared before the Geneva Society of Public Utility which included such philanthropists as Gustav Moynier, Dr. Louis Appia, and Adolph Ador, and lectured further on the theme of humanity in warfare. General Dufour of Switzerland was interested in the project, and in October 1863 a gathering of thirty-six men, half of them official delegates, resolved that national committees be formed to cooperate in time of war with the sanitary services of the army and that the universal emblem of volunteer nurses should be the red cross. Furthermore, the conference recommended to the governments of the world that during combat hospitals, medical personnel, volunteer nurses, and so forth be regarded as neutrals and that a distinctive sign be adopted by all sanitary services. In consequence of this remarkable spadework, sixteen states responded to Switzerland's bid to attend an international conference in 1864 to consider amelioration of the wounded in armies in the field; within fourteen days they concluded the first multilateral convention regulating land warfare.

The Geneva Convention of 1864 sanctioned no Red Cross society, but all parties to the compact agreed that ambulances, hospitals, and staff employed in the sanitary service, including chaplains, ought to be regarded as neutrals during hostilities; each nation obliged itself to care for the sick and wounded regardless of uniform. The reversed Swiss flag, a red cross on a white field, was adopted as the emblem for all places and personnel dedicated to the sick and wounded. Like the Declaration of Paris, the Convention was opened to states not represented at the conference and again the hearty acclamation of the world community to a law for war cheered the patient ploddings of vision-struck men and women. Thirty-one governments had ratified the treaty before the United States banished its phobia of foreign alliances in 1882 and concurred with the humane document: by the end of the century virtually all states, including Persia, Siam, and Japan, had acceded to the Geneva Convention. Clarification of certain paragraphs and new provisions for the neutralization of medical personnel and equipment in navies were proposed as additional articles to the Convention in 1868. Although these additions lacked unanimous approval, they were circumspectly observed during the Franco-Prussian and Spanish-American Wars [41].

Even before the delegates met in Geneva to circumvent the brutality of warfare, the United States was locked in a death struggle between North and South, the costliest combat between Waterloo and the Marne. Francis Lieber, professor of history and political science at Columbia University, wrote to Charles Sumner on 19 August 1861 that he should like to prepare a book on the law and usages of war affecting the combatants. While Congress paid little heed to this offer, General H. W. Halleck, author of a treatise on international law and a friend of Lieber's, fell heir to the kinky military-legal problems stirred up by fighting American rebels and occupying American states: the handling and treatment of prisoners, the use of parole, the definition and punishment of guerilla warfare, and so forth puzzled field commanders who bluntly proceeded according to the tactics dictated by the local military situation. As General in Chief of the Union, General Halleck invited Lieber to Washington to work with a War Department board charged with revising the Articles of War and preparing a code of regulations for the government of armies in the field. To the jurist the generals assigned the dazzling task of codifying the laws of warfare for the first time in history. On 20 February 1863 Lieber submitted his draft of a code to General Halleck [42]:

I have earnestly endeavored to treat of these grave topics conscientiously and comprehensively; and you, well read in the literature of this branch of international law, know that nothing of the kind exists in any language. I had no guide, no groundwork, no textbook . . . Usage, history, reason, and conscientiousness, a sincere love of truth, justice, and civilization, have been my guides; but, of course, the whole must be still very imperfect. . . .

With minor revisions the "Instructions for the Government of Armies of the United States in the Field," General Order 100, appeared in May 1863, echoing the venerable lesson of Cicero, that war is not an end in itself, and the preface of Grotius, that men do not cease to be moral beings responsible to God and humanity because of public war. Enslavement, pillage, cruelty, the destruction of private property, and the debasement of morality stigmatize barbarians, not civilized armed forces [43]. While every battle has since provoked abuses under "military necessity," Lieber's code first limited the wildest excesses of war by setting forth official rules to which the two belligerents roughly adhered.

By his skillful organization of the rules of land warfare for the United States government, Francis Lieber prepared the way for international regulation. When thirteen states assembled in Brussels in 1874 to consider Russian proposals for an international code of warfare, Baron Jomini, plenipotentiary of the Tsar, admitted that the idea had been suggested by Lieber's work.

Nearly every age has frowned upon or forbidden "inhuman" weapons of destruction: the ancient Greeks condemned the poisoning of wells in their internecine feuds; Innocent III banned the use of the crossbow and other machines for hurling projectiles against Christians; but the first international prohibition of an uncivilized instrument of warfare occurred in 1868 at St. Petersburg when seventeen states renounced the use of explosive or inflammable bullets weighing less than 400 grams. Explosive bullets, originally used to kill big animals in India, were perfected by 1867 to detonate and fragment in a substance as soft as the human body. General Milutine, the Russian Minister of War, repelled by the cruelty of jagged metal within the wounded soldier, had conveyed his thoughts to the Tsar, and the international conference at St. Petersburg ensued [44].

A more comprehensive scheme to codify the rules of land warfare emanated from Russia in 1874. To Brussels virtually every state of Europe sent delegates to consider a project of fifty-six articles extending from "military authority over the territory of the hostile state" to "armistices and reprisals." The means of injuring an enemy were defined, undefended towns declared free from attack, and the duties of prisoners of war carefully drawn. From the beginning, however, Britain had opposed the limitation of belligerent action—although not insensitive to the humanity of restraining warfare—and other objections eventually prevented the Declaration of Brussels from international ratification [45].

Nevertheless, the zealous labor to limit warfare by international compact was not lost, for the Institute of International Law, a private organization of eminent international jurists (founded in 1873 at the suggestion of Francis Lieber, Gustav Moynier, and Kaspar Bluntschli), kept prodding the governments to instruct their armies in the rules of international law [46]. By the end of the nineteenth century, the Netherlands, France, Germany, Switzerland, Serbia, Spain, and various Latin-American countries, as well as the United States, had issued manuals to their armies on the conduct of warfare although no single code, except the Geneva Convention of 1864 and the St. Petersburg Declaration of 1868, had yet secured international acceptance.

ARBITRATION AND DISARMAMENT

Concomitant with the awakened rationality of the nineteenth century toward warfare, a movement to prevent the outbreak of hostilities by negotiation and compromise attempted to stem the reckless passions of nationalism. The use of third, friendly parties to soothe the tempers of two ruffled states had long been known to history by such hopeful names as "mediation" and "good offices." Arbitration had been a resort of Greek *polei*, Italian communes, and Swiss cantons to settle disputes, but the arrogance of national princes tended to reject all referees of claims. In 1794, however, the Jay Treaty signed by the United States and Great Britain revived this salubrious practice between major states. Thorny claims for damages caused by the belligerents during the American Revolutionary War and the contentious St. Croix River boundary yielded nicely to the mollifying discussions of three commissions, and other arbitrations between Great Britain and the United States followed during the next century.

In Europe a unique five-man tribunal established by treaty among Great Britain, Austria, Prussia, Russia, and the Netherlands in 1815 awarded a disputed inheritance; Queen Victoria decided a quarrel between France and Mexico in 1839, while the King of Prussia judged an argument between Great Britain and France in 1842. Chile entered an arbitral agreement with the United States in 1858, and France agreed to a commission in 1882 to settle United States or French claims arising from the Franco-Mexican, Franco-Prussian, and American Civil Wars. More striking in their development in Latin America than elsewhere, compulsory-arbitration clauses covering all disputes were inserted into some fifty different treaties between 1820 and 1890. From every viewpoint the use of arbitration in the nineteenth century increased; J. H. Ralston listed no less than 217 instances of arbitral or other judicial tribunals which functioned among nations from 1794 to 1897 [47]. Despite this remarkable proliferation of arbitral awards, no permanent international tribunal open to the litigation of all states was yet available.

Thus, two structural beams to the rising framework of international law, the codification of rules of war and the establishment of a permanent arbitral tribunal, were ready for international architects. A third lintel for the support of peace was disarmament: Napoleon III had tried on three occasions to interest the statesmen of Europe, especially Germany, in disarmament, but without success; various unofficial peace conferences—in 1849, 1850, 1851, 1878, and 1889—had adopted resolutions urging the reduction of weapons of war. Motions to study disarmament were frequently introduced into the several European parliaments after 1870, and Lord

Salisbury called the attention of Germany to the fact that seven great powers of Europe spent 23 billion francs on their armed forces alone between 1881 and 1886 [48]. Finally, just two years before the end of the century, the Russian ministers, dismayed by the drains upon the national treasury caused by intensive competition with the more advanced Austrian guns and fieldpieces, prevailed upon the Tsar to issue an invitation to all states accredited to St. Petersburg to attend a conference "with the object of seeking the most effective means of ensuring to all peoples the benefits of a real and lasting peace and, above all, of limiting the progressive development of existing armaments [49]."

THE HAGUE PEACE CONFERENCES OF 1899 AND 1907

The Hague Peace Conferences have been regarded both as milestones in the development of international law and organization and as ceremonious shows which failed to organize the community for the maintenance of international peace. Both judgments are valid. Twenty-six nations, including the United States and Mexico from the Americas, met at The Hague on the Tsar's birthday, 18 May 1899, and in the course of two months marked by magnanimous deliberations completed three conventions and three declarations. What was most significant about the Conference was its demonstration that the states of the world could be assembled in time of peace to approve multilateral declarations and conventions which might, because of their universality, be cited as new standards and obligations for the international community.

The First Hague Peace Conference made an attempt to crystallize the nineteenth-century attitudes toward arbitration, rules of warfare, and disarmament. The use of international commissions of inquiry was recommended as a means of solving international disputes. The most important step, however, was the creation of a Permanent Court of Arbitration. In truth, the Court was not a court, but rather a panel of distinguished persons, highly competent in international law, willing to act as arbitrators in international questions. Each signatory power to the convention establishing the Permanent Court of Arbitration could nominate four persons to the list of arbitrators. When having recourse to arbitration each party to the case could choose two arbitrators from the panel and the arbitrators together would choose a fifth umpire. The states which agreed upon a Permanent Court of Arbitration, however, did not agree that all legal disputes among them *must* be settled by arbitration. In particular, the leading powers insisted that they be the judges of whether to arbitrate or not. Consequently the First Hague Peace Conference merely went on record as recognizing arbitration in questions of a legal nature as the most effective and equitable means of settling disputes where diplomacy had failed.

In respect to rules of warfare, each state promised to issue instructions to their armed forces in conformity with a single code of land warfare, while the Geneva Convention of 1864 was generally applied to maritime warfare. Every nation present, moreover, declared that it would abstain from bombing for at least five years, not use asphyxiating gases in projectiles, and prohibit expanding bullets. Although a limitation of armaments, the real incentive for the invitation to The Hague in 1899, received frigid support from a single, jejune resolution "that the restriction of military charges . . . is extremely desirable," nevertheless the other achievements of the Conference crowned the age of consultation with honor [50].

Considering the short span of international history from the inexact speculations and rambling hypotheses of the early writers on international law to the actual assembly of the leading nations of the world for the express purpose of developing international law, the work of the statesmen at The Hague was highly commendable. But it was a nineteenth-century conference, still handicapped by the traditional rules of sovereignty and the equality of each state. For example, every state had the right to be represented on every commission of the Conference, and unless there was unanimity in the commission it could not recommend a convention for adoption by the Conference! All voting in plenary sessions recognized the equality of each state, and no state was bound by the recommendations of the Conference. Some undermining of these stilted principles, however, did appear. The leading powers, for instance, controlled the committee chairmanships, and abstentions by small powers on resolutions which they opposed did not spoil the effect of the resolution. Perhaps the most valuable contribution of the First Hague Peace Conference to the history of international organization is that from its inception the assembled states looked forward to a reunion.

Such questions as the rights and duties of neutrals, the inviolability of private property in naval warfare, and the bombardment of ports, towns, and villages by a naval force had been postponed for a future conference. No action, however, was taken until 1904 when the Interparliamentary Union, an unofficial organization prominent in advancing international law, met in St. Louis—concurrent with the world fair. By unanimous vote the delegates (either active or retired members of legislative chambers throughout the world) asked the President of the United States to summon a conference to discuss the questions left in abeyance by the First Hague Peace Conference as well as the negotiation of arbitration treaties and "the advisability of establishing an international congress to convene periodically for the discussion of international questions [51]." The United

States, therefore, sounded the other powers on a second peace conference and received an encouraging response. Meanwhile, the Russo-
Japanese War terminated and the Tsar, with a courteous nod from President Roosevelt, assumed the initiative and proposed a new assembly at
The Hague.

At the insistence of the United States all the Latin-American states were
invited to the Second Hague Peace Conference, and every republic except Costa Rica and Honduras attended, thereby swelling the membership of the world assembly to forty-four, a veritable parliament of nations. The three conventions of 1899 were revised and ten new compacts
signed—including the limitation of force in recovering international contractual debts, the rights and duties of neutrals, the laying of submarine
mines, the rules of capture in naval warfare, and the institution of an
international prize court. Never ratified, the constitution of the International Prize Court clearly forecast the spirit of the coming age of collaboration, for the court would have been an appeal court from national
prize tribunals, would have provided for fifteen judges paid through an
international bureau, and would have entitled Germany, the United States,
Austria-Hungary, France, Great Britain, Japan, and Russia to permanent
seats with the balance of places occupied by the smaller powers in rotation. But the most pregnant deed, almost one hundred years after Castlereagh had first proposed fixed reunions to the leading European states,
was the resolution passed by the sixth plenary session of 21 September
1907:

The Conference recommends to the Powers the assembly of a Third Peace
Conference, which might be held within a period corresponding to that which
has elapsed since the preceding Conference . . . and it calls their attention to
the necessity of preparing the program of this Third Conference a sufficient
time in advance to ensure its deliberations being conducted with the necessary
authority and expedition [52].

Continuous collaboration, therefore, was on its way when the sullen
war clouds of Sarajevo smothered the best hopes for international peace.
The slender international machinery of conferences proved unable to
withstand the deep disturbances of international society. Sporadic consultation demonstrated more clearly every day the need for permanent
institutions to mitigate political conflicts just as the international bureaus
already established were proving the efficacy of international organization in economic and social matters. The First World War, unfortunately,
stopped a process of regular international conferences to promote international law, and it harshly demonstrated the inadequate formulation of
international law on belligerency, neutrality, and the regulation of warfare. But the very enormity of the world disaster spurred men into a new

crusade for an international organization which would promote peace by disarmament, arbitration, and the development of international law. When peace had restored reason in the Western world, men slowly and stubbornly went back to the work of raising international organization from the dust. Without the experience of the nineteenth century, without the practices and procedures of international consultation for one hundred years, without the examples of the international agencies created in two or three generations, they could never have built such a rare device as the League of Nations.

NOTES

1. For the lessons of the chief representative Stoics, Epictetus and Marcus Aurelius, see their complete extant writings in W. J. Oates (ed.), *The Stoic and Epicurean Philosophers;* see also P. Barth, *Die Stoa,* Stuttgart, Frommanns, 1903.

2. Cicero, *De officiis,* I, xi.

3. *Apology,* I, xlvi, 1–4, quoted in H. Bettenson (ed.), *Documents of the Christian Church,* New York, Oxford, 1947, p. 8.

4. *De libero arbitrio,* II, x.

5. J. Lenfant, *The History of the Council of Constance,* trans. by S. Whatley, London, A. Bettesworth *et al.,* 1730, 2 vols., Vol. I, p. 83. Eight other ecumenical councils were held between the twelfth and sixteenth centuries.

6. F. Vitoria, *De indis noviter inventis,* Sec. I, xxiii. Text and English translation by J. P. Bate are in J. B. Scott, *The Spanish Origin of International Law,* Oxford, Clarendon Press, 1934.

7. The texts and English translations of "De re militari et bello tractatus" by Belli and "De iure et officis bellicis et disciplina militari" by Ayala are in J. B. Scott (ed.), *Classics of International Law,* New York, Oxford, 1936, and New York, Carnegie Endowment, 1912, respectively.

8. A. Gentili, "De iure belli," Book I, Chap. 1, trans. by J. C. Rolfe, in *ibid.,* New York, Oxford, 1933.

9. H. Grotius, *De iure belli ac pacis,* Oxford, Clarendon Press, 1925, Prolegomena, xxviii.

10. *Ibid.,* Book II, Chap. XV, v, viii.

11. R. Zouche, *Iuris et iudicii fecialis, sive, iuris inter gentes, et quaestionum de eodem explicatio,* trans. by J. L. Brierly,

in Scott, *op. cit.,* Baltimore, Lord Baltimore Press, 1911.

12. S. von Pufendorf, *De iure naturae et gentium,* especially Book II, Chap. III, xxiii, trans. by C. H. Oldfather and W. A. Oldfather, in Scott, *op. cit.,* New York, Oxford, 1934.

13. For a short history of the publication of treaties, see D. P. Myers, *Manual of Collection of Treaties and of Collections Relating to Treaties,* Cambridge, Mass., Harvard University Press, 1922, pp. 579–604.

14. J. Dumont, *Corps universel diplomatique du droit des gens,* Amsterdam and The Hague, 1726–1731, 8 vols., Vol. I, p. 1.

15. E. Vattel, *Le droit des gens,* 1758, Préliminaires, xviii.

16. Address by J. B. Moore, *Proceedings of American Society of International Law,* 19–20 April 1907, New York, Baker, Voorhis, 1908, p. 252.

17. Thomas Clarkson, *The History of the Rise, Progress, and Accomplishment of the Abolition of the African Slave Trade by the British Parliament,* Philadelphia, 1808, 2 vols.

18. For eyewitness accounts of the horrors of slave trading, see *An Abstract of Evidence for Abolition of the Slave Trade* delivered before a select committee of the House of Commons, 1790–1791, Cincinnati, Ohio, American Reform Tract and Book Society, 1855.

19. H. A. Smith, *The Law and Custom of the Sea,* London, Stevens and Sons, 1948, pp. 43–56.

20. Napoleon restored slavery and slave trading in 1799 and extinguished it

again in a last burst of popular appeal during the Hundred Days, March 1815. For the Additional Articles to the Paris Peace Treaty of 1814, see *B.F.S.P.*, Vol. I, Part 1, p. 172.

21. W. B. Lawrence, *Visitation and Search*, Boston, Little, Brown, 1858, p. 26.

22. For the slave-trade conventions between Britain and France, see *B.F.S.P.*, Vol. XVIII, p. 641; Vol. XX, p. 286.

23. Treaty between Great Britain and others, For the Suppression of the African Slave Trade, signed at London, 20 December 1841, *B.F.S.P.*, Vol. XXX, p. 269. See also H. Fischer, "The Suppression of Slavery in International Law," *International Law Quarterly*, Vol. 3, Nos. 1, 4 (January and October 1950), London, Stevens and Son, pp. 28–51, 503–522.

24. See W. E. Dubois, *The Suppression of the African Slave Trade to the United States of America*, New York, Longmans, 1904, especially pp. 94–130.

25. General Act of the Conference of Berlin, signed 26 February 1885, Chap. II, *B.F.S.P.*, Vol. LXXVI, p. 11.

26. Ministère des Affaires Estrangères, *Conférence internationale de Bruxelles*, 18 novembre 1889–2 juillet 1890, Paris, Imprimerie Nationale, 1891, p. 12.

27. *Ibid.*, pp. 473–495.

28. For the Regulations of the Channel Fisheries between Great Britain and France, see *B.F.S.P.*, Vol. XXXI, p. 165.

29. The Convention between Great Britain, Belgium, and others, for Regulating the Police of the North Seas Fisheries, signed at The Hague, 6 May 1882, is in *B.F.S.P.*, Vol. LXXIII, p. 39. See also L. Larry Leonard, *International Regulation of Fisheries*, New York, Carnegie Endowment, 1944, for a complete study including the multilateral agreements regulating whaling and fur-sealing as well as the author's proposal for an international fisheries office.

30. Protocol of 29 October 1881, *B.F.S.P.*, Vol. LXXII, p. 1208.

31. Convention between Great Britain, the Argentine Republic, and others, for the Protection of Submarine Cables, signed at Paris, 14 March 1884, *B.F.S.P.*, Vol. LXXV, p. 356. See also Ministère des Affaires Estrangères, *Conference internationale pour la protection des câbles sous-marins, 12–21 mai 1886*, Paris, Imprimerie Nationale, 1886. The Convention for the Control of the Liquor Traffic between Great Britain, Belgium, and others, signed at The Hague, 16 November 1887, is in *B.F.S.P.*, Vol. LXXIX, p. 894.

32. C. C. Hyde, *International Law Chiefly as Interpreted and Applied by the United States*, 2d ed., Boston, Little, Brown, 1945, 3 vols., Vol. I, pp. 755–756.

33. U.S. Department of State, *Protocols of Proceedings of the International Maritime Conference*, Washington, Government Printing Office, 1890, 3 vols., Vol. I, p. 1. The report and recommendations of the United States delegates on the thirteen divisions of maritime law discussed at the Conference are in *ibid.*, Vol. III, pp. 449–499. See also Final Act, International Maritime Conference, Washington, October–December 1899, *B.F.S.P.*, Vol. LXXXI, p. 705.

34. Of exceptional interest is A. Justice, *A General Treatise of the Dominions and Laws of the Sea*, London, 1705, which contains the marine laws of Rhodes and Oléron as well as the French Code of 1691 and a collection of marine treaties concluded during the seventeenth century. See also C. Abbot (Lord Tenterden), *A Treatise of the Law Relative to Merchant Ships and Seamen*, 6th American ed. by J. C. Perkins, Boston, Little, Brown, 1850, for principles of maritime law in the mid-nineteenth century.

35. International Conventions for the Unification of Certain Rules of Law respecting (1) Collisions between Vessels; and (2) Assistance and Salvage at Sea, signed at Brussels, 23 September 1910, *B.F.S.P.*, Vol. CIII, p. 434.

36. International Convention on Safety of Life at Sea, signed at London, 20 January 1914, *B.F.S.P.*, Vol. CVIII, p. 283.

37. F. R. Stark, "The Abolition of Privateering and the Declaration of Paris," *Studies in History, Economics, and Public Law*, Vol. 8 (1896–1898), New York, Columbia University Press, is a comprehensive study. See also H. B. Thompson, *The Laws of War Affecting Commerce and Shipping*, London, Smith, Elder, 1854.

38. Ministère des Affaires Estrangères, "Congrès de Paris," *Documents diplomatiques,* Paris, Imprimerie Impériale, April 1856, pp. 132–135.

39. *Ibid.,* p. 31.

40. H. Dunant, *Un souvenir de Solferino,* 3d ed., Geneva, J. Fick, 1863, p. 165.

41. For a background of the formation of the Red Cross societies, texts of the first semiofficial international conference resolutions and the Geneva Convention of 1864, and the additional articles of 1868, see C. Barton, *The Red Cross,* Washington, American National Red Cross, 1898. See also G. Moynier, *Étude sur la Convention de Genève pour l'amélioration du sort des militaires blessés,* Paris, J. Cherbuliez, 1870.

42. T. S. Perry (ed.), *The Life and Letters of Francis Lieber,* Boston, Osgood, 1882, p. 331. See also L. D. Harley, *Francis Lieber, His Life and Political Philosophy,* New York, Columbia University Press, 1899, and F. Freidel, *Francis Lieber, Nineteenth Century Liberal,* Baton Rouge, La., Louisiana State University Press, 1947.

43. "Instruction for the Government of Armies of the United States in the Field," in R. N. Scott, *An Analytical Digest of the Military Laws of the United States,* Philadelphia, Lippincott, 1873, pp. 441–461.

44. Declaration between Great Britain, Austria, and others Renouncing the Use, in Time of War, of Explosive Projectiles under 400 Grammes Weight, signed at St. Petersburg, 11 December 1868, *B.F.S.P.,* Vol. LVIII, p. 16.

45. Correspondence respecting the Conference at Brussels between the representatives of Great Britain, Austria-Hungary, and others, including the Russian project, résumé of discussions, and modified text are in *B.F.S.P.,* Vol. LXV, pp. 1004–1111.

46. For the organization and work of the Institute of International Law, see *Revue de droit international,* Vol. 6 (1874), p. 167, and succeeding volumes. See also P. Bordwell, *The Law of War between Belligerents,* Chicago, Callaghan, 1908, for a history and commentary upon laws of war.

47. *International Arbitration from Athens to Locarno,* Stanford, Calif., Stanford University Press, 1929, Appendix A, pp. 345–355. See also H. M. Cory, *Compulsory Arbitration of International Disputes,* New York, Columbia University Press, 1933.

48. H. Wehberg, *The Limitation of Armaments,* New York, Carnegie Endowment, 1921, Chap. III.

49. Russian Circular Note Proposing the Program of the First Conference, *Foreign Relations of the United States,* Washington, Government Printing Office, 1898, p. 551.

50. J. B. Scott (ed.), *The Hague Conventions and Declarations of 1899 and 1907,* New York, Oxford, 1915, contains all the important documents with signatures, ratifications, and adhesions. For full details, see *The Proceedings of the Hague Peace Conferences, The Conference of 1899,* New York, Oxford, 1920, and F. W. Hollis, *The Peace Conference at The Hague,* New York, Macmillan, 1900.

51. The Secretary of State of the United States to the American Diplomatic Representatives Accredited to the Governments Signatory to the Acts of the First Hague Conference, *Foreign Relations of the United States,* 1904, p. 10.

52. *The Proceedings of the Hague Peace Conferences, The Conference of 1907,* New York, Oxford, 1921, 2 vols., Vol. I, p. 226.

APPENDIX 4

I. *From the Prolegomena of "De iure belli ac pacis" by Hugo Grotius* (an original translation from the Latin)

. . . for man is indeed an animal, but an animal of an exceptional kind, and he differs much more from all other species than they differ among themselves. This may be demonstrated by evidence of many things which are peculiar to the human race. And among these characteristics which are special to man is a desire for society, or a community of fellow men, not of any kind, but rather suitable to his own discernment and organized for peace. This the Stoics used to call a feeling of kinship. . . .

But just as the laws of each state look after that state's welfare, for the same reason should laws be established by agreement among all states or the majority of them; and it does seem that such laws have been established, laws not concerned with the single state, but rather safeguarding that great universal society. And this is what is called the law of nations as we customarily distinguish that title from natural law.

If no community may be preserved without law . . . then certainly that community which unites the human race or many nations needs law.

Nor should anyone be impressed by the lucky success of evil schemes. For it is enough if the justice of a case has great force in its own application even though that force, as happens in human events, may often be obstructed by the contrary action of other things. Furthermore, to keep the friendships which nations as well as individuals need for many things, the opinion that wars ought not to be undertaken recklessly or unjustly or waged impiously is worth a great deal. For no one allies himself easily with those who think that the dictates of religion, obligation, and good faith are of no value. I, for those reasons which I have mentioned, holding it to be clearly proved that there are laws for the community which are valid both in respect to war and during war, had many grave reasons why I should write on this subject. I saw throughout the Christian world a license in making war shameful even for barbarous tribes with a resort to arms for trifling causes or none whatever, and once such fighting broke out there was no respect for divine or human laws, just as if a proclamation to commit any crime without restraint had been issued.

II. *Extract from "United States v. the Schooner La Jeune Eugenie"* (United States Circuit Court, 1822)

Now the law of nations may be deduced, first, from the general principles of right and justice, applied to the concern of individuals, and thence to the relations and duties of nations; or, secondly, in things indifferent or questionable, from the customary observances and recognitions of civilized nations; or, lastly, from the conventional or positive law, that regulates the intercourse between states. What, therefore, the law of nations is, does not rest upon mere theory, but may be considered as modified by practice, or ascertained by the treaties of nations at different periods. It does not follow, therefore, that because a principle cannot be found settled by the consent or practice of nations at one time, it is to be concluded, that at no subsequent period the principle can be considered as incorporated into the public code of nations . . . I think it may be unequivocally affirmed, that every doctrine, that may be fairly deduced by correct reasoning from the rights and duties of nations, and the nature of moral obligation, may theoretically be said to exist in the law of nations; and unless it be relaxed or waived by the consent of nations, which may be evidenced by their general practice and customs, it may be enforced by a court of justice, whenever it arises in judgment.

III. *Extract from "The Antelope"* (United States Supreme Court, 1825)

The question, whether the slave trade is prohibited by the law of nations has been seriously propounded, and both the affirmative and negative of the proposition have been maintained with equal earnestness . . . Whatever might be the answer of the moralist to this question, a jurist must search for its legal solution, in those principles of action which are sanctioned by the usages, the national acts, and the general assent, of that portion of the world of which he considers himself as a part and to whose law the appeal is made. If we resort to this standard as the test of international law, the question . . . is decided in favor of the legality of the trade . . . No principle of general law is more universally acknowledged, than the perfect equality of nations . . . It results from this equality, that no one can rightfully impose a rule on another. Each legislates for itself, but its legislation can operate on itself alone. A right, then, which is vested in all by the consent of all, can be divested only by consent; and this trade, in which all have participated, must remain lawful to those who cannot be induced to relinquish it. As no nation can prescribe a rule for others, none can make a law of nations; and this traffic remains lawful to those whose governments have not forbidden it.

If it is consistent with the law of nations, it cannot in itself be piracy. It can be made so only by statute; and the obligation of the statute cannot transcend the legislative power of the state which may enact it.

If it be neither repugnant to the law of nations, nor piracy, it is almost superfluous to say in this Court, that the right of bringing in for adjudication in time of peace, even where the vessel belongs to a nation which has prohibited the trade, cannot exist. The Courts of no country execute the penal laws of another. . . .

IV. *The Closing Meeting of the Second International Peace Conference, 18 October 1907*

The President: Gentlemen: We have at last reached the end of our labors. Despite the good-will with which we undertook them, they have lasted much longer than we expected. We were obliged to exhaust the program which served as the basis of our deliberations, and, if we have not succeeded in coming to an understanding upon all of its points, a general agreement has been reached upon the majority of them, giving rise to numerous arrangements, the nomenclature of which is recorded in the Final Act, which we have just signed. It therefore seems to me proper and advisable to summarize, before we separate, the extent of the work which we have accomplished.

In the first address, gentlemen, which I had the honor to deliver at the opening session of the Conference, I thought it my duty to point out that the task which was imposed upon us had two objects in view: (1) to endeavor to prevent armed conflicts between nations, and (2) in case war breaks out, to render its effects less burdensome to those who may be affected by it directly or indirectly.

The political events which have happened since the First Conference would furnish us with plenty of material for deliberation, in so far as concerns the latter part of the problem that we had before us. The inadequacy of the arrangements relating to the rules of war on land, which were elaborated in 1899, has been seen in the course of the military operations which have taken place during the past eight years. It has also been possible to perceive how advisable it would be to regulate naval warfare and the status of neutrals, as well as certain circumstances closely connected with conditions that arise as a result of war. Such was the work, technical in nature and often most delicate, which the Second, Third, and Fourth Commissions took up. The latter two had a particularly complicated task in this respect, the difficulties of which I had more than once occasion to point out. And now that we have before us the results accomplished, I do not know whether we owe them more to the lofty spirit of conciliation displayed by all interested, or to the able guidance of the eminent presidents of the Commissions, who endeavored to avoid reefs and to discover solutions which were acceptable to all.

What is particularly remarkable in this regard are the stipulations relating to naval warfare and the status of neutrals in such warfare. This is the first time that an attempt at codification has been made in this matter, and, although we have only a beginning, the foundations have been laid, and those who are called to continue our undertaking will no doubt do justice to the workers of the first hour.

In the preventive field—means of preventing and avoiding international conflicts—the progress of the Conference has been less noticeable. It is because there has not been sufficient experience in this field to make new solutions seem urgent, and to indicate practical and universally recognized conditions to which they can be applied. The important projects presented to the First Commission for the establishment of a Court of Arbitral Justice and Compulsory Arbitrations sprang from theoretical plans, which met with insurmountable obstacles to their execution. In the matter of the Prize Court, on the contrary, the creation of which appeared to be highly desirable, a satisfactory solution, which will remain one of the monuments of this Conference, was reached. We may be assured that it will not fail to render a useful service which will help indirectly to prevent a further extension of wars.

But, gentlemen, in my opinion it is not in this that lies the principal significance of the Second Peace Conference. We cannot fail to recognize the fact that one of the principal guarantees to the maintenance of peaceful relations between nations is a more intimate knowledge of mutual interests and needs; the establishment of many and varied relations, forming an ever-spreading network, which finally creates a moral and material solidarity that, more and more, resists every warlike undertaking. The progress of the present Conference is the greatest that mankind has ever made in this direction. This is the first time that the representatives of all constituted States have been gathered together to discuss interests which they have in common and which contemplate the good of all mankind. Furthermore, by the collaboration of the representatives of Latin America, new and very precious elements have unquestionably been paid into the common treasury of international political science, the value of which we have but imperfectly known hitherto. On their part, the representatives of Central and South America have had an opportunity to acquire a more intimate knowledge of the internal situations and reciprocal relations of European States, which, with their various institutions, their historical development, their traditions and their individual peculiarities, present political conditions that are perceptibly different from those under which the younger nations of the New World live and progress. This more intimate knowledge has thus been of advantage to both, and has facilitated collaboration in the Conference, which is a genuine step forward for mankind.

We may therefore refute the accusation which some people are already trying to hurl at us, alleging that we have done nothing for the maintenance of peace, nothing for the progress of human solidarity. There is doubtless a great deal still to be done in this direction. Nations must be educated in order that they may learn to esteem and love each other, still keeping their own individuality and the traditions that are dear to them. We should also recognize the fact that the voices which have been raised around us and in the press connected with the Conference, making a recommendation to this effect to the Governments, were indeed proclaiming a principle by which the directors of the affairs of the world may profit. Besides, it is too soon to estimate at its true value the significance of the work of the Second Peace Conference. The press that showed an interest in the Conference has been kept regularly and fully in touch with its labors by the secretary general. The press has thus been able to keep the whole world informed of the progress of the work; but all conclusions must be left for a just estimate of the work as a whole, from a more distant and consequently more objective view-point.

This is our work. We all feel we have collaborated conscientiously and have done our best. It has not been possible for us to do everything. Let us leave it for those who come after us to develop what we have been able to sketch, and to prepare in their turn for future Conferences the outlines of such work as they may not succeed in accomplishing themselves. As for us, the present Conference has at any rate made its mark in the history of mankind, for it has been the first to assume a universal character by making the delegates of the whole world march hand in hand along the road of progress.

CHAPTER 5 *The First Period of Collaboration:*
The League of Nations

The nineteenth century was an age of international consultation on political affairs; the twentieth century begins a period of collaboration. A salient difference between international organization before and after the League of Nations lies in the achievement of a permanent agency through which states can collaborate continuously on the grave problems which affect the peace of the world.

The League of Nations did not spring full grown from the minds of wise statesmen. Indeed, its origins can be traced back to the various congresses of the nineteenth century culminating in the two international peace conferences at The Hague. Just as the Napoleonic Wars had interrupted the rudimentary peace parleys of the eighteenth century only to be revived in the splendid Congress of Vienna, so did the First World War suspend the universal conferences at The Hague only to realize a more articulate association of nations.

The painful, fumbling breakdown of negotiations among the chancelleries of London, Paris, Berlin, Vienna, and St. Petersburg in 1914 bore tragic witness to the need for some standing agency of international conciliation. Between 1815 and 1914 the consultations of the Great Powers had averted several crises, but the lack of any regular meetings, the failure to delegate any powers to some permanent agency for political adjustments, and the ability of any one of the Great Powers to frustrate even the calling of a conference—as on the eve of the First World War—showed the fundamental weakness of that system to prevent the quarrels that lead to war. By creating a permanent panel of jurists available for international arbitrations, the Hague Peace Conferences had pushed the amicable settlement of disputes into the spotlight of world attention. Commissions of inquiry had been recommended to find facts for the adjudication of controversies, while an international prize court and a court of arbitral justice, both permanent tribunals with full-time judges paid from an international fund, had been proposed in 1907 [1]. Neither of these permanent courts, however, came into being, and the international community badly needed some standing agency of international conciliation. On this track, therefore, the first exponents of a league of nations set their wheels.

THE DRAFTING OF THE LEAGUE OF NATIONS COVENANT

Early in 1915 a group of distinguished Americans, including Hamilton Holt, Theodore Marburg, A. Lawrence Lowell, and former President Taft, began informal discussions in New York eventually leading to a private organization called the League to Enforce Peace. Whereas the Hague conferences had nourished a spirit of arbitration and adjudication these men soon resolved that a next fateful step must be taken: the states of the world should create a League of Nations wherein all "legal" disputes would be submitted to arbitration and all nonjusticiable or political questions would be heard by a council of conciliation before any resort to force. Should any member of this League use military duress *before* bringing its grievance to a tribunal or the council of conciliation, the other states of the League would unite their strength against the renegade [2].

The kernel of the whole idea for a compulsory hearing of all international quarrels passed virtually intact from 1915 through the excited war years to 1919. Other organizations also sought a permanent association of nations: a League of Nations Society was formed in London during the spring of 1915 and adopted resolutions almost identical to those of the League to Enforce Peace; Lord Bryce presided over a British League to Enforce Peace; during April 1915 some thirty people from a dozen different countries gathered at The Hague to establish a Central Organization for a Durable Peace which urged the world to make the Hague Conferences a permanent institution meeting regularly and to require each state to submit all disputes to peaceful settlement or face the concerted action of the community; the Hague group also called for a reduction of armaments and the transfer of territories solely by plebiscites. Sometime later other societies campaigning for a League of Nations were founded in Italy and France.

Official support for a League of Nations lagged only a little behind the ardor of private groups. Lord Robert Cecil, Undersecretary of Foreign Affairs, wrote a brief memorandum to the British Cabinet in the fall of 1916 which labored the principle that international disputes must be submitted to conciliation before a state uses the bludgeon of war; any state disregarding this norm ought to be constrained by the powers—especially through cessation of all economic and financial intercourse with the outlaw. Shortly after Lord Cecil's memorandum, the Foreign Secretary appointed Lord Phillimore to head a committee which, after studying many perpetual-peace plans, drafted a covenant. This British outline contained the nucleus of eight articles finally adopted in the Covenant of the League of Nations. General Smuts of South Africa endorsed the Phillimore committee's work while advocating that territories detached from the Central Powers be transferred to the League and administered by a mandatory power [3].

As early as 1 February 1916 the President of the United States [4] had said:

What is America expected to do? She is expected to do nothing less than keep law alive while the rest of the world burns. You know that there is no international tribune, my fellow-citizens. I pray God that if this contest have no other result, it will at least have the result of creating an international tribune and producing some sort of joint guarantee of peace on the part of the great nations of the world.

Three months later, addressing the first annual assembly of the League to Enforce Peace, Wilson asserted that the United States might "become a partner in any feasible association of nations" which would "prevent any war begun either contrary to treaty covenants or without warning and full submission . . . to the opinion of the world [5]." But the Chief Executive publicly threw down the gauntlet to American isolationists when he told the Senate on 22 January 1917, "If the peace presently to be made is to endure it must be made secure by the organized major forces of mankind," and he sincerely hoped "that the people and Government of the United States will join the other civilized nations of the world in guaranteeing the permanence of peace [6]."

The Fourteen Points of President Wilson, set forth as the peace program of the United States to the first meeting of Congress in 1918, began by calling for a new day in international relations in which open covenants should be openly arrived at, and ended by declaring: "A general association of nations must be formed by treaties which would mutually guarantee the political independence and territorial integrity of all states [7]."

The French government as well as the British government, meanwhile, had appointed a commission to study the creation of a League of Nations. The French ideas, with appropriate notations by the Phillimore committee, were transmitted to President Wilson in the summer of 1918, and he turned naturally to his close friend and adviser, Colonel House, for the draft of a plan sensible to the views of the President. On 16 July 1918 Wilson received from House a scheme of twenty-three articles and a preamble. At least four of these articles copied the British proposals verbatim; others bore traces of Lord Phillimore's work; but House contributed points on an international court, disarmament, the interest of the League in all threats to peace, and his vision that the representatives of the contracting parties would virtually become an international parliament requiring continuous sessions. Wilson, himself, then proceeded to improve this draft by excision, alteration, and addition.

With a flourish and ceremony not witnessed since the Congress of Vienna, the Allied Powers prepared to dictate peace to Germany on 18 January 1919. Paris filled rapidly with a multitude of ministers, deputies, secretaries, and clerks. The British and American delegations alone numbered almost 800; no less than 500 journalists from every part of the world swarmed to the Quai d'Orsay. Two months had elapsed between the armistice and the opening of the peace conference, two months in which the Allies were still not agreed upon the chief points of procedure. The Supreme War Council of the United States, Britain, France, and Italy accepted Japan into their deliberations and without a flutter metamorphosed into a body known as the Council of Ten—two representatives from each power. This group managed the peace conference.

A devolution of work to committees had characterized one aspect of the international-conference system: the blunt methods of restoring peace in the seventeenth and eighteenth centuries had yielded to a division of labor most completely revealed in the Hague Conferences of 1899 and 1907. At Paris in 1919 only seven lifeless plenary sessions met during the peace talks, whereas some fifty-eight commissions, committees, and subcommittees debated the prickly details of territorial claims, financial indemnities, war guilt, international labor legislation, regulation of international waterways, and so forth. These committees held 1,646 meetings, and their findings were supported by another 26 local investigations. This largesse of information was funneled into the tangled deliberations of the Council of Ten, the Council of Five, or the most intimate councils of France, Britain, and the United States for final action. Indeed, the full membership of the conference received the peace treaty only one day before the Germans glumly listened to its terms [8].

At the second plenary session of the peace conference on January 25, the delegates, insistently drummed by Wilson, resolved that a League of Nations should be created as an integral part of the peace treaty. Thus, a commission headed by the President of the United States and including Léon Bourgeois, Lord Robert Cecil, General Smuts, Vittorio Orlando, and other luminaries was formed. Although the French and Italians introduced their own ideas, the commission proceeded almost immediately to analyze a draft which had resulted from a painstaking fusion of Wilson's third sketch and the British proposals [9]. After fifteen meetings extending from February 3 to April 11 the commission pared and shaped the Covenant of the League of Nations to fit within the terms of peace presented to Germany on 7 May 1919.

Meanwhile in the United States thirty-nine senators, led by Henry Cabot Lodge, had signed a resolution that the League of Nations, in the form proposed to the peace conference, should not be accepted by the United States. On 22 September 1919 Senator Reed of Missouri [10] excoriated the proposed international organization as follows:

. . . a superstate, with rights, powers, and authorities superior to those of its constituent members, who, upon acceptance of membership, become subject to its governing control . . . it possesses a supreme jurisdiction over all matters international and over many purely national rights and policies . . . member nations may be deprived of their most sacred rights in defiance of the will of their people or their governments. . . .

Based upon nineteenth-century international law and organization, the League of Nations did not resemble this caricature, but the political opposition in Congress to both Wilson and the Covenant was strong enough to vote down the articles of the League agreed upon at Versailles; in consequence, the treaty was not ratified by the United States. The zeal of Wilson, however, which had demanded the incorporation of the Covenant in the treaty of peace with Germany—despite the contrary opinion of his own Secretary of State and others—did bring the first permanent international organization for peace into existence among all the great powers except the United States.

THE STRUCTURE AND PURPOSES OF THE LEAGUE

The League of Nations operated through three major organs: (*a*) a Council, originally comprising Britain, France, Italy, Japan, and four smaller states designated by the Assembly; (*b*) an Assembly, consisting of all the member states, originally forty-two in number; (*c*) a permanent Secretariat whose chief officer, the Secretary-General, was nominated by the Council and approved by a majority of the Assembly. Even in these rough divisions the structure utilized the experience of the nineteenth century with its concert of major powers, its general assemblies such as the Hague Conferences, and the institution of dispassionate international secretariats most notably in the form of bureaus. On any matter extending beyond administrative regulations, equality of votes and unanimity of voice had ruled international procedure. The League of Nations circumspectly hewed to this line. Learning from the past, however, the Covenant required the Council to meet at least once a year and the Assembly to convene at stated intervals; in practice the Council held 106 regular sessions while the Assembly met every September between 1920 and 1940. For the first time in history, therefore, the world was provided with humming machinery to study and solve the causes of international war.

To stave off the blows of war was the chief objective of the League of Nations; to substitute a fair examination of the cause of international conflict for arbitrary aggression continued to be the organization's major premise. The League did not deny the ultimate right of a state to resort to war, but it pledged each member to submit its own controversy with another member to either judicial remedies or the Council of the League *before* firing its guns. No matter what happened, every state admitted that there should be a ninety-day "cooling-off" period between a complaint and an overt act of warfare, but if the Council should issue a *unanimous* opinion (not including the votes of the disputants), each member agreed *not* to go to war with the party which accepted this opinion. Negatively phrased, however, the Covenant skirted the very inferno of international politics.

What happened if a state violated these prescriptions, failed to apply to conciliation, and blindly seized the quick decision of battle? In the eyes of the League such a state then committed an act of war upon the community and every member promised to sever all commercial and financial relations with the aggressor immediately. If the Council should decide upon further coercion "to protect the covenants of the League," it could invite member states to supply contingents of military or naval forces. Such troops would be permitted to cross the territory of all member states in order to approach the outlaw [11].

No paragraph of the Covenant rubbed certain United States senators harder than Wilson's own contribution:

The Members of the League undertake to respect and preserve as against external aggression the territorial integrity and existing political independence of all Members of the League. In case of any such aggression or in case of any threat or danger of such aggression the Council shall advise upon the means by which this obligation shall be fulfilled [12].

Based upon the President's experience with Latin America and his stubborn conviction that each state should develop according to its own fashion, unthreatened and unafraid, Article 10 sought to extend the nineteenth-century Monroe Doctrine in good-neighbor form to the rest of the world. But the fixed guarantees seemed to pledge the United States to maintain the status quo *everywhere,* an idea as unwelcome to many Americans in the 1920's as it had been to the British in the 1820's. To avoid this apparent commitment to a rigid international order, Article 19 had been coupled with Article 10. It provided that the Assembly might advise the members to reconsider treaties whose terms burdened the maintenance of international peace. Ironically Article 10, the chief frustration to the League in the United States, was never enforced during the entire history of the organization, while its companion piece drifted aimlessly in the Covenant.

Although the provisions for channeling international frictions into a conciliatory, arbitrary, or judicial process constituted the core of the League of Nations, other sections of the Covenant also reflected the tendencies of the nineteenth century. By Article 8 the member states recognized the continuing problem of the armaments race so gingerly touched and dropped at the Hague Conferences, and the Council was prodded to formulate plans for the reduction of weapons of war. By Article 25 the member states agreed to encourage the establishment of national Red Cross societies—which had finally achieved the status of international neutrality in 1906. Highly significant and remarkably prescient, however, was the determination of the League to tackle economic and social problems, for the men of Geneva intended to strike at the roots of war as well as its full-blown menace.

Disease, communications, traffic in arms, and slavery, all subjects of nineteenth-century international regulation, fell directly or indirectly under the supervision of the League; conditions of labor and traffic in drugs, looming on the twentieth-century horizon of international cooperation, became a subject of interest to the League; finally, in one sweeping paragraph, the League proposed that the existing international bureaus and commissions be placed under its direction, but where the parties to the basic convention were not amenable to supervision the League offered at least to collect and distribute all relevant information [13]. Never in the history of international organization had any agency made such impressive strides toward a world community, for as time went by the League took an active interest in virtually all aspects of economic and social life, in their effect not only upon nations but also upon individuals. The actual work of the League lay in the collection of statistics, the dissemination of information, the planning and calling of conferences on topics of economic or social import, and a gentle but persistent pressure upon governments to take steps either by international convention or by national statutes to improve the world's welfare.

One of the most important agencies of the League of Nations was the Economic and Financial Organization. It was composed of two committees of experts appointed by the Council of the League and included both private individuals and government officials highly qualified in economic-financial matters. Investigations into such matters as tariffs, clearing agreements, and taxation provided disinterested studies for members of the League on some of the most crucial international problems, and the fiscal advice of the committees, their evaluation of loans, and their general counsel on business brought governments together in objective examinations of their mutual requirements. A second useful agency of the League in the economic-social field was the Communications and Transit Organization. It had a separate constitution originally adopted by forty-four states and approved by the Assembly of the League, for the expenses of the organization were paid out of the League's budget. Conferences were held at least every four years, and its interim work was handled by a standing transit committee. In keeping with the purposes of the League, the organization acted as a spur to international conventions in the field of communications and transportation and through its conferences fostered agreements upon maritime ports, international railways, regulations for international touring, and development of water-power projects affecting more than one state. In addition to this activity the Communications and Transit Organization also served as a storehouse of information, collecting data and frequently offering the technical advice of its staff to the League or interested governments.

Other organizations of the League of Nations were the Health Organization, the refugee organization, the Intellectual Cooperation Organization, the Advisory Committee on Traffic in Women and Children, and the Advisory Committee on Traffic in Opium and Other Dangerous Drugs, some of whose work is discussed in Chapter 8.

THE MANDATE SYSTEM FOR DEPENDENT PEOPLES

Community means social responsibility, a sense of obligation to fellow men. Especially since the colonial-mercantile period of European expansion, wars had often resulted in gross territorial exchanges with no regard to the wishes or welfare of the indigenous people. The rapacious development of Africa had first wakened the states of the world to the urgency of international surveillance over peoples unable to comprehend or resist modern "civilization." In 1876 a quasi-private organization, the International African Association, undertook scientific and humanitarian missions along the Congo River; a Committee for the Study of the Upper Congo superseded this organization, and gradually the exigencies of commerce molded a corporation, headed and financed by King Leopold II of Belgium, with dozens of trading stations, which made treaties under its own flag. The territorial claims and commercial interests of neighboring nations inevitably collided with this new Congo state and, in consequence, a conference of fourteen powers assembled in Berlin late in 1884. Within three months they signed a general act which described the boundaries of the Congo basin, provided for free navigation of the Congo and Niger

Rivers, and opened the territory to the trade of all nations. Furthermore, each state pledged to "protect the indigenous inhabitants and look after the improvement of their moral and material conditions of existence [14]." By international agreement, therefore, a kind of international state—neutral and open to the commerce of the world—had been created, but shortly thereafter Leopold assumed personal rule over the state and frustrated the animations of the Berlin conference by arbitrary government, greedy monopolies, and a cruel exploitation of natives. In 1908 the Congo became a Belgian colony.

The fifth of Woodrow Wilson's Fourteen Points set forth on 8 January 1918 asked for "a free, open-minded, and absolutely impartial adjustment of all colonial claims" which observed the principle that "the interests of the population concerned must have equal weight with the equitable claims of the government whose title is to be determined." America wanted no annexations. Conscious of the tutelary relationship of the United States toward the Philippine Islands and Cuba after the Spanish-American War, Wilson looked ahead to some comparable arrangement. This progressive outlook also prevailed in British circles. On 29 June 1917 at Glasgow and again before the House of Commons on 20 December 1917, Lloyd George asserted that future trustees of the German colonies must heed the welfare of the native peoples. During the winter of 1918 General Smuts wrote a long tract proposing the transfer to the League of territories formerly belonging to Russia, Austria, Hungary, and Turkey, such territories to be administered by a mandatory state responsible to the new international organization.

Since the war itself had shaped the *de facto* states of Poland, Czechoslovakia, Austria, Hungary, and Yugoslavia, little could be done about the transfer of imperial Austrian possessions; France peremptorily considered the provinces of Alsace and Lorraine as French, but grudgingly yielded to Wilson on the temporary creation of a Free Territory of the Saar with commissioners responsible to the League. Only the Turkish possessions and the German colonies in Africa and the Pacific were left for this unprecedented experiment in international administration, an experiment clothed in idealism, fed by philanthropy, but put to sleep by political cupidity [15]. Nevertheless, no article of the Covenant contained more sentences than the article dealing with mandates and, farcically or not, the member states recognized that the well-being and development of helpless peoples "form a sacred trust of civilization and that securities for the performance of this trust should be embodied in this Covenant [16]."

Whereas the Berlin Act of 1885 had declared what principles ought to be observed in respect to certain indigenous peoples of the internationalized Congo basin, the League of Nations clearly retained supervisory jurisdiction over thirteen areas detached from Turkey and Germany, maintained the legal right of intervention, and actually set up the first international machinery for investigating the administration of the powers to whom these territories were entrusted.

One of the most propulsive forces for international organization had been the success of nineteenth-century arbitration. Demands for a permanent tribunal to settle legal questions among states had led to the creation of a large panel of jurists from which states could select arbitrators. This panel, entitled the Permanent Court of Arbitration, admirably handled sixteen cases between 1902 and 1921, but it lacked the cohesiveness and cogency of a court empowered to decide issues, gather precedents, and serve as a judicial third leg for the League of Nations. The Court of Arbitral Justice proposed in 1907 had missed the support of the community of states, so that in 1920 the founders of a new international organization carefully capitalized on experience and finally established a truly permanent international tribunal.

THE PERMANENT COURT OF INTERNATIONAL JUSTICE

Wilson's first draft for the League at Paris (10 January 1919) had stressed the familiar channels of arbitration, with a radical innovation: arbitral awards might be set aside by qualified majorities of the Body of Delegates, forerunner of the Assembly. The British draft convention of the same period, however, anticipated the creation of a permanent court of international justice to which the Conference (Assembly) or the Council could refer certain disputes, but "the decision of the Court shall have no force or effect unless it is confirmed by the Report of the Conference or Council." After many compromises the negotiators left a modest place for the Permanent Court of International Justice: the Council should formulate the constitution of the Court and submit it to the members of the League for their adoption; the Court should be competent to determine disputes which the *parties* submitted to it; if asked, the Court could give advisory opinions to the League itself [17].

The Treaty of Versailles invested the Permanent Court of International Justice with jurisdiction over problems of waterways and labor even before that tribunal was established; five mandates approved by the Council of the League on 17 December 1921 provided for questions of interpretation or application of a mandate to be placed before the Permanent Court of International Justice. At its second session, therefore, the Council of the League moved with dispatch to appoint a special committee of distinguished jurists, including Elihu Root of the United States, which considered various proposals for an international court drafted by eminent scholars during the summer of 1920. No finer testament to the continuity of international organization was needed than the remarks of Elihu Root [18] before this advisory committee of jurists:

I would be glad to have the world know that we begin here again the course of development of the law of nations, the principle of justice in international affairs. There is throughout the world much respect and reverence for the self-sacrifice and devoted work done at the Hague. . . . I think the committee should make clear the relation which it means to bear to all that work and all that was accomplished then. . . .

In August 1920 the Council of the League received the project for the Permanent Court of International Justice and three months later submitted it with slight modifications to secure the unanimous approval of the Assembly. The Statute of the Court was then opened to the signature of individual states, for although an auxiliary of the Versailles Treaty and the League of Nations, the institution had a separate existence based upon separate agreements. Within two years thirty-five states had ratified the protocol [19]. Thus the seeds so industriously planted at the Hague Conferences at last bore fruit. The nations of the world community had finally consented to a permanent tribunal staffed by judges nominated through the panel of the Permanent Court of Arbitration and elected by an absolute majority in both the Council and the Assembly of the League of Nations. In a real sense jurists were elected by merit, with no single state ever represented by more than one judge in the court of fifteen. Some years later one of the most distinguished students of the Permanent Court of International Justice wrote: "For the first time in modern history, the world has available a permanent group of judges devoting their time to the development of international jurisprudence and ready to act in a judicial manner to develop international law as it is to be applied to the facts of life [20]."

Between 1922 and 1940 the Permanent Court of International Justice held fifty sessions, heard sixty-five cases, and delivered thirty-two judgments and twenty-seven advisory opinions. Although this record seems unimpressive by domestic standards of judicial activity, its aid to international law and its support of the League in settling international controversies were unprecedented. The original committee of jurists, moreover, would have had all "legal" disputes *automatically* submitted to the Court, that is:

1. The interpretation of a treaty.
2. Any question of international law.
3. The existence of a fact which, if established, would constitute a breach of an international obligation.

4. The nature and extent of the reparation to be made for the breach of an international obligation.

In the final draft of the Statute of the Permanent Court of International Justice, however, the jurisdiction of the Court was extended to "all cases which the parties refer to it and all matters specially provided for in treaties and conventions in force." Members of the League and other states that subscribed to the Statute could declare that they recognized as compulsory the jurisdiction of the Court in legal disputes provided, of course, that the other party to the litigation had made the same declaration. For the first time in history, moreover, advisory opinions on international legal matters by a permanent international tribunal were made available to an international organization—upon request of either the Assembly or the Council of the League of Nations. The high judicial standards of the Court gradually enhanced its reputation and authority, so that its judgments, carefully formulated and in the opinion of some critics overcautious, were invariably carried out. While the states of the world proceeded quite cautiously in placing themselves under the optional clause requiring the submission of legal disputes *ipso facto* to the Court, nevertheless by 1934 no less than forty-two states—some with reservations—had pledged to submit their nonpolitical disputes with each other to the Permanent Court of International Justice [21]. Furthermore, when the work of the Court terminated in 1939, there were about 600 international agreements in existence which allowed jurisdiction to the Court in one matter or another.

THE INTERNATIONAL CIVIL SERVICE

The idea of an international civil service had been foreshadowed in 1804 by the action of the German Empire and France in creating a director-general of the toll collectors of the Rhine River who was appointed jointly by the two states. Later the employees of international river commissions, sanitary councils, and various administrative bureaus, as well as the mixed secretaries of international political conferences after 1878, also pointed toward the development of an international civil service. But generally speaking, international secretariats before the First World War consisted of personnel supplied by one or more states for the international conference or agency. The League of Nations, on the other hand, created a truly international civil service, in both structure and spirit.

Curiously enough, neither the draft of the Phillimore committee nor that of Colonel House had mentioned a secretariat for the administration of the proposed League of Nations. The Smuts plan of 16 December 1916, however, had called for a permanent staff to assist the Council—the only agency expected to meet annually—a staff to make investigations, prepare the agenda, sort information, and coordinate the several existing international bureaus for the League of Nations. A French suggestion which envisaged the creation of an international army under the aegis of the League of Nations had hoped for a permanent international staff which would investigate all military questions affecting the League and even coordinate belligerent operations against violators of the Covenant. This grandiose plan, however, fell before the cooler counsels of the British and the Americans that the secretariat should simply be a civil service for the organization, collating documents for action by the Assembly or the Council, preparing minutes, keeping records, and aiding the various technical bureaus already in operation—in short, providing the mortar for the bricks of the multinational building [22].

The Covenant had wisely left the detailed organization of the Secretariat to the future. Except for specifying a chief officer, the Secretary-General, to be appointed by the Council with the approval of the majority of the Assembly, the secretaries and staff were to be enlisted as required. These international civil servants, mainly chosen by a merit system of competitive examinations, strived to detach themselves from narrow nationalism. To avoid partisanship, persons in the Secretariat were specifically enjoined from holding office incompatible with the discharge of their neutral duties, preparing biased speeches or articles on the politics of any country, or accepting honors and decorations—except for services performed prior to their appointment to the Secretariat. After 1932 all members of the Secretariat swore to regulate their conduct "with the interests of the League alone in view and not to seek or receive instructions from any Government or other authority [23]."

Beginning with 121 officials in 1919, the staff of the Secretariat climbed to a peak of 707 in 1931. Almost 30 per cent of these men and women were engaged as directors, chiefs of section, counselors, section members, writers, translators, and interpreters. Salaries and allowances for personnel cost the members of the League almost one million dollars per year, but the really vital tribute to the achievement of an international organization staffed by an international civil service was the distribution of nationalities: after ten years of collaboration the Secretariat of the League included the citizens of some forty different states.

The organization of the Secretariat itself was largely the work of Sir Eric Drummond, the first Secretary-General of the League. For each major responsibility of the Secretariat under the Covenant of the League of Nations or other parts of the Treaty of Versailles, a section headed by a director was established. Thus, there was a Political Section to assist the Council on political disputes, a Mandates Section, an Economic and Financial Section, a Transit and Communications Section, a Disarmament Section, a Minorities Section, and so forth. The Legal Section, for example, had the task of registering and publishing all treaties, for the members of the League had agreed that no international engagement should be binding after the formation of the organization unless registered with the Secretariat [24]. Prior to the twentieth century, no single, official collection of the international acts of states was published regularly. Not until 1919 did the nations of the world, through the League of Nations, draw together nearly all the treaties of the day into public volumes, and by 1943 the Legal Section had registered 4,822 compacts [25]. The other sections of the Secretariat, charged with other functions, performed just as notable services; the organization could never have functioned without them.

Under Drummond were two deputy secretaries-general and two under-secretaries. These posts were customarily held by citizens of the leading powers of the League, and under them were the section directors with their staffs of all nationalities. These officials of the League of Nations, when engaged on the business of the League, enjoyed diplomatic privileges and immunities that gave to the organization a unique international status of genuine value. While the Secretary-General was constitutionally the chief administrator of the League, studiously devoted to impartiality, he could not help influencing policy by the scope of his information and the framing of the issues. Nevertheless, the Secretariat under Drummond until 1932 and under Joseph Avenol of France thereafter earnestly endeavored to steer clear of the temptations to make policy and the natural bias for one's own national interest. Difficulties multiplied with the temper of the times after 1931, but the rather few exceptions to the general rule of loyalty [26] to the organization itself are a compliment to the first permanent international civil service.

CONSTITUTIONAL CHANGES OF THE LEAGUE, 1920 TO 1931

The League of Nations was never static. As in the case of all political organizations its constitution gave only a shadowy index to its prolific activities. Over the years the organization was subtly modified. Lord Cecil himself had never suspected that the Assembly would be more than a quadrennial or quinquennial conference, yet the very first meeting of that body decided, without objection, to convene every year on the first Monday of September [27]. The Council which had been enjoined by the Covenant to assemble at least once a year began in December 1923 to hold four regular sessions each year. The Council, moreover, which had been envisaged as a virile organization with the permanent membership of great powers, tended to wilt both by the dilution of its membership and the intrigues of the same great powers. Since the United States did not join the League, the permanent members of the Council were reduced to four until 1926, when Germany was admitted; in 1934 Russia gained a fixed seat in the Council, but in 1935 both Germany and Japan withdrew as the League entered its final debilitated years. Meanwhile, the non-permanent members of the Council had increased from four to nine. The Covenant had also provided that the Council or the states involved in a controversy could transfer a dispute from the Council to the Assembly: almost every dispute during the first ten years of the League was adjusted by the Council, but thereafter the Assembly seized the moral leadership of the organization as the integrity of the Council sagged under the ponderous cross-purposes of the leading powers, especially in the two crucial issues which cracked the spine of the League—the aggression of Japan against Manchuria in 1931 and the attack of Italy upon Ethiopia in 1935.

On the subject of budgetary control, to illustrate another development of the League, the Covenant had been moot, only specifying that expenses should be borne in accordance with the apportionment of expenses in the International Bureau of the Universal Postal Union. Although the Council first assumed supervision of the budget, shortly thereafter the Assembly obtained joint authority over fiscal matters. By 1923 a new scale for the allocation of expenses, based upon ability to pay, had been determined by the Assembly [28] and a supervisory (auditing) commission of the organization, though appointed by the Council, was made responsible to the Assembly. By 1928 the Assembly not only initiated and approved all expenses but also appointed the supervisory commission. This commission, finally, became the first permanent committee of the Assembly, an innovation hardly contemplated by any of the authors of the Covenant.

Another unforeseen but healthy consequence of continuous collaboration within an international organization was the abandonment of the awkward unanimity rule. The rule that no state could be bound by a decision without its consent had measured the conference system, and the League silently fell heir to the principle. All matters of procedure, of course, including the appointment of investigating committees, could be decided by majorities. In a few substantive issues, noted in the Covenant, absolute unanimity was not required, and especially in the reports of the Council or the Assembly on disputes the votes of the parties to the dispute were not counted. The Assembly annually appointed the following six main committees:

1. Constitutional and legal matters.
2. Technical organizations.
3. Armaments.
4. Administrative and financial matters.

5. Social and humanitarian matters.
6. Mandates, minorities, and political matters.

This committee organization, in which all members of the League participated, could not tolerate the obstruction of a single or few small states on some substantive matters, particularly the budget, and still remain intact. The financial committee, therefore, originated the practice of recommending resolutions to the plenary sessions by a majority vote, and this reform was copied by other committees. In the plenary session, then, it became usual to pass unanimously the resolutions which had already been approved in the committees. Opposing states simply abstained from the count. Finally, the Assembly availed itself of the difference between "decisions" and "recommendations." The latter could be passed by a simple majority, so that frequently proposals were rephrased as recommendations for the Assembly and did not run the risk of defeat by the negative vote of one state.

The virtually continuous sessions of the League, therefore, pressed by daily exigencies, served as a vehicle for the reformulation of international relations; its permanent organization, distinguished from the sporadic conferences of the nineteenth century, allowed constitutional development to be channeled through established agencies in an annual public forum.

POLITICAL DISPUTES AND THE LEAGUE IN ACTION

The pageantry of international organizations seems to follow the blare of political strife rather than the quiet grace of economic and social cooperation. For that reason the League of Nations has often been judged by its ineptitude rather than by its positive contributions to the history of international organization. From 1920 until 1931 the callow organization weathered the buffeting of international jealousy and wrath, but when the great powers deliberately assailed the thin strands of collaboration, woven and tied with artful slowness, the net broke and the community crashed into the chaos of war. Despite the inability of the organization to restrain the militarists of Japan from plundering China and despite the ineffectual international concert against the bravado of Mussolini, the record of the League of Nations for promoting peace does not lack luster. Indeed, by comparison with the period before the First World War the page is luminous.

During the first ten years of its existence some thirty disputes were brought before the League; not all of these involved the risk of war, yet each menaced the community with growing irritation and a few verged on pitched battle [29]. Probably the most notable success among a spate of other peaceful adjustments by the Council of the League was the termination of a violent controversy between Greece and Bulgaria in 1925.

The Greco-Bulgarian Crisis. On 22 October 1925 the Bulgarian foreign minister wired the Secretary-General of the League that a border incident had led to a flagrant invasion of Bulgarian territory by Greek forces. The Bulgarian government, therefore, requested a meeting of the Council of the League without delay to repair the breach of Covenant obligations. Within twenty-four hours Aristide Briand, Acting President of the Council, exhorted the two governments that until the Council heard both sides of the case, no further military movements should be undertaken and that all troops should retire at once behind their respective frontiers. Three days later the representatives of Bulgaria and Greece were confronted by a stern Council which requested that, before anything else was done, hostilities cease and each state withdraw its troops immediately from the affected area. To this unequivocal proposition the two belligerents acceded. Military attachés of Great Britain, France, and Italy hastened to the scene of the encounter to verify the actions of Greece and Bulgaria. On 31 October 1925, just nine days after the charge of aggression, the military attachés wired the Council of the League: "Reoccupation of the Bulgarian posts by the Bulgarian troops took place without any incident. There is complete calm on both sides. The Bulgarian population which had evacuated the invaded territory has nearly all returned and life is again taking up its normal course [30]."

The success of the League in first limiting, then settling the Greco-Bulgarian dispute contrasted handsomely with the clumsiness of conciliation in 1914, for as a result of the Covenant not only were these two states pledged to refrain from war but an international organization was prepared to take charge of the situation and impress upon the excited governments their obligations. The Council, moreover, concentrated upon stopping the fight first and asking questions afterward. It followed through by dispatching military attachés to supervise the neutralization of the controversial area and then sent a board of experts to recommend a fair solution of the cause of the conflict. Peace ensued.

War in the Gran Chaco. In 1928 fighting broke out in the Gran Chaco situated between Bolivia and Paraguay. Hesitant before the admonition of Article 21 that nothing in the Covenant should affect the validity of such regional arrangements as the Monroe Doctrine and painfully conscious of the absence of the United States, Mexico, and Brazil from League Councils, the organization in Geneva watched the course of distant events with trepidation, hoping that the machinery of inter-American cooperation would soon bring peace. To its credit, the Council forcefully called the attention of Bolivia and Paraguay to their obligations immediately after battle had been reported, although neither state had registered a complaint, and it constantly urged the calling of a Pan-American conference which would use its good offices to lead the parties to an amicable settlement. Speaking before the Assembly the delegate from Uruguay observed at this time:

The Council's action in this matter deserves to be emphasized, implying as it does a recognition of the fact that Latin America constitutes an integral part of the League. . . . There is nothing, either in the Covenant or elsewhere, that need restrict the League's activities. Indeed the mere fact of having signed the Covenant entitles us to hope for and to claim the benefit ensuing from it. That there is nothing to prevent the League from taking action is proved by the successful intervention of the Council on the occasion of the dispute between Bolivia and Paraguay [31].

While the American states tried to hush the squabbles in their own back yard the League waited discreetly, but the renewal of sharp hostilities in the Gran Chaco during 1932 impelled the League to send a commission of inquiry to South America despite the peevishness of the United States. Although the war was finally ended in 1936 by the exhaustion of both belligerents rather than by the concerted efforts of the international commission and the American republics, the concern of the League for the Western Hemisphere had boldly affirmed its preoccupation with peace everywhere.

Both the Greco-Bulgarian dispute and the Bolivian-Paraguay conflict high-lighted a remarkable evolution of international law through international organization. The Paris Congress of 1856 had conceded that a neutral state mediating a dispute between two unfriendly nations did not thereby compromise its neutrality; the Hague Conferences had further encouraged the use of good offices. But the Covenant of the League of Nations bluntly stated that "any war or threat of war, whether immediately affecting any of the Members of the League or not," concerns the League and the organization may take any action it thinks necessary "to safeguard the peace of nations [32]." With rare audacity the new collaborators on international organization struck a blow at the most hallowed pillar of national sovereignty: the unqualified right to declare war. One of the results of this provision of the Covenant was the appointment of international commissions of inquiry by the League to report from the field of dispute to the Geneva headquarters. Such a commission lent itself to reason rather than passion by its impartial fact gathering and its real presence as an international agency at the scene of action, a device gradually wedded to international organization.

Yet even the brazen claim of the League to interest itself in all international disputes left a wide allowance for war, since a state could legally open fire if it had submitted its controversy to arbitration, judicial settlement, or the Council of the League and waited ninety days after their decision or report. To close this gap in the Covenant, to end the tolerance of war as a legal means for settling disputes, the statesmen of Geneva in 1924 fashioned a brilliant protocol [33].

THE GENEVA PROTOCOL OF 1924

The Geneva Protocol of 1924, the most radical step ever proposed by an international organization to outlaw war, could trace its ancestry to the awkward appeals of the nineteenth century for disarmament. The circular note of the Tsar leading to the First Hague Peace Conference of 1899 had earnestly called attention to the ever-increasing financial burden of military expenditures and their inherent threat to international peace, but neither then nor in 1907 did the assembled nations accomplish any limitation of armaments. The fourth of Wilson's Fourteen Points and subsequently Article 8 of the Covenant of the League of Nations took up the challenge of international disarmament by requiring the Council to formulate plans for the reduction of national weapons. As early as May 1920, therefore, the Council instituted a Permanent Advisory Commission consisting of military, naval, and air representatives to work on the knotty problem. This group, at the behest of the Assembly, was soon enlarged to include political, economic, and labor experts and retitled the Temporary Mixed Commission. Between 1921 and 1924 three major schemes for disarmament emerged from this commission, each plan tending to emphasize that a guarantee of security must predate any scrapping of weapons. Meanwhile, encouraged by the Washington Disarmament Conference of 1922, a small group of Americans without official connection but including such celebrities as General Tasker Bliss, Isaiah Bowman, Joseph Chamberlain, Stephen P. Duggan, and David H. Miller finished and sent to Geneva a general draft treaty of disarmament and security. Circulated by the League of Nations, the American plan drew attention to a magnetic thesis: the stigma of "aggressor" must be branded upon any state which, regardless of circumstances or claims, refuses to submit its dispute with another state to an appropriate tribunal [34]. No international organization had dared to go so far.

The Fifth Assembly of the League of Nations met on 1 September 1924 in a generous mood. Conservative governments in both Great Britain and France had toppled, leaving Ramsay MacDonald and Edouard Herriot guiding their respective governments mildly leftward. A responsible statesman, Gustav Stresemann, gripped the helm of Germany. On 6 September 1924 the Assembly passed by a vote of 46 to 0 a British-French resolution requesting the armaments committee to consider again the various proposals on security and disarmament while the constitutional and legal committee should study methods of bolstering the pacific settlement of disputes. These committees soon placed before the Assembly a Protocol for the Pacific Settlement of International Disputes (Geneva Protocol) of twenty-one articles by which (a) procedures for the judicial or arbitral settlement of *all* disputes were devised; (b) an aggressor was defined quite simply as any state either refusing to submit a controversy to peaceful settlement or failing to carry out the decision of the tribunal; (c) when an aggressor had been labeled by the Council, *ipso facto* the members of the League would collaborate immediately, loyally, and effectively in applying such sanctions as the situation required. In the words of the *rapporteur* of the armaments committee, Eduard Beneš [35]:

Our purpose was to make war impossible, to kill it, to annihilate it. To do this we had to create a system of pacific settlement of *all disputes* which might arise. In other words, it meant the creation of a system of arbitration from which no international dispute, whether legal or political, could escape. The plan drawn up leaves no loophole; it prohibits wars of every description and lays down that all disputes shall be settled by pacific means.

Unfortunately this splendid vision never materialized. The Assembly of the League unanimously adopted the Geneva Protocol on 2 October 1924, but within a few weeks the first British Labor government fell and a new Conservative government under Stanley Baldwin quickly scuttled the all-embracing collective-security system of the Geneva Protocol.

Having bravely approached the ordeal of intensive international collaboration, the League of Nations now backed away, leaving the Great Powers to work out their own limited and specific guarantees through the Locarno treaties of 1925. During the next five years the League meandered toward a new general-security system by encouraging and promoting special or collective agreements on arbitration: in 1931 it framed a General Convention to Strengthen the Means of Preventing War, and with waning hope waited for the signature of all states in the world. But the golden hour of opportunity had ticked away: unemployment racked the world and hunger mocked the patience of nations as they turned to the tin shelter of dictators. On the night of 18 September 1931 Japan grabbed at Manchuria, slowly paralyzed Geneva, and then callously brushed the League aside.

The Manchurian Crisis. The Council of the League of Nations learned of an "incident" between Japan and China on the South Manchurian Railway, which the Japanese operated and policed by virtue of a ninety-nine-year lease, just one day after the occurrence. The Japanese delegate immediately stated that his government had taken all possible measures to prevent this local incident from leading to undesirable consequences, but two days later the Chinese representative invoked Article 11—the article used in the Greco-Bulgarian struggle—to summon the Council of the League, for Japan had manifestly bombarded arsenals and barracks, disarmed Chinese troops, and occupied the cities of Mukden and Antung. For several days thereafter the Council strived through informal negotiations and public meetings to restore peace: the Japanese reiterated that they had no territorial designs upon Manchuria and that they fully intended to withdraw as soon as the lives and property of their nationals were safeguarded. When the Chinese proposed that a neutral commission of inquiry be dispatched to the scene of distress, the same technique employed so successfully in the Greco-Bulgarian dispute, not only did Japan block the proposal in the Council but the United States, involved by the Nine-Power Treaty of 1922 and the Kellogg-Briand Pact of 1928, frowned from across the Atlantic. To the United States Minister in China, Secretary of State Henry L. Stimson had telegraphed on 24 September 1931 that "the idea of sending a military commission to Manchuria to establish the facts disturbed us . . . That the Japanese nationalistic element would be immensely strengthened and that it would unite Japan behind the military element, is our principal fear," and the Department could only endorse a commission appointed solely by Japan and China [36].

Thus, twelve days after the flare of hostilities in Manchuria, the Council had reassuring statements from both states, but no commission had been appointed to report from the point of action and no time limit had been set for the withdrawal of troops. Requesting both powers "to do all in their power to hasten the return of normal relations," the Council formally adjourned for two weeks.

The bombing of Chinchow, a city more than fifty miles from the railway zone, by Japanese airplanes on October 9 peeled the mask from the deceptive face of Japanese policy. The passing weeks brought no prospect of peace, as the circle of fire widened. After innumerable private consultations, the Council on October 24 finally called upon Japan to withdraw her troops to the railway zone before 16 November 1931. Every member of the Council voted for this resolution except Japan, thereby technically invalidating the resolution, but world opinion had spoken in unmistakable terms. That the Japanese coveted nothing less than all Manchuria and that none of the Great Powers was prepared to resist this aggression by force became tragically evident as the representatives of the Mikado stalled for time to complete the conquest: the Japanese themselves suggested a commission of inquiry on November 21, and the Council, now receiving an affirmative nod from the United States of America, resolved to send a group of five headed by the Earl of Lytton to investigate the Manchurian situation. This commission did not arrive in the Far East until the end of February 1932, more than five months after the outbreak of violence.

Meanwhile China had requested the transfer of the controversy from the Council to the Assembly. Although world sympathy rallied against aggression, the intransigence of Japan prevented any peaceful settlement. Even before the Lytton commission made its findings public, Japan recognized and signed a treaty with the puppet state of "Manchukuo" on 15 September 1932. Still the League labored incessantly through the weary months, talking, reporting, pleading, hoping to persuade Japan to yield. Finally, when forty-two members of the Assembly unanimously recommended (Japan objecting, Siam abstaining) the withdrawal of Japanese troops to the South Manchurian Railway zone, the restoration of an administration in Manchuria under Chinese sovereignty, and direct negotiation between the two parties to settle all outstanding difficulties, Japan walked out of the League of Nations [37]. On the same day, 24 February 1933, the parliament of Paraguay prepared to declare war on Bolivia, the U.S. Department of Commerce reported that thirty-five major commercial nations had lately erected new barriers to international trade, and frenzied Adolf Hitler raised his hand to smash German democracy by converting the Prussian police into an auxiliary of the Nazi party [38]. The tide of international organization ebbed into dark and muddy flats.

The Italo-Ethiopian War. On the afternoon of 5 December 1934 the second major attack was made upon international collaboration at Geneva. An armed conflict between Ethiopian and Italian troops at the Ethiopian oasis of Wal Wal, more than fifty miles from the Italian Somaliland border, led to mutual diplomatic protests with Italy loudly demanding apologies and reparations. Ethiopia offered to arbitrate the whole matter, but Italy spurned arbitration, and on 14 December 1934 Ethiopia appealed to the League of Nations under Article 11 of the Covenant. The timidity of Britain and France shaken by the bluster of Italy delayed the mere inscription of the complaint upon the Council's agenda, but at length international opinion stirred the Council to request both parties to arbitrate their disputes under a bilateral treaty of friendship which they had signed in 1928.

As early as January 1935, however, Emilio de Bono had been dispatched by Premier Mussolini to Eritrea as High Commissioner of East Africa with instructions "to make active preparations" in view of any settlement of the Ethiopian controversy unsatisfactory to the Italian government [39]. By March it was apparent that Italy had little taste for arbitration: increasing numbers of Fascist troops sailed through the Suez Canal to

Eritrea and Somaliland. Ethiopia, therefore, fearfully invoked Articles 10 and 15 before the Council of the League. To allay world opinion and particularly Great Britain, made uneasy by this new African chauvinism, Italy abruptly declared its readiness to nominate arbitrators. When the Council met on 15 April 1935, therefore, it willingly forestalled action to await the outcome of arbitration between the two disputants, although retaining the complaint upon the agenda. The arbitration dragged through a mire of obstinate procedure for several months, finally culminating in a pitiful agreement on 3 September 1935 that "neither the Italian Government nor its agents on the spot can be held responsible in any way for the actual Wal Wal incident" and although the local authorities of the Ethiopian government "may have given the impression that they had aggressive intentions . . . it has not been shown that they can be held responsible for the actual incident of December 5th [40]."

The Council of the League had agreed to meet "in any event" on 4 September 1935 to consider the Italo-Ethiopian dispute. At this meeting the Italian delegate brusquely announced that any possibility of further peaceful cooperation between Italy and Ethiopia had vanished, especially since that uncivilized state was now threatening the Italian frontier; on the following day Ethiopia earnestly appealed to Article 15 of the Covenant, but instead of clamping a vise upon the dispute, the Council appointed a committee of five of its own members to attempt once more to conciliate the parties. In the face of Italian determination to act, this committee on September 26 admitted its failure to relieve the tension. The Council then made a last effort to maintain peace by setting up a committee of all the members of the Council except Italy and Ethiopia, but its work was stultified when, seven days later, exactly one month after the arbitral decision and coinciding perfectly with the end of the rainy season in East Africa, General de Bono ordered his Italian troops in Eritrea to cross the Mareb River into Ethiopia [41].

In the very teeth of aggression, beset by a world of economic misery and moral despair, the Council of the League made an important entry in the annals of international organization on 7 October 1935. Without reservation, every member of the Council of the League (except Italy) approved its committee report that "the Italian government has resorted to war in disregard of its covenants under Article 12 of the Covenant of the League of Nations," and the President of the Council also noted that the fulfillment of duties under Article 16 was now incumbent upon every member of the League [42]. For the first time in history an international organization of fifty-four states prepared to invoke economic and financial sanctions against an outlaw nation.

The Assembly of the League had convened in September as usual, and on October 9 President Beneš placed before the organization a letter and documents concerning the Italo-Ethiopian dispute. Except for Italy, Albania, Hungary, and Austria, the entire membership of the Assembly rallied behind the spirit of severing economic connections with an aggressor. Even if some nations doubted the efficacy of sanctions, the League had courageously plunged into a veritable pool of international intrigue which lapped at the foreign policies of Great Britain, France, Germany, and the Soviet Union. No international organization, faithful to a sixteen-year-old contract, each member risking war itself, had ever before attempted such thoroughgoing strangulation of a giant.

The first experiment with economic coercion in the history of international collaboration lasted only nine months. Between 10 October 1935, when the League established the committee to coordinate the application of sanctions, and 6 July 1936, when the same committee recommended the abandonment of sanctions, Italy overwhelmed the puny forces of Ethiopia. The realities of the international political situation in 1935, with Japan disturbing the Far East and Hitler's Third Reich on the rise in Europe, constrained Great Britain and France to proceed cautiously against Italy. The application of sanctions by the League of Nations, therefore, was designed to turn Italy away from its imperialistic aggression, keep the faith of the Covenant in collective security, but not sting Italy into a war with Great Britain and France. The Coordination Committee of fifty delegates proceeded to study the sanctions to be applied and made the proposals of sanctions which individual states should apply. Led by Great Britain, the committee *first* agreed that all exports of arms to Italy ought to be stopped. The members of the committee, with the exception of Switzerland and Luxembourg, further concurred that Ethiopia should be permitted to buy arms. *Second,* it was agreed that no further credit should be extended to the Italian government or to Italian companies. After long discussion and some disagreement by states like Yugoslavia, Rumania, Switzerland, Austria, and Hungary, a *third* sanction upon imports from Italy was approved, with the provision that states losing their trade thereby with Italy should be assisted by a rechanneling of trade with other states. *Fourth,* and most crucial, was the proposed sanction upon raw materials or manufactures exported to Italy by members of the League. Those items which League members generally controlled (rubber, tin, manganese, etc.) were placed under sanctions, but those items which Italy might buy from such alternate sources as the United States, Germany, Japan, or Brazil (oil, coal, steel, etc.) were not included.

The sanctions, even though not applied by all states and even though not including some of the most vital war materials, had a telling effect.

Italy soon fell into financial difficulties, and by the end of November the gold value of the lira had been cut 25 per cent. Monthly exports to Britain were reduced from $3,000,000 to $100,000, and Italian sales to France fell 90 per cent. Despite enormous Italian exertions the gold reserves of the country were rapidly disappearing. If the League had endorsed the application of sanctions upon oil and steel, Italy would have been strangled. But neither Britain nor France had given up the idea of appeasing Italy, and even while sanctions were being applied their foreign ministers were exploring plans for delivering parts of Ethiopia to Italy in exchange for Mussolini's halting of belligerent action. When the Hoare-Laval proposals came to light in December 1935, world opinion which had been mobilizing behind the Covenant was shocked. The delays of these negotiations, even though unfruitful, and the subsequent caution at Geneva in consequence of it, hampered the work of the Coordination Committee, so that the application of the sanction against sending to Italy the most vital war materials never was undertaken. On 7 March 1935 Adolf Hitler denounced the Locarno treaties and marched into the Rhineland. The new menace in Europe was much more formidable to France and Great Britain than Italian imperialism in Africa. With the ever-ready hope that Italy would eventually join them against Germany, they could go no further in collective security through the League of Nations.

Perhaps Maxim Litvinov of the Soviet Union best summed up the failure of the first attempt at collaboration against aggression on 1 July 1936: "We have met here to complete a page in the history of the League of Nations. . . . I assert that Article 16 equipped the League of Nations with such powerful weapons that, in the event of their being fully applied, every aggression can be broken [43]." To be sure, four members of the League refused to apply any sanctions whatsoever, and some who raised no objection to sanctions never actually applied all those which the coordination committee had approved. But the application of economic sanctions by an international organization for the principle of collective security against a great power was utterly unprecedented and, in the light of history, came within an inch of astonishing success. Unfortunately France, rigid and white with fear of Germany, refused to hit hard at Italy, and where France would not follow, Great Britain refused to lead.

Finally, although the nations had collaborated on economic sanctions, they were still not ready to recognize that in the long run they would have to be ready to enforce those sanctions with military force if necessary. Speaking before the House of Commons, Sir Samuel Hoare [44] defended his policy of appeasing Italy as stark realism:

. . . it is essential if collective defense is to be really effective . . . that we have actual proof by action from the member states concerned . . . We alone have taken military precautions. There is a British fleet in the Mediterranean. There are British reinforcements in Egypt, Malta, and Aden. No ship, no machine gun, no man has been moved by any other State . . . we must have something more than general protestations of loyalty to the League. . . .

A BALANCE SHEET OF THE LEAGUE OF NATIONS

Whatever the reality of aggression proved, the fledgeling international organization in 1931 and 1936 could not soar beyond its own limitations: the provincialism of the United States, the pessimism of France, the opportunism of the Soviet Union, the conservatism of Great Britain, all shuddered under the ruthless arrogance of Japan, Italy, and Germany while the small states, too, frequently played with callous ambition or petty covetousness.

Yet for all these adolescent disorders the organization carried on its work. Throughout the twenty years of its brief life the League of Nations steadfastly promoted international administration. Cautious world cooperation was filled with new energy and, culling the weeds of the past from old bureaus, the League's international economic and social programs flowered in the fields of commerce, health, communications, and protection of helpless peoples. The Permanent Court sponsored by the League gained the respect of the world, and no reticulation of international law had ever spread so rapidly. Both at Geneva and in the cities of different continents the League encouraged conferences and consultations among statesmen, some of whom became close friends and sympathetic with other national views. In its best years, from 1924 to 1931, the foreign ministers of Great Britain, France, Germany, Poland, Czechoslovakia, Holland, and the Scandinavian countries frequently represented their states in the Council, giving to the international organization a political weight and center unparalleled in modern times. Not only were responsible ministers represented in the Council, but distant states, notably Brazil and Argentina, appointed special representatives to Geneva with ambassadorial status to sit with the Council instead of utilizing on a part-time basis one of their envoys to a European state. Even the blasts of derision leveled at the military impotency of Geneva in later years could not alter the fact that no other international organization had ever united to condemn and punish a major state for violating its covenants to keep the peace [45].

The days of the League were unhappily numbered in the docket of security from international aggression. After helplessly expelling the Soviet Union on 14 December 1939 for its attack upon Finland, the League faded into the twilight of a shattered world at war. Japan and Italy had been revealed as blustering criminals in a community of nation-states, but their success in getting away with their loot forecast the doom of the first period of international collaboration. The weakness of the League of Nations to enforce its judgments, however, did not mean the end of international organization for the maintenance of peace; it indicated rather the urgency of shoring up its hollow structure. Scarcely had the Second World War blazed across Europe than men of vision set themselves to the task of creating a new charter for international collaboration.

NOTES

1. See *The Project Relative to a Court of Arbitral Justice*, New York, Carnegie Endowment, 1920.

2. Resolutions passed by the Fourth Dinner Conference for the purpose of formulating proposals for the constitution of a League of Peace (League of Nations), 9 April 1915, J. H. Latané (ed.), *Development of the League of Nations Idea, Documents and Correspondence of Theodore Marburg*, New York, Macmillan, 1932, 2 vols., Vol. II, p. 717.

3. The most valuable study of the making of the League of Nations by official acts is D. H. Miller, *The Drafting of the Covenant*, London and New York, Putnam, 1928, 2 vols. Also see H. R. Winkler, *The League of Nations Movement in Great Britain, 1914–1919*, New Brunswick, N.J., Rutgers University Press, 1952.

4. Address at Des Moines, Iowa, partly reprinted in *Chronology of Woodrow Wilson*, comp. by J. R. Bolling *et al.*, Philadelphia, Stokes, 1927, p. 68.

5. *Ibid.*, pp. 79–80.

6. *Foreign Relations of the United States*, 1917, Supplement 1, pp. 24–29.

7. *Ibid.*, 1918, Supplement 1, 2 vols., Vol. I, pp. 15–16.

8. H. W. V. Temperley (ed.), *A History of the Peace Conference at Paris*, London, Frowde, Hodder, and Stoughton, 1920–1924, 6 vols., is an exhaustive study. A briefer but valuable insight to the conference is provided in Lord Riddell, C. K. Webster, A. Toynbee, *et al.*, *The Treaty of Versailles and After*, New York, Oxford, 1935. See also "Documents Regarding the Peace Conference," *International Conciliation*, No. 139 (June 1919), New York, Carnegie Endowment, and H. Nicolson,

Peacemaking, 1919, Boston, Houghton Mifflin, 1933.

9. The so-called Hurst-Miller Draft. Cecil Hurst and David H. Miller were legal advisers to the foreign offices of Great Britain and the United States respectively. On 31 January 1919 President Wilson and Lord Cecil agreed to have these men draft a reconciliation of the American and British views. See Miller, *op. cit.*, Vol. I, especially Chap. VI.

10. *Congressional Record*, Vol. 58, Part 6 (13 September–4 October 1919), p. 5701.

11. Covenant of the League of Nations, Arts. 12–16. For official French and English texts see League of Nations, *Official Journal*, No. 1 (February 1920), pp. 3–12. A good study of the history of the League of Nations and its actual work between 1918 and 1935 is A. Zimmern, *The League of Nations and the Rule of Law*, London, Macmillan, 1936, especially Part III.

12. Covenant of the League of Nations, Art. 10.

13. *Ibid.*, Art. 24.

14. General Act of the Conference of Berlin of the Plenipotentiaries of Great Britain, Austria-Hungary, etc., signed at Berlin, 26 February 1885, *B.F.S.P.*, Vol. LXXVI, pp. 4–20. See also F. B. Sayre, *Experiments in International Administration*, New York, Harper, 1919, pp. 79–87, and A. Debidour, *Histoire diplomatique de l'Europe*, Paris, Librairie Felix Alcan, 1916–1919, 2 vols., Vol. I, Part I, pp. 90–94.

15. For the Smuts proposals on mandates, see Miller, *op. cit.*, Vol. II, Doc. 5, especially pp. 27–36. A valuable study is G. L. Beer, *African Questions at the Paris*

Peace Conference with Papers on Egypt, Mesopotamia and the Colonial Settlements, New York, Macmillan, 1923. See also T. A. Bailey, *Woodrow Wilson and the Lost Peace,* New York, Macmillan, 1944, especially Chap. 11, "The White Man's Burden."

16. Covenant of the League of Nations, Art. 22.

17. For a comparison of Wilson's draft and the British proposals on the judicial process, see Miller, *op. cit.,* Docs. 7, 10, pp. 65, 106. Compare the Covenant of the League of Nations, Art. 14.

18. E. Root, "The Constitution of an International Court of Justice," *American Journal of International Law,* Vol. 15 (1921), p. 1. See also "Report on the Organization of a Permanent Court of International Justice Submitted by M. Léon Bourgeois," League of Nations, *Official Journal,* No. 2 (March 1920), pp. 33–38.

19. League of Nations, Advisory Council of Jurists, Permanent Court of International Justice, *Procès-verbaux of the Proceedings of the Committee,* 1920. See also M. O. Hudson, "The First Year of the Permanent Court of International Justice," *American Journal of International Law,* Vol. 17 (1923), pp. 15–28.

20. M. O. Hudson, "The Advisory Opinions of the Permanent Court of International Justice," *International Conciliation,* No. 214 (November 1925).

21. An excellent study of the Court, its origins, organization, and procedure, is M. O. Hudson, *The Permanent Court of International Justice,* New York, Macmillan, 1943. The statistics cited are based upon Appendixes 11 and 12.

22. For the basic organization of the Secretariat, see League of Nations, *Records of the Second Assembly,* Fourth Committee, Annex 2, "Organization of the Secretariat and the ILO," 1921, pp. 174–203.

23. League of Nations Secretariat Staff Regulations, Art. 3, par. 1, quoted by E. F. Ranshofen-Wertheimer in his excellent study, *The International Secretariat,* New York, Carnegie Endowment, 1945, p. 245.

24. Covenant of the League of Nations, Art. 18.

25. Ranshofen-Wertheimer, *op. cit.,* p.

104. See also D. P. Myers, *Manual of Collection of Treaties,* Cambridge, Mass., Harvard University Press, 1922, pp. 600–604, and M. O. Hudson, "The Registration and Publication of Treaties," *American Journal of International Law,* Vol. 19 (1925), pp. 273–292. Although various nations had begun official collections of their international acts and some private anthologies had impressive contents, there was no single, official bureau for gathering all the documents. Encouraged by the Swiss Federal Council, the Institute of International Law had adopted a draft convention in 1892 for an international union to publish treaties. Eighteen nations met in Geneva in 1894 to discuss the proposal; although several nations supported it, the lack of unanimity, with apathy and economy, dragged the project down to oblivion.

26. The problem of the "loyalty" of international civil servants to an international organization is acute in respect to citizens of a totalitarian state which, by definition, tolerates no parallel or competing loyalties. In the League of Nations, for example, there were peculiar difficulties for Italian officials at Geneva after the advent of Mussolini, and the restraints upon Soviet officials are obvious. Another more recent problem is the employment by an international organization of individuals whose state considers them "disloyal" or "poor security risks."

27. League of Nations, *Records of the First Assembly, Plenary Meetings,* 11th Plenary Meeting, 30 November 1920, pp. 214–241.

28. League of Nations, *Resolutions and Recommendations Adopted by the Assembly during Its Third Session,* 4–30 September 1922, p. 13; see also F. Morley, *The Society of Nations,* Washington, Brookings, 1932, pp. 511–526, for shift in financial responsibility, and League of Nations, *Ten Years of World Cooperation,* 1930, especially "The Financial Administration of the League," pp. 388–397.

29. For a résumé of the more important political disputes throughout the League's history, see J. I. Knudson, *A History of the League of Nations,* Atlanta, Ga., T. E. Smith, 1938, pp. 67–113. Particulars of each controversy may be found

in the appropriate year of League of Nations, *Official Journal*.

30. League of Nations, *Official Journal*, 1925, p. 1717. For the complete report of the commission of inquiry on the frontier incidents between Greece and Bulgaria, see *ibid.*, 1926, pp. 196–209.

31. League of Nations, *Official Journal*, *Special Supplement 75*, "Records of the Tenth Ordinary Session of the Assembly," 1929, pp. 38–39.

32. Covenant of the League of Nations, Art. 11.

33. Two special studies of the Geneva protocol are D. H. Miller, *The Geneva Protocol*, New York, Macmillan, 1925, and P. T. Noel-Baker, *The Geneva Protocol for the Pacific Settlement of Disputes*, London, King, 1925.

34. For the American contributions toward disarmament and the Geneva protocol, see J. T. Shotwell, "A Practical Plan for Disarmament," *International Conciliation*, No. 201 (August 1924).

35. League of Nations, *Records of the Fifth Assembly, Meetings of the Committees*, Annex 16, "Arbitration, Security, and Reduction of Armaments," 1924, p. 134. The complete text of the Protocol for the Pacific Settlement of International Disputes is in *ibid.*, Annex 18, pp. 136–140. For discussion leading to the Assembly resolution of 6 September 1924, see League of Nations, *Records of the Fifth Assembly, Text of the Debates*, 1924. See also A. Wolfers, *Britain and France between Two Wars*, New York, Harcourt, Brace, 1940, pp. 343–354, and W. Rappard, *The Quest for Peace*, Cambridge, Mass., Harvard University Press, 1940, pp. 252–261.

36. *Foreign Relations of the United States, Japan 1931–1941*, Washington, 1943, 2 vols., Vol. I, p. 10.

37. Details of the Sino-Japanese dispute before the Council can be pursued through League of Nations, *Official Journal*, 1931, 1932; for the role of the Assembly, see League of Nations, *Official Journal, Special Supplements 102, 111, 112,* and *113*, 1932, 1933. An excellent study of the controversy based upon the official documents is W. W. Willoughby, *The Sino-Japanese Controversy and the League of Nations*, Baltimore, Johns Hopkins Press, 1935.

38. *The New York Times*, 25 February 1933.

39. E. M. de Bono, *Anno XIII, the Conquest of an Empire*, London, Cresset Press, 1937, p. 58. For another view of the mobilization and conduct of the Italian campaign in Ethiopia, see P. Badoglio, *La guerra d'Etiopia*, Milan, A. Mondadori, 1936.

40. Pitman B. Potter, *The Wal Wal Arbitration*, New York, Carnegie Endowment, 1938, Annex P, "Decision of the Commission," p. 182.

41. League of Nations, *Official Journal*, November 1935, pp. 1133–1145.

42. *Ibid.*, Minutes of the Council, 89th Session, November 1935, pp. 1209–1223.

43. League of Nations, *Official Journal, Special Supplement 151*, "Records of the Assembly, Text of the Debates," 1936, p. 36. An excellent volume treating the whole Italo-Ethiopian conflict between 1928 and 1936 is A. Toynbee, "Abyssinia and Italy," in *Survey of International Affairs*, 1935, Vol. II (Royal Institute of International Affairs), London, Oxford, 1936.

44. *The New York Times*, 14 December 1935.

45. For a complete and most valuable study of the League of Nations, see F. P. Walters, *A History of the League of Nations*, London, Oxford, 1952, 2 vols.

APPENDIX 5

The Covenant of the League of Nations, 1919

The High Contracting Parties,

In order to promote international co-operation and to achieve international peace and security

by the acceptance of obligations not to resort to war,

by the prescription of open, just and honourable relations between nations,

by the firm establishment of the understandings of international law as the actual rule of conduct among Governments, and

by the maintenance of justice and a scrupulous respect for all treaty obligations in the dealings of organised peoples with one another,

Agree to this Covenant of the League of Nations.

ARTICLE 1

1. The original Members of the League of Nations shall be those of the Signatories which are named in the Annex to this Covenant and also such of those other States named in the Annex as shall accede without reservation to this Covenant. Such accession shall be effected by a declaration deposited with the Secretariat within two months of the coming into force of the Covenant. Notice thereof shall be sent to all other Members of the League.

2. Any fully self-governing State, Dominion or Colony not named in the Annex may become a Member of the League if its admission is agreed to by two-thirds of the Assembly, provided that it shall give effective guarantees of its sincere intention to observe its international obligations, and shall accept such regulations as may be prescribed by the League in regard to its military, naval and air forces and armaments.

3. Any Member of the League may, after two years' notice of its intention so to do, withdraw from the League, provided that all its international obligations and all its obligations under this Covenant shall have been fulfilled at the time of its withdrawal.

ARTICLE 2

The action of the League under this Covenant shall be effected through the instrumentality of an Assembly and of a Council, with a permanent Secretariat.

ARTICLE 3

1. The Assembly shall consist of Representatives of the Members of the League.

2. The Assembly shall meet at stated intervals, and from time to time as occasion may require at the Seat of the League or at such other place as may be decided upon.

3. The Assembly may deal at its meetings with any matter within the sphere of action of the League or affecting the peace of the world.

4. At meetings of the Assembly each Member of the League shall have one vote, and may have not more than three Representatives.

ARTICLE 4

1. The Council shall consist of Representatives of the Principal Allied and Associated Powers, together with Representatives of four other Members of the League. These four Members of the League shall be selected by the Assembly from time to time in its discretion. Until the appointment of the Representatives of the four Members of the League first selected by the Assembly, Representatives of Belgium, Brazil, Spain and Greece shall be members of the Council.

2. With the approval of the majority of the Assembly, the Council may name additional Members of the League whose Representatives shall always be members of the Council; the Council with like approval may increase the number of Members of the League to be selected by the Assembly for representation on the Council.

3. The Council shall meet from time to time as occasion may require, and at least once a year, at the Seat of the League, or at such other place as may be decided upon.

4. The Council may deal at its meetings with any matter within the sphere of action of the League or affecting the peace of the world.

5. Any Member of the League not represented on the Council shall be invited to send a Representative to sit as a member at any meeting of the Council during the consideration of matters specially affecting the interests of that Member of the League.

6. At meetings of the Council, each Member of the League represented on the Council shall have one vote, and may have not more than one Representative.

ARTICLE 5

1. Except where otherwise expressly provided in this Covenant or by the terms of the present Treaty, decisions at any meeting of the Assembly or of the Council shall require the agreement of all the Members of the League represented at the meeting.

2. All matters of procedure at meetings of the Assembly or of the Council, including the appointment of Committees to investigate particular matters, shall be regulated by the Assembly or by the Council and may be decided by a majority of the Members of the League represented at the meeting.

3. The first meeting of the Assembly and the first meeting of the Council shall be summoned by the President of the United States of America.

ARTICLE 6

1. The permanent Secretariat shall be established at the Seat of the League. The Secretariat shall comprise a Secretary-General and such secretaries and staff as may be required.

2. The first Secretary-General shall be the person named in the Annex; thereafter the Secretary-General shall be appointed by the Council with the approval of the majority of the Assembly.

3. The secretaries and staff of the Secretariat shall be appointed by the Secretary-General with the approval of the Council.

4. The Secretary-General shall act in that capacity at all meetings of the Assembly and of the Council.

5. The expenses of the Secretariat shall be borne by the Members of the League in accordance with the apportionment of the expenses of the International Bureau of the Universal Postal Union.

ARTICLE 7

1. The Seat of the League is established at Geneva.

2. The Council may at any time decide that the Seat of the League shall be established elsewhere.

3. All positions under or in connection with the League, including the Secretariat, shall be open equally to men and women.

4. Representatives of the Members of the League and officials of the League when engaged on the business of the League shall enjoy diplomatic privileges and immunities.

5. The buildings and other property occupied by the League or its officials or by Representatives attending its meetings shall be inviolable.

ARTICLE 8

1. The Members of the League recognize that the maintenance of peace requires the reduction of national armaments to the lowest point consistent with national safety and the enforcement by common action of international obligations.

2. The Council, taking account of the geographical situation and circumstances of each State, shall formulate plans for such reduction for the consideration and action of the several Governments.

3. Such plans shall be subject to reconsideration and revision at least every ten years.

4. After these plans have been adopted by the several Governments, the limits of armaments therein fixed shall not be exceeded without the concurrence of the Council.

5. The Members of the League agree that the manufacture by private enterprise of munitions and implements of war is open to grave objections. The Council shall advise how the evil effects attendant upon such manufacture can be prevented, due regard being had to the necessities of those Members of the League which are not able to manufacture the munitions and implements of war necessary for their safety.

6. The Members of the League undertake to interchange full and frank information as to the scale of their armaments, their military, naval and air programmes and the condition of such of their industries as are adaptable to warlike purposes.

ARTICLE 9

A permanent Commission shall be constituted to advise the Council on the execution of the provisions of Articles 1 and 8 and on military, naval and air questions generally.

ARTICLE 10

The Members of the League undertake to respect and preserve as against external aggression the territorial integrity and existing political independence of all Members of the League. In case of any such aggression or in case of any threat or danger of such aggression the Council shall advise upon the means by which this obligation shall be fulfilled.

ARTICLE 11

1. Any war or threat of war, whether immediately affecting any of the Members of the League or not, is hereby declared a matter of concern to the whole League, and the League shall take any action that may be deemed wise and effectual to safeguard the peace of nations. In case any such emergency should arise, the Secretary-General shall, on the request of any Member of the League, forthwith summon a meeting of the Council.

2. It is also declared to be the friendly right of each Member of the League to bring to the attention of the Assembly or of the Council any circumstance whatever affecting international relations which threatens to disturb international peace or the good understanding between nations upon which peace depends.

ARTICLE 12

1. The Members of the League agree that if there should arise between them any dispute likely to lead to a rupture, they will submit the matter either to arbitration or to enquiry by the Council, and they agree in no case to resort to war until three months after the award by the arbitrators or the report by the Council.

2. In any case under this Article the award of the arbitrators shall be made within a reasonable time, and the report of the Council shall be made within six months after the submission of the dispute.

ARTICLE 13

1. The Members of the League agree that whenever any dispute shall arise between them which they recognize to be suitable for submission to arbitration and which cannot be satisfactorily settled by diplomacy, they will submit the whole subject-matter to arbitration.

2. Disputes as to the interpretation of a treaty, as to any question of international law, as to the existence of any fact which, if established, would constitute a breach of any international obligation, or as to the extent and nature of the reparation to be made for any such breach, are declared to be among those which are generally suitable for submission to arbitration.

3. For the consideration of any such dispute the court of arbitration to

which the case is referred shall be the court agreed on by the parties to the dispute or stipulated in any convention existing between them.

4. The Members of the League agree that they will carry out in full good faith any award that may be rendered, and that they will not resort to war against a Member of the League which complies therewith. In the event of any failure to carry out such an award, the Council shall propose what steps should be taken to give effect thereto.

ARTICLE 14

The Council shall formulate and submit to the Members of the League for adoption plans for the establishment of a Permanent Court of International Justice. The Court shall be competent to hear and determine any dispute of an international character which the parties thereto submit to it. The Court may also give an advisory opinion upon any dispute or question referred to it by the Council or by the Assembly.

ARTICLE 15

1. If there should arise between Members of the League any dispute likely to lead to a rupture, which is not submitted to arbitration in accordance with Article 13, the Members of the League agree that they will submit the matter to the Council. Any party to the dispute may effect such submission by giving notice of the existence of the dispute to the Secretary-General, who will make all necessary arrangements for a full investigation and consideration thereof.

2. For this purpose, the parties to the dispute will communicate to the Secretary-General, as promptly as possible, statements of their case with all the relevant facts and papers, and the Council may forthwith direct the publication thereof.

3. The Council shall endeavour to effect a settlement of the dispute, and if such efforts are successful, a statement shall be made public giving such facts and explanations regarding the dispute and the terms of settlement thereof as the Council may deem appropriate.

4. If the dispute is not thus settled, the Council either unanimously or by a majority vote shall make and publish a report containing a statement of the facts of the dispute and the recommendations which are deemed just and proper in regard thereto.

5. Any Member of the League represented on the Council may make public a statement of the facts of the dispute and of its conclusions regarding the same.

6. If a report by the Council is unanimously agreed to by the members thereof other than the Representatives of one or more of the parties to the dispute, the Members of the League agree that they will not go to war with any party to the dispute which complies with the recommendations of the report.

7. If the Council fails to reach a report which is unanimously agreed to by the members thereof, other than the Representatives of one or more of the parties to the dispute, the Members of the League reserve to themselves the right to take such action as they shall consider necessary for the maintenance of right and justice.

8. If the dispute between the parties is claimed by one of them, and is found by the Council, to arise out of a matter which by international law is solely within the domestic jurisdiction of that party, the Council shall so report, and shall make no recommendation as to its settlement.

9. The Council may in any case under this Article refer the dispute to the Assembly. The dispute shall be so referred at the request of either party to the dispute, provided that such request be made within fourteen days after the submission of the dispute to the Council.

10. In any case referred to the Assembly, all the provisions of this Article and of Article 12 relating to the action and powers of the Council shall apply to the action and powers of the Assembly, provided that a report made by the Assembly, if concurred in by the Representatives of those Members of the League represented on the Council and of a majority of the other Members of the League, exclusive in each case of the Representatives of the parties to the dispute, shall have the same force as a report by the Council, concurred in by all the members thereof other than the Representatives of one or more of the parties to the dispute.

ARTICLE 16

1. Should any Member of the League resort to war in disregard of its covenants under Articles 12, 13 or 15, it shall *ipso facto* be deemed to have committed an act of war against all other Members of the League, which hereby undertake immediately to subject it to the severance of all trade or financial relations, the prohibition of all intercourse between their nationals and the nationals of the covenant-breaking State, and the prevention of all financial, commercial or personal intercourse between the nationals of the covenant-breaking State and the nationals of any other State, whether a Member of the League or not.

2. It shall be the duty of the Council in such case to recommend to the several Governments concerned what effective military, naval or air force the Members of the League shall severally contribute to the armed forces to be used to protect the covenants of the League.

3. The Members of the League agree, further, that they will mutually support one another in the financial and economic measures which are taken under this Article, in order to minimise the loss and inconvenience resulting from the above measures, and that they will mutually support one another in resisting any special measures aimed at one of their number by the covenant-breaking State, and that they will take the necessary steps to afford passage through their territory to the forces of any of the Members of the League which are co-operating to protect the covenants of the League.

4. Any Member of the League which has violated any covenant of the League may be declared to be no longer a Member of the League by a vote of the Council concurred in by the Representatives of all the other Members of the League represented thereon.

ARTICLE 17

1. In the event of a dispute between a Member of the League and a State which is not a Member of the League, or between States not Members of the League, the State or States not Members of the League shall be invited to accept the obligations of Membership in the League for the purposes of such dispute, upon such conditions as the Council may deem just. If such invitation is accepted, the provisions of Articles 12 to 16 inclusive shall be applied with such modifications as may be deemed necessary by the Council.

2. Upon such invitation being given, the Council shall immediately institute an enquiry into the circumstances of the dispute and recommend such action as may seem best and most effectual in the circumstances.

3. If a State so invited shall refuse to accept the obligations of membership in the League for the purposes of such dispute, and shall resort to war against a Member of the League, the provisions of Article 16 shall be applicable as against the State taking such action.

4. If both parties to the dispute when so invited refuse to accept the obligations of membership in the League for the purposes of such dispute, the Council may take such measures and make such recommendations as will prevent hostilities and will result in the settlement of the dispute.

ARTICLE 18

Every treaty or international engagement entered into hereafter by any Member of the League shall be forthwith registered with the Secretariat and shall as soon as possible be published by it. No such treaty or international engagement shall be binding until so registered.

ARTICLE 19

The Assembly may from time to time advise the reconsideration by Members of the League of treaties which have become inapplicable and the consideration of international conditions whose continuance might endanger the peace of the world.

ARTICLE 20

1. The Members of the League severally agree that this Covenant is accepted as abrogating all obligations or understandings *inter se* which are inconsistent with the terms thereof, and solemnly undertake that they will not hereafter enter into any engagements inconsistent with the terms thereof.

2. In case any Member of the League shall before becoming a Member of the League have undertaken any obligations inconsistent with the terms of this Covenant, it shall be the duty of such Member to take immediate steps to procure its release from such obligations.

ARTICLE 21

Nothing in this Covenant shall be deemed to affect the validity of international engagements, such as treaties of arbitration or regional understandings like the Monroe doctrine, for securing the maintenance of peace.

ARTICLE 22

1. To those colonies and territories which as a consequence of the late war have ceased to be under the sovereignty of the States which formerly governed them and which are inhabited by peoples not yet able to stand by themselves under the strenuous conditions of the modern world, there should be applied the principle that the well-being and development of such peoples form a sacred trust of civilization and that securities for the performance of this trust should be embodied in this Covenant.

2. The best method of giving practical effect to this principle is that the tutelage of such peoples should be entrusted to advanced nations who, by reason of their resources, their experience or their geographical position, can best undertake this responsibility, and who are willing to accept it, and that this tutelage should be exercised by them as Mandatories on behalf of the League.

3. The character of the mandate must differ according to the stage of the development of the people, the geographical situation of the territory, its economic conditions and other similar circumstances.

4. Certain communities formerly belonging to the Turkish Empire have reached a stage of development where their existence as independent nations can be provisionally recognized subject to the rendering of administrative advice and assistance by a Mandatory until such time as they are able to stand alone. The wishes of these communities must be a principal consideration in the selection of the Mandatory.

5. Other peoples, especially those of Central Africa, are at such a stage that the Mandatory must be responsible for the administration of the territory under conditions which will guarantee freedom of conscience and religion, subject only to the maintenance of public order and morals, the prohibition of abuses such as the slave trade, the arms traffic and the liquor traffic, and the prevention of the establishment of fortifications or military and naval bases and of military training of the natives for other than police purposes and the defence of territory, and will also secure equal opportunities for the trade and commerce of other Members of the League.

6. There are territories, such as South West Africa and certain of the South Pacific Islands, which, owing to the sparseness of their population, or their small size, or their remoteness from the centres of civilisation, or their geographical contiguity to the territory of the Mandatory, and other circumstances, can be best administered under the laws of the Mandatory as integral portions of its territory, subject to the safeguards above mentioned in the interests of the indigenous population.

7. In every case of mandate, the Mandatory shall render to the Council an annual report in reference to the territory committed to its charge.

8. The degree of authority, control or administration to be exercised by the Mandatory shall, if not previously agreed upon by the Members of the League, be explicitly defined in each case by the Council.

9. A permanent Commission shall be constituted to receive and examine the annual reports of the Mandatories and to advise the Council on all matters relating to the observance of the mandates.

ARTICLE 23

Subject to and in accordance with the provisions of international conventions existing or hereafter to be agreed upon, the Members of the League:

(a) will endeavor to secure and maintain fair and humane conditions of labor for men, women and children, both in their own countries and in all countries to which their commercial and industrial relations extend, and for that purpose will establish and maintain the necessary international organisations;

(b) undertake to secure just treatment of the native inhabitants of territories under their control;

(c) will entrust the League with the general supervision over the execution of agreements with regard to the traffic in women and children, and the traffic in opium and other dangerous drugs;

(d) will entrust the League with the general supervision of the trade in arms and ammunition with the countries in which the control of this traffic is necessary in the common interest;

(e) will make provision to secure and maintain freedom of communications and of transit and equitable treatment for the commerce of all Members of the League. In this connection, the special necessities of the regions devastated during the war of 1914–1918 shall be borne in mind;

(f) will endeavour to take steps in matters of international concern for the prevention and control of disease.

ARTICLE 24

1. There shall be placed under the direction of the League all international bureaux already established by general treaties if the parties to such treaties consent. All such international bureaux and all commissions for the regulation of matters of international interest hereafter constituted shall be placed under the direction of the League.

2. In all matters of international interest which are regulated by general conventions but which are not placed under the control of international bureaux or commissions, the Secretariat of the League shall, subject to the consent of the Council and if desired by the parties, collect and distribute all relevant information and shall render any other assistance which may be necessary or desirable.

3. The Council may include as part of the expenses of the Secretariat the expenses of any bureau or commission which is placed under the direction of the League.

ARTICLE 25

The Members of the League agree to encourage and promote the establishment and co-operation of duly authorised voluntary national Red Cross organisations having as purposes improvement of health, the prevention of disease and the mitigation of suffering throughout the world.

ARTICLE 26

1. Amendments to this Covenant will take effect when ratified by the Members of the League whose Representatives compose the Council and by a majority of the Members of the League whose Representatives compose the Assembly.

2. No such amendments shall bind any Member of the League which signifies its dissent therefrom, but in that case it shall cease to be a Member of the League.

ANNEX

I. Original Members of the League of Nations, Signatories of the Treaty of Peace

United States of America	Haiti
Belgium	Hejaz
Bolivia	Honduras
Brazil	Italy
British Empire	Japan
Canada	Liberia
Australia	Nicaragua
South Africa	Panama
New Zealand	Peru
India	Poland
China	Portugal
Cuba	Roumania
Ecuador	Serb-Croat-Slovene State
France	Siam
Greece	Czechoslovakia
Guatemala	Uruguay

States Invited to Accede to the Covenant

Argentine Republic	Persia
Chile	Salvador
Colombia	Spain
Denmark	Sweden
Netherlands	Switzerland
Norway	Venezuela
Paraguay	

II. First Secretary-General of the League of Nations

The Honourable Sir James Eric Drummond, K.C.M.G., C.B.

CHAPTER 6 *The Second Period of Collaboration: The United Nations*

Three monstrous wars have led to three sane attempts to institutionalize peace by international organization. The consuming struggles of Napoleon drove the world powers to consultation; the raw excesses of the First World War, which cost no less than 180 billion dollars and 10 million lives, further impelled men and women to seek a system of collaboration against international violence; and, out of the maw of the Second World War, more terrible than all the hecatombs of the past, came the plans for the United Nations.

Despite the magnitude of the conflict after September 1939, no general war aims were formulated until Prime Minister Winston Churchill and President Franklin D. Roosevelt met on the Atlantic Ocean on 14 August 1941 and declared their hopes for a better future after the destruction of Nazi tyranny. Rejecting territorial aggrandizement for themselves, acknowledging the right of peoples to choose their own forms of government, and stressing the need for economic cooperation, the two great war leaders envisaged world-wide disarmament, "pending the establishment of a wider and permanent system of general security [1]." Less than four months later the bombing planes of Japan scourged Pearl Harbor and plunged the United States into a scalding blood bath of global war.

DECLARATION OF THE UNITED NATIONS AGAINST GERMANY, ITALY, AND JAPAN

On 13 December 1941 M. M. Hamilton, chief of the Division of Far Eastern Affairs in the U.S. Department of State, began drafting a joint declaration to be made by the nations at war with Germany, Italy, or Japan. The document, after review by Secretary of State Cordell Hull, his assistants, British Ambassador Halifax, his aides, and their chiefs, Prime

Minister Churchill and President Roosevelt, declared that all the signatory nations regarded the Atlantic Charter as their common program of purposes and principles; it pledged each state, moreover, to wholehearted cooperation in the war effort and not to make a separate armistice or peace with the enemies. "On the morning of December 31, while Prime Minister Churchill was having a bath at the White House, the President came to him and suggested that the Joint Declaration carry the title, 'Declaration of the United Nations.' The distinguished bather agreed, and thus the term 'United Nations' came into being [2]." By the end of 1942 twenty-nine nations had signed the declaration, and in the next year fifteen more states joined the United Nations.

The U.S. Department of State set a committee in motion at the very outbreak of war to study the consequences of peace. In Washington one committee soon branched into another; memorandum was piled upon memorandum, each urging the need for a future international organization to guarantee world peace. With rare skill and fortunate insight the United States Congress and the American people were gradually introduced to the idea of participating in some council to safeguard all nations from aggression, for, above all, a new world order would depend upon the great arsenal of democracy. The dire experience of America's snub to the League of Nations ominously lurked in the background.

ORIGINS OF THE UNITED NATIONS

By 1943 military events had outdistanced political arrangements among the Allies. Cooperation between the U.S.S.R. and the Western Powers, however, was epitomized when Moscow announced the dissolution of the Communist International (Comintern) on 22 May 1943. Two months later Benito Mussolini resigned, signaling an early end to the Italian campaign. The crowded minutes of the war ticked insistently toward an hour of political decision on the future organization of the world. Roosevelt and Churchill, unable to persuade Stalin to attend a top-level conference, had met in Quebec in August 1943 and, among other agreements, affirmed their desire to see a new international organization created for the maintenance of international peace. The United States House of Representatives on 21 September 1943 lent further support to the participation of America in such an organization by voting 360 to 29 in favor of the Fulbright resolution [3].

In the meantime the Soviet press had intimated that a conference of foreign ministers, if not chiefs of state, might prove fruitful. The United States and Great Britain snapped at this suggestion to reach an accord with Russia on a number of uneasy military and political issues. On 19

October 1943 the Moscow Conference, attended by Anthony Eden for Great Britain, Cordell Hull for the United States, and V. Molotov for the U.S.S.R., began. Out of the travail of this meeting the United Nations was born.

Pressing matters on measures of war against Germany, including a statement on Hitlerian atrocities, the democratization of Italian government, and the future of Austria were discussed at Moscow, but the most significant achievement for the history of international organization was the Declaration of Four Nations on General Security by which the United States, the Soviet Union, the United Kingdom, and China—at the insistence of the United States—recognized "the necessity of establishing at the earliest practicable date a general international organization, based on the principle of sovereign equality of all peace loving states, large and small, for the maintenance of international peace and security [4]."

Through all the vicissitudes of the ensuing eighteen months of war, two fundamental principles of the organization first proposed at Moscow remained: that it would seek the maintenance of international peace and security and that it would be based upon the sovereign equality of all peace-loving states. Both these phrases were incorporated in the very first articles of the Charter of the UN, leaving no doubt as to the continuity of the new organization with the League of Nations as a device for bringing independent states together to collaborate on preserving international peace.

THE DRAFTING OF THE CHARTER

Dumbarton Oaks. At the Teheran Conference of December 1943 which brought President Roosevelt, Prime Minister Churchill, and Premier Stalin together for the first time, future peace plans were only sketched in a single grand flourish. The three leaders declared that they would seek the cooperation of all nations dedicated to the elimination of tyranny, slavery, intolerance, and oppression, welcoming them, "as they may choose to come, into a world family of Democratic Nations." Much more conclusive was the secret agreement to launch a "second front" against Germany through France in May 1944 (delayed until June) which, in time, doomed Hitler to defeat and brought the first rainbow of peace. Meanwhile, however, the U.S. Department of State had been continuously planning the structure which the new world organization might take. Although both Roosevelt and Churchill first leaned toward a regional organization of the world, perhaps capped by a small world council, the views of men like Isaiah Bowman, Norman Davis, Myron C. Taylor, James C. Dunn, Benjamin Cohen, Stanley Hornbeck, Harley A. Notter, Green

Hackworth, and Leo Pasvolsky under the supervision of the U.S. Secretary of State eventually prevailed in favor of a universal organization [5]. By spring of 1944 the United States had shaped a rough draft of the proposed international organization for initial discussion. With sound diplomacy Cordell Hull submitted this draft to three outstanding independent Americans, Charles Evans Hughes, John W. Davis, and Nathan L. Miller (two of them Republicans!), for review. Thereafter he fastidiously arranged conferences on the proposals with a subcommittee of the powerful Senate Foreign Relations Committee headed by Tom Connally and Arthur H. Vandenberg while he kept the House of Representatives informed through its majority and minority party leaders as well as the key men of the Foreign Affairs Committee. On 30 May 1944 the United States notified Great Britain and the Soviet Union that it was ready to proceed with informal talks on the proposed security organization and conversations actually began on August 21 at Dumbarton Oaks, Washington, D.C.

During the summer London, Moscow, and Washington exchanged their drafts on the international organization which, because of many informal notes and conversations, roughly paralleled each other in foreseeing a small executive Council, an Assembly of all member nations, and an international Secretariat. The Russian draft, however, would have shunted economic and social matters from the planned security organization to another agency; both the British and the Russians assigned a less important place to the Assembly than the Americans, and they looked longingly at establishing an international air force; the United States sought a permanent seat on the Council for Brazil, and Russia asked that all sixteen republics of the U.S.S.R. be admitted to membership in the organization; President Roosevelt thought that the Assembly ought to meet in a different city of the globe each year, while the Council would alternate its sessions between the Azores and the Hawaiian Islands!

Dexterity of negotiations and patient compromises by all three wartime allies enabled the conferees at Dumbarton Oaks to conclude their work by the end of September. In view of the fact that Russia was not at war with Japan, Great Britain and the United States consulted separately with China; on 9 October 1944 the proposals for a general international organization agreed to by all four powers were released to the public with much fanfare [6].

The Yalta Conference. Three major items had been deliberately cut from further discussion at the Dumbarton Oaks Conference: first, the British (and the U.S. Joint Chiefs of Staff) had strenuously opposed the injection of the colonial issue and the disposition of mandates from the League of Nations; second, Russia had persisted in advocating membership in the Assembly for all sixteen Soviet republics; and, third, the Anglo-

American plea that a party to an international dispute be excluded from voting on the issue in the Council had been sharply rejected by the Russians. Only another top-level conference, therefore, among the three chiefs of state could resolve these differences before assembling the allied nations to draft a charter upon which the Great Powers were essentially agreed. With great fortitude, President Roosevelt in the last year of his life traveled halfway around the world to join Marshal Stalin, who refused to leave the borders of the Soviet Union, and Prime Minister Churchill at Yalta in the Crimea on 4 February 1945.

At this moment the inner walls of Hitler's Nazi bastion had begun to crumble, and the Yalta Conference considered the future of a prostrate Germany and its liberated satellites, reparations, the role of France, and the government of Poland. Most secretly, Russia was offered concessions in China for her promise to enter the war against Japan soon after the defeat of Germany. But the crowning achievement for international organization was reached, first, when Russia agreed that a party to a dispute should be excluded from voting in the Council *where the Council is simply recommending a pacific mode of settlement;* second, when the United States accepted the idea of admitting Byelorussia and the Ukraine to separate membership in the new organization, plainly giving the U.S.S.R. three votes; and, third, when Great Britain conceded further discussion on territorial trusteeship—limited, however, to existing mandates of the League of Nations and territories detached from Germany, Italy, or Japan. The Big Three then fixed the date of 25 March 1945 for the inauguration of a conference in the United States to consider the Dumbarton Oaks Proposals supplemented by the Yalta protocols on the international organization as the basis for the Charter of the UN [7].

The San Francisco Conference. Whereas the Covenant of the League of Nations had been drafted along with the peace terms for Germany in 1919, the proponents of the UN deliberately met before the Second World War had ended. San Francisco played host to a scintillating, teeming international conference unsurpassed in the twentieth century. Fifty governments addressed 260 delegates to the task of writing a charter which would guarantee world peace and security. These delegates, moreover, were surrounded by no less than 1,400 assistants and aided by a secretariat of over 1,000 people. From the scattered surfaces of the earth reporters, photographers, and commentators converged by the thousands upon the Golden Gate city to relay to waiting millions the picture of great states studiously engaged in the collective enterprise of fashioning world order.

The Dumbarton Oaks Proposals of the four sponsoring states (France had demurred an invitation to act as a sponsor) with the Yalta protocol formed the nucleus of an elaborate agenda. The actual work of clarifying, adding, and amending the bare statements devolved upon four commissions: (*a*) general provisions, (*b*) General Assembly, (*c*) Security Council, and (*d*) International Court of Justice, further subdivided into twelve committees. Subsequently the final texts, guided by a steering and executive committee, received the approval of at least two-thirds of the plenary sessions.

Although the instant success of the Conference and, indeed, the UN itself could only be assured by the unanimity of the powerful sponsors, smaller nations did not hesitate to chisel or varnish the articles set before them with an impressive democratic exuberance. Bold ideas and bolder structures were introduced with lines of rhetoric designed to enliven the gaunt phrases of the Dumbarton Oaks Proposals. At times the zealous deliberations of the delegates, added to other Conference notices, records, and correspondence, piled up a million sheets of mimeograph paper in a single day [8].

For two milling months the hard-working delegations scrutinized every chapter and article of the proposals set before them by the Great Powers. Sentence by sentence, word by word, the committees and commissions either revamped the articles or hammered their grudging approval until on 26 June 1945 the Charter of the UN was completed. At the last session of the Conference Field Marshal Smuts [9] of the Union of South Africa, a living link between the drafting of the Covenant of the League of Nations and the UN Charter, said:

Our Charter is not a perfect document by any means. It is full of compromises over very difficult and tangled problems. But at least it is a good, practical, workmanlike plan for peace—a very real and substantial advance on all previous plans for security against war. It provides for a peace with teeth; for a united front of peace-loving peoples against future aggressors; for a united front among the great powers backed by the forces of the smaller powers as well. It provides also for lesser combinations for prompt defense on a regional or local basis. And it provides for central organization and direction of the joint forces for peace.

The UN opened the second period of collaboration in the history of international organization, for by origin, by principle, by structure, and by operational code the UN continued the trail-blazing endeavors of the League of Nations to maintain peace through collective international action. Both organizations emerged from a world clawed by war and sickened by the horror that drove millions into economic misery and moral collapse. Both organizations valiantly attempted to reconcile the virtues of national independence and sovereignty with the patent need for a supernational force to rebuff arrogance and destroy aggression. Both organizations took shape through multilateral treaties open to other members of the international community. The Covenant of the League of Nations began, "The High Contracting Parties," while the Charter of the UN ends, "The states signatory to the present Charter . . . will become original members of the United Nations on the date of deposit of their respective ratification."

THE STRUCTURE AND PURPOSES OF THE UNITED NATIONS

The six organs of the UN grew out of both the Concert of Europe and the League of Nations. The idea of a select council of great states to manage vital security problems, as seen through the nineteenth-century international conferences, has been supplemented in the twentieth century by the democratic notion of an assembly of all states, large and small, to make petitions and recommendations which, by force of opinion, also determine international issues. The UN Charter, therefore, provides for, *first*, a General Assembly which, like the Assembly of the League, includes all members of the organization. Each member is entitled to one vote. There are some modifications in the role of the General Assembly of the UN from the Assembly of the League, but essentially its function as a world forum and world conscience is retained.

The Council of the League of Nations has been transformed to the *second* organ of the UN, the Security Council, which has "primary responsibility for the maintenance of international peace and security." While the Council of the League began with the representatives of the Principal Allied and Associated Powers as permanent members, that is, the chief victors of the First World War, the Security Council gives permanent seats to the United States, the United Kingdom, the Soviet Union, France, and China, the victorious coalition of the Second World War.

The *third* organ of the UN is the International Court of Justice. With growing faith in the endurance of international organizations, the Dumbarton Oaks Proposals merely clipped the word "permanent" from the respected Permanent Court of International Justice which had been associated with the League for twenty-five years. Joining the UN now signifies *ipso facto* adherence to the Statute of the Court.

Finally, the League had dispelled all lingering doubt as to the necessity of a permanent secretariat. The *fourth* organ of the UN, the Secretariat, had been proposed at Dumbarton Oaks with little question; the San Francisco Conference, though debating the term of the Secretary-General, the number of his deputies, and the role of the chief administrative officer, never challenged the necessity for an international civil service.

Thus the UN entered its career with four organs directly evolved by the League of Nations. With slight mutations caused by the slide of power and the expansion of their responsibilities, the General Assembly, the Security Council, the International Court of Justice, and the Secretariat of the UN are lusty, lineal descendants of the League.

But the smaller states at San Francisco, consulted on the Dumbarton Oaks Proposals, wanted more than just a cold security organization. They added a preamble to the Charter, for instance, which resounded with the phrases "to reaffirm faith in fundamental human rights," "to promote social progress and better standards of life," and "to employ international machinery for the promotion of the economic and social advancement of all peoples." They insisted, therefore, upon two additional organs for the UN: the Economic and Social Council and the Trusteeship Council. Even here League footprints led the way. As the League was gradually numbed by the aggression of Japan in 1931 and Italy in 1935, a sincere effort was made to prop up the League's prestige by strengthening its economic and social activities. The Council of the League had appointed a small, distinguished committee, headed by Stanley Bruce, to study the further development of the economic-social activities of the League, particularly in view of the United States interests in these fields. On 22 August 1939 the Bruce committee recommended a new Central Committee for Economic and Social Questions with power to nominate personnel, control the budget, and supervise the programs of the technical organizations and committees of the League. Ten days later, however, at dawn and without any preliminary warning, Adolf Hitler began his brutal assault upon Poland. The Second World War had started. Plans for the postwar organization, however, kept the idea of a central coordinating agency for economic-social affairs, and the Dumbarton Oaks Proposals had included an Economic and Social Council. But "in its first draft it was a somewhat anemic document" and the delegates at San Francisco transformed it into "a full-blooded document which should carry to the peoples of the world a hope that in the days to come wars cannot only be prevented by force, but the conditions which make wars possible will themselves be gradually removed [10]." Thus, the Economic and Social Council took its place as the *fifth* organ of the UN.

Mandates over dependent peoples under the surveillance of a permanent international organization were also the invention of the League of Nations. Mandates had been handled by a ten-member Permanent Mandates Commission abetted by a section of the Secretariat. During the planning of the UN, the U.S. Department of State had ardently urged the inclusion of the trusteeship principle, but the Dumbarton Oaks Proposals had postponed a decision on the matter. The San Francisco Conference on its own accord established the *sixth* major organ of the UN, the Trusteeship Council. Said Lord Cranborne [11] of the British delegation:

The chapter on Trusteeship . . . is in some ways . . . the most remarkable achievement of the Conference . . . the Trusteeship Committee had nothing, merely a blank sheet of paper. On this it had to write a complete and balanced chapter, covering the whole of a vast and complicated subject. That this should have been achieved in the course of a few short weeks is no mean feat.

With the Economic and Social Council and the Trusteeship Council raised to the level of major organs, the UN Charter stood girded and ready to meet the challenge of a strenuous international life. The time for reminiscence upon the mournful ghost of the League of Nations had ended. On 10 January 1946 the General Assembly met in London to organize itself, elect the nonpermanent members of the Security Council and the Economic and Social Council, and then joined with the Security Council in selecting the judges of the International Court of Justice and the Secretary-General. Since no territories had been entrusted to the UN at this time, the Trusteeship Council was not formed until two months later. A tentative budget of $21,500,000 with a capital fund of $25,000,000 based upon contributions of the member states finally launched the UN into solvency. On 8 April 1946 the Assembly of the League of Nations disbanded itself, transferring its assets, including the buildings at Geneva, to the UN.

The UN did not begin auspiciously. Six months after the first session of the General Assembly, Secretary-General Trygve Lie asked, "Has the United Nations succeeded in capturing the imagination and in harnessing the enthusiasm of the peoples of the world?" and replied, "I, for one, do not feel that it has done so in the degree that might be hoped for." He emphasized that the UN was not designed to perform the functions of a peace conference. Indeed, the Charter specifically acknowledged that the governments primarily responsible for the defeat of the Axis powers in the Second World War would determine the peace terms. Furthermore, the Secretary-General maintained that the UN was not equipped to act as a referee among the Great Powers. "I appeal . . . especially to those Powers with special rights and obligations under the Charter, to ponder the dangers to which I have called attention and to exert every effort to overcome them [12]." With this grim preface the UN has struggled for eight years, carrying on its mission despite the bitter dregs left by the Second World War, the deep cleavages between the views of the Soviet Union and those of the United States, and the ever-ready cynicism of international politics.

THE GENERAL ASSEMBLY

Sixty nations of the world have joined the UN. As a meeting place for global opinion, therefore, the General Assembly is unexcelled. The General Assembly may discuss any question or any matter within the scope of the UN Charter. It may, moreover, make recommendations to members of the UN or the Security Council or both, not only on economic and social matters but also on the settlement of an international dispute—provided that the Security Council is not exercising its functions in respect to the dispute.

The Charter provides that the General Assembly meet in annual session on the third Tuesday in September, but constitutional practice which has so deftly molded the history of all international organizations has already extended the meetings of this plenary organ of the UN. In addition to the regular annual sessions, sometimes divided into two, even three, parts, the General Assembly has met in special sessions; in 1947 it instituted the Interim Committee of the General Assembly. The object of American and British policy, in view of the Soviet Union's perverse minority position in the Security Council and its ability to veto virtually any substantive recommendation, was to transfer some action to a standing committee of the General Assembly, a committee which would meet between the sessions of the main body of the UN. This committee, to consist of all members of the UN and with no veto in voting, was designed to assist the General Assembly in all questions referred to it and especially to help the General Assembly make recommendations for the *peaceful* adjustment of a dispute where the Security Council was not "exercising the functions assigned to it." Although the Soviet bloc protested vigorously against the Interim Committee and steadfastly refused to participate in its work as encroachments upon the functions of the Security Council, the General Assembly renewed the mandate of the Interim Committee in 1948 and in 1949 practically gave it a permanent status. Because the "Little Assembly," as the Interim Committee has been styled, works without the Soviet bloc, its effectiveness is questionable, but it has pointed to the need for some standing body of the General Assembly, meeting between sessions, to carry out the burdensome job of making preliminary studies and recommendations for international problems which may arise at any time.

To assist in discussing matters relating to peace and security or in making recommendations to its own members and the Security Council, the General Assembly can establish subsidiary organs. In consequence, the several political frays of the opening years of the UN have evoked special commissions of the General Assembly charged with a particular investigation. At the first special session of the General Assembly in April 1947 at Flushing Meadow, New York, a committee of eleven states, purposely excluding the Great Powers, was created to investigate and report on the issue of Palestine between Jews and Arabs. At its second regular session in October–November 1947 the General Assembly brought two more special commissions into being: one to observe and help carry out a resolution that Albania, Bulgaria, and Yugoslavia should do nothing to abet the guerrillas harassing the Greek government; the other to arrange elections in Korea for a national government while witnessing the withdrawal of all occupation troops. In December 1948, with an independent Israel at war with Egypt, Syria, Lebanon, Iran, and Jordan, the General Assembly appointed a conciliation commission. In 1949 the General Assembly, loaded with the responsibility of disposing of the former Italian colonies of Libya and Eritrea, established two more commissions for these territories. Another commission of the General Assembly went to work in 1951 to investigate conditions for holding free elections in Germany, and on 22 December 1952 a good offices commission was appointed to assist in the negotiations between India and the Union of South Africa on the treatment of Indians in South Africa [13].

The exact success of each of these "political" commissions of the General Assembly is rather difficult to gauge. Events outside the UN have sometimes carried their work along like a chip upon a flooded brook. The Palestine conciliation commission, for instance, did not solve the partition of that country, but its vigilance in offering conciliation between Arabs and Jews has dampened excessive chauvinism and given the parties a sound basis for negotiation. The Balkans commission did not close the Albanian, Bulgarian, or Yugoslav frontiers to the Greek guerrillas, but again it spoke loudly for the UN and kept world attention focused on a tinderbox of war. The commission for Libya successfully brought that territory into existence as a sovereign state, and the commission for Eritrea approved the federation of that territory with Ethiopia. On the other hand, the commission to investigate conditions for holding free elections in Germany was not allowed to operate in the Soviet zone of occupation and simply disbanded in 1952, while the government of the Union of South Africa refused to recognize the good offices commission to aid her relations with India in 1953. The Korean commission, finally, remained in Korea as a watchdog after the Republic of Korea had been constituted by UN action. This commission fortunately verified on 24 June 1950 an aggression which led to the most sensational act of international collaboration in the history of international organization. As forces from north Korea drove across the thirty-eighth parallel at the Republic of Korea, the commission, composed of Australia, China, El Salvador, France, India, the Philippines, and Syria, reported [14]:

Commission met this morning 1000 hours and considered latest reports on hostilities and results direct observation along parallel by UNCOK military observers ending 48 hours before hostilities began. Commission's present view on basis this evidence is, first, that judging from actual progress of operations northern regime is carrying out well-planned, concerted, and full-scale invasion of South Korea, second, that South Korean forces were deployed on wholly defensive basis in all sectors of the parallel, and third, that they were taken completely by surprise as they had no reason to believe from intelligence sources that invasion was imminent.

On the basis of this report the Security Council recommended that the UN furnish the assistance to the Republic of Korea necessary to restore international peace in the area, and since October 1950 the General Assembly has been represented by the UN Commission for the Unification and Rehabilitation of Korea.

All decisions on "important" questions in the General Assembly require a two-thirds majority of those present and voting—especially recommendations with respect to the maintenance of international peace and security. Such decisions speak for the whole organization and morally bind all members. Yet on more than one occasion in its brief history the states have simply ignored the declarations of the General Assembly. For example, a General Assembly resolution in 1946 asking all members to recall their ambassadors and ministers plenipotentiary from Madrid in view of Franco's fascist government received feeble compliance. Four years later some twenty members of the UN were maintaining ambassadors and ministers plenipotentiary in Madrid. Similarly, a General Assembly resolution in 1950, backed by an advisory opinion of the International Court of Justice, urged the Union of South Africa to place the former mandates of the League of Nations under the United Nations trusteeship system, meanwhile submitting reports on the administration of the territory and allowing petitions to the United Nations from its inhabitants. Repeated appeals to the Union of South Africa have not won compliance.

The most unsettling feature of the checkered history of the General Assembly thus far has been the antagonism of the U.S.S.R. and its satellites to most other members of the UN partial to views of the United States. With monotonous regularity, in committees and plenary session, Russia, Byelorussia, the Ukraine, Poland, and Czechoslovakia have voted as a monolith, cold to compromises and vituperative against all opposition. The work of the Interim Committee and all the special political committees has been vitiated by the denunciation and noncooperation of a state in the very first rank of power.

As a permanent minority, moreover, the U.S.S.R. and its satellites have not only impugned most acts of the UN but have loudly resisted the encroachment of the General Assembly upon Security Council functions—where the single dissenting vote of Russia can block all decisions. Contrariwise the Western Powers, blocked in the Security Council, have attempted to emphasize the role of the General Assembly where no veto obtains. After creating the Interim Committee in 1947, the General Assembly adopted on 3 November 1950 the Uniting for Peace Resolution by a vote of 52 to 5 of the Soviet bloc—with India and Argentina abstaining. This resolution, introduced by the United States delegation, empowers the General Assembly to meet in emergency session within twenty-four hours and make recommendations to the members of the UN for collective measures to maintain international peace and security—including the use of armed forces—if the Security Council *because of a lack of unanimity among the permanent members* fails to discharge its responsibility. The resolution, furthermore, established a peace observation commission of fourteen members, including the five Great Powers, as a permanent investigating committee for troubled areas of the world and recommended that member states maintain elements within their national forces which could promptly be made available for service as UN units. Finally, the resolution set up a Collective Measures Committee (without the Soviet Union), somewhat reminiscent of the League's Coordination Committee, whose function was to formulate a plan for the application of sanctions against an aggressor.

The Uniting for Peace Resolution was, of course, complementary to the circumstances and conduct of the Korean action of the UN. The attempt to give the General Assembly a greater responsibility for security and peace reflects the basic division of the Great Powers within the Security Council. It is still open to debate whether such a transfer of function will prove the wisest course in the development of the UN. Fortunately there is no question as to the concern of the General Assembly for economic, social, administrative, and legal matters.

In addition to its ability to discuss and recommend in the field of economic and social international cooperation, the General Assembly elects the entire Economic and Social Council and part of the Trusteeship Council, receives their reports and recommendations, approves agreements placing nonstrategic trust territories under the UN, and approves the budget of the entire UN. The general administration of the organization as well as the promotion of the progressive development of international law lie within the purview of the General Assembly. To facilitate this multitude of duties, the General Assembly operates through six main committees:

1. Political and Security.
2. Economic and Financial.
3. Social, Humanitarian, and Cultural.
4. Trusteeship.
5. Administrative and Budgetary.
6. Legal.

An *ad hoc* committee shares the burden of political issues with the first committee while the General Committee, comprising the President of the Assembly, the seven vice-presidents, and the chairmen of the six main committees, completes the administrative structure [15].

THE ECONOMIC AND SOCIAL COUNCIL

The eighteen members of the Economic and Social Council are elected by the General Assembly for a term of three years. The period of membership is staggered in such a way, however, that six members are elected each year. No state is a permanent member of the Council, and each state has one vote. Decisions are made by a majority of those present and voting. Although the General Assembly can elect any eighteen members of the UN to the Economic and Social Council, it invariably takes into account the larger interests of the Great Powers in economic-social matters and also strives for geographical-cultural diversification.

Under the authority of the General Assembly the Economic and Social Council strives to promote higher standards of living, the solution of international economic, social, and health problems, cultural cooperation, and a universal respect for human rights. To implement such a stupendous undertaking, the Economic and Social Council since its first session on 23 January 1946 has created twelve commissions which have a marked affinity with certain sections, committees, and commissions of the League of Nations:

1. Economic, Employment and Development Commission.
2. Transport and Communications Commission.
3. Statistical Commission.
4. Commission on Human Rights.
5. Commission on the Status of Women.
6. Social Commission.
7. Commission on Narcotic Drugs.
8. Fiscal Commission.
9. Population Commission.

In addition to these nine functional commissions, the Economic and Social Council makes use of three regional commissions to facilitate economic reconstruction by raising economic activity and encouraging trade in specific areas:

10. Economic Commission for Europe.
11. Economic Commission for Asia and the Far East.
12. Economic Commission for Latin America.

In his sixth annual report to the General Assembly in 1951 the Secretary-General remarked that "despite ever growing difficulties in the political sphere, the United Nations has pursued with undiminished vigor" the international economic and social objectives outlined in the Charter. The long list of studies and publications processed by the Economic and Social Council—with the aid of the Department of Economic Affairs in the Secretariat—would have staggered the imagination of the pioneers in international organization. How else could one obtain such objective and comprehensive works as *World Economic Report, National and International Measures for Full Employment, Review of International Commodity Problems, Public Finance Surveys, International Tax Agreements, Statistical Yearbook, Demographic Yearbook, Yearbook of International Trade,* and *Yearbook of Human Rights,* to cite but a few studies of the UN.

This profusion of paper work, moreover, has been accompanied by several spurs to international organization itself: the Economic and Social Council convened the conference and recommended the constitution of the World Health Organization which absorbed the League of Nations Health Organization and the Office International d'Hygiène Publique; it established the committee which proposed the International Refugee Organization to cope with the problems of the thousands of refugees left in the wake of the Second World War. The Economic and Social Council recommended to the General Assembly the creation of the International Children's Emergency Fund; it drew attention to the need for an international bill of human rights and assisted in the adoption of the Universal Declaration of Human Rights as well as the drafting of a covenant to ensure such rights by international law. Responsibility for powers once exercised by the League of Nations over international traffic in dangerous drugs, women and children, and obscene publications fell upon the Economic and Social Council; it initiated the study of technical assistance to underdeveloped countries which, since July 1950, has expanded into a program involving 25 million dollars annually, almost 1,600 experts of 61 nationalities having been sent to 55 different countries, with no less than 527 projects in existence or completed, and about 2,700 officials from 70 governments having received fellowship aid to study development techniques in some 45 states [16].

Never intended as an operating agency, although it became involved in policy making for the children's fund and technical assistance, the Economic and Social Council pursues its objectives by means of studies, reports, and recommendations with respect to international economic, social, and cultural matters to the General Assembly, the members of the UN, and the specialized agencies concerned. One facet of its work is the stimulation of international conventions necessary to the welfare of mankind. Another vital part of its operation has been to graft several independent, nonpolitical, international organizations to the body of the UN. While the League of Nations had proposed that all existing international bureaus and commissions be placed under its direction, the lack of universal membership in the League (*e.g.*, the United States) and the habitual resistance of independent agencies to controls undermined the plan of the Covenant. The UN Charter started afresh. It provided that the various international agencies for economic, social, cultural, health, and related purposes "shall be brought into special relationship with the United Nations."

The Economic and Social Council was empowered to negotiate agreements with such "specialized agencies," defining the terms upon which they might affiliate with the UN, subject to the approval of the General Assembly. On 16 February 1946 the Economic and Social Council appointed a committee to approach the International Labor Organization, the United Nations Educational, Scientific, and Cultural Organization, the Food and Agricultural Organization, the International Monetary Fund, and the International Bank for Reconstruction and Development. An agreement with the International Civil Aviation Organization entered into force on 13 May 1947; later the Economic and Social Council began negotiations with the Universal Postal Union, the International Telecommunication Union, and the World Meteorological Organization. By the middle of 1950 eleven agreements between the United Nations and the specialized agencies were in force.

All public agencies are marked by the bombast of ambitious bureaucrats and the torment of empire building; international administrations are no exception to the rule. The challenge to the UN has been to control the proliferation of functions and personnel of the specialized agencies, weeding out eager, empty projects and putting genuine talents to their most efficient use. To eliminate duplication of projects and puncture the inflation of both budgets and personnel is no mean task, especially since each of the specialized agencies owes its existence to a separate multilateral treaty, not to the compact binding the UN together. The agreements between the UN and the specialized agencies, therefore, are intended to review and coordinate the various endeavors in the international economic-social field. Representatives of the specialized agencies may participate in the Economic and Social Council, the Trusteeship Council, or even the General Assembly in a consultative capacity—and vice versa. There is a reciprocal obligation to include items on their agenda when proposed by a specialized agency or an organ of the UN. The UN may make recommendations to the specialized agencies which are bound to report annually on their work to the UN. By exchanging information and documents with the UN, making use of common statistical and administrative services, and maintaining similar standards of personnel recruitment, pay, and other conditions of employment, the specialized agencies can make the most efficient use of their resources. In the interests of economy all agreements, save those of the International Bank for Reconstruction and Development and the International Monetary Fund, have required the specialized agencies to confer with the UN in the preparation of their administrative budgets and to transmit them annually for examination by the General Assembly.

An imaginative program of technical assistance for underdeveloped areas of the world, moreover, has been initiated by the UN and five of its specialized agencies: International Labor Organization, Food and Agriculture Organization, UNESCO, and World Health Organization. No less than fifty governments in the summer of 1950 pledged their support to the generous idea of exchanging knowledge between well-to-do and poor countries by sending missions of experts in labor, agriculture, education, air navigation, and health to countries in need of them and thereby teaching techniques of increasing productivity. Novel to the history of international organization, the technical-assistance program, coordinated by the Technical Assistance Board and Technical Assistance Committee in the UN, focuses another ray of hope on the difficult task of raising living standards in backward economic areas of the world [17].

The results of review and coordination of the work of the specialized agencies by the UN have frequently been disappointing. Some of the agencies are much older than the UN and cling to their long-standing prerogatives. All the agencies are constituted by separate multilateral conventions, and the membership in each of them is by no means uniform. The governments that send delegates to specialized agencies and the UN have shown no great zeal in coordinating their instructions; the governments have sometimes voted for programs either overburdening the resources of the specialized agency or duplicating the work of another agency. Nor have the secretariats been exempt from the inclination to build little empires or the disinclination to cooperate with other staffs. For all these complaints, however, the fact remains that for the first time in history coordination among virtually autonomous international agencies is being attempted under the guidance of a universal international organization for peace. The inertia of tradition is heavy. But no one can deny that the task of efficient public administration severely taxes the energy and wit of national governments on their domestic scene with results often quite discouraging. How much more onerous is the job of bringing international organizations into an efficient and harmonious relationship with each other. The defects of the international system have been glaringly highlighted in the course of the history of international organization; now the remedies of collaboration are available if the nations of the world choose to use them.

THE TRUSTEESHIP COUNCIL

In both the Trusteeship Council and the International Court of Justice the sterling work of the League of Nations endures. By making the Trusteeship Council a separate organ and filling its membership with the five Great Powers, the trustee nations, and an equal number of nontrustee states, the UN has recognized its grave responsibility for dependent peoples. Various "strategic" territories, however, have been removed from the surveillance of the Trusteeship Council. The work of the Council under the aegis of the General Assembly is chiefly administrative and is more fully described in Chapter 7, "Twentieth-century Society and International Administration."

THE INTERNATIONAL COURT OF JUSTICE

The International Court of Justice looks back solemnly to the score of years wisely used by the Permanent Court of International Justice. Except for minor changes, the Statute guiding the International Court of Justice is the same as the document laboriously drawn in 1920 by the committee of jurists advisory to the Council of the League of Nations. By the end of 1945 the UN Charter with the Statute of the International Court of Justice had been ratified by all the signatory states at San Francisco, and on 6 February 1946 the fifteen judges began their terms of office. Two months later, without ceremony, the final session of the League of Nations dissolved the Permanent Court of International Justice [18].

The International Court is open to all member states of the UN, for it is the principal judicial organ of the UN. Other states, not members of the UN, however, may become parties to the Statute of the International Court by special agreement with the UN, under conditions to be determined by the General Assembly upon the recommendation of the Security Council. States involved in a dispute, moreover, which are not members of the UN or parties to the Statute of the Court may have recourse to the Court subject to conditions laid down by the Security Council for the case before the Court. The chief function of the International Court of Justice is to decide in accordance with international law such disputes as are submitted to it by states. Treaties frequently confer jurisdiction upon the Court in the event of disagreement upon the interpretation or application of the treaty. The Court may also give advisory opinions on any legal question upon the request of the General Assembly or the Security Council, while other organs and specialized agencies of the UN may be authorized by the General Assembly to request advisory opinions.

But accessibility to the high judicial standards of the Court does not compel use of its facilities, however excellent. In both 1946 and 1947 the International Court met only thirty-one days of the year. Not until 22 May 1947 was the first case transmitted to the Court when Albania, not a member of the UN or a party to the Statute, was accused by the United Kingdom of international negligence in failing to notify the maritime world of mines lying within her territorial waters. As a result two British destroyers and forty-five lives were lost. At the end of almost three years of litigation a judgment for damages of $2,365,000 was granted by the Court in favor of the United Kingdom. Still the record of the Court seemed dismal. Manley O. Hudson [19] wrote:

Almost four years have passed since the Court was reorganized for the resumption of its judicial activity in the changed international order. In this period it has had before it but one contested case; and it has handed down two advisory opinions. In these three cases it has functioned smoothly and efficiently, and significant contributions have been made to the Court's jurisprudence. This is hardly a satisfactory record of usefulness, however. Compared with the first four years of the Court, from 1922 to 1925 the record is somewhat disheartening . . .

The next year, however, 1950, saw two new judgments and four advisory opinions on the Court's calendar; in 1951 the Court handed down another judgment, gave two advisory opinions, and issued three orders; and in 1952 the Court judged three more cases.

With a cautious tread among the veritable pitfalls of international adjudication, the Court has warily decided that (*a*) Colombia should not continue giving asylum to a Peruvian political refugee in her embassy at Lima, but otherwise Colombia was under no obligation to surrender him to Peru! (*b*) Norway had not violated international law in fixing her territorial waters at a distance of four miles out to sea—calculated from base lines drawn between forty-eight points on the mainland, islands, and rocks along the coast; (*c*) France cannot discriminate against American imports into Morocco or interfere with American consular jurisdiction over American citizens under treaties of 1787 and 1836 and the Act of Algeciras in 1906; (*d*) the Court does not possess jurisdiction over the Anglo-Iranian oil dispute, for the concession of 1933 was not a treaty and the Iranian government's declaration to recognize the compulsory jurisdiction of the Court on situations and facts arising out of treaties applies only to treaties after 1932; and (*e*) the United Kingdom was obliged to submit to arbitration its difference with Greece on the validity of a Greek citizen's claim (N. E. Ambatielos) under procedures referred to in a treaty of commerce and navigation of 1886 and supplemented by a declaration of 1926. The Court, upon the request for an advisory opinion, has counseled the UN that (*a*) it has the capacity to sue a state for damages done to a UN agent; (*b*) members of the UN should not make their consent to the admission of an applicant to the UN contingent upon conditions other than those expressly provided in the Charter; and (*c*) the Union of South Africa, acting alone, does not have the competence to alter the status (mandate) of the Territory of Southwest Africa.

Other judgments, opinions, orders, and applications have gone into the records of the Court as it has slowly edged its way into the stream of international disputes. Fifteen reasonable men, sitting in The Hague and tied to an annual budget of $600,000, relying solely upon respect for international law to enforce their judgments, are not the powerful guardians of world justice one might wish. It is lamentable, also, that scarcely more than half the members of the UN have agreed to the compulsory jurisdiction of the Court over all their international legal disputes with each other, and even of this number many have put crippling reservations in their agreements. Yet the Court exists and thrives. For thirty-one years it has contributed its mite to the golden collection of international organizations seeking peace with justice.

THE SECRETARIAT

The Secretariat is the mortar which holds the loose bricks of the UN together. Headed by a Secretary-General, who was nominated by the Security Council and elected by the General Assembly in 1946 for a term of five years, the international civil service has shuffled its temporary headquarters from London to the Sperry Gyroscope Building at Lake Success and, finally, to its gleaming glass and marble abode in New York City. About 700 members of the Secretariat work at the UN office at Geneva where the headquarters of the Economic Commission for Europe, the Narcotic Drugs Supervisory Board, the Permanent Central Opium Board, and the High Commissioner for Refugees are located. Starting with about 1,200 people, the UN Secretariat has expanded to some 4,000 men and women working at a score of posts throughout the world. When combined with a like number employed by the specialized agencies, the total represents the most spectacular increase in history of personnel in the full-time service of international organization.

The Charter is deliberately laconic on the composition and duties of the Secretariat. Only the Secretary-General, as the chief administrative officer, is named, and he recruits such additional staff as the organization requires on as wide a geographical basis as possible. All members of the international corps pledge allegiance to the UN and impartial conduct of their duties regardless of national interest. Center of the entire system and in many ways the personification of the UN itself is the Secretary-General, who may sit in any meeting of any organ and who is enjoined to report annually on the work of the UN. The Secretary-General, moreover, has been granted a power unusual in the tradition of international bureaucracy, for he may call the attention of the Security Council to any matter which in his opinion threatens international peace and security.

With alacrity the first Secretary-General, Trygve Lie of Norway, impressed his quasi-political responsibilities upon the UN: not only has the annual report gone beyond a cool account of the organization's activities to positive admonitions on the state of the world, but the Secretary-General has made recommendations, given legal opinions inescapably partial, and developed a "Twenty-year Programme for Achieving Peace through the United Nations" which he personally presented in 1950 to the President of the United States and the prime ministers of France, the United Kingdom, and the Soviet Union in a dramatic round-the-world flight [20]. Inevitably such activities nettled the Great Powers—although the Secretary-General had granted no special favors: in 1946 he agreed with the Soviet Union that the Iranian dispute should be removed from the Security Council's agenda; in 1950 he also buttressed the argument of the Soviet Union which had demanded the replacement of the Nationalists of Chiang Kai-shek by the Communists of Mao Tse-tung in the UN when he said that "the government which has the power should represent China in the United Nations." Yet his vigorous support of the UN action to repel the Korean aggression stung the Soviet Union into vetoing his renomination by the Security Council late in 1950. Since the United States threatened to block any other candidate, the General Assembly seized the situation and voted 46 to 5 to continue Trygve Lie in office until 1 February 1954, but on 10 November 1952 the Secretary-General tendered his resignation to the General Assembly. Five months later the Security Council recommended Dag Hammarskjold, a Swedish civil servant and economist, to this key UN post; on 7 April 1953 he was elected by the General Assembly.

The Secretariat has been divided into departments, headed by assistant secretaries-general, which are designed to service the several organs, committees, and programs of the UN. While the Executive Office of the Secretary-General takes primary responsibility for the chores of the General Assembly itself, the Departments of (a) Security Council Affairs, (b) Economic Affairs, (c) Social Affairs, and (d) Trusteeship Affairs cling to the other major divisions of the UN. In addition, there is (e) a Legal Department, (f) a Department for Conferences and General Services, (g) a Department of Public Information, and (h) a Department of Administrative and Financial Services. The Technical Assistance Board, while not a department, has special functions and personnel of its own. During 1953 the General Assembly had under consideration a proposal of the Secretary-General to reorganize the Secretariat under three deputy secretaries-general rather than the eight assistant secretaries-general, drawing together for economy and efficiency (a) political and public affairs, (b) social and economic affairs, and (c) administrative and conference services, with legal matters being the direct concern of the Secretary-General [21].

The Legal Department attends the UN International Law Commission, which seeks the progressive development and codification of international law, and it maintains liaison with the International Court of Justice. Year by year it continues the registration and publication of treaties sent to it, and no treaty may be invoked before any organ of the UN without this formality. In a period of three recent years, for example, the Legal Department registered, filed, and recorded 1,372 treaties.

The sun never sets on a UN conference. Arranging thousands of meetings with hundreds of delegates in scores of countries and working in five official languages, the Department for Conferences and General Services has its hands full. In a single year the UN makes 15,000 travel or hotel reservations and drives its own cars a million miles. During one fiscal year the headquarters alone made 273 million impressions of documents. The Department of Public Information carries on all the functions of publicizing the UN through press, radio, film, and special services. Nineteen information centers in nineteen countries ranging from Russia to Liberia and Argentina to Pakistan encourage the dissemination of information about the UN. While all these activities may seem to be mere trappings, nevertheless they are the requisites of an international organization in the twentieth century which spreads its balm over the inflamed membranes of a distressed world. Some of the UN work is tediously repetitive; some of the quixotic projects are tilting at windmills; but the grain, not the chaff, counts upon the scales of achievement, and the Secretariat spends many long days and nights in the service of sixty nations seeking security through international organization.

Budgets are dull reading, but indispensable to administration. The Department of Administrative and Financial Services not only supervises the recruitment, training, and payment of UN personnel but also prepares the budget and spends the appropriations of the UN—as approved by the General Assembly. The entire annual budget of the UN would run the national government of the United States for about six hours. Each year a little more than 40 million dollars has been collected from all the contributions of the member states, and to this is added miscellaneous income (interest from deposits, donations, sale of UN stamps, etc.), totaling about 6 million dollars in 1953.

The fact that the United States has paid more than one-third of all the UN cost year after year and that the contributions of the United States, Great Britain, and France have accounted for more than half the budget is a cause of grave concern. While the UN has striven to adjust this disproportion, declaring that after 1 January 1954 no member shall contribute more than one-third of the UN expenses in any one year, nevertheless real contrasts among the national wealths of the member states, not to mention a reluctance to increase their shares on the part of some members, give a lopsided look to the assessments. Fifty-three of the sixty states of the UN in 1953 contributed less than $900,000 each to the organization's budget. In terms of per capita income, the assessment of the United States for 1953 of 35.12 per cent of the budget may be just, but it does raise serious questions of influence upon the UN itself in personnel, program, and so forth.

It should be noted, however, that the UN is primarily a means of collaborating on projects, not operating them. The combined budgets of the specialized agencies like the Food and Agriculture Organization, the International Labor Organization, the International Refugee Organization, UNESCO, and the World Health Organization have added up to another 40 million dollars. The moneys of the International Monetary Fund and the International Bank for Reconstruction and Development for stabilizing currencies and making large-scale international loans stand entirely separate from UN appropriations. The United Nations Korean Reconstruction Agency, the United Nations Relief and Works Agency for Palestine Refugees in the Near East, and the United Nations International Children's Emergency Fund have all operated from funds or services contributed voluntarily by governments, public or private organizations, and individuals. Finally, the technical-assistance program uses a special account entirely separate from the regular UN budget [22].

From the administrative point of view, the steady standardization of pay scales, leave policies, and opportunities for retirement pensions among the international bureaus is a help in attracting the able personnel so necessary to the improvement of international organizations. The UN and its specialized agencies do offer good salaries, increments for merit and service, generous vacation and sick leaves, and reasonable pensions. Working for an international organization is still hazardous: national governments have been suspicious of the loyalty of their citizens engaged in the services of international organizations, appropriations fluctuate from year to year according to the economy, the interest, or even the caprice of the subscribing states, and there are the difficulties of living away from home, perhaps sacrificing a political career in the national government. Needless to say, international organizations are more vulnerable to the upsets of a world war than domestic agencies. Despite these disadvantages, a competent international civil service is in the making, profiting from the League's experience and going on to serve in new, difficult tasks. With deserved pride, for example, the Secretary-General reported that during 1951 over 40 per cent of the UN personnel had chalked up at least five years of continuous service.

Another interesting development in the history of international organization is the extension of privileges and immunities to international organizations by national governments. Before 1920 the grant of privileges and immunities to international organizations was rare, but since then the members and agents of international river commissions, reparations commissions, organs created by the Paris peace treaties after the First World War, and other agencies have enjoyed privileges and immunities from the state in which they were working or traveling. Under the League of Nations the higher officials were granted the immunities generally conferred upon the staff of a diplomatic mission by international law. The General Convention on the Privileges and Immunities of the United Nations provides for not only the inviolability of its premises, immunity of its assets and property from legal process, but exemption from direct taxes, customs duties, and import-export restrictions; it also extends such privileges and immunities as immunity from personal arrest; inviolability for all papers and documents; right to use codes and sealed bags for papers or correspondence; exemption from immigration restrictions, alien registration, or national-service obligations for themselves and their spouses; the same facilities for currency exchange accorded representatives of foreign governments; and privileges for their personal baggage to the representatives of members of the UN and to the Secretary-General and assistant secretaries-general *"while exercising their functions and during their journey to or from the place of meeting"* (italics added). Lesser officials of the UN are conceded lesser immunities under the Convention, to which most states, including the Soviet Union, have acceded. The United States has made a separate agreement with the UN in respect to the headquarters, representatives, and Secretariat which spells out more precisely the privileges and immunities of the UN under United States Federal, state, and local law, but it broadly complements the General Convention. These concessions by national governments to the UN and other international agencies recognize the importance of international organizations in the modern world and the necessity of allowing them to function without the hindrances which strict national jurisdiction might create [23].

As an inconspicuous yet important innovation of international organization, the growth of the UN field service should be noted. The assassination of Count Folke Bernadotte in Israel on 17 September 1948 while working for the UN as mediator between Arabs and Jews shocked the international community. The need for some protection of UN personnel in areas where international tension was great and local governments could not afford adequate security impelled the General Assembly fourteen months later to resolve upon a UN field service and panel of observers. The object was to provide trained personnel for rendering telecommunications, transport, and security services to field missions. Beginning with only ten men on 5 July 1950, the field service has schooled over a hundred "guards" in typing, radio transmission, maintenance of vehicles, first aid, and principles of security. Here stands no international army or international police, but a simple response of an international organization determined to carry out its responsibilities effectively. Inadvertently, perhaps, it has opened another fissure in the mountain of sovereignty by lessening—very slightly —the dependence of UN missions upon national services and protection. For the first time in history, at any rate, an international organization has trained its own personnel to be constantly on call to go anywhere in the world and help it perform its delicate duties—even to the point of carrying a pistol!

THE SECURITY COUNCIL

The Security Council has the primary responsibility of maintaining international peace and security. Nowhere in the world or ever in history has there been assembled such a potential for preventing international war. Upon the Security Council, by virtue of its exclusive membership and its constitutional power, rests the final responsibility for the success or failure of the UN as it is now constituted for keeping the peace. Although the General Assembly has attempted to seize the initiative in security matters when the Security Council has been frustrated by a veto of one of the Great Powers, not only does the Charter intend the Security Council to be the executive organ of the UN but it also recognizes that without Great

Power agreement the chances for success of the UN in repelling aggressions are very limited.

The Dumbarton Oaks Proposals had carefully sketched the membership of the Security Council to include the United States, the United Kingdom, the Soviet Union, China, and, "in due course," France with permanent seats, with six additional states to be elected by the General Assembly for a term of two years. Furthermore, the proposals asked that the Security Council be organized to function continuously and that each member of the Council be permanently represented at the headquarters of the UN. For more than a century statesmen had bewailed the lack of a continuous conference of the Great Powers to settle international squabbles promptly before governments used violence; in the solidarity of a wartime alliance the Great Powers in 1944 finally agreed. Because the Security Council was to be given primary responsibility for the maintenance of international peace and security, a burden that would certainly fall upon the broad shoulders of the United States, Russia, and Great Britain, each of the Great Powers insisted upon having a veto in any substantive decisions taken by the Council. The U.S.S.R. considered the principle of unanimity among them as inviolable. To a group of United States senators on 12 May 1944, moreover, Secretary of State Hull [24] said:

The veto power is in the document primarily on account of the United States. It is a necessary safeguard in dealing with a new and untried world arrangement . . . We should not forget that this veto power is chiefly for the benefit of the United States in light of the world situation and our own public opinion.

He added, however:

In all the discussion with my associates in postwar planning, two important conditions had been understood and repeatedly stated in connection with the veto. The first was that none of the permanent members of the Council would exercise its veto capriciously or arbitrarily . . . The second condition was that we were thinking largely of the application of the veto power to military or other means of compulsion.

The chief bone of contention between the Russians and the Anglo-American negotiators at Dumbarton Oaks on the voting principle was whether a member of the Security Council involved in a dispute should have the right to cast a vote on the issue. To the British and Americans this seemed contradictory to all rules of justice, so the question was left open for a top-level decision. At the Yalta Conference of February 1945, therefore, Stalin, Churchill, and Roosevelt compromised by agreeing that decisions of the Security Council on all substantive matters should be made "by an affirmative vote of seven members including the concurring votes of the permanent members," but where the Security Council is receiving a complaint or merely investigating a dispute or recommending *pacific procedures* for settling a dispute, the parties involved should abstain from voting. If the Security Council decides upon an interruption of economic relations, the rupture of communications, severance of diplomatic relations, or the use of armed force as a course of action, all members of the Security Council, even if parties to the dispute, have the right to vote.

The San Francisco Conference in April 1945 could not poach upon this preserve of the Great Powers. Without the concurrence of the most powerful states in the world upon a Security Council, there would have been no UN. The delegates did raise France to unequivocal membership in the Council and suggested that due regard be paid by the General Assembly to contributions to peace and geographic location in electing the nonpermanent members of the Security Council. Led by Australia, moreover, the small states tried to get the Great Powers to abandon their prerogative of veto, at least on decisions taken by the Security Council which only called upon the disputants to make use of commissions of conciliation, arbitration, the International Court of Justice, and so forth. On May 22 the little states addressed twenty-three questions to the big states about the exercise of the veto power. The giants patiently responded, but the essence of their claim to privilege in all decisions was blunt, that "in view of the primary responsibilities of the permanent members, they could not be expected . . . to assume the obligation to act in so serious a matter as the maintenance of international peace and security in consequence of a decision in which they had not concurred [25]." And so the matter has rested—almost.

POLITICAL DISPUTES BEFORE THE SECURITY COUNCIL

Unlike the dispassionate International Court of Justice, the Security Council has not lacked business since its first meeting on 17 January 1946. Through the smoke, particularly around the burning issue of the veto power, it is possible to make out a design in the management of the most crucial international disputes. For eight years five Great Powers joined by six other states elected by the General Assembly have argued and appealed, wheedled and threatened, proposed, opposed, and reposed in a Council watched by all governments of the world.

While evidence of sound decisions and happy solutions to disputes brought before this powerful panel of the UN seems woefully scant, some complaints have withered away with time and others have been settled in the shadow of the UN without drumming up the garrisons of the five continents: (*a*) The first complaint to come before the Security Council was the charge of Iran that the Soviet Union was interfering in the internal affairs of the nation, a situation which might have led to international friction. Although the Security Council did nothing except request the parties to negotiate their difference and although the Soviet Union sulkily boycotted the discussions after the Council refused to remove the item from its agenda, nearly all Russian troops withdrew from Iran within three and a half months from the date of the complaint. (*b*) Also in 1946 the complaint of the Syrian and Lebanese delegations to the UN against the presence of British and French troops in their countries came before the Security Council. Although the U.S.S.R. vetoed a simple resolution looking forward to the withdrawal of these forces, thereby legally voiding all action of the Security Council, the British and French soon retired their armies from Syria and Lebanon. (*c*) Probably the most serious threat to world peace during the adolescence of the Security Council occurred in 1948, when the Soviet Union closed all land communications between the United States–United Kingdom–French zones of occupation in Germany and their Berlin enclaves located within the Russian zone. The Western Powers presented their complaint to the Security Council on September 29, and once more in protest against the insertion of this item upon the agenda, the U.S.S.R. withdrew from the discussions. Nevertheless, negotiations between the Soviet Union and the United States continued informally and privately at the UN headquarters, so that on 4 May 1949 the Security Council was informed that a satisfactory agreement between the parties concerned had been reached on the Berlin question [26].

Other issues have been swept into convenient oblivion by the rush of circumstances. (*a*) On 8 July 1947 Egypt complained against the maintenance of British troops in the country against the will of the people. Three different resolutions with several amendments failed to obtain the required number of affirmative votes in the Security Council. Nothing more happened. (*b*) In the summer of 1948 Hyderabad, later supported by Pakistan, complained of violent intimidations by India. Although the Council voted 8 to 0 to place the matter on its agenda, a few weeks later the occupation and control of Hyderabad by Indian military forces was a *fait accompli*. Nothing more happened. (*c*) The United Kingdom asked the Security Council to consider its dispute with Iran over the nationalization of the British-controlled Anglo-Iranian Oil Company on 28 September 1951, since Iran had failed to comply with a temporary restraining order of the International Court of Justice. Iran denied the competence of the Security Council and maintained that any decision of the Court on this matter was not binding. After six weeks the Council adjourned debate until the International Court should rule on its own competence. Late in 1952 the International Court of Justice decided that it did not have jurisdiction over this case.

At times the Security Council has dropped the hot coal of a dispute into the open palms of the General Assembly. (*a*) Early in 1946 Poland and the Soviet Union called the attention of the Security Council to the activities of the Franco government in Spain as a menace to international peace and insisted that the Security Council keep the matter under its continuous observation. Later in the year, however, Poland asked that the Spanish question be removed from the agenda of the Security Council so that the General Assembly might make recommendations upon it. The Security Council concurred unanimously. (*b*) Acting upon the complaint of Greece, a commission of the Security Council in 1947 investigated alleged provocations along the frontiers of that nation by its Balkan neighbors. The majority of the commission found evidence of aid to Greek guerrillas by Yugoslavia, Bulgaria, and Albania, although not whitewashing the Greek record. When the Soviet Union disagreed with this report and vetoed a United States resolution which charged the three Greek neighbors with threats to the peace, the issue was removed from the purview of the Council and placed at the disposal of the General Assembly. (*c*) In the taut, tangled problem of Palestine the issue zigzagged back and forth between the cluttered desk of the Security Council and the noisy forum of the General Assembly. A special session of the General Assembly in May 1947 began the study of the future status of this League of Nations mandate riven by Jews and Arabs. A special committee, after arduous investigation, recommended—but not without substantial dissent —a partition of Palestine to the General Assembly in the fall of 1947. In consequence a five-man commission was appointed by the General Assembly to help implement the recommendations of partition under the guidance of the Security Council. With Arabs and Jews shooting each other, however, nothing but heavy sanctions or a display of UN force could ensure the partition. Two months after its appointment, the United Nations Palestine Commission beseeched the Security Council for help. After calling for a truce between Jews and Arabs, and appointing a truce commission of the resident consular officers of Belgium, France, and the United States, the Security Council requested the Secretary-General to convoke another special session of the General Assembly. The General Assembly responded by empowering a mediator, selected by the five Great Powers, to promote a peaceful adjustment of the situation. On that very day, 14 May 1948, the British terminated their mandate, Israel declared its independence, and full-scale war broke out in Palestine.

Even the innocuous or negative actions of the Security Council, saved by time or laterally passed to the General Assembly, have been anodynes for international peace. Furthermore, in a few instances real progress toward the quelling of international unrest can be attributed to the Security Council. (*a*) The mediator and the truce commission in Palestine kept pushing the Arabs and Jews for an armistice; although each side jealously guarded its own military advantages, the very presence of an international organization put a third party into the fray and afforded the enemies a ready means of negotiation. On 11 June 1948 a truce was secured and on July 7 it expired; on July 18 another truce was announced, but by October minor sorties had grown to large-scale fighting. New armistice negotiations arranged by the UN began in July 1949 on the isle of Rhodes; on 24 February 1950 Israel and Egypt signed a general armistice agreement soon followed by others between the Arab states and Israel. (*b*) In January 1947 the United Kingdom brought its complaint against Albania before the Security Council for failing to notify other nations of the floating mines in Albanian waters which caused the explosion of two British ships. Within three months, by a vote of 8 to 0, the Soviet Union and Poland abstaining, the Security Council recommended the immediate submission of the case to the International Court of Justice, where it was ultimately settled. (*c*) In the summer of 1947 both Australia and India called the Security Council's attention to the fighting between Republican forces and Dutch troops in Indonesia. With the aid of a committee of good offices a general standfast and cease-fire agreement was reached aboard the U.S.S. "Renville" in January 1948 by the Republic of Indonesia and the Netherlands. Eighteen political principles on future relationships between the two governments, however, proved more difficult to settle and hostilities again broke out in December. The Security Council kept pressing the Netherlands to stop its "police action" and release the arrested leaders of the Republican government. To the Indonesians the Security Council addressed a call to halt all guerilla activities. After several months of nerve-racking negotiation, the Security Council committee, renamed the United Nations Commission for Indonesia, succeeded in bringing the parties to a peaceful discussion; in November 1949 delegates of the Netherlands and the Republic of Indonesia arrived at a comprehensive political settlement in The Hague without further risk of bloodshed. (*d*) On 1 January 1948 India complained to the Security Council that Pakistan was supporting forces invading the states of Jammu and Kashmir. After hearing counter-charges by Pakistan, the Security Council voted 9 to 0 to establish a commission for investigation and report. In April the United Nations Commission for India and Pakistan was instructed to facilitate peace and order in the area by assuring the withdrawal of Pakistan elements and the reduction of Indian troops to the minimum necessary for law enforcement and by arranging a free plebiscite to determine whether the people wished to join India or Pakistan. Exactly one year after the complaint had been submitted to the Security Council the Commission succeeded in obtaining a cease-fire agreement between India and Pakistan. But details of the truce proved sticky. Without avail the Security Council appointed United States Admiral Nimitz to supervise a plebiscite and Canadian General McNaughton to mediate between India and Pakistan on troop withdrawals. In April the Commission's responsibilities were transferred to Sir Owen Dixon of Australia as UN representative, but five months later, after fruitless negotiations, he resigned. In the spring of 1951 Frank P. Graham of the United States, aided by the paper resolutions of the Security Council and a puny team of military observers, was selected to stand between the two glowering, embittered rivals for Kashmir, holding the heavy weight of peace by a single thread of international organization. Month after month and point by point he has tried to bring India and Pakistan to an agreement upon the demilitarization of the troubled area before holding a plebiscite. After two years of negotiation a final solution had not been reached in 1953, but neither had India or Pakistan made war upon the other.

THE KOREAN WAR AND INTERNATIONAL COLLABORATION

None of the foregoing decisions of the Security Council had recourse to sanctions for the settlement of the international dispute. But on 27 June 1950 the Security Council, in an act unprecedented in the entire history of international organization,

Having determined that the armed attack upon the Republic of Korea by forces from North Korea constitutes a breach of the peace,
Having called for an immediate cessation of hostilities . . .
Having noted from the report of the United Nations Commission that the authorities in North Korea have neither ceased hostilities nor withdrawn their armed forces to the 38th parallel and that urgent military measures are required to restore international peace and security,
Recommends that the Members of the United Nations furnish such assistance to the Republic of Korea as may be necessary to repel the armed attack and to restore international peace and security in the area [27].

Because the Soviet Union had refused to sit with the representative of the Chinese (Nationalist) government in the Security Council, one permanent member was absent when the historic vote was taken. Moreover, Yugoslavia dissented and Egypt later abstained. But the United States, the United Kingdom, France, Cuba, Norway, Ecuador, and later India all favored the resolution in the Security Council. The legality of the act under the terms of the Charter will ever remain moot. Clearly political consideration, the engine of change in every structure of law, had overridden the constitution laid down at San Francisco in 1945. To be sure, all the members of the Security Council had already acquiesced in regarding abstentions by the Great Powers as tantamount to the concurrence required by the Charter; furthermore, it could be argued that the absence of one permanent member from the Security Council, if not regarded as abstaining, could effectively terminate the functions of the Security Council and destroy the UN. But the crux of the matter was the attempt of an international organization, founded on the theory of Great Power unanimity, to deal with a violent dispute upon which the Great Powers themselves were angrily divided.

The United States rushed to the support of south Korea with land, sea, and air forces, and on 7 July 1950 was placed in charge of a UN command by the Security Council. The Soviet Union scathingly denounced the decisions of the Council by blaming south Korea for the aggression, maintaining that the war was civil, not international, and contending that the refusal to seat the Chinese (Communist) government rendered all acts of the Security Council illegal. Nevertheless forty-six states promptly affirmed the stanch decisions taken by the Security Council. At last international collaboration in the UN was put to the test of fire.

The governments of the smaller countries, mindful of the two crushing armadas of the United States and the Soviet Union, moved hesitantly into the uncharted waters of a UN crusade. To the Secretary-General's inquiry of 14 July 1950 on what assistance they could give, many members replied politely that the matter was "under consideration" or simply acknowledged receipt of the letter. When units of Communist China entered the battle on October 25, gradually increasing to more than a quarter of a million men by the end of the year, the UN line shuddered and fell back along the Korean peninsula. The UN Commanding General Douglas MacArthur reported to the Security Council on 31 January 1951 that ten nations had combat forces sustaining the heavy blows: Korea and the United States supplied over 90 per cent of the men supported by choice units of Australia, Greece, France, the Netherlands, the Philippines, Thailand, Turkey, and the United Kingdom [28]. Battered by terrible mass assaults of Chinese infantrymen the UN line dug in and held. Within the year fresh military contingents from the farthest corners of the earth landed in Korea. Speaking before the United States Congress on 22 May 1952 General Matthew Ridgway [29], who succeeded General MacArthur as UN Commander, said:

In the scant eighteen months beginning with that early July day in 1950 when those first few immortal riflemen and airmen saw the Communist aggressors over their guns and bomb sights, the 8th Army, comprising our own forces and those of the Republic of Korea, the British Commonwealth, Turkey, Greece, India, France, Ethiopia, Belgium, the Netherlands, Luxemburg, the Philippines,

Thailand, Denmark, Sweden, Norway, Colombia, and Italy, has left a record of fidelity, valor, and cooperation unsurpassed in all military history.

After thirty-seven months of hostilities which killed 72,500 UN personnel and wounded 250,000, an armistice was signed on 27 July 1953 between Lt. Gen. William K. Harrison for the UN and Lt. Gen. Nam Il for the Korean Peoples Army and the Chinese People's Volunteers at Panmunjom, Korea. The world's first collective action to repel aggression in which sixteen nations sent military forces to the UN command had closed a chapter, and the terms of the armistice looked forward to a political conference "to settle through negotiation" the future of Korea.

History may deal with the merits of the Korean War; history may record the conflicting national policies of the Soviet Union and the United States, the brutal struggle between Chinese and Chinese, Korean and Korean; history may even question the pretensions of international organization to solve a fundamental power rivalry between two great nations. But whatever qualification may eventually be pinned to the UN action in Korea, it was the first of its kind. Fifteen years before June 1950 only one member of the League of Nations had moved troops and none had fired a gun to resist the brazen aggression of Italy against Ethiopia. Not only did the UN receive offers from twenty-five governments for military assistance of one kind or another, but no less than forty-three states volunteered equipment and supplies—such as meat from Argentina, sugar and blood plasma from Cuba, a hospital ship from Denmark, rice from Ecuador, cod-liver oil from Iceland, opiates from Israel, a field-hospital unit with personnel from Italy and Sweden, a field-ambulance unit and jute bags from India, wheat from Pakistan, and blankets from Uruguay [30].

Five years after the high hopes of San Francisco the UN had been dragged down by the rankling division of the world into two ideologies and two armed camps. In Greece, Indonesia, Palestine, India, and South Africa, admonitions of the Security Council too often had gone unheeded. While the national interest of the United States opposed the subordination of Korea to the Soviet Union, the UN badly needed some demonstration that outright aggression would be swiftly condemned and repelled. Only a Great Power could have initiated such a faith-restoring deed.

The dismal record of the Security Council in regulating weapons of war had accounted in part for the low morale of the UN until the Korean aggression. Neither the Atomic Energy Commission, established in 1946, nor the Commission for Conventional Armaments, established in 1947, could bridge the ugly chasm between the Soviet Union and the Western Powers on the perennial issue of disarmament or the new, grisly threat of atomic warfare. A new Disarmament Commission composed of the members of the Security Council and Canada to prepare comprehensive and coordinated plans for the international control of all armaments and armed forces made little progress in 1952 and 1953. The Military Staff Committee of the Security Council, which was organized under Article 47 of the Charter and consists of the chiefs of staff of the five Great Powers or their representatives, was completely paralyzed after 1947. Even simple applications for membership to the UN submitted by Albania, Austria, Bulgaria, Ceylon, Finland, Hungary, Ireland, Italy, Jordan, Mongolia, Nepal, Portugal, Rumania, and other states were lost in the bitter division between the Great Powers. While the devastation of Korea, therefore, bears the curse of the bipolar world, it has finally needled an increasingly apathetic international organization into making a grave decision and assuming a momentous responsibility.

Since the passage of the Uniting for Peace Resolution by the General Assembly in 1950 the importance of the Security Council has been considerably undermined. Emanating from the circumstances of the UN action in Korea and the desire of the United States to rally as many nations of the world as possible against the aggression of the north Korean–Chinese forces without the frustrating veto of the Soviet Union in the Security Council, the resolution has considerably blurred the distinction between the General Assembly and the Security Council in security matters. During 1953 the Collective Measures Committee of the General Assembly was asked to suggest specific ways of encouraging preparatory collective-security action by states of the United Nations. Nevertheless the Security Council continues its work. It still has primary responsibility for the maintenance of international peace, partly for legal reasons, but chiefly because the inability of the UN to coerce one of the Great Powers without war is realistically reflected by the veto power in the Security Council.

THE UNITED NATIONS AND THE HISTORY OF INTERNATIONAL ORGANIZATION

The history of the UN, the second trial of international collaboration by a world organization for peace, has too many new pages for a seasoned analysis. The many facets of its international activities—in security matters, in economic, social, and cultural affairs—beggar an adequate description, and the mere account of its ever-proliferating conferences, commissions, and committees would make a dizzy array of details. But the continuity of the UN in many respects with the League of Nations gives the eight postwar years some perspective. For dependent and colonial peoples the UN has carried a beacon of hope and a plea for equality unknown to the past degradations of slavery and exploitation. For the improvement of mankind through international economic and social cooperation it has afforded new insights and bold projects captivating the imagination on the limitless possibilities of improving health, nutrition, employment, education, science, and morals through international organization. All these things enrich the soil and the climate of international peace and security. For the deadly quarrels of nation-states the UN has provided a means of accommodation, a permanent forum, and a permanent tribunal; it has offered to all disputants its good offices and has successfully driven every state, large or small, to the bar of world opinion. The UN is an international organization, not a world government: as such, it bumps along the twisting, rocky, perilous trail first opened in the nineteenth century. Given a pliable, multilateral treaty for a constitution, an expert international Secretariat, and the honest will of nation-states to work together for peace, the UN can make the twentieth century a golden era of civilization.

NOTES

1. Atlantic Charter. This and succeeding documents of recent American foreign policy referred to in this chapter have been conveniently collected and edited by F. O. Wilcox and T. V. Kalijarvi in *Recent American Foreign Policy, Basic Documents, 1941–1951,* New York, Appleton-Century-Crofts, 1952.

2. Cordell Hull, *Memoirs,* New York, Macmillan, 1948, 2 vols., Vol. II, p. 1124.

3. On 6 November 1943 the Senate passed the Connally resolution by a vote of 85 to 5 favoring the participation of the United States in a general international organization to maintain peace and security.

4. Wilcox and Kalijarvi, *op. cit.,* p. 9.

5. The most exhaustive study of policy planning in the U.S. Department of State in respect to the wartime conferences and the committees dealing with the proposed international organization is *Postwar Foreign Policy Preparation,* U.S. Department of State Publication 3580, 1949. See especially pp. 167–185, 270–338.

6. Many private organizations dedicated themselves to the study of future international organizations during this period. Two of the most notable were the Commission to Study the Organization of the Peace, directed by Clark M. Eichel-

berger, and the Universities Committee on Post-war International Problems, representing no less than forty major American universities. For a compilation of the many current remarks and criticisms of the Dumbarton Oaks Proposals by statesmen, publicists, and academicians, see R. E. Summers (ed.), *Dumbarton Oaks,* New York, H. W. Wilson, 1945.

7. For the Yalta Conference and its diplomacy, see two books by two former U.S. Secretaries of State, E. Stettinius, *Roosevelt and the Russians,* New York, Doubleday, 1949, and J. Byrnes, *Speaking Frankly,* New York, Harper, 1947, especially Chap. II. Text of the Crimean Conference, 4–11 February 1945, may be found in Wilcox and Kalijarvi, *op. cit.,* pp. 16–23.

8. The basic reference work for the San Francisco Conference on the United Nations is United Nations Information Organization, *Documents of the United Nations Conference on International Organization, San Francisco, 1945,* 1945, 15 vols. and index. See also U.S. Department of State, *The United Nations Conference on International Organization— Selected Documents,* Washington, 1946, for an excellent abridgment. G. L. Kirk and L. K. Chamberlain, "The Organiza-

tion of San Francisco Conference," *Political Science Quarterly,* Vol. 60 (September 1945), pp. 321–342, contains a short, lucid account of the management of the Conference. For a sound commentary on the UN Charter, analyzed article by article, see L. Goodrich and E. Hambro, *The Charter of the United Nations,* rev. ed., Boston, World Peace Foundation, 1949. Also see H. Kelsen, *Law of the United Nations,* New York, Library of World Affairs, 1950.

9. *The United Nations Conference on International Organization—Selected Documents,* p. 934.

10. Remarks of H. Evatt, Australian delegate, at the second meeting of Commission II, 11 June 1945, Doc. 909, in *The United Nations Conference on International Organization—Selected Documents,* p. 675.

11. *Ibid.,* p. 692.

12. United Nations, *Annual Report of the Secretary-General on the Work of the Organization,* Doc. A/65, 30 June 1946, pp. v–vi.

13. A valuable series of publications has been issued on each of the UN commissions by the UN under the title of *Organization and Procedure of the United Nations Commissions.* See also H. Field Haviland, *The Political Role of the General Assembly,* New York, Carnegie Endowment, 1951.

14. United Nations, Security Council, *Official Records,* Fifth Year, 474th Meeting, 27 June 1950, No. 16, p. 2. For a summary of events, United States policy, and UN action up to the Korean aggression, see *Background Information on Korea,* Report of the House Committee on Foreign Affairs, 81st Cong., 2d sess., 1950.

15. For more details on the structure and operations of the UN, consult United Nations, Secretariat, Department of Public Information, *Everyman's United Nations,* 4th ed., 1953, or such books as N. Bentwich and A. Martin, *A Commentary on the Charter of the United Nations,* New York, Macmillan, 1950; L. Larry Leonard, *International Organization,* New York, McGraw-Hill, 1951; J. Maclaurin, *The United Nations and Power Politics,* London, G. Allen, 1951; and A. Vandenbosch and W. N. Hogan, *The United Nations,* New York, McGraw-Hill, 1952.

16. *United Nations Bulletin,* Vol. 14, No. 2 (15 January 1953), p. 84. For the first year of the technical-assistance program, see United Nations, General Assembly, *Annual Report of the Secretary-General on the Work of the Organization, 1 July 1950–30 June 1951,* 1951, p. 131.

17. See United Nations, *Measures for the Economic Development of Underdeveloped Countries,* Doc. E/1986; ST/ECA/10, Report by a Group of Experts Appointed by the Secretary-General, 1951. For the technical assistance of the specialized agencies of the UN, see their annual reports to the General Assembly.

18. On the drafting of the Statute of the International Court of Justice, see *The International Court of Justice,* U.S. Department of State Publication 2491, 1946.

19. M. O. Hudson, "The Twenty-eighth Year of the World Court," *American Journal of International Law,* Vol. 44, No. 1 (January 1950), p. 36.

20. See United Nations, *Development of the Twenty-year Programme for Achieving Peace through the United Nations—Progress Report by the Secretary-General,* Doc. A/1902, 1951.

21. United Nations, Secretariat, *Organization of the Secretariat,* 8 June 1951, gives the full details of organization and responsibilities. See also S. M. Schwebel, *The Secretary-General of the United Nations: His Political Powers and Practice,* Cambridge, Harvard University Press, 1952.

22. See United Nations, *Information Annex II to Budget Estimates for the Financial Year 1952,* Doc. A/1812/Add. 1, 1951; United Nations, Advisory Committee on Administrative and Budgetary Questions, *Second Report of 1951 to the General Assembly,* Doc. A/1853; and United Nations, *Report of the Committee on Contributions,* Doc. A/1859, 1951, for details about UN money.

23. The General Convention on the Privileges and Immunities of the United Nations and the United Nations–United States Agreement Regarding the Headquarters of the United Nations are conveniently reprinted, in the main, in H. Briggs (ed.), *The Law of Nations,* 2d ed., New York, Appleton-Century-Crofts, 1952.

24. Hull, *op. cit.*, pp. 1662, 1663.

25. Text of the "Statement by the Delegations of Four Sponsoring Governments on Voting Procedure in the Security Council" from Goodrich and Hambro, *op. cit.*

26. The brief accounts of the cases brought before the Security Council were taken from three sources: United Nations, Security Council, *Official Records;* United Nations, General Assembly, *Report of the Security Council to the General Assembly;* and *Annual Report of the Secretary-General on the Work of the Organization.*

27. United Nations, Security Council, *Official Records,* Fifth Year, 474th Meeting, 27 June 1950, No. 16, p. 4.

28. *United States Policy in the Korean Conflict,* U.S. Department of State Publication 4263, September 1951, covers the July 1950–February 1951 period in detail.

29. *The New York Times,* 23 May 1952.

30. See United Nations, General Assembly, *Report of the Collective Measures Committee,* 1951, 1952, for the Korean measures of collective security. For additional documentation, see *The United States and the Korean Problem, Documents 1943–1953,* U.S. 82d Cong., 2d Sess., Doc. 74, 1953.

APPENDIX 6

I. *Bibliographical Notes on the United Nations*

To study the United Nations in detail one should properly begin with *United Nations Documents Index* which, since January 1950, has been issued monthly and which indexes by subject all the documents and publications of both the UN and the specialized agencies received by the UN Library. Publications of the Food and Agriculture Organization, the International Civil Aviation Organization, the International Refugee Organization, the Interim Commission of the International Trade Organization, the International Telecommunication Organization, the United Nations Educational, Scientific and Cultural Organization, the Universal Postal Union, the World Meteorological Organization, the International Labor Organization (since January 1951), the International Bank and the International Monetary Fund (since November 1951), and the World Health Organization (since November 1951), as well as the major organs of the UN, can be conveniently located in this index. All documents of the UN itself may be obtained from the International Documents Service, Columbia University Press, New York. The means of obtaining publications of the specialized agencies are indicated in the *United Nations Documents Index*.

For a general and exhaustive survey of the work of the entire UN in any year one can consult the *Yearbook of the United Nations*, while to keep up to date on UN activities one can read the biweekly *United Nations Bulletin*. An extremely useful summary of the year's performance of the UN, shorn of excessive detail, is the *Annual Report of the Secretary-General on the Work of the Organization* made to the General Assembly.

Not only the Secretary-General but the Security Council, the Economic and Social Council, and the Trusteeship Council report annually to the General Assembly on their work. These reports, therefore, are excellent recitals of what has transpired within each of the major organs of the UN during the year. For further details, one can pursue the *Official Records* of the Security Council, the Economic and Social Council, the Trusteeship Council, and the General Assembly.

Special statistical, economic, financial, social-welfare, public-information, and legal studies, issued by the various departments of the Secretariat, may be located through the *United Nations Documents Index*.

The International Court of Justice at The Hague issues most notably its *Reports of Judgments, Advisory Opinions, and Orders* soon after a judgment, opinion, or order is delivered, as well as an annual *Index* to these dicta. Furthermore, the *Yearbook* summarizes the work of the Court in each twelve-month period.

II. *Major Organs of the United Nations, 1945*

The General Assembly   All the members of the UN in annual or special sessions.
The Security Council   Six members of the UN elected by the General Assembly

for two years (three new members being elected each year) and the five permanent members: the United States, the Soviet Union, the United Kingdom, France, and China.

The Secretary-General   Appointed by the General Assembly upon the recommendation of the Security Council for a term regulated by the General Assembly.

The Economic and Social Council   Eighteen members of the UN elected by the General Assembly, six members elected each year for a term of three years.

The Trusteeship Council   The permanent members of the Security Council, members administering trust territories, and as many other members as needed to balance trustee states with nontrustee states to be elected by the General Assembly for three-year terms.

The International Court of Justice   Up to four persons, no two of whom may be nationals of the same state, may be nominated by national groups in the Permanent Court of Arbitration or national groups appointed by their governments for this purpose. The fifteen members of the Court, no two of whom may be nationals of the same state, are elected by the General Assembly and the Security Council independent of each other, an absolute majority being required in each election. Five judges are elected every three years for nine-year terms.

III. *Key Articles of the United Nations Charter Pertaining to the Security Council*

ARTICLE 27

1. Each member of the Security Council shall have one vote.

2. Decisions of the Security Council on procedural matters shall be made by an affirmative vote of seven members.

3. Decisions of the Security Council on all other matters shall be made by an affirmative vote of seven members including the concurring votes of the permanent members; provided that, in decisions under Chapter VI, and under paragraph 3 of Article 52, a party to a dispute shall abstain from voting.

CHAPTER VI

Pacific Settlement of Disputes

ARTICLE 33

1. The parties to any dispute, the continuance of which is likely to endanger the maintenance of international peace and security, shall, first of all, seek a solution by negotiations, enquiry, mediation, conciliation, arbitration, judicial settlement, resort to regional agencies or arrangements, or other peaceful means of their own choice.

2. The Security Council shall, when it deems necessary, call upon the parties to settle their dispute by such means.

ARTICLE 34

The Security Council may investigate any dispute, or any situation which might lead to international friction or give rise to a dispute, in order to determine whether the continuance of the dispute or situation is likely to endanger the maintenance of international peace and security.

ARTICLE 35

1. Any Member of the United Nations may bring any dispute, or any situation of the nature referred to in Article 34, to the attention of the Security Council or of the General Assembly.
2. A state which is not a Member of the United Nations may bring to the attention of the Security Council or of the General Assembly any dispute to which it is a party if it accepts in advance, for the purposes of the dispute, the obligations of pacific settlement provided in the present Charter.
3. The proceedings of the General Assembly in respect of matters brought to its attention under this Article will be subject to the provisions of Articles 11 and 12.

ARTICLE 36

1. The Security Council may, at any stage of a dispute of the nature referred to in Article 33 or of a situation of like nature, recommend appropriate procedures or methods of adjustment.
2. The Security Council should take into consideration any procedures for the settlement of the dispute which have already been adopted by the parties.
3. In making recommendations under this Article the Security Council should also take into consideration that legal disputes should as a general rule be referred by the parties to the International Court of Justice in accordance with the provisions of the Statute of the Court.

ARTICLE 37

1. Should the parties to a dispute of the nature referred to in Article 33 fail to settle it by means indicated in that Article, they shall refer it to the Security Council.
2. If the Security Council deems that the continuance of the dispute is in fact likely to endanger the maintenance of international peace and security, it shall decide whether to take action under Article 36 or to recommend such terms of settlement as it may consider appropriate.

ARTICLE 38

Without prejudice to the provisions of Articles 33 to 37, the Security Council may, if all the parties to any dispute so request, make recommendations to the parties, with a view to a pacific settlement of the dispute.

CHAPTER VII

*Action with Respect to Threats to the Peace, Breaches of the
Peace, and Acts of Aggression*

ARTICLE 39

The Security Council shall determine the existence of any threat to the
peace, breach of the peace, or act of aggression and shall make recommendations, or decide what measures shall be taken in accordance with Articles 41
and 42, to maintain or restore international peace and security.

ARTICLE 40

In order to prevent an aggravation of the situation, the Security Council may,
before making the recommendations or deciding upon the measures provided
for in Article 39, call upon the parties concerned to comply with such provisional measures as it deems necessary or desirable. Such provisional measures
shall be without prejudice to the rights, claims, or position of the parties concerned. The Security Council shall duly take account of failure to comply with
such provisional measures.

ARTICLE 41

The Security Council may decide what measures not involving the use of
armed force are to be employed to give effect to its decisions, and it may call
upon the Members of the United Nations to apply such measures. These may
include complete or partial interruption of economic relations and of rail, sea,
air, postal, telegraphic, radio, and other means of communication, and the
severance of diplomatic relations.

ARTICLE 42

Should the Security Council consider that measures provided for in Article 41
would be inadequate or have proved to be inadequate, it may take such action
by air, sea, or land forces as may be necessary to maintain or restore international peace and security. Such action may include demonstrations, blockade,
and other operations by air, sea, or land forces of Members of the United
Nations.

ARTICLE 43

1. All Members of the United Nations, in order to contribute to the maintenance of international peace and security, undertake to make available to
the Security Council, on its call and in accordance with a special agreement
or agreements, armed forces, assistance, and facilities, including rights of
passage, necessary for the purpose of maintaining international peace and security.

2. Such agreement or agreements shall govern the numbers and types of
forces, their degree of readiness and general location, and the nature of the
facilities and assistance to be provided.

3. The agreement or agreements shall be negotiated as soon as possible on the initiative of the Security Council. They shall be concluded between the Security Council and Members or between the Security Council and groups of Members and shall be subject to ratification by the signatory states in accordance with their respective constitutional processes.

Article 44

When the Security Council has decided to use force it shall, before calling upon a Member not represented on it to provide armed forces in fulfillment of the obligations assumed under Article 43, invite that Member, if the Member so desires, to participate in the decisions of the Security Council concerning the employment of contingents of that Member's armed forces.

Article 45

In order to enable the United Nations to take urgent military measures, Members shall hold immediately available national air force contingents for combined international enforcement action. The strength and degree of readiness of these contingents and plans for their combined action shall be determined, within the limits laid down in the special agreement or agreements referred to in Article 43, by the Security Council with the assistance of the Military Staff Committee.

Article 46

Plans for the application of armed force shall be made by the Security Council with the assistance of the Military Staff Committee.

Article 48

1. The action required to carry out the decisions of the Security Council for the maintenance of international peace and security shall be taken by all the Members of the United Nations or by some of them, as the Security Council may determine.

2. Such decisions shall be carried out by the Members of the United Nations directly and through their actions in the appropriate international agencies of which they are members.

Article 49

The Members of the United Nations shall join in affording mutual assistance in carrying out the measures decided upon by the Security Council.

Article 50

If preventive or enforcement measures against any state are taken by the Security Council, any other state, whether a Member of the United Nations or not, which finds itself confronted with special economic problems arising from the carrying out of those measures shall have the right to consult the Security Council with regard to a solution of those problems.

ARTICLE 51

Nothing in the present Charter shall impair the inherent right of individual or collective self-defense if an armed attack occurs against a Member of the United Nations, until the Security Council has taken the measures necessary to maintain international peace and security. Measures taken by Members in the exercise of this right of self-defense shall be immediately reported to the Security Council and shall not in any way affect the authority and responsibility of the Security Council under the present Charter to take at any time such action as it deems necessary in order to maintain or restore international peace and security.

CHAPTER VIII

Regional Arrangements

ARTICLE 52

1. Nothing in the present Charter precludes the existence of regional arrangements or agencies for dealing with such matters relating to the maintenance of international peace and security as are appropriate for regional action, provided that such arrangements or agencies and their activities are consistent with the Purposes and Principles of the United Nations.

2. The Members of the United Nations entering into such arrangements or constituting such agencies shall make every effort to achieve pacific settlement of local disputes through such regional arrangements or by such regional agencies either on the initiative of the states concerned or by reference from the Security Council.

3. This Article in no way impairs the application of Articles 34 and 35.

ARTICLE 53

1. The Security Council shall, where appropriate, utilize such regional arrangements or agencies for enforcement action under its authority. But no enforcement action shall be taken under regional arrangements or by regional agencies without the authorization of the Security Council, with the exception of measures against any enemy state.

2. The term enemy state as used in paragraph 1 of this Article applies to any state which during the Second World War has been an enemy of the signatory of the present Charter.

ARTICLE 54

The Security Council shall at all times be kept fully informed of activities undertaken or in contemplation under regional arrangements or by regional agencies for the maintenance of international peace and security.

IV. *Competence of the International Court of Justice, Articles 34, 35, 36 of the Statute*

ARTICLE 34

1. Only states may be parties in cases before the Court.

2. The Court, subject to and in conformity with its Rules, may request of public international organizations information relevant to cases before it, and shall receive such information presented by such organizations on their own initiative.

3. Whenever the construction of the constituent instrument of a public international organization or of an international convention adopted thereunder is in question in a case before the Court, the Registrar shall so notify the public international organization concerned and shall communicate to it copies of all written proceedings.

ARTICLE 35

1. The Court shall be open to the states parties to the present Statute.

2. The conditions under which the Court may be open to other states shall, subject to the special provisions contained in treaties in force, be laid down by the Security Council, but in no case shall such conditions place the parties in a position of inequality before the Court.

3. When a state which is not a Member of the United Nations is a party to a case, the Court shall fix the amount which that party is to contribute towards the expenses of the Court. This provision shall not apply if such state is bearing a share of the expenses of the Court.

ARTICLE 36

1. The jurisdiction of the Court comprises all cases which the parties refer to it and all matters especially provided for in the Charter of the United Nations or in treaties or conventions in force.

2. The state parties to the present Statute may at any time declare that they recognize as compulsory ipso facto and without special agreement, in relation to any other state accepting the same obligation, the jurisdiction of the Court in all legal disputes concerning:

a. the interpretation of a treaty;

b. any question of international law;

c. the existence of any fact which, if established, would constitute a breach of an international obligation;

d. the nature or extent of the reparation to be made for the breach of an international obligation.

3. The declaration referred to above may be made unconditionally or on condition of reciprocity on the part of several or certain states, or for a certain time.

4. Such declarations shall be deposited with the Secretary-General of the

United Nations, who shall transmit copies thereof to the parties to the Statute and to the Registrar of the Court.

5. Declarations made under Article 36 of the Statute of the Permanent Court of International Justice and which are still in force shall be deemed, as between the parties to the present Statute, to be acceptances of the compulsory jurisdiction of the International Court of Justice for the period which they have to run and in accordance with their terms.

6. In the event of a dispute as to whether the Court has jurisdiction, the matter shall be settled by the decision of the Court.

V. *Uniting for Peace Resolution of the General Assembly, 3 November 1950*

The General Assembly, . . .

A

1. Resolves that if the Security Council, because of lack of unanimity of the permanent members, fails to exercise its primary responsibility for the maintenance of international peace and security in any case where there appears to be a threat to the peace, breach of the peace, or act of aggression, the General Assembly shall consider the matter immediately with a view to making appropriate recommendations to Members for collective measures, including in the case of a breach of the peace or act of aggression the use of armed force when necessary, to maintain or restore international peace and security. If not in session at the time, the General Assembly may meet in emergency special session within twenty-four hours of the request therefor. Such emergency special session shall be called if requested by the Security Council on the vote of any seven members, or by a majority of the Members of the United Nations;

2. Adopts for this purpose the amendments to its rules of procedure set forth in the annex to the present resolution;

B

3. Establishes a Peace Observation Commission which for the calendar years 1951 and 1952, shall be composed of fourteen Members, namely: China, Colombia, Czechoslovakia, France, India, Iraq, Israel, New Zealand, Pakistan, Sweden, the Union of Soviet Socialist Republics, the United Kingdom of Great Britain and Northern Ireland, the United States of America and Uruguay, and which could observe and report on the situation in any area where there exists international tension the continuance of which is likely to endanger the maintenance of international peace and security. Upon the invitation or with the consent of the State into whose territory the Commission would go, the General Assembly, or the Interim Committee when the Assembly is not in session, may utilize the Commission if the Security Council is not exercising the functions assigned to it by the Charter with respect to the matter in question. Decisions to utilize the Commission shall be made on the affirmative vote of two-thirds of the members present and voting. The Security Council may also utilize the Commission in accordance with its authority under the Charter;

4. Decides that the Commission shall have authority in its discretion to appoint sub-commissions and to utilize the services of observers to assist it in the performance of its functions;

5. Recommends to all governments and authorities that they co-operate with the Commission and assist it in the performance of its functions;

6. Requests the Secretary-General to provide the necessary staff and facilities, utilizing, where directed by the Commission, the United Nations Panel of Field Observers envisaged in General Assembly resolution 297 B (IV);

C

7. Invites each Member of the United Nations to survey its resources in order to determine the nature and scope of the assistance it may be in a position to render in support of any recommendations of the Security Council or of the General Assembly for the restoration of international peace and security;

8. Recommends to the States Members of the United Nations that each Member maintain within its national armed forces elements so trained, organized and equipped that they could promptly be made available, in accordance with its constitutional processes, for service as a United Nations unit or units, upon recommendation by the Security Council or General Assembly, without prejudice to the use of such elements in exercise of the right of individual or collective self-defence recognized in Article 51 of the Charter;

9. Invites the Members of the United Nations to inform the Collective Measures Committee provided for in paragraph 11, as soon as possible of the measures taken in implementation of the preceding paragraph;

10. Requests the Secretary-General to appoint, with the approval of the Committee provided for in paragraph 11, a panel of military experts who could be made available, on request, to Member States wishing to obtain technical advice regarding the organization, training, and equipment for prompt service as United Nations units of the elements referred to in paragraph 8;

D

11. Establishes a Collective Measures Committee consisting of fourteen Members, namely: Australia, Belgium, Brazil, Burma, Canada, Egypt, France, Mexico, Philippines, Turkey, the United Kingdom of Great Britain and Northern Ireland, the United States of America, Venezuela and Yugoslavia, and directs the Committee, in consultation with the Secretary-General and with such Member States as the Committee finds appropriate, to study and make a report to the Security Council and the General Assembly not later than 1 September 1951, on methods, including those in Section C of the present resolution, which might be used to maintain and strengthen international peace and security in accordance with the Purposes and Principles of the Charter, taking account of collective self-defence and regional arrangements (Articles 51 and 52 of the Charter);

12. Recommends to all Member States that they cooperate with the Committee and assist it in the performance of its functions;

13. Requests the Secretary-General to furnish the staff and facilities necessary

for the effective accomplishment of the purposes set forth in Sections C and D
of the present resolution. . . .

VI. *Scale of Assessments against Members of the United Nations for
Expenses of the Organization*

State	1952	1953
Afghanistan	0.08	0.08
Argentina	1.62	1.45
Australia	1.77	1.75
Belgium	1.35	1.37
Bolivia	0.06	0.06
Brazil	1.62	1.45
Burma	0.15	0.13
Byelorussian S.S.R.	0.34	0.43
Canada	3.35	3.30
Chile	0.35	0.33
China	5.75	5.62
Colombia	0.37	0.35
Costa Rica	0.04	0.04
Cuba	0.33	0.34
Czechoslovakia	1.05	1.05
Denmark	0.79	0.78
Dominican Republic	0.05	0.05
Ecuador	0.05	0.04
Egypt	0.60	0.50
El Salvador	0.05	0.05
Ethiopia	0.10	0.10
France	5.75	5.75
Greece	0.18	0.19
Guatemala	0.06	0.06
Haiti	0.04	0.04
Honduras	0.04	0.04
Iceland	0.04	0.04
India	3.53	3.45
Indonesia	0.60	0.60
Iran	0.40	0.33
Iraq	0.14	0.12
Israel	0.17	0.17
Lebanon	0.06	0.05
Liberia	0.04	0.04
Luxembourg	0.05	0.05
Mexico	0.65	0.70
Netherlands	1.27	1.25
New Zealand	0.50	0.48
Nicaragua	0.04	0.04
Norway	0.50	0.50
Pakistan	0.79	0.79
Panama	0.05	0.05
Paraguay	0.04	0.04

State	1952	1953
Peru	0.20	0.18
Philippines	0.29	0.39
Poland	1.36	1.58
Saudi Arabia	0.08	0.07
Sweden	1.73	1.65
Syria	0.09	0.08
Thailand	0.21	0.18
Turkey	0.75	0.65
Ukrainian S.S.R.	1.30	1.63
Union of South Africa	0.90	0.83
U.S.S.R.	9.85	12.28
United Kingdom	10.56	10.30
United States	36.90	35.12
Uruguay	0.18	0.18
Venezuela	0.32	0.35
Yemen	0.04	0.04
Yugoslavia	0.43	0.44
Total	100.00	100.00

CHAPTER 7 *Twentieth-century Society*
and International Administration

The avenue of international organization, fringed by the piked fences of security, often hides its serpentine course from the panorama of history. But the sections of the road are clearly marked by the innumerable international administrative agencies for economic and social cooperation which, strung together, trace a long street of progress.

Impelled by the curious dialectic of history which opened every crack of the earth to the invention of the industrial revolution while enclosing peoples in national compartments, the first trials of international economic and social cooperation proved successful, encouraged other attempts, and led to a virtual maze of twentieth-century agencies. How difficult it would be for the fathers of the first Rhine River Commission to recognize as their offspring the present-day Permanent International Association of Navigation Congresses with its 36 government members, approximately 400 affiliated corporations, 1,950 individuals, including both the Central Commission for the Rhine and the Suez Canal Commission [1]! But the noisy advance of natural and social science in the twentieth century has constantly echoed the fiction of national boundaries and posed new problems for international administration.

THE MATURATION OF NINETEENTH-CENTURY
INTERNATIONAL AGENCIES

To the body of the International Telegraphic Union of 1865, oldest member of the family of international administrative agencies, the states of the world subtly grafted new agencies to fulfill the needs of twentieth-century communications: the first regulations for international telephone service were signed in 1885, and twenty-seven states adhered to the International Radiotelegraph Convention in 1906. The basic compacts relating

215

to the telegraph, telephone, and radio finally blended into the International Telecommunication Convention of 1932 with a single administrative union. Two years after the defeat of Japan in the Second World War seventy-two nations signed a new convention establishing the International Telecommunication Union as a specialized agency of the United Nations. No explorer of early international telegraphic administration could ever have dreamed of an agency which in the mid-twentieth century handles more than half a million documents of telecommunications each year, coordinates technical research through three international committees, and insinuates itself into the delicate diplomacy of allocating international high-frequency radio channels or hearing complaints of jamming propaganda broadcasts [2].

During 1949 the Universal Postal Union celebrated its seventy-fifth anniversary at Berne. At least 100 states or territories affiliated with the Union issued stamps commemorating one of the most successful acts in the history of international organization. Without fanfare the Universal Postal Union has adjusted to the demands for improved international service during the better part of a century, its bureau clearing the postal accounts of virtually every government in the world while coordinating the prompt, safe, and inexpensive exchange of letters, cards, air mail, parcels, phonograph records, cash-on-delivery articles, insured items, and periodicals between nations. In a single year the Union arranged for the manufacture and distribution of over 12,000,000 international reply coupons, 600,000 postal identity cards, and 1,000 traveler's orders; it published hundreds of invaluable circulars and bulletins including postal statistics, directories, and guides to land, sea, and air routes; each month it circulates to its members *L'Union Postale*—now printed in six languages. Certainly Postmaster General Montgomery Blair of the United States, who suggested in 1863 that the heads of the national postal administrations discuss a basic international agreement to facilitate the exchange of mail, never envisaged such a benign octopus [3].

The prolonged consultations of the sanitary conferences during the nineteenth century had eventually led to the creation of a permanent Office International d'Hygiène Publique at Paris in 1908. The League of Nations, prompted by the Red Cross, wished to establish a universal health organization based upon the existing Office, but the obstinacy of the United States and fear of losing autonomy prevented this reasonable connection. A compromise resulted in the plenary body of the Paris organization and the Council of the League each electing half the membership of a health committee. Serving this committee, then, was the Health Section of the Secretariat of the League while the Office International d'Hygiène Publique, with needless duplication, continued its bureau at Paris. On 22 July

1946, following the dislocations of the Second World War, the international prevention of disease was greatly improved as sixty-one nations signed the constitution of the World Health Organization.

Nothing emphasizes the response of the new health organization to the special challenge of the twentieth century more than a list of its duties: in addition to its traditional function of preventing the spread of disease, the World Health Organization is interested in mental hygiene, nutrition, housing, accident prevention, and medical care. Furthermore, at Geneva its epidemiological office can chart the incidence of infectious diseases by reports from the Far Eastern Bureau at Singapore and some twenty-four air or sea ports from the five continents of the earth. These reports are transmitted to every interested public-health agency in the world by bulletin, cable, and broadcast over eleven radio stations. During the fall of 1947, for example, 19 governments collaborated in containing and exterminating an outbreak of cholera in Egypt which, at the peak of incidence, claimed 581 lives in a single day. Less than one hundred years ago the disease would have brutally ravaged the Near East and Europe, yet in 1947 a mere handful outside of Egypt were contaminated by the epidemic, and the scourge passed away. How would Louis Napoleon, calling for the First International Sanitary Conference of 1851, regard a program of 200 international fellowships in medicine, the first efforts to standardize all health reports and statistics, a *pharmacopoeia universalis*, and an international digest of all the national laws, regulations, and bills dealing with public health? In 1952, finally, one of the most interesting developments in international organization occurred when the thirteen conventions relating to health-control measures at frontiers which were in force during the early twentieth century were virtually superseded by the International Sanitary Regulations of the World Health Organization. Adopted unanimously by the representatives of the sixty member states of the Organization to the Fourth World Health Assembly, the Sanitary Regulations automatically come into force among the member states—unless they make specific reservations or rejections of them within nine months. In effect, an international organization has been given far-reaching authority to make sanitary regulations for every member state of the Organization without any other special treaty or convention unless the state puts up a definite objection within a limited time. Such an encroachment upon sovereignty is subtle, but genuine and highly indicative of the potentialities of international organization [4].

On 28 January 1948 the International Institute of Agriculture, for which David Lubin had worked so long and earnestly at the close of the nineteenth century, was liquidated. This first official international organization for agriculture gave way to a newer and more comprehensive institution;

indeed, its very assets and liabilities were assumed by the Food and Agriculture Organization, first of the permanent UN agencies to succeed the Second World War. Once again international society of the twentieth century cleaved to the line of development taken by the pioneers of international organization; once again a structure was refurbished, an organization revamped to fit the exigencies of an atomic era, and what men had formerly scoffed at became the marrow of world order.

Although the FAO plainly starts with the respectable function of collecting, analyzing, and disseminating information relating to nutrition, food, and agriculture, the signatories of the convention which established the FAO on 16 October 1945 also provided for the promotion of research, improvement of education, conservation of natural resources, and adoption of international policies for agricultural commodity arrangements. During the first five years of its life the membership of the FAO increased from forty-four to sixty-six, but this universality only pointed to a more significant achievement as, for the first time in history, international agencies were given the means (through the expanded technical-assistance program of the UN) of extending direct aid to states seeking to improve their wellbeing. By 1953 the budget of the FAO under the expanded program amounted to about 6 million dollars, and agreements had been reached with 52 countries providing for 890 experts in the field. Drought in Yugoslavia, an Indo-Pacific fisheries council, a logging training center in the Philippines, a eucalyptus study tour in Australia—all come under the eye of the FAO. As befits the memory of David Lubin and the International Institute of Agriculture, the FAO headquarters has been removed from Washington to its true birthplace, Rome [5].

Not only the technical improvement of agriculture but also the production and marketing of certain basic food commodities have gradually come under the tent of international supervision. The International Sugar Agreement of 1902, the first important intergovernmental commodity control, fell apart during the First World War, but in 1931 another international agreement pin-pointed the problems inherent in this inelastic commodity so susceptible to the violent fluctuations of supply and price. India, Ceylon, and the Netherlands East Indies signed the first International Tea Agreement in 1933, while in the same year twenty-one governments subscribed to the International Wheat Agreement. In 1939 seven states joined in allocating export quotas of beef to Great Britain.

Other commodities, notably tin, rubber, timber, and wool, also succumbed to international production-marketing agreements. A coffee commission of fifteen states of the Inter-American Economic and Social Council studies problems of coffee, and an international cotton advisory committee cooperates with the FAO in keeping the world cotton position under review. Still other commodity arrangements exist, but prior to the Second World War no single international agency was organized to study, compare, and perhaps coordinate the activities of commodity-control groups.

Proposals for the expansion of world trade and improved labor standards, fundamental goals of President Franklin D. Roosevelt and Prime Minister Winston Churchill enunciated in the Atlantic Charter of 1941, led to a draft charter of an International Trade Organization which, among other things, would elaborate principles for international commodity agreements and endeavor to coordinate the work of all interested groups. Pending the establishment of the International Trade Organization, however, an interim coordinating committee for international commodity agreements, consisting of a chairman nominated by the interim committee of the ITO, a second member designated by the FAO, and a third member primarily interested in nonagricultural commodities, has been proceeding under the supervision of the UN Economic and Social Council. Private producers and marketing agencies naturally play a vital, often decisive role in the formulation of intergovernmental commodity agreements, but from the narrow efforts of a few states to regulate trade in commodities like sugar, international organization has spawned a school of commodity arrangements at least indicating one path to a gigantic planning agency for the more rational distribution of the world's thin resources.

Although the ITO has not come into being, the most comprehensive action ever taken toward the reciprocal reduction of international trade barriers was alternately stimulated by the agitation for such an organization. On 30 November 1947 a General Agreement on Tariffs and Trade was signed by twenty-three states, granting reciprocal trade concessions on some 45,000 items. New negotiations at Annecy, France, in 1949 and Torquay, England, in 1950 included more nations and further trade concessions. By 1953 some thirty-three states were participating in the General Agreement on Tariffs and Trade. While the convention itself and the sessions held for discussions and negotiation on trade policy are outside the UN, the Economic and Social Council has a continuing interest in this important area of world cooperation; certainly the foundation for a specialized international organization in this field is being laid [6].

Thus, the International Telecommunication Union, the Universal Postal Union, the World Health Organization, and the Food and Agriculture Organization, all affiliated today with the UN, reach back to the nineteenth century for their origins and now face the spinning currents of twentieth-century international society with integrity and an unshakable faith in their mission. Concomitantly the International Bureau of Weights and Measures, founded in 1875, has continued its work, going beyond the simple standardization of the meter and the kilo to fixing units of light, measurement of electricity, and a scientific scale of temperatures. The World Meteorological Organization came into being on 23 March 1950, when thirty states and a number of territories ratified a convention which continued and improved the activities of the International Meteorological Organization started in 1878. The present-day International Union for the Protection of Industrial Property, the International Union for the Publication of Customs Tariffs, and the International Penal and Penitentiary Commission similarly owe their beginnings to the generous hope for international cooperation in the nineteenth century.

NEW FIELDS OF INTERNATIONAL ADMINISTRATION

The international administration of rivers beginning with the Octroi of the Rhine in 1804 and continued by the Congress of Vienna down through the nineteenth century, the several commissions and conventions applied to international canals, and the development of railroad associations spanning national boundaries after 1847 bluntly poked the thumb of international organization into the ribs of commerce. An entirely new carrier, therefore, the airplane, which pushed proud states closer to each other by collapsing time and space, could not go roaring over a shrinking planet for long without an international compass—or muffler.

Aviation. Immediately after the great French Revolution, when ascent to the sky by human beings had proved feasible, police regulations increased for the protection of persons and property against flying balloons. By the end of the nineteenth century, even before the conclusive demonstration of the Wright brothers at Kitty Hawk that heavier-than-air machines would be the future of world aviation, individual jurists and statesmen had begun to inquire about the licensing of aircraft, the responsibility of aviators, the salvage of aerial wrecks, and whether pilots should be treated as spies or belligerents in time of war. At the invitation of the French government in 1889 the first international aerial conference met in Paris with representatives, though not plenipotentiaries, of six states. In 1890, 1906, 1909, and 1911 both France and Italy played host to conferences which discussed the mechanics of flying as well as customs regulation, collisions, responsibility for criminal acts, and the right of free passage over foreign territory. Private initiative did not lag during these years. The Institute of International Law, distinguished for its roster of jurists from all states, tediously worked its way through a tangle of drafts and resolutions to arrive at a few fundamental principles of aerial law, while the International Judicial Committee for Aviation, founded in 1909 at Paris, not only enrolled the support of local committees in Europe and America but managed to convene three assemblies in 1911, 1912, and 1913 specifically attendant upon framing a comprehensive aerial code.

The French view of aerial law generously appealed to the widest circulation of international air traffic with a minimum of national restrictions; this philosophy colored practically all conferences until 1910. On the eve of the First World War France again invited the nations of the world to a conference on aviation—this time to draft international regulations. Eighteen European states responded and completed a draft convention on nationality, registration, licensing, landing rules, customs, and so forth. But no treaty was ratified, for the British adhered to a strict interpretation of the exercise of sovereignty over national air space. The bombardments of 1914 halted further negotiation [7].

Out of the terrible distress of the First World War emerged some glimmering achievements of international cooperation, notably the Inter-Allied Aviation Committee to coordinate the air forces of the principal Allies. At the peace conference in 1919 it was suggested that this organization be continued for peacetime international regulation, and a little later an aeronautical commission, comprising representatives of the United States, Britain, France, Italy, and Japan, undertook the drafting of both the terms of peace relating to aircraft and a new international convention for the future regulation of aviation.

On 13 October 1919, therefore, the first multilateral air treaty in the history of international organization was opened for signature. By 11 July 1922 fifteen states had ratified the document. The experience of the war had chastened the French championship of free air passage, and without further ado the 1919 agreement recognized "that every power has complete and exclusive sovereignty over the air space above its territory [8]." Other sections of the convention indicate the achievements of the international accord: nationality of aircraft; certificates of airworthiness and competency; admission to air navigation above foreign territory; rules to be observed on departure, when under way, and on landing; and prohibited transport. Finally, a permanent International Commission for Air Navigation was established to service the provisions of the convention in collecting and communicating information on all matters relative to aviation and to regulate, in general, aircraft and air traffic through standard markings, certificates of airworthiness, signals, minimum qualifications for licensing pilots, maps, and so forth.

Because only a score of states participated in the International Commission for Air Navigation, the French government initiated a new, more catholic international air conference in 1925 to discuss the ramifications of private air law. This conference led to the creation of the International Technical Committee of Juridical Aerial Experts, a panel of jurists from several states who painstakingly prepared draft conventions for air law after individual consultations with interested governments. In consequence, for example, the Second International Conference on Private Air Law at Warsaw in 1929 smoothly agreed upon a convention defining the liability of shippers in air traffic. In the long view, the value of the Committee of Juridical Aerial Experts lay in its sophisticated technique of international legislation.

When Germany invaded France in 1940 thirty-three states belonged to the International Commission for Air Navigation, but the United States and most of the Latin-American states never subscribed to the 1919 convention. Instead, the Fifth Inter-American Conference at Santiago in 1923 authorized a commission to draft a comprehensive aerial convention. This document was presented to the Sixth Inter-American Conference in 1928 at Havana. A substantial number of American states, including the United States, eventually ratified the agreement which, however, did not provide for a permanent commission. Except for an inoperative Ibero-American Convention of Aerial Navigation signed at Madrid in 1926, therefore, the Paris convention of 1919 and the Havana convention of 1928 were the chief multipartite instruments controlling public international aviation prior to the Second World War [9]. Numerous bilateral accords already covered the skies, but international organization had set its sights on a broader horizon.

On 1 November 1944, while Allied bombers were still pounding Germany and Japan, Franklin D. Roosevelt sent a message to the opening plenary session of the International Civil Aviation Conference at Chicago which read in part: "I hope you will not dally with the thought of creating great blocs of closed air, thereby tracing in the sky the condition of future wars. I know that you will see to it that the air which God gave to everyone shall not become the means of domination over anyone [10]." Of fifty-five nations invited by the United States to attend the Conference, only Saudi Arabia and the Soviet Union failed to send delegates.

Earlier bilateral conversations between the United States and states vitally interested in the renewal and expansion of civil aviation when hostilities stopped enabled the Conference to proceed with commendable alacrity in shaping a provisional international organization which became permanent on 4 April 1947. Following the constitutional pattern of international organizations, the new International Civil Aviation Organization is composed of an assembly of all member states, an executive council of twenty-one states elected by the assembly for three years, and a permanent secretariat of international civil servants with headquarters in Montreal.

No real break with the past of international civil aviation occurred, for as the Paris convention of 1919 and the Havana convention of 1928 burned out, the ICAO rose like a phoenix from the ashes. Furthermore, although every state was urged to contribute to the work of the old International Technical Committee of Juridical Aerial Experts as soon as peace should restore its vigor, in November 1946 that organization decided to turn its business over to a legal committee of ICAO; its final meeting was held at the instant of the first assembly of ICAO in May 1947. In addition to these organic developments the Chicago conference produced a new general convention on international aviation and two agreements to extend reciprocal privileges for free transit and certain landings of planes of member states. Starting from the rigid doctrine of national sovereignty over the skies, economic conflicts on passenger and cargo routes, frequency of service, and ports of call have hardly been solved. In 1952, for instance, the council of the ICAO gave consideration to the first dispute between contracting states ever submitted to its jurisdiction—a difference between India and Pakistan over Indian aircraft flying across Pakistan territory. With a budget of little more than 3 million dollars annually, the ICAO at least clarifies issues and brings publicity to air negotiations. It has entered the program of technical assistance, particularly in the training of flying and ground personnel, aeronautics inspection, and navigation. With little public notice for its vital job, the ICAO has advanced standards of air commerce and communications as well as catalyzing multilateral legal agreements relating to the air, all of which improve the sense of world community and responsibility [11].

LABOR

At the close of the First World War no less than 314 private and official international organizations were already in existence [12]. The entry of the League of Nations into the orchestra of international organization, however, gave twentieth-century world society new resonance. Haphazardly the various international administrative agencies had sprung to the special needs of the community, but until 1919 no general organization planned to coordinate these institutions had been created. Indeed, Article 23 of the Covenant staked out conditions of labor; treatment of native inhabitants; traffic in children, women, or drugs; trade in arms; freedom of commerce; and prevention of disease as proper concerns of the League of Nations. Furthermore, Article 24 desired all international bureaus and commissions to be placed under the direction of the League. Of this grand plan of international organization only a part was completed, but the autonomous institution most closely linked to the League of Nations was the International Labor Organization. Like the Covenant, its very constitution was chiseled into the articles of peace dictated to the Germans at Versailles [13]. Membership in the League of Nations automatically signified membership in the ILO, and the expenses of the ILO were met by the general funds of the League.

As early as 1818 Robert Owen had addressed a memorial on behalf of the working classes to the Great Powers conferring at Aix-la-Chapelle. Twenty years later Jérôme Adolphe Blanqui, professor of political economy at Paris, intimated an international remedy for the abuses of labor when he asked, "Heretofore, the Powers have signed treaties binding them to kill men; why could they not draw up modern agreements to preserve and enrich human life [14]?"

The convulsions of 1848 drove segments of labor into extremist camps, especially the subversive International Workingmen's Association (the First International) founded in 1864 which corralled republicans, socialists, communists, and anarchists under one fluttering banner for the universal emancipation of working people [15]. It was Switzerland, however, which tendered the first official invitation to the major industrial states of Europe in 1880 to discuss international labor treaties, but the circular met an icy rebuff; nine years later the Swiss tried again, but the zest of the young German Emperor William II whisked away to Berlin the honor of convening the first international assembly on problems of labor. Twelve states gathered there to study working conditions in mines, a day of rest, child labor, and the regulation of women's work, but little of concrete benefit emerged from many inflated platitudes of good will.

The cloudy discussions of the Berlin conference and two other assemblies in 1897 gradually precipitated into an epoch-making—though unofficial—congress at Paris in 1900 at which the International Association for the Legal Protection of Labor was founded. In 1901 a permanent International Labor Office began to function at Basle. While the bureau supplied periodic reports on legislation and various labor statistics to the members of the Association, general conferences met to prod the states of the world into legislation benefiting the health and safety of working people. By treaty in 1904 France and Italy extended the advantages of workingmen's insurance, factory inspection, and free transfer of the savings of working people to the nationals of both states; between 1904 and 1913 twenty other bilateral treaties were signed which contained terms protecting labor [16]. The International Association for the Legal Protection of Labor reached a splendid success when two of its resolutions, (*a*) prohibiting the manufacture of white phosphorous matches and (*b*) regulating the night work of women in industry, solidified into international conventions signed by seven and fourteen states respectively. Until the First World War, therefore, the Association and its office vociferously championed labor before the councils of the nations, but the organization lacked any official charter, basing itself upon some fifteen relatively independent national committees, and its funds trickled to the treasury from these national committees or from subsidies by interested governments [17].

During the war years of 1914 to 1918 opinion mounted for curing the economic causes of war, particularly by allaying the insecurity of the proletariat. The peace conference at Versailles gladly encouraged the work of a commission headed by Samuel Gompers, president of the American Federation of Labor, which met thirty-five times and drafted the constitution of a new International Labor Organization. Even before the League started to function, the first annual International Labor Conference, plenary body of the organization, assembled in Washington on 29 October 1919 to be welcomed by the Secretary of Labor of the United States:

From the days when Moses was the spokesman, the angel, the walking delegate of the brickmakers of Israel until the present time, the relationship that should exist between employers and employees, the best means of securing the acme of production while safeguarding those who toil, and the equitable distribution of that which has been produced, have been ever present questions. . . . This institution represents the first concerted effort on the part of the nations of the earth to deal with problems of labor in a concerted manner [18].

The ILO has cut a unique swath in the field of international organization, for while adhering to the standard triune plan of other international administrative agencies, that is, (*a*) the plenary conference, (*b*) the governing or executive board, and (*c*) the permanent bureau, the ILO is constituted so that each member state sends four representatives to the plenary conference: two spokesmen for the government, one representative of labor, and one representative of the employers within a country. The Governing Body consists of thirty-two members: eight representing employers, eight representing labor, and sixteen representing government. Voting, moreover, follows individual preference, and a national delegation may sometimes be divided two, three, or even four ways. Thus, for the first time in the history of international organization, private citizens representing labor and management groups have obtained equal representation with their government's delegates in drafting either recommendations for national labor laws or conventions for international ratification. Should either a recommendation or a convention be approved by two-thirds of the conference, each member state has pledged to act upon it—positively or negatively—within eighteen months.

Between 1919 and 1939 the ILO held twenty-five plenary sessions, launching no less than sixty-six recommendations to national governments on labor legislation and approving some sixty-seven conventions to be submitted to states for their ratification. Only the insincere could hide the plain fact that the recommendations received only passing courtesy while the general average of states which ratified the labor conventions fell from 50 per cent during the first ten years of the ILO's life to a scant 10 per cent after 1930. The twenty-sixth session of the International Labor Conference, nevertheless, meeting under dismal war conditions, courageously admitted its frailties and then affirmed its continuing purpose of elevating working standards everywhere through international organization [19].

Attached to the League of Nations, the ILO easily transferred its mooring from the defunct Geneva organization to the UN on 2 October 1946. Cooperating with the World Health Organization and the Food and Agriculture Organization, the ILO has lately assailed such problems as dust diseases affecting workers and the training of agricultural labor. Granted a special fund of a million dollars, it has struck at the evil of confused mass migrations in postwar Europe, selecting and training workers for labor-hungry areas. Branch offices operate in seven states, and with field offices in São Paulo, Brazil, or Bangalore, India, the ILO at Geneva implements the technical-assistance program of the UN. Although the Second World War brought ratifications of the precious international labor conventions practically to a halt, nevertheless, since the end of hostilities there has been a steady, if not meteoric, increase in number. By 1953, of the 103 labor conventions adopted by the International Labor Conferences, 73 were in force among some states. For example, a convention on crew quarters which was adopted by the 1946 Conference came into force on 29 January 1953, and it requires the ratifying states to assure specified minimum standards of accommodations for the crews aboard their merchant ships. Another Convention on the Right to Organize and Collective Bargaining adopted by the ILO in 1949 has been ratified by a dozen states.

Working with a budget of slightly more than 6 million dollars a year, the ILO has progressed from its early admonitions against Sunday work and the employment of young children to preparing a comprehensive international labor code and delving into problems of labor conciliation and arbitration, holidays with pay in agriculture, cooperation between public workers' unions and public authorities, and the protection of the health of workers in places of employment, thus intelligently tailoring its administration to the cloth of twentieth-century international society [20].

TRUSTEESHIP FOR DEPENDENT PEOPLES

Another thrust into international administration energized by the League of Nations was the mandate system. Article 22 of the Covenant recognized that territories containing peoples unable to weather "the strenuous conditions of the modern world" ought to be placed under the tutelage of an advanced nation which would then administer the area as a sacred trust on behalf of the League of Nations and international society. Although "mandates" had been given by a conference of powers to a single state during the nineteenth century—Britain over the Ionian Islands in 1815 and over Cyprus in 1878, France in the Lebanon in 1860 to protect Christian minorities, King Leopold of Belgium over the Congo basin in 1885, and the police power granted to France and Spain over Morocco in 1906 —no single coordinating agency which fixed international responsibility upon the mandatory power existed until the League of Nations took shape. Indeed, the Covenant only inscribed the principles of the mandate system; it wisely left the actual allocation of territories to the peace settlement of 1919.

The idea of mandates was by no means wholly altruistic. Within Britain and the United States in particular (and in France among some socialists), there had been a "no annexations" cry from liberals opposed to economic exploitation of colonies and conservatives interested in humanitarianism. But the need for meeting the promises of independence made to the Arabs while keeping control over their strategic areas also motivated Britain and France in advocating mandates for the Middle East, while Britain had special problems with her Dominions of the Union of South Africa, Australia, and New Zealand which pressed for annexations of nearby territory but were eventually persuaded to accept mandates over them [21]. At the time of the armistice of the First World War, General Smuts was thinking of applying mandates to central European territories and Russian border areas; Great Britain imagined that Armenia, Albania, Persia, Constantinople with the straits, Anatolia, and the Belgian Congo might be put under the new international system of accountability. President Wilson rashly proposed to the United States Senate that the United States assume a mandate over Armenia. The Supreme War Council of the Allied Powers finally ground down all claims, sifted the arguments, and limited the mandates to the former German colonies in Africa and the Pacific Ocean as well as Iraq, Syria-Lebanon, Palestine, and Transjordan.

Undeniably the mandates given to certain states over dependent territories detached from Germany and Turkey veiled an outright control by the victors of the First World War. On the other hand the mandatory powers made certain pledges for the improvement of the peoples under their administration to an international organization. In A mandates, such as Iraq, independence of the state was anticipated; in B mandates, such as Tanganyika, the mandatory power was required to maintain an administration separate from its other colonial possessions; in C mandates, such as New Guinea or South-West Africa, the territory was virtually integrated with the administering state. In addition to being responsible for peace, order, and good government within the mandated territory, the mandatory powers—Great Britain, France, Japan, Belgium, the Union of South Africa, Australia, and New Zealand—pledged to promote the material and moral well-being of the inhabitants; not to establish military bases within the territory or use the inhabitants for military service except in defense of the territory; to prohibit slavery or forced labor; and to control traffic in arms, ammunition, and liquor. In some mandates equal economic rights for all nationals of member states of the League were guaranteed.

The organization devised to exercise supervision over the mandatory powers was the Permanent Mandates Commission. It consisted of eleven persons appointed by the Council of the League of Nations, with the requirement that each member of the Commission be a private citizen and that a majority of them should be chosen from nonmandatory states. Meeting fifty or sixty days each year, the Commission sedulously attended to its high purposes with the ever-ready support of the Mandates Section of the Secretariat. The principal device which the Commission relied upon for the international supervision of the mandates was the annual report submitted by the mandatory powers on the territories under their administration. These reports were studied and forwarded to the Council of the League with recommendations. The Permanent Mandates Commission was also granted a very limited right of inspection of the territories themselves in agreement with the administering power. F. P. Walters, formerly Deputy Secretary-General of the League, has said, "The Mandates Commission left behind it a record as satisfactory as that of any of the institutions created by the League. . . . In its last years the Commission was consulted and trusted by mandatory and non-mandatory powers alike." A splendid tribute to the international administration of mandates has been paid by H. Duncan Hall:

The Commission held steadily to its course year after year, examining and analyzing the Annual Reports. Each member, a specialist in some aspect, put questions to the accredited representatives of the mandatory powers as they took their seats in turn at the table . . . Year after year as the mass of Annual Reports by governments passed over one's table together with the minutes and reports of the Commission, certain impressions began to form. One began to get the feeling that something was happening with great rapidity in the sphere of international administration which had taken centuries to develop in the national sphere [22].

The Second World War terminated the League of Nations and the mandates system, but as early as August 1942 a special subcommittee on international organization began to draft a proposed international trust system for the U.S. Department of State [23]. At the Moscow and Teheran Conferences of the Allied Powers in 1943, international trusteeship of dependent territories received peripheral attention, but by the time of the Crimea Conference of 1945 the matrix of future international trusteeship, following American recommendations quite closely, had been set: existing mandates of the League, territories to be detached from enemy powers, and any other territory voluntarily placed under trusteeship should come under the supervision of a general international organization.

Three chapters of the Charter of the UN are devoted to the political, economic, and social advancement of the millions of people in non-self-governing territories. Apart from the four territories in the Pacific and the seven territories in Africa (Italian Somaliland was placed under Italian administration with complete independence anticipated in 1960), each member of the UN has also accepted the obligation, new in the history of international organization, of transmitting to the Secretary-General of the UN certain information on all the non-self-governing territories under its own flag. This amounts to about sixty annual reports with comparative data on schools, health facilities, social services, and progress toward political responsibility, all put under the close scrutiny of an international organization.

The UN trusteeship system carries the mandates system further, integrating the old administration with the new. Focus has been slightly altered with a new lens, but the picture of international responsibility for the wards of twentieth-century society is the same.

Opening the first session of the Trusteeship Council on 26 March 1947 the Secretary-General of the UN indicated one difference of mechanism between the League and the UN, in that "for the first time in history a permanent international body, whose membership is composed solely of official representatives of Governments, is assembled to deal exclusively with the problems of non-self-governing peoples [24]." Whereas the Council of the League acted through its Permanent Mandates Commission of private citizens, the General Assembly (except for strategic trust territories which are reported directly to the Security Council) acts through the Trusteeship Council composed equally of trustee and nontrustee states —including the five permanent members of the Security Council. While some frankness and impartiality may have been sacrificed by the substitution of official representatives for private citizens, the recommendations of the Trusteeship Council bear the weight and responsibility of governments. Whereas the members of the Mandates Commission rarely visited a mandated territory, under the UN annual visits have been arranged for four-man visiting teams by the Trusteeship Council in collaboration with the administering powers. Within the first three years of its existence the Council sent visiting missions to East Africa, West Africa, and the Pacific. Late in 1952, for example, a four-man team representing Australia, El Salvador, Belgium, and China visited the Togolands and the Cameroons under British and French administrations, while early in 1953 another team representing the Dominican Republic, Great Britain, France, and Syria was dispatched to the Pacific islands placed under the United States administration, Nauru and New Guinea under Australian administration, and Western Samoa under New Zealand's administration.

Whereas the League permitted written petitions to be sent from a territory only *through* the mandatory power, the rules of the Trusteeship Council allow the Secretary-General to accept petitions either through the administering authority or *directly* for submission to the Council. In some instances even oral testimony from a petitioner is permitted. While many of the petitions have been trivial, they are another device to publicize actions within a trust territory, and they do come under the eye of fellow states who may call for an explanation. At its tenth session in 1952, by way of illustration, the Trusteeship Council went to work on 301 petitions from African territories and 1 from New Guinea. Seventy-one petitions were actually examined, and decisions were granted on 35. Thus, the Trusteeship Council and the General Assembly, with its universal forum to discuss the recommendations of the Trusteeship Council and make further recommendations of its own, have pursued the shining ideals of the Permanent Mandates Commission and the League. Certainly the Trusteeship Council has been stymied at times by the jealousy, inertia, or downright obfuscation of the administering power, but it has constantly probed, exposed, and encouraged the very conscience of international society in respect to dependent peoples [25].

INTERNATIONALIZED TERRITORY

In addition to assigning the administration of territories to mandatory or trustee states, three novel attempts have been made by an international organization to supervise the government of an area: in Danzig, the Saar, and Trieste. Limited success has attended these pioneer efforts to provide for a lasting peace under an international organization's supervision in disputed territories.

Danzig. The Treaty of Tilsit (1807) had guaranteed the independence of the Free City of Danzig by Prussia, Saxony, and France, although a military governor of Napoleon really controlled the artificial state until 1814. Then a century of Prussian-German sovereignty preceded Woodrow Wilson's declaration that a resurrected Poland should have access to the sea at the end of the First World War. The natural outlet for Warsaw commerce was Danzig. Article 102 of the Versailles Treaty, ratified 10 January 1920, placed a new Free City of Danzig under the protection of the League of Nations, and the fledgling international organization itself guaranteed the constitution of the city. A High Commissioner, appointed by the Council of the League, dealt with any differences arising between Danzig and Poland, which were now linked in tariffs and foreign relations. Through its agent, therefore, and its right to permit military installations, obtain reports on public affairs, and sanction nationality laws, the League of Nations experimented with a bold form of international government. The squabbles between Poland and Danzig soon overwhelmed the High Commissioner, and in the next decade they filled the docket of the Council of the League and the Permanent Court of International Justice with testimony. The rise of Adolf Hitler finally tipped the flimsy tripod of League, Poland, and Danzig under the Constitution of the Free City. After April 1933 the Nazi party controlled a majority of the Senate of the city, gradually extinguishing its obligations to any superior save Germany, and in September 1939 the Third Reich formally annexed Danzig [26].

The Saar. The Saar, squeezed between Germany and France and coveted by both nations for its abundant coal, fell by compromise under more direct government by the League of Nations than Danzig. During the First World War France had secretly played for annexation of the territory to compensate for the destruction of French coal mines by Germany, but neither Lloyd George nor Woodrow Wilson would tolerate this demand at the Paris peace conference. Instead the Versailles Treaty stated: "Germany renounces in favor of the League of Nations, *in capacity of trustee*, the government of the territory defined [27]." (Italics supplied.) The Saar coal mines were given to France, but a five-man commission, including representatives of France, the Saar, and three other nations, governed the state efficiently for fifteen years when, according to treaty, the Saarlanders were polled as to their preference for remaining under the League or being integrated with either France or Germany. Thoroughly German in sentiment, though perhaps not fully conscious of the character of Nazism, the debt-free Saar delivered itself from the League of Nations into the hands of Hitler in 1935.

Trieste. These two ventures into government by an international organization were not lost to the memory of statesmen as compromises for a tendentious peace settlement. The first treaty ending the Second World War ran full speed into the problem of drawing a new boundary line between Yugoslavia and Italy. The area of Trieste, confounded by an ethnic mixture of Slovenes and Italians, yet economically dependent upon the trade of Austria and neighboring states, became a hot iron of dispute during the peace negotiations at Paris in 1946. In the face of intransigent attitudes, the Soviet Union and the Western Allies agreed to establish a Free Territory of Trieste ruled by a local legislature and a governor appointed by and responsible to the Security Council of the UN. Degenerating relations between the United States and Russia during 1947 and 1948, however, precluded this expedient compromise, and in March 1948 Britain, France, and the United States openly advocated the return of the whole territory to Italy. Whether or not military government by the West and Yugoslavia continues, the only plan for direct international government in recent years has entered the limbo of discarded hopes [28].

FINANCE

Prior to the First World War a fine mesh of international lending and borrowing suspended private entrepreneurs and national banking institutions on a gently swaying gold standard. With London as the world's banker guaranteeing convertibility of currencies already pegged upon ounces of yellow metal, international trade shuttled across the oceans and lands with filaments of sterling. The First World War jostled the fixed channels of exchange; the Great Depression of 1930 to 1934 shattered them. International economic conferences during the nineteen twenties timidly discussed remedies for restoring the friendly flow of international trade; indeed, the first international bank, the Bank for International Settlements, was created as an integral part of the Young Plan of 1929 to facilitate the transfer of German reparations to the victorious Allies in useful currency. The economic turbulence churned in the interwar years, however, made the prophets of the new world order immediately conscious of safeguarding mankind from both fear and want through "the fullest collaboration between all nations in the economic field [29]." Two international organizations, unique in history, stemmed directly from mid-twentieth-century economic strife: the International Monetary Fund and the International Bank for Reconstruction and Development.

After the Great Depression of 1930 to 1934 and throughout the Second World War, the "garrison state" economy of both democracies and dictatorships constricted all normal trade arteries. Instead of a free international market governed by supply and demand, states resorted to internal subsidies of high-cost industries or farming, export-import licensing, and currency controls, all of which fostered national price structures only remotely connected with a multilateral foreign exchange. As early as 1943 Great Britain proposed a new international clearing union, a brain child of the economist John Maynard Keynes, while the United States, guided by Harry D. White, suggested an international stabilization fund. Extended consultations led to the inauguration, in March 1946, of the International Monetary Fund, which has sought to free and develop international trade from the several restrictions of foreign exchange and the injury of currency depreciation. A member state, embarrassed by the lack of convertible currency, can borrow from the Fund the requisite money—in proportion to its own share of the Fund. As a corollary, every state promises to maintain a par value for its own currency, only variable within 10 per cent without permission from the Fund, and to abolish exchange controls. Between 1 March 1947 when the Fund began operations and 30 April 1952, the Fund effected exchange transactions equivalent to 850 million dollars for twenty members. In 1953, to illustrate further the work of the Fund, Greece and Bolivia eliminated multiple currency practices after consultation with the international organization, and Austria also discontinued a multiple exchange rate after her schilling was given a par value in U.S. dollars. Yet the chronic disequilibrium of trade resulting from the fat economy of the United States, the evaporation of European capital, the ruptures of the Asiatic and African markets, and the grim march toward state control of the economy everywhere has thus far haunted and hampered this attempt to oil the creaking wheels of universal trade by means of international monetary stabilization [30].

The International Bank for Reconstruction and Development, the sister of the International Monetary Fund, also shaped in 1946 to heal the fractures of the twentieth-century world economy, has fared better. The Bank, called "the first venture of permanent international cooperation in long term foreign lending [31]," was intended to *guarantee* private loans for the reconstruction and development of countries devastated by the Second World War or intent upon improving their productivity as well as to *make* loans where private capital was not forthcoming on reasonable terms. By the end of 1952, however, the Bank was virtually a lending agency for its fifty-four member governments. Any loan made to a political subdivision of a state or a private enterprise must be guaranteed by the government. Since its first grant to France in May 1947 the Bank has made scores of loans—for general purposes of reconstruction or for specific projects of power improvement, irrigation, communications, renewing or expanding steel industries, port facilities, woodworking, and many others—to dozens of states or enterprises all over the world. During the fiscal year 1952, for example, the Bank not only received 26.5 million dollars of income from over 1 billion dollars in outstanding loans but granted another 300 million dollars in new loans. The Bank's activities are not confined to making loans, for it has given advice on a wide range of technical and financial matters when requested, and its survey missions, visiting a country and examining a project for which a loan may be requested, have often influenced governments in their development plans.

Both the International Monetary Fund and the International Bank for Reconstruction and Development have a system of weighted voting; member states receive a number of votes in proportion to their contributions to the capital funds of each institution. Both organizations consist of a Board of Governors, comprising all the member states, and a Board of Executive Directors, comprising the five members which have made the largest contributions and nine others elected from geographical groups in the Board of Governors. Policy making, in fact, has passed into the hands of the fourteen-member Board of Executive Directors.

While the work of the International Monetary Fund and the International Bank for Reconstruction and Development has been hamstrung by the basic disequilibrium of economies left in the world after the Second World War as well as an increasing tendency of governments to manage all fiscal and trade policies in view of "political" considerations, both organizations nevertheless represent an effort to minimize economic difficulties among states by international cooperation. Trade is encouraged through the stabilization of currencies and help for their convertibility; productivity is encouraged by provision of capital to projects which promise benefits to individual countries and, in the long run, the community at large. Of subtle but significant importance to the history of international organization has been the sale of the Bank's bonds, totaling more than half a billion dollars, to private investors in order to increase its funds, for it is a rare instance of an international organization dealing directly with individuals. By no means a panacea to all the economic ills of a war-devastated world burdened with a lopsided distribution of wealth and arrogant nationalism, the Fund and the Bank are endeavoring to meet a new challenge for international organization in a way never before attempted [32].

RELIEF AND REFUGEES

Private ethics inescapably gauge social policy. The compassion for mankind felt by the individual rises first to the level of personal kindness, then organized philanthropy, and, in a day of tremendous tasks requiring tremendous resources, government action. No less has the work of international organization in charity lately recognized the responsibility of the official community to succor the needy, refresh the weak, and sustain the dispossessed.

During the nineteenth century disaster relief had been the charge of high-minded private chapters such as the Red Cross, but the magnitude of human suffering caused by the First World War, relayed about the globe by modern communications, demanded better palliatives. Only intergovernmental cooperation offered a remedy. The president of the Italian Red Cross, therefore, at the Tenth International Red Cross Conference of 1920, called for a new international organization designed to coordinate the work of national governments and voluntary agencies when an overwhelming catastrophe required prompt action. After long years of cautious negotiation—even upon such a patent need—with timid gestures and windy debates, an International Relief Union for this purpose, carefully circumscribed in power, was founded.

The League of Nations, moreover, one month after it began to operate in 1920 was confronted with the problem of almost a quarter of a million prisoners of war suffering famine and disease in the camps of the new revolution-racked Soviet Union. Desperate efforts for relief by the Red Cross societies and the International Young Men's Christian Association still left an estimated 120,000 men scheduled to die of privation. In April 1920 Dr. Fridtjof Nansen, acting under the aegis of the League of Nations, began an amazing mission of securing the cooperation of all interested governments in arranging transport and obtaining relief moneys. Within fourteen months 350,000 men had been returned to their own countries.

But an even greater calamity inflicted upon helpless people was the Russian Revolution and the ensuing civil war which scattered almost 2 million refugees from Shanghai to Paris, piling up human wreckage in Constantinople, Gallipoli, the isle of Lemnos, Warsaw, Sofia, and points west. Deprived of home and personal goods these victims of politics suffered doubly in the postwar employment blight. Worse than that, some 800,000 persons were without protection of law, being "stateless," without citizenship or passport [33]. Early in 1921 the Director-General of the Red Cross called the League's attention to this deplorable situation, and although the international organization lacked enthusiasm for the onerous task, it was forced by events to accept responsibility. In the fall of the same year Dr. Nansen was appointed High Commissioner for Refugees to coordinate the distracted efforts of private and government agencies.

Not only destitute Russians sought refuge in the twenties, for the violently nationalistic Turks expelled 1.5 million Greeks with thousands of Assyrians and Armenians from their soil in 1922 and 1923. International organization again thwarted epidemic disease as private groups and governments mobilized soup kitchens and medical aid while the Fourth

Assembly of the League itself voted funds [34]. In the cold annals of history the generous cooperation of nations often lies buried under a granite obelisk immortalizing war, but Dr. Nansen [35] once said:

> I wish I could make you feel what it is to see a whole people on the road, fleeing for their lives in a wild panic of fear; or to visit a people stricken by famine, to enter huts where men, women and children lie motionless, no longer complaining, but just waiting for death; or the nightmare of the country where corpses are dug up from the churchyards, to be used for food, and where mothers, in mad desperation, kill and eat their own children.

Against such barbarity the states of the world began organizing. Beyond sheer economic assistance, an identity certificate (known as the Nansen passport) giving legal status to refugees was adopted by fifty-one governments during the nineteen twenties, while the International Labor Organization anxiously sought jobs for honest people willing to work.

Hardly had one group of uprooted men and women been settled than another crowded upon the attention of international organization, for Adolf Hitler beat the Jews into exodus or death from 1933 to 1939, and the Spanish Civil War, beginning in 1936, drove hundreds of thousands of exiles across the French border. The League of Nations continued its High Commission for Refugees except for persons of German or Austrian extraction who now fell under the protection of a new Intergovernmental Committee on Refugees in which the United States participated. The Second World War compounded the distress of refugees, and as the League disintegrated the Intergovernmental Committee assumed wider functions. The havoc of the blasting and bombing shook millions of people from their homes, villages, cities, and nations; prisoners of war in Italy or Russia, refugees in France or Britain, resettled populations in Germany or Poland all added up to a fantastic total of broken families with no place to live, no place to work, no place to go. Only international organization led by the wealthiest state, the United States, could mitigate the human suffering.

On 9 November 1943, with forty-four nations initialing an agreement to aid the populations of liberated areas and help repatriate both prisoners and exiles, the United Nations Relief and Rehabilitation Administration began its brief, brave career [36]. In the wake of liberation the occupying armies of the Allied forces quickly assisted most of the 5 million displaced persons home. UNRRA followed hard on the heels of misery and distributed nearly 4 billion dollars' worth of goods to the needy within two years. While the United States paid 73 per cent of the bill, no less than fifty other states and numberless private agencies also bore the tragic burden. In addition to its magnanimous relief activities, UNRRA was also concerned over the plight of many people from Eastern Europe who were unwilling to return to their homes—now under the jurisdiction of the Soviet Union or Communist-controlled governments. The Intergovernmental Committee, meanwhile, continued its work with refugees, but early in 1946 the UN Economic and Social Council recommended a single, temporary agency to deal exclusively with refugees and displaced persons. Thus was the International Refugee Organization, born of the horror of two world wars. Three years after it began its work, the Organization could say without boasting: "The program of the International Refugee Organization has been the first great test in peacetime of the notion that practical international problems can be dealt with successfully and efficiently on a large-scale operating basis by a cooperative international administration [37]." In 1951 the International Refugee Organization began a gradual self-liquidation and, again following the model of the League, the UN established a High Commissioner for Refugees. In its final report, the International Refugee Organization noted that between 1946 and 1952 it had repatriated 73,000 people to their countries of origin or former residence while more than 1 million people had been resettled. From 1 July 1947 to 7 February 1952 the Organization had received almost 400 million dollars from member states [38].

By the mid-twentieth century, therefore, many states had assumed a broad responsibility to cooperate through an international agency for the relief of war victims and displaced persons. But international charity, like private charity, is often inadequate. Earnestly working for the protection of refugees and stateless persons by law and conventions, the UN High Commissioner has a special problem in the weak, the old, and the occupational specialist whom no country seems willing to admit for settlement. Authorized to solicit 3 million dollars for emergency aid for refugees in February 1952, the UN High Commissioner secured no more than $800,000 from the voluntary contributions of governments within the next eleven months. Fortunately a Ford Foundation grant of $2,900,000 enabled the High Commissioner to allot funds to various international voluntary agencies in order to promote the integration of refugees in communities in which they live or to aid their resettlement abroad. The original term of the Office of the UN High Commissioner for Refugees expired at the end of 1953, and at the time of writing the General Assembly is considering the renewal of the Office. Furthermore, as a result of the hostilities in Palestine in 1948 about 750,000 Arabs became refugees. The UN established a Relief and Works Agency for Palestine Refugees in the Near East, but by 1953 the reintegration of these refugees by either repatriation in Israel or resettlement in other countries of refuge had not been realized, thereby thrusting an additional burden of direct relief activities of some 20 million dollars annually upon the Organization. These funds must be sought from the

voluntary contributions of states. So, too, Korea raises new refugee problems, as must every outbreak of war in the twentieth century. In this field
international organization has a hard task, but the challenge of human
suffering itself has fostered cooperation and a sense of community which
misfortune makes states remember.

PROTECTION OF WOMEN AND CHILDREN

The protection of women and children through international organization, like the administering of relief and the care of refugees, was preceded by the agitation of private groups and a slow, steady evolution. The
First International Congress of Benevolent Societies met in 1890, and the
work of this private organization encouraged governments to sign a convention in 1904 to suppress the white-slave traffic. At the Fifth Congress
of Benevolent Societies in 1911, moreover, the treatment of abnormal
children and the legal rights of minors were discussed. Two years later,
at the invitation of the Belgian government, forty-two states and a large
number of private societies sent delegates to the First Congress for the
Protection of the Child. In 1919, finally, the peace conference at Versailles
charged the League of Nations with organizing international cooperation
for the benefit of women and children.

The League of Nations not only promoted the protection of women and
children from white slavery, through various conferences on the subject,
but in 1924, at the prompting of the International Association for the
Promotion of Child Welfare, it established the Advisory Committee on
the Traffic of Women and Child Welfare. Cooperating with other agencies and affiliates of the League, the child-welfare section of this committee
performed valorous service in guarding the physical, mental, and moral
well-being of children everywhere. Nothing, however, compared to the
calamity visited upon children by the ferocity of the Second World War.
Infant-mortality rates in postwar Europe soared to the appalling total of
400 per 1,000 live births in some places while injury, disease, and shock
maimed the bodies and minds of children.

By a resolution of the UN General Assembly in December 1946, the
International Children's Emergency Fund was created. By the end of
1947 this hardy organization was delivering enormous quantities of skim
and whole milk, fats, and fish-liver oils to needy children. The shortage of
milk, unsanitary housing, and the general debility of youngsters breached
normal defenses against the assaults of tuberculosis. In cooperation with
the Danish Red Cross, UNICEF facilitated the vaccination of more than
11 million children. With raw materials procured by the international
organization, 1,850,000 pairs of shoes, 400,000 layettes, 1,300,000 diapers

and vests, 850,000 stockings, and 67,000 blankets were fabricated to alle-
viate the misery which war had inflicted upon the most innocent victims
of politics. Seventy-two countries and over 17 million children received
aid through UNICEF during 1952: about 4 million children were vacci-
nated against tuberculosis, over 3 million were examined for yaws and
syphilis and a third of these given treatment; another 7 million were
given protection against malaria. Child-health centers and maternity training form an integral part of the busy program. Such relief for children
depended upon the voluntary contributions of thirty-two states which
gave almost 10 million dollars to UNICEF, again indicating the grave
responsibilities which the nations of the world have shouldered in the
twentieth century and the tendency to use international organizations both
to carry out their will and to answer their conscience [39].

INTELLECTUAL COOPERATION

UNESCO rings with a curiously melodic sound among the alphabetic
contractions of government agencies. Yet this starry-eyed child of international organization which is dedicated to the elimination of ignorance, suspicion, and mistrust among peoples follows in the footsteps of her more
prosaic sister institutions in the fields of communications, health, agriculture, aviation, and finance.

The acceleration of learning and the growing storehouse of knowledge
in the nineteenth century underlined the inadequate exchange of information and ideas across national frontiers. In 1895 the unofficial International
Office of Bibliography encouraged a Union of International Associations,
which held its first congress in 1910. This organization, composed solely
of noncommercial groups, actively promoted the cause of a league of nations—naturally stressing the importance of education and intellectual
cooperation. No less than 230 international societies were affiliated with
the union by 1914.

Although the peace conference of 1919 and the Covenant of the League
of Nations gave no official recognition to the purposes of the Union of International Associations, one of the founders of the organization, Henri
Lafontaine of Belgium, eloquently urged the First Assembly of the League
to provide facilities for information and centers of collaboration for exchanging the intellectual work of all nations. Impressed by his argument,
the Assembly turned the matter over to the Council, and on 15 May 1922
the Council appointed a twelve-man committee (later increased to fifteen) entitled the Intellectual Cooperation Committee. This organization
of distinguished scholars and statesmen met regularly in Geneva once a
year and reported to the Council. By patiently molding its imaginative en-

terprise to the activities of other committees of the League, nongovern-
mental international agencies, and national committees, the unique organization modestly tried to further education, culture, scientific achievement, and a spirit of internationalism. But meeting once or twice a year
on a meager budget, the Committee could scarcely maintain adequate liaison with the far-flung intellectual centers of the world. Lacking a permanent center of work for research, study, and exchange of information,
the committee almost gave up its ill-appreciated job in 1924 when, in
the nick of time, the French government offered to subsidize an International Institute of Intellectual Cooperation at Paris. France and the League
of Nations agreed that the Intellectual Cooperation Committee should
become the governing board of the Institute, but under the chairmanship
of a French member with the office located in Paris rather than in Geneva.
From the governing body, moreover, a committee of five executive directors was selected and, to complete the pattern of twentieth-century international administrative agencies, a director with a permanent staff was
appointed.

Because the budget, building, and staff came chiefly from France, the
Institute of Intellectual Cooperation appeared as an embarrassed, back-
door entrant to international organization. Similarly the International
Educational Cinematographic Institute gained the sponsorship of the
Italian government in 1928. Yet both organizations had organic ties to
the League, which appointed virtually all the members of both governing bodies and supervised their programs, and in their later years received
contributions from most members of the League, as well as from certain
American foundations.

No subject can be more controversial for an international organization
than education, for it necessarily involves a philosophy and psychology
of politics. Barely three months before the first battles of the Second World
War the Director of the International Institute of Intellectual Cooperation
reported:

Like every international movement, Intellectual Cooperation found it hard to
make the people aware of its existence. For many years, only a minority of in-
tellectuals showed any interest in it . . . It is no part of our present task to
examine why so many dangers nevertheless still threaten peace. The Intellectual
Cooperation Organization, in its own field, and to the extent of its means, seeks
to play its part in warding off those dangers . . . [The] factor which gives that
movement its justification, its original features, its reason for existence: the
quest of an intellectual atmosphere in which the life of the mind can freely
develop [40].

The cataclysm of the Second World War counted among its horrible
casualties hundreds of ruined museums and scientific laboratories, thou-

sands of shattered schools, and millions of burned books. A conference of Allied ministers of education assembled at London as early as October 1942 to meet the problem, but one pressing educational need yielded to another, and the scope of the required program could not be handled by any temporary conferences. On 12 July 1945, therefore, it was resolved to request the British government to convene a conference to discuss a permanent international educational and cultural organization of the UN. Forty-four nations responded to the invitation late in 1945, and the constitution of the United Nations Educational, Scientific, and Cultural Organization with its challenging preamble—"since wars begin in the minds of men, it is in the minds of men that the defences of peace must be constructed"—became effective 4 November 1946.

The connection between UNESCO and the Intellectual Cooperation Committee is self-evident: twentieth-century society, however, demands more work and, therefore, more organization of international administrative agencies. In education, UNESCO seeks to achieve a minimum educational level of literacy; in science, UNESCO has begun field-science cooperation offices in Asia, Latin America, and Africa to promote the exchange of ideas, equipment, and personnel among well-endowed centers of science and needy areas; in the social sciences and the humanities, UNESCO has held conferences of experts, encouraged studies of international tensions, and prepared exhaustive bibliographies or formidable translations of classic writings; through UNESCO a deluge of books, film projectors, radios, and musical instruments has poured into villages, towns, and cities thirsty for mind- and spirit-lifting things [41]. One year finds UNESCO surveying the press, film, and radio needs of 120 countries and territories, trying to service 200,000 Arab children with minimum educational facilities, or appropriating $100,000 for emergency school requirements in Korea; another year witnesses UNESCO preparing an international social-science research center, setting up a public library pilot project in Latin America, convening a conference of 300 artists in Venice, publicizing and assisting international fellowships, or abetting a universal copyright convention, signed by 35 states, to give writers, artists, and scientists extensive legal protection for their creative works.

The diverse and manifold activities of UNESCO have frequently run the gauntlet of stern criticism. Jean Desy, the delegate from Canada to the organization, minced no words at the fifth session of the General Conference:

We do not think it essential to publish monographs on free and compulsory education, to issue popular articles to broadcasting organizations, to produce film strips or pictures for the use of lecturers, to trace the stages in the constitutional development of Specialized Agencies, or to collect photographs and illustrations supplied by scientific or technical societies. There is too much urgent work awaiting our attention for us to waste time on such enterprises [42].

In 1952, the eighteen-member Executive Board of UNESCO, which is elected by the General Conference, now comprising sixty-one states, also discussed focusing on limited programs and tailoring them to the annual budget of about 9 million dollars for the organization. The Director-General, however, vigorously protested curtailment of UNESCO activities— and later resigned when the general conference sliced 10 per cent from his estimates of UNESCO's financial needs for 1953–1954.

Despite these problems for an organization which is admittedly difficult to orient and operate in such controversial areas as education and culture, what strikes the historical record is the vitality of international cooperation moving in all directions to touch both the robust, extrovert activities of nations and the fragile, inmost thoughts of their peoples. Economic and social cooperation, moreover, through international organization, proves nothing less than the competence of men to govern themselves with kindness on a precious earth often assailed by envy and greed. Policemen must forever curb the criminal imperfections of man, but good neighbors have many things in common. Responding to the pulse of the twentieth century, the international administrative agencies have taken new strength and quickened their steps. They must acknowledge an infinite debt to those enlightened private agencies and early official meetings which first forced down the brazen ramparts of sovereignty. Despite the gloomy remarks of critics and the angry posture of the world in general they keep moving on with their business.

NOTES

1. *Patterns of Cooperation,* U.S. Department of State Publication 3735, International Organization and Conference Series I, 9, p. 130. For the regulation of international waterways up to the Second World War, see O. Mance, *International River and Canal Transport,* London, Oxford, 1945.

2. For a general résumé of the history, work, etc., of the International Telecommunication Union and the other specialized agencies of the United Nations, see the *Yearbook of the United Nations,* published annually. The *Report of the International Telecommunication Union* is submitted each year to the United Nations Economic and Social Council. Detailed operations of the organization are de-

scribed in the trilingual *Journal des communications,* issued monthly. See also O. Mance, *International Communications,* London, Oxford, 1944.

3. A handsome survey of the history and work of the Universal Postal Union is *L'Union Postale; sa fondation et son development, 1874–1949,* published by the organization at Bern in 1949. The *Report of the Universal Postal Union,* submitted annually to the United Nations Economic and Social Council, gives valuable information; detailed operations may be found in the monthly periodical *L'Union Postale.*

4. For the proceedings of the World Health Assemblies, see the *Official Records* of the organization. The *Report of*

the *World Health Organization* is submitted annually to the United Nations Economic and Social Council. For the text of the International Sanitary Regulations (WHO Regulations No. 2), see *Official Records*, No. 37, pp. 335–365. For background material, see C. E. A. Winslow, "World Health Organization," *International Conciliation*, No. 437 (March 1948), New York, Carnegie Endowment, and C. S. Ascher, "Current Problems in the World Health Organization," *International Organization*, Vol. 6 (1952), pp. 27–50.

5. For the work of the organization, see United Nations, Economic and Social Council, *Report of the Food and Agriculture Organization of the United Nations*, submitted annually.

6. For interesting documents on commodities, see United Nations, Department of Economic Affairs, Interim Coordinating Committee for International Commodity Arrangements, *Review of International Commodity Arrangements*, 1947; *Review of International Commodity Problems, 1948*, 1948; and *Review of International Commodity Problems, 1949*, 1950. For a bibliography on multilateral trade arrangements, see General Agreement on Tariffs and Trade, *Short List of Official Material Relating to the General Agreement on Tariffs and Trade*, 2d ed., Geneva, March 1952.

7. K. W. Colegrove, *International Control of Aviation*, Boston, World Peace Foundation, 1930, is an excellent study and a mine of information with texts of the early aviation conventions.

8. International Commission for Air Navigation, *Convention Relating to the Regulation of Aerial Navigation dated October 13, 1919*, Paris, 1929, Chap. I, Art. 1.

9. See O. J. Lissitzyn, *International Air Transport and National Policy*, New York, Council on Foreign Relations, Inc., 1942, especially Chap. XV, "The Diplomacy of Air Transport."

10. U.S. Department of State, *Proceedings of the International Civil Aviation Conference at Chicago November 1–December 7, 1944*, Washington, Government Printing Office, 1948, p. 43.

11. The first three years of ICAO are neatly summarized in U.S. Department

of State, *International Civil Aviation, 1945–1948*, a report of the representative of the United States to the International Civil Aviation Organization, Washington, 1948. For the annual work of the ICAO, see *Report of the International Civil Aviation Organization*, submitted to the United Nations Economic and Social Council; the Assembly of the ICAO records its work in the *Proceedings* and the Council publishes *Actions*. In addition to special studies, reports, and lists, the ICAO publishes a monthly bulletin of its activities.

12. Tallied from League of Nations, *Handbook of International Organizations*, 1921, pp. 32–128.

13. J. T. Shotwell (ed.), *The Origins of the International Labor Organization*, New York, Columbia University Press, 1934, 2 vols., is a comprehensive study of the ILO's history and establishment under the Versailles Treaty, with many valuable constitutional documents.

14. Quoted in P. Perigord, *The International Labor Organization*, New York, Appleton-Century-Crofts, 1926.

15. See E. Villetard, *Histoire de l'Internationale*, Paris, Garnier Frères, 1872, for the formation, organization, and principles of the First International. The appendix includes the constitution of the International and the national section of Paris, as well as resolutions of the International and documents of the Paris Commune of 1871.

16. For a compilation of labor legislation during this period, see B. E. Lowe, *The International Protection of Labor*, New York, Macmillan, 1921, pp. 171–329.

17. See G. N. Barnes, *History of the International Labour Office*, London, Williams & Norgate, 1926.

18. League of Nations, *International Labor Conference, First Annual Meeting, 29 October 1919–29 November 1919*, 1920.

19. See especially the speech of Sir John Ballingall Forbes Watson, director of the British Employers Confederation, in International Labor Organization, *A New Era: The Philadelphia Conference and the Future of the ILO*, Montreal, 1944, pp. 63–69. Consult also International Labor Organization, *The International Labour Code, 1939*, Montreal, 1941, for the list of conventions and recom-

mendations adopted by International Labor Conferences. F. G. Wilson, "The International Labor Organization," *International Conciliation*, No. 284 (November 1932), is a good study of the early history of the organization.

20. The data on ratification of conventions are taken from the *Seventh Report of the International Labour Organisation to the United Nations,* 1953, p. 100. In addition to the annual reports to the UN, information on the International Labor Organization and its work can be found in the *Provisional Records* (for the general conferences), the *Minutes* of the governing body, the *International Labour Review,* published by the International Labor Office, and the several reports of the special committees of the ILO.

21. See E. B. Haas, "The League and Colonial Policy Aims," *International Organization,* Vol. 6, No. 4 (November 1952), pp. 521–536, for a good study of mandate motivations.

22. See F. P. Walters, *A History of the League of Nations,* London, Oxford, 1952, 2 vols., Vol. I, p. 173, and H. Duncan Hall, *Mandates, Dependencies, and Trusteeship,* New York, Carnegie Endowment, 1948, p. 50. See also Q. Wright, *Mandates under the League of Nations,* Chicago, University of Chicago Press, 1930.

23. *Postwar Foreign Policy Preparation, 1939–1945,* U.S. Department of State Publication 3580, General Foreign Policy Series, 1949, pp. 109–110.

24. United Nations, Trusteeship Council, *Official Records,* First Year, First Session, 26 March 1947–28 April 1947, p. 1.

25. For a comprehensive pamphlet on the workings of the trusteeship system, see United Nations, Department of Public Information, *The International Trusteeship System and the Trusteeship Council,* 1949. For the work of the organization in detail, see the *Official Records* and the annual *Report of the Trusteeship Council to the General Assembly.* Of special note are the separate trusteeship agreements between the trust power and the UN, approved by the General Assembly, which set forth the terms of the administration of the trusteeship. For procedure on petitions, see United Nations, *Rules of Procedure for the Trusteeship Council,* Doc.

T/1/Rev. 1, 23 April 1947, especially rules 76–93, pp. 16–19.

26. I. F. D. Morrow, *The Peace Settlement in the German-Polish Borderlands,* London, Oxford, 1936, includes an extensive bibliography of publications issued by the government of Danzig, the League of Nations, and other sources. See especially pp. 15–180.

27. Versailles Treaty, Part III, Sec. IV, Art. 49. Italics added. A thorough study is F. M. Russell, *The Saar,* London, Oxford, 1951.

28. See G. J. Mangone, "Trieste Pawn in Struggle Over Yugoslavia," *Foreign Policy Bulletin,* Vol. 29, No. 2 (21 October 1949). For current developments, see the several reports of the military commanders of Zone A and Zone B to the Security Council of the UN.

29. From the declaration of principles, known as the Atlantic Charter, by President Franklin D. Roosevelt of the United States and Prime Minister Winston Churchill of the United Kingdom, 14 August 1941.

30. See N. S. Buchanan and F. A. Lutz, *Rebuilding the World Economy,* New York, Twentieth Century Fund, 1947; also R. F. Mikesell, "The International Monetary Fund, 1944–1949: A Review," *International Conciliation,* No. 455 (November 1949), and C. P. Kindelberger, "Bretton Woods Reappraised," *International Organization,* Vol. 5, No. 1 (February 1951). For the work of the International Monetary Fund, see the *Annual Report of the Executive Directors,* Washington.

31. A. Basch, "The International Bank for Reconstruction and Development, 1944–1949: A Review," *International Conciliation,* No. 455 (November 1949).

32. For the activities of the International Bank for Reconstruction and Development, see the *Annual Report* as well as the several *Loan Agreements* between the Bank and the borrowing states, all published in Washington.

33. See M. Vichniac, "Le statut international des apatrides," *Recueil des cours, 1933,* Vol. 43, Paris, Academy of Law, Librairie de Recueil Sircy, pp. 119–243, for a comprehensive treatment of the legal status of refugees after the First World War.

34. League of Nations, *Ten Years of World Cooperation*, 1930, Chap. VIII, and H. R. Greaves, *The League Committees and World Order*, London, Oxford, 1931, Chap. III, relate further details.

35. Fridtjof Nansen, *Adventure, and Other Papers*, London, Hogarth, 1927, p. 57.

36. The definitive work on UNRRA is *UNRRA: The History of the United Nations Relief and Rehabilitation Administration*, prepared by a special staff under the direction of George Woodbridge, New York, Columbia University Press, 1950, 3 vols.

37. United Nations, International Refugee Organization, *Third Annual Report to the United Nations*, Doc. E/2005, 6 June 1951. See also R. Ristelhueber, "The International Refugee Organization," *International Conciliation*, No. 470 (April 1951).

38. For an excellent review of the problems of statelessness as well as recommendations for further improvement of the situation through conventions, see United Nations, Secretariat, Department of Social Affairs, *A Study of Statelessness*, August 1949. See also United Nations, *Refugees and Stateless Persons and Problems of Assistance to Refugees, Report of the United Nations High Commissioner for Refugees*, Doc. A/2011, 1952, and *Report of the United Nations High Commissioner for Refugees*, Doc. A/2394, 1953.

39. For early background of child-welfare activities, see *Ten Years of World Cooperation*, pp. 297–299, and Greaves,

op. cit., Chap. X. For the International Children's Emergency Fund, see United Nations, *Final Report of First Executive Board of UNICEF, December 1946– 31 December 1950*, Doc. E/1908, E/ICEF/160, 1951; UNICEF, *General Report of the Executive Director*, Doc. E/ICEF/163, 1951; and UNICEF, *Financial Report and Accounts for the Year Ended 31 December 1952 and Report of the Board of Auditors*, Doc. A/2396, 1953.

40. League of Nations, International Commission on Intellectual Cooperation, *Work of the Twenty-first Plenary Session*, Doc. C.231.M.153 1939 XII, 10 August 1939, pp. 16–17.

41. T. Bestermann, *Unesco, Peace in the Minds of Men*, New York, Praeger, 1951, is a comprehensive study of the activities of the organization with an extensive bibliography.

42. *Records of the General Conference of UNESCO, Fifth Session, Florence, 1950*, 1950, p. 76. The work of the organization can be followed in the annual *Report of the United Nations Educational, Scientific, and Cultural Organization* to the Economic and Social Council of the United Nations. The *Records* of the General Conferences contain both proceedings and resolutions of the conferences; the Executive Board publishes *Resolutions and Decisions Adopted*, which indicates its main work. Various *Reports* to both the General Conferences and the Executive Board, sometimes by the Director-General of the organization, give other pertinent information.

I. *Extract—Fifth Report of the International Labor Organization to the United Nations, 1951*

It is the primary responsibility of the international organizations at the present time to re-emphasize that the attainment of the objective of a lasting world peace is more than ever dependent on vigorous action directed at laying the foundations of social and economic well-being. Political tension does not diminish but rather increases the importance of this task. There must be no diminishing of the international effort in which these organizations are engaged. The Economic and Social Council, in its resolution of 13 March 1951, emphasized that the unprecedented international effort of the United Nations and the specialized agencies in the economic and social fields is already proving to be of benefit to the world.

II. *Selected List of Meetings Convened by the International Labor Organization*

April 1950	Second Session of the Chemical Industries Committee	Geneva
April 1950	Preliminary Migration Conference	Geneva
June 1950	First Session of Asian Advisory Committee	Geneva
July 1950	Conference on Rhine Boatmen	Paris
November 1950	Third Session of Textiles Committee	Lyons
December 1950	First Session of Committee on Work on Plantations	Bandung
December 1950	Asian Technical Conference on Cooperation	Karachi
January 1951	First Session of the Committee of Experts on Indigenous Labor	La Paz
February 1951	Third Session of the Building, Civil Engineering and Public Works Committee	Geneva
October 1952	Third Session of Petroleum Committee	Scheveningen
October 1952	Second Session—Joint ILO-WHO Committee on Occupational Health	Geneva

III. *Typical Loans Made by the International Bank for Reconstruction and Development, 1946–1953*

Belgium: $30,000,000 for ten-year development plan in the Belgian Congo. September 1951.

Brazil (Guarantor): $15,000,000 for electric-power development. Sao Francisco Hydroelectric Co. May 1950.

Brazil: $3,000,000 for financing a highway program in the State of Rio de Janeiro. April 1953.

Colombia: $25,000,000 for importing equipment and services to improve the national railways. August 1952.

Ethiopia: $7,000,000 for road program and foreign exchange for new development bank. September 1950.

Ethiopia: $1,500,000 for rehabilitation and extension of telephone and telegraph systems. February 1951.

Finland: $2,300,000 for timber-production equipment. October 1949.

Iraq: $12,800,000 for construction of a flood-control project. June 1950.

Iceland: $854,000 to help finance a nitrogen fertilizer plant. August 1952.

Netherlands (Guarantor): $12,000,000 for the purchase of six merchant vessels. Four Dutch shipping companies. July 1948.

Union of South Africa: $20,000,000 for expansion of transport facilities. January 1951.

Yugoslavia: $28,000,000 for equipment for productive projects in electric power, mining, manufacturing, agriculture, fisheries, and transportation. October 1951.

IV. *Classification and Salary Scales of the Internationally Recruited Staff of the International Civil Aviation Organization, 1953*

The figures shown are net, that is, after deductions for the Staff Assessment Plan in lieu of national taxation on such income.

President of the Council	$20,290 (plus representation allowance of $3,600)
Secretary-General	15,000 (plus representation allowance of $1,800)
Assistant Secretary-General	10,700–11,500
Director	9,500–10,400
Principal Officer	8,750– 9,500
P–5	8,250– 9,250
P–4	7,300– 8,500
P–3	6,000– 7,525
P–2	4,800– 6,200
P–1	3,600– 5,000

In addition to this internationally recruited staff of professional workers, there are also General Service workers who are recruited locally and whose salaries range from $1,836 (Net—G–1) to $4,328 (Net—G–5). Staff in Director, Principal Officer, and Professional categories also receive an additional cost-of-living allowance of $500 per year. All the above figures are in Canadian funds. About 400 men and women are employed by this specialized international organization.

V. *The Structure of a Representative Specialized International Organization (UNESCO).*

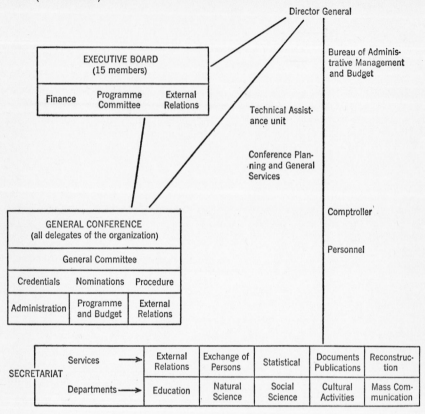

Director General

EXECUTIVE BOARD
(15 members)

| Finance | Programme Committee | External Relations |

Bureau of Administrative Management and Budget

Technical Assistance unit

Conference Planning and General Services

Comptroller

Personnel

GENERAL CONFERENCE
(all delegates of the organization)

General Committee

| Credentials | Nominations | Procedure |

| Administration | Programme and Budget | External Relations |

SECRETARIAT

Services →

Departments →

| External Relations | Exchange of Persons | Statistical | Documents Publications | Reconstruction |
| Education | Natural Science | Social Science | Cultural Activities | Mass Communication |

CHAPTER 8

The Rise of Regional International Organization

While the tide of international organization has been advancing up the shoals of world communications, commerce, health, agriculture, and education, reaching high-water marks with the League of Nations and the United Nations, several other channels to international collaboration have been cut by smaller regional groupings of states. The UN, indeed, expressly acknowledges regional organizations as playing an essential role in the maintenance of international peace and security [1], but recent political developments have aroused heated controversy over the type of regional arrangement permissible under the Charter.

The admonition of the Egyptian delegate to the UN Conference on International Organization in 1945 admirably clarified the meaning of regional arrangement, for he called it wrong to extend the term to alliances of a purely military character, these resting upon fortuitous political circumstances rather than affinities which would make them permanent organizations [2]. Transitory alliances which seek a quick military advantage over a particular enemy and do not combine economic cooperation, cultural exchange, and the progressive development of international law— all within the framework of a multilateral treaty—scarcely classify as regional international organizations. Invariably regional international organizations provide a secretariat to carry on the day-to-day work formulated and decided by the participating states.

THE INTER-AMERICAN SYSTEM

Standing alone for its continuity, its range of interests, and its unique promotion of international peace through collective security is the inter-American system which has fostered the Organization of American States.

The example of the federation of the colonies of North America after

249

their revolution and independence from Great Britain in 1776 fixed itself in the memory of Simón Bolívar, the great Liberator of South America. This amazing man, who roused a continent against Spain through personal eloquence and heroism, envisaged a league of nations "truly American, not formed merely on the principles of an ordinary alliance for offense and defense," and with unbounded energy devoted himself to the independence and federation of the South American colonies [3]. In 1815, disheartened by the first collapse of revolution in Venezuela, he wrote:

Would to God that someday we may have the good fortune to convene there [Isthmus of Panama] an august assembly of representatives of republics, kingdoms, and empires to deliberate on the high interests of peace and war with the nations of the other three-quarters of the globe. This type of organization may come to pass in some happier period of our regeneration [4].

Then, for nine grim years, Bolívar advanced, retreated, and advanced again, fighting in jungle coastlands, on scorched plains, and on sky-high mountains, to triumph ultimately in Venezuela, Colombia, Ecuador, Peru, and Bolivia. In 1822 negotiation began for the First Pan-American Congress, which Bolívar defined as "a counsel in the great conflicts, as a point of contact in great dangers, and as a faithful interpreter of public treaties, in case any doubt occur, and as a conciliator in differences which may arise [5]."

Bolívar dreamed one hundred years ahead of reality. The United States and Chile dawdled over the invitation to the conference until their delegates arrived too late; neither Bolivia, Brazil, nor Argentina heeded the call to action; and Great Britain, toward which Bolívar inclined most favorably as a protector of any South American organization, sent Edward James Dawkins under instructions not to participate in the discussions of the assembly. The handful of delegates from Colombia, Central America, Peru, and Mexico who gathered on the Isthmus of Panama 22 June 1826 soon crumpled the bold program of the Liberator into a small ball of paper resolutions. For the first time in the history of international organization the principle of general arbitration—with devices for mediation and conciliation—was introduced into a council of states, only to be chilled and put to rest for several generations. The key document signed by the delegates, entitled A Treaty of Perpetual Union, League, and Confederation, languished with one ratification. Independence had now been completely wrested from Spain, and the bright hour of unity split into ugly seconds of bickering and quarrels: Buenos Aires struck at Brazil; Mexico shuddered with political upheaval; El Salvador and Guatemala, Peru and Colombia came to blows; and Venezuela broke its tie with Colombia. Exhausted at the age of forty-seven, Simón Bolívar died with the bitter remark, "We have plowed the sea."

In an age of consultation rather than of continuous collaboration, the delegates at Panama in 1826 had singularly failed to provide for regular meetings and a permanent secretariat. Only the momentary panic of a military danger had impelled the gathering. Again in 1847 fear of aggression drove five states into the Congress of Lima to sign mutual-defense pacts, but the danger passed before the treaties were ratified. Similarly in 1856 and 1864 spontaneous conferences were held by Latin-American neighbors who sought safeguards for their national defense through alliances and provisions for the peaceful settlement of disputes. While the term "confederation" was slowly whittled into "family of nations," none of the proposed multilateral treaties secured the necessary complement of ratifications [6].

On 29 November 1881 James G. Blaine, U.S. Secretary of State, addressed a circular note to the United States diplomatic representatives in the capitals of Latin America directing them to invite each state to send two commissioners to a general congress to be held in Washington on 24 November 1882 "for the purpose of considering and discussing the methods of preventing war between the nations of America." The President, said Secretary Blaine, "desires that the attention of the congress shall be strictly confined to this one great object." In the meantime, however, President Garfield was assassinated and Chester Arthur, who succeeded him, did not hesitate to accept Blaine's resignation. Desultory war between Chile and Bolivia-Peru as well as the apathy of the United States Congress persuaded the new Secretary of State, Frederick T. Frelinghuysen, on 9 August 1882 to call off the congress entirely.

But the idea of an American assembly lingered in Washington. Six years later, the United States Congress appropriated $75,000 for a conference to consider measures to preserve the peace and prosperity of the American states, especially through the formation of an American customs union; improved communications; uniform weights, measures, and coinage; and "a definite plan of arbitration of all questions, disputes, and differences that may now or hereafter exist among them [7]." Thus it happened that at the call of the United States, the state regarded most suspiciously by Latin America, Simón Bolívar's rare vision of an organization of American states achieved the first outline of reality.

THE INTERNATIONAL UNION OF THE AMERICAN REPUBLICS

Thirty-seven delegates from eighteen American countries met in Washington during the fall of 1889. The First International American Conference passed a score of recommendations ranging from uniform weights and measures to the extradition of criminals and drafted an elaborate, farsighted plan of obligatory arbitration, but it seemed to achieve little in definitive action other than gallant courtesies, pompous speeches, and inflated toasts to the future. Prevailing opinion pronounced the Conference a failure. Nevertheless the wheels of a regional international organization were set in motion by a minor resolution of 29 March 1890 that the governments should create a bureau for the collection, tabulation, and publication of information as to production and commerce in American countries. On 14 April 1890 the Conference adopted a report of its committee on customs regulations which established the International Union of American Republics, with a bureau to be called the Commercial Bureau of the American Republics for gathering and disseminating information on customs tariffs, official shipping regulations, quotations from commercial treaties, and important statistics. An annual budget of $36,000 was prorated among the eighteen republics on the basis of population—with the United States paying half and Costa Rica as little as $75. The Bureau began so modestly that only nine employees, including a messenger and a porter, were assigned to the Director. But during the first four months 700 inquiries poured into the office and the initial 271-page Bulletin, which contained everything from historical notes on early American explorations and the recent cultivation of the banana to statistics on geography, consular regulations, and trade-mark laws, was distributed to no less than 50,000 subscribers during the first year [8].

The success of the Commercial Bureau of the American Republics was marked by publication of some seventy books, directories, and bulletins in the next five years. On 1 April 1896 the chief Washington diplomats of all except five states of the International Union of American Republics gathered at the U.S. Department of State offices to discuss the future of the Bureau and the enlargement of its work. A committee brought forth a plan which opened with the statement: "The Bureau of the American Republics is, for all purposes, to be considered as an international organization," and then went on to recommend that a permanent executive committee be established to meet once a month. Up to this time the Bureau had been virtually an adjunct of the U.S. Department of State, but with the unanimous adoption of the committee's plan the pace of internationalizing the activities of the Bureau (even on its actual budget of $28,000) accelerated. Henceforth, applicants for positions with the new International Bureau were to be examined by two examiners appointed by the U.S. Secretary of State *and* a board of the executive committee [9].

The International Union of American Republics had been created for a period of ten years by the delegates to the First International Conference of American States—with the expectation of ten-year renewals. On 15 August 1900, the Foreign Minister of Mexico invited the governments of the American states to participate in the Second International Conference of American States. Forty-six delegates from nineteen states met on 22 October 1901 to consider, for the first time, a program which had been prepared and submitted by the executive committee of the International Bureau of the American Republics. The scope of the Conference's work is indicated by the host of committees, including arbitration and court of arbitration, water transportation, commerce and reciprocity, Pan-American railway, patents and trade-marks, interoceanic canal, sanitary regulations, and practice of learned professions. While a score of protocols, conventions, and resolutions were adopted, the machinery of the regional organization whirred into higher gear. For the first time complete authority over the International Bureau was vested in a Governing Board comprising all members of the Union; the Director of the Bureau was granted the right to attend all meetings of the Governing Board and its committees; and the governments pledged to fulfill their quota of the Bureau's budget six months in advance instead of allowing the United States to bear the financial responsibility until contributions trickled in. By such gradual amendments, seemingly minor and unpolitical, the American states steadily moved in the direction of more permanent and more articulated international cooperation [10].

A single resolution of the Second International Conference of American States confirmed the continuity of the inter-American system. In part it read:

That the Third International Conference shall meet within five years. . . .

It is also resolved to recommend to each one of the Governments that they present to the next Conference a complete report of all that has been done . . . in obedience to the recommendations adopted by the First and Second Conferences.

In consequence, the republics of America met again in 1906 in Rio de Janeiro with fifty-three representatives from nineteen states. Almost the first order of business was a bold expansion of the functions of the Bureau: to supply information on educational matters, to assist in obtaining the ratification of resolutions and conventions adopted by the Conference, and to act as the permanent committee of the conferences by keeping records and recommending topics for future programs. The Director of the Bureau, for the first time, was *required* to attend the sessions of the Governing Board and was given wider powers over budget and personnel.

UNION OF AMERICAN REPUBLICS—PAN AMERICAN UNION

Step by step the successive inter-American conferences tightened the cords of international organization. In 1910 the Fourth Conference of the International Union of American Republics dropped the "International" from its title and changed the name of its Bureau, which had just moved into a new million-dollar building in Washington, to the Pan American Union.

The First World War postponed the Fifth Conference until 1923; at the Sixth Conference in Havana all twenty-one republics of the Americas were in attendance with no less than eighty-two delegates; the Seventh International Conference of American States met in Montevideo during December 1933. The magnitude of the First World War, the frequently mailed fist of United States diplomacy in Latin America, and the increasing interest in economic-social problems distinctly diverted the swollen agenda from the original items of commercial relationships to methods of maintaining international peace and the development of international law, communications, health, and cultural exchange.

GOOD OFFICES, CONCILIATION, MEDIATION, AND ARBITRATION

A landmark in the regional organization was reached in 1923 when a treaty was signed and ratified by a dozen American states which required all disputes not settled by diplomacy to be submitted to a commission of inquiry for an advisory report. Then, in 1928, among the fifty-odd resolutions of the Conference, the American republics took another step forward by accepting the principle of compulsory international arbitration in all juridical or "legal" controversies. This progressive act led to a General Treaty of Inter-American Arbitration in 1929, eventually ratified by no less than sixteen states. Finally, the Montevideo Conference of 1933 adopted a Convention on the Rights and Duties of States which emphasized "that no state has the right to intervene in the internal or external affairs of another" and that no territory or concession obtained by threat or coercion should be recognized.

Neither the Treaty to Avoid and Prevent Conflicts (1923), which pledged the American states to submit controversies to investigation and report of a commission of inquiry, the General Convention of Inter-American Conciliation (1929), which pledged the American states to use conciliation through a commission of conciliation, nor the Treaty of Non-Aggression and Conciliation (1933), which condemned aggressive war and denied all territorial changes made through violence, stopped the fierce Chaco War between Bolivia and Paraguay from 1932 to 1935. The Seventh Conference laboriously obtained a truce, but hostilities flared again within two weeks. Early in 1936, therefore, President Franklin D. Roosevelt took the initiative in calling an extraordinary assembly of the American states to "consider their joint responsibility and their common need of rendering less likely in the future the outbreak or the continuation of hostilities between them." In consequence a strong declaration of regional solidarity announced that every act susceptible of disturbing the American peace justified the initiation of consultation by the American states to find and adopt peaceful means of peaceful cooperation. Two treaties and two conventions reaffirmed and strengthened the procedures of good offices, mediation, conciliation, and arbitration as means to prevent conflicts.

Year by year, by fits and starts, the American states narrowed the irresponsible action of reckless national sovereignty. A series of conferences and consultations, the growth of a community forum and community opinion, and the hard facts of economic-social interdependence nicked both the blustering objections of national honor and the arrogance of total domestic jurisdiction. By 1938 the 21 republics represented by 118 delegates at the Eighth International Conference of American States at Lima were ready to confront a program on the organization of the peace which included (a) the perfection and coordination of existing inter-American arrangements, (b) the creation of an Inter-American Court of International Justice, (c) the creation of a league or association of American nations, and (d) a declaration with respect to nonrecognition of territory acquired by force [11]. No less than 112 declarations, resolutions, and agreements upon every facet of inter-American cooperation were approved in 1938, but the paramount addition to the regional organization was the Declaration of Lima which stoutly affirmed the continental solidarity of the American republics, proclaimed a common concern and determination to make that solidarity effective, and provided for consultations of American foreign ministers whenever necessary. Of less importance, but consistent with the historical trend of internationalizing the Pan American Union, was the recommendation that the Union make available to other international bodies information at its disposal, exchange points of view, and coordinate their investigations as much as possible.

STRUCTURAL CHANGES AND WARTIME CONSULTATION

In the meantime, the formal organization of the inter-American system changed to meet its widening international responsibilities. The U.S. Secretary of State had customarily headed the Governing Board, but in 1923 the chairman and vice-chairman were declared elective positions. Five years later, at the Sixth Conference, the Director-General of the Pan American Union received authority to appoint the personnel (with the approval of the Governing Board) necessary to the work of the organization, "endeavoring as far as possible to distribute the positions among the nationals of the countries members of the Union." For the first time, moreover, the organs of the Union of the American States were specified as (*a*) the International Conferences of American States, (*b*) the Pan American Union under the direction of a Governing Board, and (*c*) every organ that may be established by virtue of conventions among American states. Finally, each government was asked to establish a national Pan-American committee within its foreign office to facilitate the connection and exchange between the international organization and the individual state. At the Lima Conference of 1938 these national committees were given technical and administrative autonomy within the national governments as well as the right to correspond directly with the Washington secretariat [12].

In rapid succession three serious crises soon hit the smug isolation of the Americas from the world. Each time the ministers of foreign affairs anxiously met for consultation; each time another link in the chain of a regional organization was forged. The onslaught of Germany upon Poland in 1939 and the embroilment of France and Great Britain caused the first meeting of consultation at Panama, in September 1939, which agreed upon the general neutrality of the American states, designated a maritime zone to be free of belligerent activities, and passed resolutions upon contraband, humanization of warfare, and subversive activities. After France had fallen to the Nazi blitzkrieg and Europe lay gasping for breath, the ministers again drew together in the summer of 1940 at Havana, where they drafted a Convention on the Provisional Administration of European Colonies and Possessions in the Americas. Additional resolutions upon neutrality and continental solidarity bubbled to the surface of discussion. The catastrophe of Pearl Harbor, which actually extended the Second World War to the American shores, summoned the twenty-one states to Rio de Janeiro for immediate consultation in January 1942. After considerable nudging, the United States managed to have the meeting approve a resolution to break off diplomatic relations with the Axis Powers while reaffirming the good-neighbor policy and creating an Inter-American Defense Board, composed of military officers of the twenty-one republics, to study and recommend measures necessary for collective defense against aggression.

Chile had originally proposed a permanent consultative organ in 1938, and the United States had hoped for at least annual meetings of the foreign ministers. The objections of Argentina to a regional organization with genuine political functions had led to a watered version of meetings to be held "when desirable." Nevertheless, the logic of consultation in international crisis compelled three meetings within four years, and the Secretary-General of the Pan American Union studiously noted in 1942 that the meetings had already developed beyond their original purpose; indeed, with an extensive agenda of economic-social items, the meetings of the foreign ministers promised to displace the International Conferences of American States [13].

THE INTER-AMERICAN (RIO) TREATY OF RECIPROCAL ASSISTANCE

The closing months of the Second World War brought the American states to the brink of a complete regional organization. Dominated by the idea of continental security against enemies either within America or beyond the seas and urged to lace the economic-social strings of cooperation more tightly, the American republics (except Argentina) closed their ranks in 1945 at Mexico City. A new economic charter for the Americas and a resolution for the reorganization, consolidation, and strengthening of the inter-American system were proposed. The luster of the Conference on Problems of War and Peace, as it has been called, came from the polished Act of Chapultepec which succinctly and cogently summarized the principles of settling disputes by pacific means that had been affirmed at previous conferences and then, with dramatic clarity, declared: "That every attack of a State against the integrity or the inviolability of a territory, or against the sovereignty or political independence of an American state, shall . . . be considered as an act of aggression against the other states which sign this declaration [14]." Finally, the Act recommended that following the establishment of peace, the governments of the American republic should consider the conclusion of a treaty to establish procedures, such as breaking diplomatic relations, economic sanctions, and the use of armed force to prevent or repel aggression.

In June 1947 Brazil invited the American republics to a conference at Petrópolis in the state of Rio de Janeiro to conclude the Inter-American Treaty of Reciprocal Assistance suggested by the Act of Chapultepec, and 20 states (Nicaragua being absent) on 15 August 1947 assembled more than 250 delegates, advisers, and other assistants. Added weight to the signal importance of the treaty as a keystone to regional stability within the UN collective-security system was lent by the presence of sixteen foreign ministers and the attendance of the Secretary-General of the UN as an observer. George C. Marshall, U.S. Secretary of State, said: "We have for years been a community of nations, with deep traditions of cooperation and mutual respect. We turn now to the drafting of a treaty to establish community responsibility, to defend by collective action any member of our regional group that may be the victim of aggression [15]."

The sting of the Inter-American Treaty of Reciprocal Assistance was lodged in Articles 8 and 20, which provided that the Organ of Consultation (Meetings of Ministers of Foreign Affairs) could, in the event of aggression, rebuke the aggressor by calling for a rupture of consular and/or diplomatic relations, interruption of communications, or economic sanctions, and, should any such measures be approved *by a two-thirds vote* they would be *binding upon all parties* to the treaty. No state, however, would be required to use armed force without its consent.

THE ORGANIZATION OF AMERICAN STATES

The Act of Chapultepec and the Rio treaty had prepared the way for the triumphal Ninth International Conference of American States which met in Bogotá, Colombia, in 1948 to present a full-blown constitution to the Organization of American States. So carefully had the inter-American system been developed that the process of integrating the several components of the regional organization required little effort. The Inter-American Conference, convened every five years, became the supreme power of the Organization of American States; the Governing Board of the Pan American Union changed its name to "Council" while extending its function to supervision of the whole activity of the new organization—including an Inter-American Economic and Social Council, a Council of Jurists, and an Inter-American Cultural Council. The Meeting of Consultation of Foreign Ministers, in existence since 1938, merely settled under the wing of the Organization of American States and quietly took the title of the Organ of Consultation. The durable Pan American Union naturally continued as the secretariat, with its Director to be called Secretary General in keeping with the recent practice of international organizations. For the first time, moreover, the Organization of American States recommended that the budget of the Pan American Union be apportioned among the member states according to their ability to pay rather than prorated by population [16].

ECONOMIC-SOCIAL ACTIVITIES

Special conferences among the American states on pressing topics of legal, economic, social, or cultural importance had been held since the first American Congress of Jurists in 1877 to 1879 at Lima. In the next half century hundreds of technical conferences met to discuss health, agriculture, transportation, communications, international law, and so forth. Some of these conferences led to the formation of permanent committees, commissions, or organizations: the Pan American Sanitary Organization, most notably, dated from 1902; the American Institute for the Protection of Childhood, from 1927; the Pan American Coffee Bureau, from 1936; and the Pan American Statistical Institute, from 1940. No less than sixty "nonpolitical" treaties in the course of sixty years bear witness to the achievements of inter-American cooperation. The intergovernmental bodies hitherto established by these multilateral agreements were now swept into the new system with the duty of reporting periodically to the Council of the Organization of American States on their work and their budget.

Along with the monumental Organization of American States a treaty, known as the Pact of Bogotá, received the approbation of the Conference. It deftly gathered all the frayed ends of the various accords between 1923 and 1946, designed to prevent war by amicable adjustments, and proposed the stern obligation of all American states to settle their controversies by regional pacific procedures running the gamut of good offices, mediation, obligatory judicial decisions on legal matters, arbitration by majority vote, appeal to the ministers of foreign affairs, and a last resort to the Security Council of the UN.

By no means have all the bold plans and conventions of the inter-American system matured. Indeed, the hopes for a strong international organization both in the past and in the present are often buried under reams of paper; sometimes their weaknesses are covered by flimsy proclamations. It must also be recognized that the twenty republics south of the Rio Grande or in the Caribbean, with a population exceeding 150 million and including Spanish-Portuguese descendants, mixed Indian-whites, pure Indians (in Bolivia, for example, the major group), and Negro grandchildren or great-grandchildren of French, Spanish, and Portuguese slaves, have had an uneven historical development and hardly represent a single outlook upon constitutional order. The weaknesses of the national governments are naturally reflected in the weaknesses of the international organization which binds them together most closely. Long-standing rivalries among the Latin-American countries, the instability of some governments, and the fact that the United States is incomparably stronger than any of the other members of the region have all caused problems for the Organization of American States. Nevertheless, the achievements of the inter-American system in commercial information and assistance, in health, in legal procedures, in social welfare, particularly for women and children, and in cultural exchange are considerable. Regional international organization has facilitated and strengthened this work so fundamental to the environment of peace.

INTER-AMERICAN COLLECTIVE SECURITY

Scarcely a week after the Rio treaty had gone into effect the Organization of American States met a challenge to the security of the region when Costa Rica on 11 December 1948 applied to the Council in a dispute which alleged an invasion from Nicaragua. Within two months the Council, acting swiftly and effectively as a provisional organ of consultation, settled the controversy and brought the two parties to sign a new pact of friendship. The next appeal that stirred the Council to consultative action occurred on 3 January 1950, when Haiti charged the Dominican Republic with abetting a plot against the Haitian government. Three days later the Dominican Republic countered Haiti's charges with denunciations involving both Cuba and Guatemala as threats to Caribbean security. Again the Council, acting as a provisional organ of consultation, speedily set up a committee which visited all the states mentioned in the accusations. The findings of the Council, based upon the committee's report, exonerated none of the aforementioned states and bluntly called upon them to adopt measures ensuring the American principle of nonintervention by preventing any group, hostile to another country, from organizing on a military basis within their territory. On 30 June 1950 the Council's committee for supervising the implementation of these resolutions reported that "the tension in the Caribbean had been eased in large measure and the firmness and authority of the OAS has been thoroughly demonstrated [17]."

In the field of foreign relations the Council of the Organization of American States correctly took its cue from the UN action in Korea and on 28 June 1950 acknowledged unanimously its role as a regional agency of the UN while calling upon its members to comply with decisions of the Security Council. In the eyes of the United States the continued aggressive policy of international communism seemed to be an urgent matter of importance to the whole American community. The United States representative, therefore, requested of the Council of the Organization of American States in the spring of 1951 that a fourth Meeting of Consultation of Foreign Ministers be held. With counselors and technicians, the meeting eventually totaled some 400 people. Four directors of the Pan American Union assisted at the meeting, while ten observers from the UN were present. In the two-week session which closed in April 1951, a score of resolutions reiterated the theme of continental solidarity against aggression, expressed the determination of all to resist Communist subversion, and declared a willingness to coordinate military preparedness with economic development throughout the hemisphere [18].

It is not easy to assess the value of the Organization of American States. Perfection remains an aspect of God, not of political systems. Far from homogeneous, the American states admittedly suffer the evils of ignorance, poverty, and bad government. Too often declarations and resolutions have simply followed the lead of rich Uncle Sam who can bestow many favors on poor countries; too often the treaties and conventions so roundly applauded at inter-American conferences await long trials of ratification or find themselves thwarted by many reservations. Beginning with a meager budget of $26,000, the Pan American Union now spends over $2,500,000 annually to service the manifold activities of the Organization of American States. The contribution of the United States is two-thirds of that total. In the short course of their history, nevertheless, the American states have taken a good step forward by their consultation and collaboration on regional problems—economic, social, and political. A stout mechanism in the Treaty of Reciprocal Assistance and the Organization of American States is available to them, and it has already shown its value. The list of effective conventions in health, legal standards, commerce and communications, and human welfare grows. This kind of international organization seems to be a sound block in the building of the UN.

ARAB NATIONALISM

Another regional international organization to appear in the midtwentieth century was the Arab League, a group of eight states sworn to cooperation on the coarse, sun-beaten deserts and around the green crescent where once Rameses, Sargon, Cyrus, and Alexander had clanged and trumpeted with battling hordes.

For centuries the Arab peoples had slept in the murky dream of ancient caliphates while the Ottoman Turks rode over them, leaving behind native and foreign sheiks to command and plunder with ferocious rivalry. As the scepter of sovereignty slipped from the palsied hand of the "sick man of Europe," British and French weapons, money, and ideas arrived. Some brazen chiefs gained virtual autonomy. But pressed between the protection of western Europeans and the gasping efforts of the Sultan to centralize control in Constantinople, the will to complete Arab independence at the time of the First World War steeled itself.

Kingpin of the Arab revolt was the Sherif Husein of Mecca who cagily ruled the Holy Cities. He acknowledged the Ottoman suzerainty, but raised his staff of authority against all the prying of Turkish administration.

By October 1914, Turkey having joined the Central European Powers in war against the Allies, British diplomatists were vaguely promising to support an Arab nation in exchange for a concerted revolution against the Turkish command. The son of Husein, Feisal, visited secret nationalist societies in Syria, and they agreed upon an independent Arab kingdom comprising Arabia, Palestine, Syria, and Iraq as a condition for aligning themselves with the St. Petersburg–Paris–London coalition. When T. E. Lawrence finally stirred the Arab tribes of the peninsula to march on to Damascus against the Turkish forces, the Syrian nationalists took new heart from their ancient desert brothers. Meanwhile, Egypt, under the thumb of British advisers since 1882, reacted violently to the protectorate imposed in 1914. The nationalists, led by Saad Zaghlul, swarmed the streets of Cairo, shouting in the dust and heat for the independence of Egypt. In October 1916 the Sherif Husein was proclaimed King of the Arabs; in March 1920 a Syrian congress approved a new constitution making Husein's son, Feisal, King of Syria and Palestine; in the same month at Damascus a congress of Mesopotamians resolved to form an independent kingdom of Mesopotamia (Iraq) with Husein's other son, Abdullah, as sovereign; at exactly the same time the Egyptian Assembly passed a resolution for independence. Filled with historic memories, a common language, and the great faith of Islam, Arab nationalism bulged everywhere with expectations.

But these high Arabian hopes were soon dashed to the ground by three factors: French insistence upon control over Syria; British determination to guard her communications and investments in the Suez-Mesopotamian area; and Zionism. In consequence, France procured a mandate over Syria from the League of Nations, driving out King Feisal. Britain then accepted Feisal as King of Iraq, but forced through a treaty putting effective controls of the government in British hands. Abdullah, meanwhile, received the compensation of a new state, Transjordan, also firmly anchored to British money and arms. And while London solemnly pronounced Egypt to be sovereign in 1922, the special rights accorded to British troops left no doubt as to the ultimate political decisions. Finally, the British mandate over Palestine, driven like a wedge between the aroused Arab nationalists, thwarted their independence and allowed the free immigration of Jews into an overwhelmingly Arab community. Most Arabs discovered, therefore, that not only had the First World War merely transferred the reins of power from the Turks to the British and French but also that a foreign people were to be transplanted in their midst. Loud calls for Arab unity echoed in the streets of Cairo, Jerusalem, Damascus, and Baghdad, from the minarets to the bazaars and across the blazing desert [19].

ARAB COOPERATION OVER PALESTINE AND SYRIA

Between the two world wars the restiveness of the Syrians under the French rule and the steady filtering of Jews into Palestine especially encouraged Arab cooperation throughout the Middle East. In 1931 a Pan-Arab conference at Jerusalem had affirmed that "the Arab lands are a complete and indivisible whole." When, in 1936, the persecution by Hitler in Germany had driven thousands of Jews to seek refuge in Palestine, the Zionist issue made the Arabs bristle. Not only was the Higher Committee, led by Haj Amin el-Husseini, the Mufti of Jerusalem, formed of all Arab parties in Palestine to resist the further immigration of Jews, but a sputtering general strike called by the committee aroused the attention of neighboring Transjordan, Iraq, and Arabia—where ibn-Saud had ousted old Sherif Husein of Mecca in 1924. The rulers of these three states dispatched identical appeals to the Arab Higher Committee on 10 October 1936 "to resolve for peace in order to save further shedding of blood. In doing this we rely on the good intentions of our friend, Great Britain, who has declared she will do justice. You must be confident that we will continue our efforts to assist you [20]."

After the Royal (Peel) Commission of Great Britain proposed the partition of Palestine in 1937, the Arab Higher Committee sought the advice of the Arab rulers, and in the same year another national Arab congress was held in Syria to discuss Palestine. Slowly revolt, kindled by the Mufti of Jerusalem, burst into flames; by October 1938 a large part of Palestine had fallen into the hands of Arab patriots and cutthroats. After quelling the revolt, the British invited a delegation of the Arab Higher Committee to London in 1939, but no accord between Arabs and Zionists could be reached. The British government finally resolved to allay Arab discontent as the larger political menace of foreign relations and announced that only 75,000 more Jews were to be admitted into Palestine over the next five years, after which there was to be no further immigration of Jews without the consent of the Arabs; secondly, in some areas of Palestine, land sales to non-Arabs were to be prohibited.

The Second World War momentarily discredited the Mufti of Jerusalem, who engineered an unsuccessful revolt against the British in Iraq in 1941 and thereafter served the Axis cause [21]. The Jews in Palestine, meanwhile, girded themselves to break the 1939 restrictions upon immigration as soon as conditions would permit. In 1944, as the war moved to a close, the British Labour party (not yet in office) supported unlimited immigration to Palestine and both Presidential candidates in the United States came out for the Jewish cause. The Arabs watched fretfully.

Except for some Lebanese Christians, the Syrian congress of March 1920 had been overwhelmingly in favor of a modern independent Arab state. Nevertheless in April the Allied conference granted France a mandate over Syria; for the next five years France governed the Arabs with exceptional incompetence. The military commissioners, the stiff bureaucracy, the ragged economic measures, and the ignorance of Arab nationalism harvested revolution in 1925. Six months of grim fighting put almost all Syria, except Lebanon, under nationalist control. Even Damascus was briefly occupied. But French bombing planes, an increased garrison, and ruthless tactics gradually recovered the field. In 1926 Lebanon was splintered from Syria and declared a republic, yet French fingers pulled all the important political strings. Negotiations with the Syrian nationalists, meanwhile, dragged on until 1936 when a treaty was proposed which would have made Syria almost independent, allowing France certain diplomatic and military privileges. Even this precious agreement crashed to pieces in the increasingly fearful, conservative French parliament, and the High Commissioner suspended the Syrian government in July 1939. Two years later the Free French, determined to continue the struggle against Germany although France had been occupied, announced their intention of ending the mandatory regime over Syria and Lebanon, but they moved slowly in implementing the promise. Only the strikes of the populace and the diplomatic pressure of the British constrained the French to yield a large measure of autonomy to the Arabs in 1944, but the concessions, made during the war and unconfirmed by any French parliament, remained precarious. Again the Arabs watched the maneuvers of the Great Powers fretfully.

FORMATION OF THE ARAB LEAGUE

In 1944, therefore, the time was ripe for Arab collaboration. Little in the way of legal ties had bound the Arab states together prior to the Second World War, apart from a treaty of brotherhood for the peaceful settlement of disputes between Iraq and Saudi Arabia in 1936 which had been adhered to by Yemen. Although the Middle East Supply Center, established by the British to allocate and control the exports and imports of the Arab states during the war, had further tended to treat the region as a unit, it was not until 1943 that Nuri as-Said, the Prime Minister of Iraq, definitely proposed the formation of Greater Syria joined to Iraq in a league, a league based upon the union of countries of closest political and social conditions [22]. But the plan raised some fears among the Arab nationalists, and the tide of war events—with Syria's independence in doubt and Iraq sagging from an aborted revolution—soon swept the leadership of the Arab world to Egypt, the largest Arab state, a center of communications, and a hotbed of nationalism.

Urged by Iraq, the Prime Minister of Egypt, Mustafa Nahas Pasha, sounded out the leaders of the Arab states during 1943 and early 1944 on the advisability of a general conference on Arab cooperation. Accordingly, representatives from Egypt, Iraq, Syria, Lebanon, Transjordan, Saudi Arabia, Yemen, and the Arabs in Palestine met in Alexandria from 25 September to 8 October 1944 to discuss an Arab League. The protocol completed at Alexandria resounded with phrases appealing to "the Arab world," "the Arab peoples," and "the Arab nation," while it proposed a League to watch over and coordinate the interests of all Arabs; it called for pacific measures to settle disputes among member states, it required a uniform foreign policy on the part of the League—obviously against the French in Syria—and maintained that the rights of Arabs in Palestine could not be impaired without disturbing the tranquillity of the entire Arab world. Finally, the protocol boldly envisaged the League as the first step toward a more perfect Arab union. One Middle Eastern commentator wrote, "The preparatory conference at Alexandria, spurred on by the pressure of public opinion, produced results which exceeded almost all expectations [23]."

Five months later at Cairo the Arab states signed a Covenant of the League of Arab States along the lines of the Alexandria protocol, but sufficiently modified to stress the sovereignty of all member states: the article requiring a common foreign policy was politely omitted and the clauses looking forward to further unity completely scuttled [24].

The object of the Arab League is set forth as the coordination of political programs to achieve real collaboration among the members—extending similarly to trade, tariffs, currency, agriculture, industry, communications, cultural affairs, nationality passports, extradition of criminals, public health, and so forth. The major organ of the League is the Council, normally convened twice a year, which can act by simple majority in juridical disputes calling for mediation or arbitration, and, in event of aggression, may decide appropriate measures of restraint by unanimous decision. Subsidiary to the Council are a set of committees, notably the very active political committee, and various economic-cultural committees to formulate Arab agreements for general consideration. Permanence is given to the organization by a Secretary-General, appointed by a two-thirds vote of the League members, and his staff of the Secretariat located in Cairo [25].

The Covenant of the Arab League had been completed the month before the assembly of San Francisco met to draft the Charter of the UN. The founders of the League, therefore, keeping in mind the Palestine and

Syrian issues, craftily noted that methods of collaboration with the future UN were a major concern of the new regional organization. Special appendixes, moreover, asserted the *de jure,* if not the *de facto,* independence of Palestine, provided for a Palestine Arab representative to sit with the Council, and also foreshadowed cooperation with other Arabs aspiring to independence—implicitly the North African countries.

The end of the war in Europe in June 1945 exposed the wretched weakness of proud France and her utter incapacity to bring rebellious Syria and Lebanon to heel. With recognized independent governments, the Syrian and Lebanese delegates at the UN, vigorously supported by their sister states, made a final complaint in February 1946 over the presence of French and British troops in their territories. Shortly thereafter the European contingents were meekly withdrawn. Palestine now became the tempest center of all Arab agitation and the tortuous trial of the Arab League.

THE ARAB-ISRAELI WAR

During 1946 the British puffed and plodded through smoky conferences in London, gritting their teeth on the rancor of the Arabs and Jews but still plugging for a peaceful compromise. The United States elections in November, however, dragged American politics into the scene and spoiled the slim chance of moderation. On October 4 President Truman called for the immediate admission of 100,000 Jews into Palestine and the creation of a viable Jewish state; two days later Governor Dewey, also cocking an eye toward the New York Jewish vote, called for the admission of not 100,000 but several hundreds of thousands of Jews into Palestine [26]. The Arab League Council angrily recommended at its fifth session in Cairo that all member states immediately wire their delegates at the UN to protest this interference.

In Palestine itself terror shivered along the spine of the populace. The moderate Zionist groups could no longer control the violence of some Jews who took matters into their own hands. While the Arabs mobbed isolated Jewish settlements and slaughtered the helpless inhabitants, the Irgun Zvai Leumi and the Stern gang resorted to dynamite and savage assaults to drive out both British and Arabs. By February 1947 Great Britain, sick of the endless, hateful wrangling and the drain upon her resources, decided to lay the case before the UN. A special committee of the UN, composed of eleven neutral nations, recommended the partition of Palestine to the General Assembly in the fall of 1947; although this view, supported by the United States and two-thirds of the member states of the UN, prevailed, no state, including the United States, showed the courage necessary to enforce the decision on the reluctant peoples of Palestine. At the end of their patience, the British abandoned their mandate over Palestine on 16 May 1948; war broke out immediately.

During this period the Arab League seemed to act with vigor. In October 1947 the Mufti arrived in Beirut to join the Council in discussing the restriction of land sales to Jews, the collection of defense funds, the boycotting of Jewish goods, and military precautions to be taken on the Palestine borders. In December another secret Council session was held on the Palestine issue. In February 1948 economic retaliation against those states voting for participation in the UN was considered. When open hostilities finally began, the League decided to send regular armies into Palestine, and in April the League's military committee met in Amman, Transjordan, to coordinate these tactics. Still seven states of the Arab League, representing 40,000,000 people, completely lost the war to 650,000 Jews with their backs to the Mediterranean. How did this happen?

Stripped of rhetorical camouflage, Hashimite Jordan and Iraq entertained no affection for ibn-Saud, who had deposed the Husein family; some Syrian nationalists hungered for the annexation of Lebanon and Iraq; and King Farouk of Egypt showed overweening pride in tinseled ambitions. A wise Arab has written most candidly:

> In the face of the enemy the Arabs were not a state, but petty states; groups, not a nation; each fearing and anxiously watching the other and intriguing against it. What concerned them most and guided their policy was not to win the war and save Palestine from the enemy, but what would happen after the struggle, who would be predominant in Palestine, or annex it to themselves, and how could they achieve their own ambitions. Their announced aim was the salvation of Palestine, and they said that afterward its destiny should be left to its people. This was said with the tongue only. In their hearts all wished it for themselves; and most of them were hurrying to prevent their neighbors from being predominant, even though nothing remained except offal and bones [27].

Partly because of UN mediation and partly because of the collapse of their campaign against the Jews, the Arab states sulkily agreed to an armistice with Israel in the spring of 1949.

OTHER INTERESTS OF THE ARAB LEAGUE

Considerably discredited by the Palestine fiasco, the Arab League still found enough heat in the Jewish issue to keep the pot boiling: in May 1951, for example, the Council announced the creation of a central office in Damascus to coordinate the boycott of all trade with Israel; a few months later the political committee of the League, meeting at Alexandria, wholly supported Egyptian shipping restrictions on commerce bound for

Israel. But the obsession with Israel did not entirely eliminate other interests of an international organization for the Arab League. On 20 November 1946, for example, a cultural treaty for the exchange of teachers and students, the promotion of sports events, the consolidation of contacts between museums and libraries, and so forth was drafted under the auspices of the League. In September of the following year a general cultural conference, an engineers' conference, and an archaeological conference met under the League's aegis. On 15 April 1950 a Joint Defense and Economic Cooperation Treaty was drawn up in Cairo and, the signatures and ratifications of six Arab states having been secured, came into force in the summer of 1952. The notoriety of the League has largely been due to its concern with political issues like Syria, Palestine, or more recently the independence of Tunis and Morocco. But in 1951 the first inter-Arab economic conference met in Damascus to discuss the unification of currencies, the relaxation of customs barriers, and the removal of foreign-exchange controls to facilitate Arab trade. In 1952 the League, through its Council, dealt with such matters as the extradition of criminals, the facilitation of refugee movement between Arab states, and the creation of an office within the Secretariat to handle affairs dealing with Palestine and the plight of the thousands of refugees as a result of the war [28].

The coarse vanity of some selfish Arab rulers, their demonstrated incompetence in coordinating the Israeli war, and their apathy toward the welfare of the people explain the cynical attitude toward the Arab League as a regional international organization. During 1953, however, Libya joined the Arab League and General Naguib gave new leadership to Egypt. The ethnic and cultural ties are indisputable. Considering the paucity of the resources in the area, the level of education, and the little experience with independent government, one may be impressed with the inherent difficulty of the situation and the real achievement of the Arab states in forming a regional organization which is far from moribund and may germinate a peaceful, prosperous unity.

THE CALL TO EUROPEAN UNITY

Although the modern state system began in Europe and the history of international organization may best be traced through European conferences of the nineteenth century, a third major regional international organization, the Council of Europe, dates only from 1949.

Voices had been lifted for centuries to urge the establishment of a permanent association of European states. Some men, like William Penn or the Abbé de Saint-Pierre or Immanuel Kant, called for free leagues [29]; others, like Napoleon Bonaparte or Adolf Hitler, would have held unruly

Europe in an iron fist. While the League of Nations, supported by Great Britain and France, had a distinctive European design, its membership and interests spanned the seas and continents. The exhausting loss of political power and leadership by Europe to the American and Soviet-Eurasian hemispheres, however, as a consequence of two world wars, scored the plight of a small, many-peopled continent once a proud lady in the great show of international politics. Shorn of all her costly raiment by greedy wars and crammed between the juggernauts of East and West, Europe desperately looked to her own defense and her own rehabilitation.

Aristide Briand's brave proposal to the League of Nations in 1930 for a federation of Europe and Count Coudenhove-Kalergi's long crusade for a European parliamentary union [30] received scant popular support before the Second World War. At the end of that six-year cataclysm, however, a number of groups began agitating for the integration of Europe: the Socialist Movement for the United States of Europe, the European Union of Federalists, the Economic League for Cooperation, the French Council for a United Europe, and a Catholic drive, *Nouvelles Équipes Internationales*—all led by distinguished persons—were among the foremost. Real momentum was given to the idea of a European regional association by Winston Churchill, the Prime Minister of Great Britain through most of the Second World War, in a speech delivered at Zurich University in 1946 [31]:

We must build a kind of United States of Europe. In this way only will hundreds of millions of toilers be able to regain the simple joys and hopes which make life worth living. . . . There is no reason why a regional organization of Europe should in any way conflict with the world organization of the United Nations. . . . And why should there not be a European grouping which can give a sense of national patriotism and common citizenship to the distracted people of this turbulent and mighty continent, and why should it not take its rightful place with other great groupings and help to shape the destinies of man?

Late in 1947 the several unofficial groups working in the cause of European unity merged in an international committee and resolved to convene a Congress of Europe at The Hague. A stellar assembly of 300 dignitaries gathered in the Riddersaal on 8 May 1948 to be welcomed by Princess Juliana. They heartily adhered to resolutions calling for a United States of Europe with an assembly to be chosen by the national parliaments from their own members, a court of justice, and a charter of human rights. In the ensuing months a European Movement group, studded with such names as Winston Churchill, Léon Blum, Alcide de Gasperi, and Paul-Henri Spaak, unloosed a barrage of propaganda to sink the remaining doubts of the European governments as to the efficacy of action.

ORGANIZATION FOR EUROPEAN ECONOMIC COOPERATION

Meanwhile the worsening economic crisis of Europe and the menacing gestures of the Soviet Union on the eastern perimeter of the Continent had already roused intergovernment cooperation. In February 1947 the withdrawal of British aid to Greece dramatized the dwindling resources of the United Kingdom, and in June 1947 U.S. Secretary of State George C. Marshall proffered American aid for the rehabilitation of Europe. "The initiative," he remarked, "must come from Europe. The program should be a joint one, agreed to by a number of, if not all, Europeans." Even before a committee on European economic cooperation in Paris had time to report its plans, the President of the United States had to call a special session of Congress in November in order to appropriate 597 million dollars for emergency aid to France, Italy, and Austria. Nevertheless on 16 April 1948 fourteen European nations signed a convention establishing the Organization for European Economic Cooperation for the allocation and distribution of approximately 5 billion American dollars a year.

This official cooperative economic enterprise in Europe was paralleled by significant defense treaties. By the end of 1947 Great Britain despaired of further progress on postwar problems through the Council of Foreign Ministers (the United Kingdom, the United States, the Soviet Union, and France) "while one of those four Powers proceeds to impose its political and economic system on the smaller states." With these words British Foreign Minister Ernest Bevin introduced the hope to the Westminster Parliament in January 1948 that treaties with Belgium, the Netherlands, and Luxembourg could be signed along the lines of the Anglo-French alliance of March 1947 [32].

THE BRUSSELS PACT

The Communist coup in Czechoslovakia in the next month was the final nudge needed to join the five European states in the Brussels Pact on 17 March 1948. The key article promised all military and other aid and assistance by each party to any of the others subjected to an armed attack in Europe. Other provisions of the treaty sought the coordination of economies, the application of conventions on social matters, and the promotion of cultural exchange. For the purpose of consulting on all matters specified in the treaty, a Consultative Council was organized [33]. This Consultative Council remarkably proved to be the sire of the Council of Europe.

To the July meeting of the Brussels Consultative Council Georges Bidault of France suddenly proposed a complete economic and customs union as well as a federal parliament for all Europe. Great Britain flatly rejected this scheme. Again in October 1948 a plan for a European parliamentary assembly fired the agenda of the Brussels Consultative Council; again the British refused to involve themselves in such a comprehensive organization, but yielded an inch to forming a special committee for discussing a counterproposal—an all-European ministerial council.

While the European Movement group kept drumming on the need for a European assembly, the special committee of the Brussels Consultative Council met during November and December. As so frequently happens in the history of international organization, the aims of exuberant private associations and the conservative policies of national governments met, clashed, and compromised. The special committee recommended, therefore, that there should be a European committee of ministers, meeting in private, assisted by an assembly meeting in public and in a purely consultative capacity. Still piqued by the notion of an assembly and ever cautious about its role, Great Britain at length invited the representatives of Denmark, Norway, Sweden, Italy, Eire, and the other four Brussels Pact partners to London. On 5 May 1949 ten nations signed the statute constituting the Council of Europe [34].

THE COUNCIL OF EUROPE

The Council of Europe seeks greater unity among its members by discussing questions of common concern and agreements upon economic, social, cultural, scientific, and legal matters—indeed, all matters *except national defense*. Great emphasis is placed on human rights and fundamental freedoms, in the traditional European sense, as a qualification for membership in the organization. Greece, Turkey, Iceland, and Western Germany have been admitted to the Council of Europe as equal partners since 1949, thus enrolling the entire Continent outside the Soviet orbit—except occupied Austria, Yugoslavia, Spain, Portugal, and perennially neutral Switzerland.

The Committee of Ministers, including normally the foreign minister of each member state, acts upon all important matters by a unanimous voice and considers any definite action necessary to further the purposes of the Council of Europe. Unique to this organization, however, is the provision for a Consultative Assembly composed of representatives appointed by the several states in the proportions shown in the accompanying table. Furthermore, representatives are appointed to the Consultative Assembly "in such manner as Parliament shall decide," and in practice this has meant that members of national parliaments themselves, in numbers reflecting

Britain, France, Italy, Western Germany	18 representatives each
Turkey	10 representatives
Belgium, Netherlands, Greece	7 representatives each
Sweden	6 representatives
Denmark, Norway	5 representatives each
Eire	4 representatives
Iceland, Luxembourg, Saar	3 representatives each

the party divisions within their countries, have gone to Strasbourg. In the Assembly, finally, they sit not by states or by parties clustered together but as individuals in alphabetical order, and they both speak and vote as individuals. The powers of the Consultative Assembly are limited to declarations, resolutions, and recommendations which must receive a two-thirds majority vote of those present and voting [35]. In brief, the Consultative Assembly proposes and the Committee of Ministers disposes, but the Council of Europe, like other modern international organizations, has been able to jump the wall of a constitution and follow the lane of its political interests, at times subtly modifying the legal powers of the organization.

At its very first session in August 1949 the Consultative Assembly challenged the right of the Committee of Ministers to limit its program of work and, despite the majority opposition of the Committee of Ministers, special committees of the Consultative Assembly have met between sessions of the plenary body. A standing committee now meets four times a year to coordinate and facilitate the work of the Consultative Assembly. Although the statute prescribes annual sessions for the Assembly, the practice is to meet twice a year at Strasbourg. And how could any gathering of 132 European parliamentarians forgo the discussion of national defense in the mid-twentieth century?

With its surprising infant strength, the Consultative Assembly has asked the Committee of Ministers to consider the nomination of a minister of European affairs in the government of each member state, to temper the principle of unanimity in the Committee of Ministers, and to find a way of placing recommendations of the Consultative Assembly *directly* before the national parliaments. While the Committee of Ministers gave a rebuff to these far-reaching ideas, it could not ignore the pressure in the direction of freeing the Council of Europe from the ropes of absolute national sovereignty, and it did approve a new joint committee composed of five ministers and six members of the Consultative Assembly to maintain good relations between the two bodies of the organization.

Both the Committee of Ministers and the Consultative Assembly participate in nominating the Secretary-General of the organization who, in turn, appoints an international staff numbering over 200 men and women of various nationalities roughly proportionate to the populations of the member states. The six senior officers under the Secretary-General are respectively French, British, Italian, Dutch, Belgian, and German. The annual budget of the Council of Europe, about 2 million dollars, is also prorated among the member states on the basis of population, so that no member pays as much as 20 per cent of the total.

UNITING EUROPE

The Council of Europe is a young international organization, but it has gone a long way in four years. Although the President of the Consultative Assembly, Paul-Henri Spaak, resigned in disgust at the timidity of the governments to get on with the work of unifying Europe, the Council of Europe has kept nibbling at the cord of sovereignty with some effect. For example, the Consultative Assembly, which marks a radical departure in representation to an international organization, has acted as a vigorous sounding board of European opinion and a frank critic of national governments. Several times it has been a stimulant to the plans for legal, cultural, economic, military, and political integration of Europe. The first major achievement of the Council of Europe, the European Convention on Human Rights, had its origin in the Consultative Assembly. This document, signed by all members and ratified by some, including Britain, Germany, Norway, and Sweden, looks forward to a Commission of Human Rights, elected by the Committee of Ministers, and a Court of Human Rights, elected by the Consultative Assembly, to watch over the personal rights of life, liberty, security of person, free expression, free assembly, and other human rights of the people of fifteen states. While access to the Commission by *individuals*, a remarkable provision in the Convention, and the *compulsory* jurisdiction of the Court depend upon a specific declaration of the contracting states, the mechanism is available and at the very least governments have made binding pledges to observe human rights and can take legal action against each other under the Convention [36].

THE EUROPEAN COAL AND STEEL COMMUNITY

More famous than the Convention on Human Rights, however, has been the achievement of the first specialized authority under the Council of Europe—the European Coal and Steel Community, generally known as the Schuman Plan. At its first session in 1949 the Consultative Assembly discussed the necessity of internationalizing certain basic industries for the common benefit of Europe. A draft convention for "European companies" was prepared which contemplated interstate companies exempt from customs dues and multiple taxation, functioning under a European companies office. National governments, meanwhile, were wrestling with the same problem, and on 4 May 1950 Robert Schuman of France wrote a letter to the Secretary-General of the Council of Europe expressing interest in the European companies proposal. Five days later he made a historic statement on the necessity of pooling the coal and steel resources of Europe which eventually led to the European Steel and Coal Community. Throughout the negotiations among the six states concerned— France, Italy, Germany, Belgium, the Netherlands, and Luxembourg— which led to the signing of the convention in April 1951, the Council of Europe acted as a catalyst and constructive critic of the plan and, finally, was brought into a special relationship with the new Authority.

In the fall of 1952 the European Coal and Steel Community through its High Authority (eight members appointed by the governments of the contracting states and the ninth member elected by the other eight) undertook the task of establishing a single market in coal and steel, reducing interference with the free movement of these products by the elimination of customs barriers, import or licensing restrictions, discriminatory freight rates, and the impediments to the free movement of labor. The pricing practices of the producers are supervised by the High Authority and prices may be set (maxima-minima) if necessary. New borrowing and security issues for investment in these industries must be passed upon by the High Authority, while it may itself borrow for initiating investment in such ways as will "rationalize" the coal and steel community's production and marketing. A Council of Ministers representing each state serves as the official— and implementing—link between the High Authority and the national governments, but there is an Assembly with eighteen delegates each from France, Germany, and Italy, ten from Belgium and the Netherlands, and four from Luxembourg, which not only reviews the work of the High Authority but may, by a two-thirds vote, force the resignation of the High Authority. There is, moreover, a close relationship between the Council of Europe and the European Coal and Steel Community. The ministers of six states are identical in the Council of Ministers and Committee of Ministers of the two organizations; the members of the European Coal and Steel Community Assembly are drawn from the members of the Consultative Assembly of the Council of Europe whose states are parties to the Community. Strasbourg is not far from Luxembourg, and liaison through meetings, reports, and discussions has not been lacking.

The difficulties inherent in such a bold idea are readily apparent. Six states have been willing to lay aside for the moment their long-standing heartfelt economic nationalism and work together on the most essential industries for modern economy. By the end of 1953 the European Coal and Steel Community was in full operation—involving more than 400 steel mills and 800 coal mines. It had abolished customs duties, quotas, and various restrictions on currency exchange. Double pricing of coal and steel, as well as discrimination in transport rates, had fallen under its control. Without exception, so far, the orders of the High Authority have been followed and the rules of the Community's Court of Justice obeyed. The planning and organization are international. From such direct collaboration on a fundamental economic problem it is more than a hope that political integration will follow [37].

THE EUROPEAN DEFENSE COMMUNITY

The second and more crucial specialized authority of the Council of Europe is the emerging European Defense Community. To make an effective fighting force from Western Europe against potential aggression from the East required not only the close cooperation of the Western democracies as it emerged in the North Atlantic Treaty Organization of 1949 but also the use of German manpower, still greater than that of any other country of Europe outside the Soviet Union.

To regulate the ticklish relationship between new armed forces of Germany and the rest of Europe, a European Defense Community of six nations (Germany, France, Italy, Belgium, the Netherlands, and Luxembourg) was planned by treaty on 27 May 1952. Under its terms there would be a true fusion of national military contingents into an international European army, something utterly unprecedented in the history of international organization. Operating with a common defense budget, the six governments of the European Defense Community would appoint an administrative commission of nine men to supervise the military training program and a council of six ministers to harmonize the Community's policies with national policies. Unanimity on the total budget, the size and location of forces, and the appointments to high commands, however, would be required. Finally, an assembly, chosen as directed by the national parliaments, would be created to examine the budget and the reports of the administrative commission, while a high court would be established to settle any controversies arising out of the treaty [38].

The stunning plan for an internationally organized army is tied to the North Atlantic Treaty Organization by a concise agreement that an attack upon the European Defense Community would be regarded as an attack upon the North Atlantic Treaty members. The likelihood of the European Defense Community treaty taking effect depends upon France, which still fears the military dominance of Germany. Nevertheless, the plan, which tears at the very essence of sovereignty in national defense, has suggested even further the desirability of uniting Europe under one political community, and the focal point of official agitation lies in the Council of Europe. Following the resolution of the Consultative Assembly of the Council of Europe for drafting a constitution for a political community and the expectation in Article 38 of the European Defense Community that political integration would eventually be necessary for Western Europe, the Assembly of the European Coal and Steel Community met as an *ad hoc* or constitutional assembly in September 1952. The Assembly appointed a twenty-six-member committee with thirteen observers to draft a treaty of political federation for the six states of the European Coal and Steel Community and the nascent Defense Community. In March 1953 the constitutional assembly approved the draft treaty, which would establish two houses, both with weighted votes, under the supervision of a committee of ministers representing the national governments in the early stages only. Eventually the union would give France seventy seats, Western Germany and Italy sixty-three each, the Netherlands and Belgium thirty each, and Luxembourg twelve in the lower house, while in the Senate each of the large nations would have twenty-one seats, Belgium and the Netherlands ten each, and Luxembourg four. In the fall of 1953, therefore, delegates from France, Italy, West Germany, Belgium, the Netherlands, and Luxembourg assembled in Rome to elaborate a constitution for the proposed political community.

Other specialized authorities—in health and agriculture—for the Council of Europe are under discussion, and the Council is constantly interested in achieving legal standardization through conventions on extradition, reciprocal treatment of aliens, and visa regulations as well as the promotion of regional trade through such an organization as the European Payments Union, created in September 1950, to facilitate the convertibility of currency. Skeptics still nod knowingly about the stiff national independence which will bristle at any future inroads into self-determination and sovereignty. As a regional organization, however, the young Council of Europe has cut a notch upon the stock of history. No better evaluation of its place could be made than this:

. . . the work of the Council, with all its impotence, friction, and frustration, nevertheless, comes closer to a government of Europe than anything ever before attempted on any basis of free choice and voluntary collaboration. It likewise serves, albeit indirectly and painfully, the human needs and common interests of free Europeans more effectively than they have ever before been served on a European level. It is therefore certain that the Council of Europe will not die, but live [39].

International organizations vibrate with the promise of new things, of wider horizons, of bold undertakings, and in at least three regions of the world the pulse of international cooperation has been quickened by an elixir of fear and hope. The barrier is down and the track is clear. Under the larger purposes and powers of a universal international organization, regional associations like the Organization of American States, the Arab League, and the Council of Europe can take honorable places.

NOTES

1. Charter of the United Nations, Art. 52.

2. U.S. Department of State, *The United Nations Conference on International Organization—Selected Documents*, 1946, p. 194.

3. See J. B. Trend, *Bolívar and the Independence of Spanish America*, New York, Macmillan, 1948, for a succinct study and a very comprehensive bibliography. A recent, lively biography of the Liberator is W. Frank, *Birth of a World*, Boston, Houghton Mifflin, 1951.

4. See H. A. Bierck, Jr. (ed.), *Selected Writings of Bolívar*, comp. by Vincente Lecuna, trans. by L. Bertrand, New York, Colonial Press, 1951.

5. Quoted from D. F. O'Leary, "The International Congress of Panama," *American Editorial*, 82, in T. H. Reynolds (ed.), *The Progress of Pan Americanism*, Washington, Public Affairs Press, 1942, p. 17.

6. For this period, see J. Fred Rippy, *Historical Evolution of Hispanic America*, New York, Appleton-Century-Crofts, 1932; M. W. Williams, *The People and Politics of Latin America*, Boston, Ginn, 1938; and L. Duggan, *The Americas: The Search for Hemisphere Security*, New York, Holt, 1949.

7. For the notes of Blaine and Frelinghuysen and the text of the invitation to the Conference of 1889, see International American Conference, *Reports and Recommendations, together with the Messages of the President and the Letters of the Secretary of State Transmitting the Same to Congress*, Washington, Government Printing Office, 1890.

8. Bureau of the American Republics, *Handbook of the American Republics*, Bulletin 1, Washington, January 1891. See also H. Tavares de Sá, "The First 60 Years," *Americas*, Vol. 2, No. 3 (March 1950), Washington, Pan American Union.

9. Bureau of the American Republics, *Annual Report of the Director, 1896*, Washington, Government Printing Office, 1897, pp. 12–15.

10. Carnegie Endowment, *The International Conferences of American States, 1889–1928*, ed. by J. B. Scott, New York, Oxford, 1931, contains a convenient collection of the conventions, recommendations, resolutions, reports, and motions adopted by the first six International Conferences of American States; textual references have been taken from this volume.

11. *The International Conferences of American States, First Supplement, 1933–1940*, New York, Carnegie Endowment, 1940, contains the conventions, recommendations, resolutions, etc., of the Seventh and Eighth International Conferences of American States, the 1936 Inter-American Conference for the Maintenance of Peace, and the first and second meetings of consultation. Textual references have been taken from this volume.

12. See Eighth International Conference of American States, *Report on the Activities of the Pan American Union, 1933–1938*, Washington, Pan American Union, 1938.

13. See M. Margaret Ball, *The Problem of Inter-American Organization*. Stanford, Calif., Stanford University Press, 1944, p. 58.

14. See *The Department of State Bulletin*, 4 March 1945, for the text of the Act of Chapultepec.

15. *Inter-American Conference for the Maintenance of Continental Peace and Security*, U.S. Department of State Publication 3016, 1948, p. 8.

16. The Charter of the Organization of American States is in U.S. Department of State, *Ninth International Conference of American States*, Washington, Government Printing Office, 1948, pp. 166–186. Other relevant documents of the Conference are also included in this volume.

17. Pan American Union, "The Annual

Report of the Secretary General for the Financial Year 1949–1950," *Annals of the Organization of American States*, Vol. 3, No. 1 (1951), p. 24. See also *Peace in the Americas*, U.S. Department of State Publication 3964, 1950, for a résumé of measures undertaken through the Organization of American States.

18. "Fourth Meeting of Consultation of Ministers of Foreign Affairs of American States," *Annals of the Organization of American States*, Vol. 3, No. 2 (1951), pp. 126–157. For further study of the Organization of American States, see the *Annals* issued quarterly by the Pan American Union, Washington, which contain all official documents of the Organization as well as the annual report of the Secretary General.

19. A condensed account of the Arab world is G. E. Kirk, *A Short History of the Middle East*, Washington, Public Affairs Press, 1949. Of particular value for the study of Arab nationalism are H. Kohn, *A History of Nationalism in the East*, New York, Harcourt, Brace, 1929; G. Antonius, *The Arab Awakening*, London, H. Hamilton, 1938; and A. H. Hourani, *Syria and Lebanon*, London, Royal Institute of International Affairs, 1946.

20. J. Marlowe, *Rebellion in Palestine*, London, Cresset Press, 1946, p. 166.

21. The Nation Associates, *The Arab Higher Committee, Its Origins, Personnel, and Purposes: The Documentary Record Submitted to the United Nations*, New York, 1947, graphically portrays the connections between the Mufti and the Axis Powers.

22. For details of the plan, see M. Khadduri, "The Scheme of Fertile Crescent Unity," in R. Frye (ed.), *The Near East and the Great Powers*, Cambridge, Mass., Harvard University Press, 1951, pp. 137–177.

23. H. A. R. Gibb, "Toward Arab Unity," *Foreign Affairs*, Vol. 24, No. 1 (October 1945), pp. 119–129.

24. See C. A. Hourani, "The Arab League in Perspective," *Middle East Journal*, Vol. 1, No. 2 (April 1947), pp. 125–136.

25. For additional background on the Arab League, see V. McKay, "The Arab League in World Politics," *Foreign Policy Reports*, Vol. 22, No. 17 (15 November 1946), pp. 206–215, and J. C. Hurewitz, "Crisis in the Arab East," *ibid.*, Vol. 25, No. 20 (1 March 1950), pp. 246–255.

26. K. Roosevelt, "The Partition of Palestine," *Middle East Journal*, Vol. 2, No. 1 (January 1948), pp. 1–6, is an excellent illustration of domestic politics and their impact upon foreign policy.

27. M. Alami, "The Lesson of Palestine" (condensed from the book of the same title, Beirut, 1949), *Middle East Journal*, Vol. 3, No. 4 (October 1949), p. 385. See also P. Seabury, "Debacle of a Regional Agreement," *International Organization*, Vol. 3, No. 4 (November 1949), pp. 633–642. For a good account of the Israel-Arab war, see K. Bilby, *New Star in the Near East*, New York, Doubleday, 1950. An interesting personal report on the gestation and birth of Israel is A. Koestler, *Promise and Fulfillment, Palestine 1917–1949*, New York, Macmillan, 1949.

28. Text of Joint Defense and Economic Cooperation Treaty is in *Middle East Journal*, Vol. 6, No. 2 (spring 1952), pp. 238–240. For recent developments of the Arab League see *Middle East Journal* and *International Organization*, both issued quarterly.

29. For descriptions of proposed leagues and federations, see E. Wynner and G. Lloyd, *Searchlight on Peace Plans*, New York, Dutton, 1944, or S. J. Hemleben, *Plans for World Peace through Six Centuries*, Chicago, University of Chicago Press, 1943, as well as I. Jennings, *Federation of Western Europe*, London, Cambridge University Press, 1940.

30. R. N. Coudenhove-Kalergi, *Crusade for Pan-Europe*, New York, Putnam, 1943.

31. *The New York Times*, 20 September 1946, p. 2, has the text of the Zurich address. For a clear, brief summary of the major European international organizations developed after the Second World War, see American Committee on United Europe, *United Europe, A Statement of Progress*, New York, January 1951 and March 1952.

32. For the text of the Anglo-French Treaty of Alliance, see United Nations, *Treaty Series*, Vol. 9, No. 132.

33. The texts of the Benelux Customs

Union and the Brussels Pact, both keys to the formation of the Council of Europe, may be conveniently found in R. Strausz-Hupé and S. T. Possony, *International Relations*, New York, McGraw-Hill, 1950, pp. 918–924. Two good background studies are R. G. Hawtrey, *Western European Union*, London, Royal Institute of International Affairs, 1949, and "The Problem of European Integration," *Major Problems of United States Foreign Policy, 1949–50*, Washington, Brookings, 1949, pp. 403–472.

34. The text of the Statute of the Council of Europe may be found in *American Journal of International Law*, Vol. 43, No. 4 (October 1949), pp. 162–172. The Council of Europe publishes *Agendas and Minutes of Proceedings, Official Reports, Working Papers,* and *Compilations of Recommendations and Resolutions of the Consultative Assembly,* available from the Columbia University Press, New York. Also see *The Union of Europe: Its Progress, Its Problems, Its Perspectives, Its Place in the Western World*, Strasbourg, 1951, and American Committee on United Europe, *The Council of Europe: Consultative Assembly, A Report on the Third Session*, New York, 1952, Part II, as well as *Europe Today and Tomorrow*, published monthly, for recent accounts.

35. Council of Europe, Directorate of Information, *Concise Handbook of the Council of Europe*, Strasbourg, 1951, is the official guide.

36. Council of Europe, Directorate of Information, *The European Convention on Human Rights*, Strasbourg, 1952, contains both the text of the convention and background material particularly illustrative of the efficacy of international organization in strengthening international law.

37. Council of Europe, Directorate of Information, *The Council of Europe and the Schuman Plan*, Strasbourg, 1952, shows the relationship between the Council of Europe and the Coal and Steel Community. For other—very cautious—views of the Schuman Plan, see J. McKesson, "The Schuman Plan," *Political Science Quarterly*, Vol. 67, No. 1 (March 1952), pp. 18–35; W. N. Parker, "The Schuman Plan—A Preliminary Prediction," *International Organization*, Vol. 6, No. 3 (November 1952), pp. 381–395; and C. B. Randall, "The Schuman Plan," *Barron's National Business and Financial Weekly*, 17 November 1952, p. 5.

38. Succinct data on the European Defense Community may be found in S. B. Fay, "Towards the Defense of Europe," *Current History*, Vol. 22, No. 129 (May 1952), pp. 257–264.

39. F. Schuman, "The Council of Europe," *American Political Science Review*, Vol. 45, No. 3 (September 1951), p. 740.

APPENDIX 8

I. *Sections of the Annual Report of the Secretary-General of the Organization of American States for the Fiscal Year 1949–1950*

Time will show that our hemisphere's greatest contribution to human civilization is the political concept of international organization. It certainly cannot be said that the idea originated in the Americas, but ours has been the privilege of trying to put it into practice as soon as the weight of new powers in world politics was sufficient to gain recognition for their moral and juridical principles. Simultaneously with the United States entrance into the circle of the great nations came this republic's demand that traditional international politics be abandoned and a solution be found in international organization for the perennial problem of war.

But although our regional agency has met with great success, and it antedates by many years other experiments in international organization, its survival is nonetheless intimately linked with the fortunes of the United Nations. The OAS has a clear claim to the title of forerunner of the world organization. But the fame of precursors, however eminent, cannot be greater than the fame of those who actually make the dream come true. Should the world organization prove to be unworkable, the regional organization would find itself beset by all sorts of dangers. And in the end it would succumb, among other reasons because the United States would be obliged to make radical changes in their foreign policy to protect their security in a manner similar to that employed by other world powers. Our organization could perhaps become a military alliance of nations bound together by common strategic motives, but it would then lose its present high juridical and moral value. The American States are therefore staking the success of their international policy on a single trump card, which is collective security through international organization. And all fluctuations in the respect commanded by the United Nations, both in this hemisphere and elsewhere, must be a matter of serious concern to the OAS and every one of its members.

The OAS Charter is the most solid achievement of the American nations in their desire to provide a logical structure for their complicated system of multilateral relationships, which had developed unevenly, subject to the vagaries of propitious circumstances. As the Charter's influence on the organization's structure makes itself felt, in greater clarity and efficiency, public opinion understands better the real purposes of the organization and is more willing to support it. The governments themselves, pressed by many well-meaning groups to sponsor the widest variety of projects, whose only common denominator was inter-American cooperation, can now see clearly that our system is really just that, and that as such it has limitations, controls, balance, and interdependence among its parts. This is a definite advantage, because while it is true that the chaotic period of inter-governmental good will did produce cooperative activities in many fields, these were not always useful, nor did they have solid foundations, as indicated by the inactivity and the failure of many agencies that have died out in spite of a certain amount of government support.

It looks as though the days of vocal enthusiasm for Pan Americanism are over; and they no doubt left behind a number of net gains. But today the Organization must be made ever more the product of conscious and deliberate expressions of the will of the governments, and of their desire to assume additional obligations and to fulfill them as thoroughly as possible. The Charter, and the fundamental treaties that complement it, will be repositories for years to come of all that was stated as a hope, maintained as a principle, and sometimes recorded in the form of a convention, even though in some cases the instrument may have lacked juridical perfection. If, as seems likely, the time has come when all the efforts of sixty years are to bear fruit, the generations of living Americans and those to come will reap the harvest of the most persistent aspiration of the nations located in this part of the world.

II. *Teeth of the Inter-American Treaty of Reciprocal Assistance* (Rio de Janeiro, 2 September 1947) *and Charter of the Organization of American States* (Bogotá, 29 April 1948)

ARTICLE VII

In the case of a conflict between two or more American States, without prejudice to the right of self-defense in conformity with Article 51 of the Charter of the United Nations, the High Contracting Parties, meeting in consultation shall call upon the contending States to suspend hostilities and restore matters to the "status quo ante bellum," and shall take in addition all other necessary measures to re-establish or maintain inter-American peace and security and for the solution of the conflict by peaceful means. The rejection of the pacifying action will be considered in the determination of the aggressor and in the application of the measures which the consultative meeting may agree upon.

ARTICLE VIII

For the purposes of this Treaty, the measures on which the Organ of Consultation may agree will comprise one or more of the following: recall of chiefs of diplomatic missions; breaking of diplomatic relations; partial or complete interruption of economic relations or of rail, sea, air, postal, telegraphic, telephonic, and radiotelephonic or radiotelegraphic communications; and use of armed force.

ARTICLE XI

The consultations to which this Treaty refers shall be carried out by means of the Meetings of Ministers of Foreign Affairs of the American Republics which have ratified the Treaty, or in the manner or by the organ which in the future may be agreed upon.

ARTICLE XII

The Governing Board of the Pan American Union may act provisionally as an organ of consultation until the meeting of the Organ of Consultation referred to in the preceding Article takes place.

ARTICLE XVII

The Organ of Consultation shall take its decisions by a vote of two-thirds of the Signatory States which have ratified the Treaty.

ARTICLE XX

Decisions which require the application of the measures specified in Article VIII shall be binding upon all the Signatory States which have ratified this Treaty, with the sole exception that no State shall be required to use armed force without its consent.

III. *Scale of Assessments and Contributions of Member States for Support of the Pan American Union, Year Ending 30 June 1953*

Country	Percentage	Amount
Argentina	7.31	$ 209,044
Bolivia	0.35	10,009
Brazil	9.54	272,815
Chile	2.06	58,910
Colombia	2.17	62,056
Costa Rica	0.24	6,863
Cuba	1.94	55,478
Dominican Republic	0.30	8,579
Ecuador	0.30	8,579
El Salvador	0.30	8,579
Guatemala	0.35	10,009
Haiti	0.24	6,863
Honduras	0.24	6,863
Mexico	3.83	109,527
Nicaragua	0.24	6,863
Panama	0.30	8,579
Paraguay	0.24	6,863
Peru	1.17	33,459
United States	66.00	1,887,402
Uruguay	0.99	28,311
Venezuela	1.89	54,048

IV. *The Organization of American States*

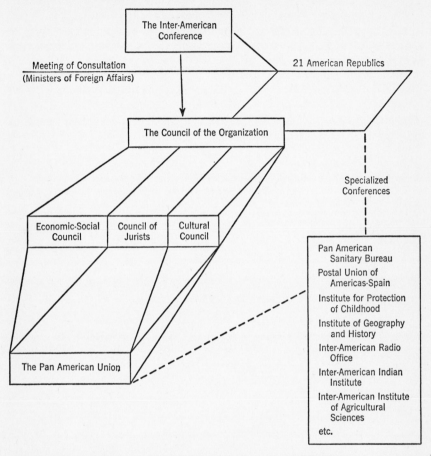

V. *The Covenant of the Arab League* (Cairo, 22 March 1945)

ARTICLE I

The League of the Arab States shall be composed of the independent Arab States signatories to this Covenant.

Each independent Arab State shall have the right to adhere to the League. If it be desirous of adhesion (to the League), it shall lodge a petition to this effect, to be deposited with the Permanent Secretariat-General and submitted to the Council at the first session convened after the lodging of the petition.

ARTICLE II

The object of the League shall be to strengthen the ties between the participant States, to co-ordinate their political programmes in such a way as to effect real collaboration between them, to preserve their independence and sovereignty, and to consider in general the affairs and interests of the Arab countries.

Likewise, a further object shall be close collaboration of the participant States, in accordance with the regime and conditions prevailing in each (individual) State, in the following matters:

1. Economic and financial affairs, comprising trade reciprocity, tariffs, currency, agricultural and industrial matters.
2. Communications, comprising railways, roads, aviation, navigation, posts and telegraphs.
3. Cultural affairs.
4. Matters relating to nationality, passports and visas, execution of judgements, and extradition of criminals.
5. Matters relating to social questions.
6. Matters relating to public health.

ARTICLE III

The League shall have a Council to be composed of representatives of the States participant in the League. Each State shall have a single vote without regard to the number of its representatives.

The Council's function shall be the realization of the objects of the League and to give effect to such agreements as may be concluded between the participating States relating to the matters indicated in the previous article and elsewhere.

A further concern of the Council shall be to decide upon methods of collaboration with the international organizations which may, in the future, be created for the preservation of peace and security and the regulation of economic and social relations.

ARTICLE IV

For each subject specified in Article II, a special committee shall be formed in which the States participant in the League shall be represented. These committees shall be responsible for formulating the bases, extent, and form of collaboration, in the shape of draft-agreements to be laid before the Council for consideration, preparatory to their presentation to the afore-mentioned States.

Members representative of the other Arab countries are permitted to participate in the afore-mentioned committees. The Council shall define the conditions under which those representatives may participate, and the regulations for representation.

ARTICLE V

Recourse to force to resolve disputes between two or more League States is inadmissible. If a difference should arise between them, not pertaining to the independence, sovereignty, or territorial integrity of [any of the] States [concerned], and the contending parties have recourse to the Council to settle it, then its decision is executory and obligatory.

In this eventuality, the contending States shall have no part in the proceedings and resolutions of the Council.

The Council shall mediate in any dispute which causes apprehension of a state of war between one of the League States and another, or one not [belonging to the League], in order to effect reconciliation between the two of them.

Decisions of arbitration and mediation shall be issued by majority opinion.

Article VI

Should aggression by a State against a member State of the League take place or be apprehended, it is for the State which has suffered, or is threatened with aggression, to demand that the Council be summoned to meet immediately.

The Council shall decide upon the appropriate measures to check this aggression, and shall issue a decision by unanimous assent. If the aggression emanates from one of the League States, the view of the aggressor State shall not affect the unanimity of assent.

If aggression should take place in such fashion as to render the injured State's Government unable to communicate with the Council, its representative at the Council may demand that it be convened for the purpose set forth in the foregoing clause. If it is impossible for the representative to communicate with the League Council, any of its member States has the right to demand that it be convened.

Article VII

Decisions of the Council by unanimous assent shall be obligatory on all the States participant in the League. Decisions of the League by majority [vote] shall be obligatory on those who accept them.

In either case, the decisions of the Council shall be executed in each State in accordance with its fundamental constitution.

Article VIII

Each State participant in the League shall respect the existing regime obtaining in the other League States, regarding it as a (fundamental) right of those States, and pledges itself not to undertake any action tending to alter that regime.

Article IX

Those Arab States desirous of closer collaboration with each other, and stronger ties than those specified by this Covenant, have a right to conclude such agreements between themselves towards the realization of these objects, as they desire.

Treaties and Agreements previously concluded, or which may be concluded with any other State, by any State belonging to the League, shall not be obligatory or binding on the other members.

Article X

Cairo shall be the permanent seat of the League of Arab States. The League Council may assemble in whatsoever place it appoints.

Article XI

The Council shall normally be convened twice a year, each March and October. Extraordinary sessions shall be convened whenever occasion demands, on the request of two of the League States.

ARTICLE XII

The League shall have a Permanent Secretariat-General, consisting of a Secretary-General, Assistant-Secretaries, and an appropriate staff of officials.

The League Council shall appoint the Secretary-General by a two-thirds majority of the League States. In consultation with the Council, the Secretary-General shall appoint the Assistant-Secretaries and the principal officials of the League.

The League Council shall create internal administrative machinery to deal with the functions of the Secretariat-General and matters of personnel.

The Secretary-General shall hold ambassadorial status, and the Assistant-Secretaries the status of Ministers-Plenipotentiary.

The first Secretary-General to the League shall be nominated in the appendix to this Covenant.

ARTICLE XIII

The Secretary-General shall prepare the draft Budget of the League, and submit it to the Council for approval before the commencement of each financial year.

The Council shall allocate the proportion of the expenses to be borne by each League State, and can review [the relative proportions in each case] as required.

ARTICLE XIV

Members of the League Council, members of its Committees, and those of its officials specified in the internal administration, shall enjoy diplomatic privileges and immunity during the performance of their duties.

The inviolability of buildings occupied by bureaux of the League shall be observed.

ARTICLE XV

The Council shall be convened on the first occasion at the instance of the Head of the Egyptian Government, and subsequently, at the instance of the Secretary-General.

At each ordinary meeting the representatives of the League States shall preside over the Council by rotation.

ARTICLE XVI

Apart from the conditions defined in this Covenant, a majority opinion will suffice for the Council to make effective decisions on the following subjects:
1. Matters [relating to] personnel.
2. Approval of the budget of the League.
3. The creation of an internal administration covering the Council, Committees, and Secretariat-General.
4. The decision to adjourn the sessions of a meeting.

ARTICLE XVII

The States participant in the League shall deposit with the Secretariat-General, texts of all the Treaties and Agreements which have been concluded, or may conclude with any other State belonging to, or outside the League.

ARTICLE XVIII

If any of the League States contemplates withdrawal from the League, it shall give notice to the Council of its decision to withdraw, a year before it puts the decision into effect.

The League Council has the right to regard any State not fulfilling the obligations of this Covenant, as having ceased to belong to the League. This shall be effected by a decision issued by unanimous assent of the States, excepting the State indicated.

ARTICLE XIX

It is permissible by agreement of two-thirds of the League States, to amend this Covenant, in order, especially, to render the ties between them firmer and closer, to found an Arab Court of Justice, and to co-ordinate the relations of the League with the international organizations which may, in future, be created to guarantee peace and security.

No amendment shall be passed except at the meeting following the meeting at which the proposal was [originally] presented.

Any State which does not accept the amendment has the right to withdraw on its becoming effective, without coming under the provisions of the Article preceding.

(N.B. The preamble, mode of ratification, and appendixes have been omitted.)

VI. *Excerpts from an Address by M. Stikker (Netherlands), Chairman of the Committee of Ministers and Chairman of the Council of the Office of European Economic Cooperation, to the Consultative Assembly of the Council of Europe, 7 May 1951*

The Reports which have been distributed among you illustrate, in my opinion, most convincingly that the Council of Europe is embracing an ever-widening field of activities and is also making progress in organising its functions in such a manner that searching analyses and studies of relevant problems can be made.

An ever-increasing part of the preparatory work is being done quietly by other organs than the Assembly and the Committee of Ministers established by the Statute. The creation of the Joint Committee of Ministers and Representatives of the Assembly has proved already to be a useful organ for mutual consultation. The work of the Committee of Ministers is prepared and expedited by meetings of the Advisers of the Ministers; experts drawn from the departmental organisations in various countries are studying complicated technical problems to prepare resolutions or conventions, which later have to be debated in the Assembly. Finally, the Secretariat has grown from the very modest body serving both

Ministers and Assembly into a fully-fledged international apparatus enjoying the assistance of excellent experts in a great variety of fields.

Even the most confirmed cynic will be unable to deny that the habit of European consultation is growing. This habit, I am glad to state, is growing far more rapidly than the constitutional framework which was set up for the work of the Council. Habits produce conventions, and conventions result in convictions. The short stretch we have gone on the road to European unity makes it difficult for us to assess exactly how much progress we have made. I for one believe that we are inclined to be too critical of ourselves.

It took Europe over seven centuries since its last unified effort in the Crusades to create a beginning of the realisation of the dreams of the Abbé de St. Pierre, the Duc de Sully and so many others.

Within the two years of its existence the Council of Europe has not only found a home in the city that once was symbolic of the strife between two of the great civilisations of Europe and has now become the symbol of the new unity, but the Council of Europe is also there to stay: to stay for much longer than the beautiful temporary building, in which we are now housed and which is only guaranteed for about ten years.

The functional integration of large sectors of European activity is hampered by very real difficulties. There is general agreement that the reduction of trade barriers would in the long run bring great benefits to the world, but the distribution of these benefits among various countries and among groups of producers and consumers would be uneven. In the short run the problems of adjustment, especially for producers, who have only been able to stay in business because of effective protection from international competition, seem to be insurmountable. It would be a false hope to suppose that the success of the policy of removing quantitative restrictions through liberalisation will be followed automatically by the removal of tariff barriers. The reparation of damage caused by the war and the injection of Marshall dollars have increased the possibilities for commercial intercourse, rendering superfluous the stringent restrictive measures of the period immediately following World War Two.

The functional integration policy needs far longer periods of transition and adaptation. A unified market is possible only when tariff barriers, which sometimes have protected industries for over a century, are effectively abolished. Certainly these are not walls which, like those of Jericho, will collapse after the trumpets have sounded seven times. Our problem, however, has this in common with that of the heroes of the Old Testament, who had to conquer the formidable fortress forbidding their entry into the Holy Land: that Faith remains essential in order to accomplish miracles.

The time is past when the world was divided into watertight national compartments which had few, if any, relations with one another. Even the federalisation of Europe, in which I firmly believe as a goal to be reached, will not atrophy but, on the contrary, will intensify the many links which unite the continent with the outside world. Not only to the casual onlooker, but even to one like myself who spends much of his time on the road or in the air travelling from one international meeting to another, the endless variety of global, regional, functional, statistical and dynamic organisations, official and private, seems bewildering. I am told that a "Handbook of International Organisations" has been issued numbering over 600 pages. Clearly, much effort is being wasted on organisational and legal work, which in fact goes by the board at the next unexpected turn of international politics. This, of course, is regrettable, but some of it is unavoidable, and the waste seems trivial compared with the heavy burdens, which the nations again have to shoulder for their defence; the military expenditure is the inevitable consequence of our failure to reach a common understanding with other nations on the globe, to whom we feel we can talk with confidence when backed up by sufficient strength.

The fact that Dutch and British, French and Germans, Italians and Greeks and the citizens of so many other nations who have fought countless wars against one another, now sit peacefully in this Assembly-hall to discuss our common problems, gives me confidence, a deep confidence, that we may eventually be successful in extending the spirit of co-operation also to those nations which so far have remained outside this or other peaceful associations.

The moral force of a harmonious Europe can still win a peaceful victory over those who are as yet unwilling to give priority to the power of reason over the weight of brutal force.

VII. *The Council of Europe and the European Coal and Steel Community*

The Committee of Ministers

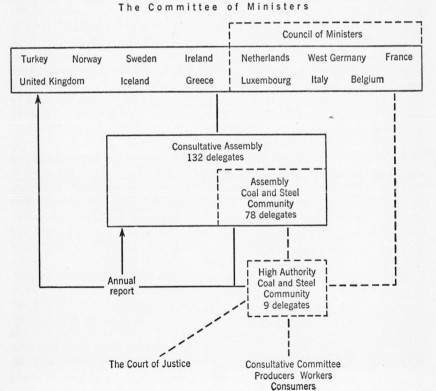

CHAPTER 9   *The Future of International Law and Organization*

The succession of international organizations now entering the stream of history defies count, and it would be impossible to do justice to each of them. Every year new intergovernmental councils, committees, and commissions—not to mention the host of private international groups—increase the flood. Some recent organizations, like the European Coal and Steel Community, arise from the hope of making an equitable and peaceful use of a powerful economic combine; others, like the North Atlantic Treaty Organization, spring from purely military considerations, but may have the capacity of developing in other directions; still others, like the Caribbean Commission or the South Pacific Commission, merely give advice for the administration of dependent territories. All of them, however, are trying to add threads to the web of international law over the untamed earth.

THE NORTH ATLANTIC TREATY ORGANIZATION

NATO was precipitated by the rapid deterioration of the alliance between the Soviet Union and the Western democracies made during the Second World War. Less than three years after the Potsdam Conference in August 1945 which set forth the Allied policy on defeated Germany, Russian-dominated governments had seized power in Bulgaria, Rumania, Hungary, and Poland. Turkey was threatened by Russia on the Dardanelles. Communists in France polled 5½ million votes, and in Italy they won the favor of almost one-third of the entire electorate. Germany lay prostrate, divided under four-power control unable to agree upon political-economic unity, and increasingly wretched. A Communist coup in Czechoslovakia during February 1948 finally pricked the lethargy of Western Europe. By the Brussels Pact of 17 March 1948, the United Kingdom,

France, the Netherlands, Belgium, and Luxembourg agreed to assist each other fully and automatically in the event of an attack upon any of them. Negotiations between these states and the United States and Canada, where the reaction to the Brussels Pact had been overwhelmingly favorable, began after the President of the United States had declared that his state would match the determination of the free peoples of Europe to protect themselves and the United States Senate passed a (Vandenberg) resolution which called for "the association of the United States, by constitutional processes, with such regional and other collective arrangements as are based on continuous and effective self-help and mutual aid, and as affect its national security."

Gradually the alliance was expanded beyond the original Brussels Pact partners to include Norway, Denmark, Iceland, Italy, and Portugal as well as the United States and Canada, so that on 4 April 1949 twelve states signed the North Atlantic Treaty. Early in 1952 both Greece and Turkey were admitted to the pact [1].

The North Atlantic Treaty is a short document, and its proponents have called it a "collective self-defense" arrangement under Article 51 of the United Nations Charter. In any case, after certain vague pronouncements on international cooperation in the opening articles, the high contracting parties agree that an attack upon one of them shall be considered an attack against them all and that they will take forthwith such action as they deem necessary, including the use of armed force, to restore and maintain the security of the North Atlantic area. While the Brussels Pact was worded more strongly, requiring all parties automatically to render all the assistance possible to an attacked member, nevertheless, this was the first time in history that the United States had committed herself in peacetime to go to the aid of a nation outside the Western Hemisphere in the event of attack.

To implement the treaty, a Council of Ministers able to meet promptly and decide policy was established. At present the Council of Ministers, consisting of foreign ministers, finance ministers, or other cabinet officers, meet two or three times a year, while a permanent representative from each state carries on the day-to-day business of the Council in Paris. A number of committees have been formed under NATO, all concerned with military-economic cooperation for defense, but the most important of all is the Military Committee, comprising the chiefs of staff of the North Atlantic Treaty states, and under it the Standing Group, a full-time military executive agency which meets continuously in Washington. The Standing Group, taking into consideration the national views on military matters which may be presented through the designates of the chiefs of staff in the Military Representatives Committee, is responsible for higher strategic direction, military guidance, and instructions for such NATO commands as the Supreme Headquarters, Allied Powers, Europe, and Supreme Allied Commander, Atlantic [2].

At the ninth meeting of the Council in Lisbon, during February 1952, not only was Paris selected as the permanent headquarters for the organization but it was decided to appoint a secretary-general, the final nail in the building of an international organization. Three years from the day of the signing of the treaty establishing NATO, Lord Ismay of the United Kingdom took the challenging position. Working under him are a Dutch deputy secretary-general, a French assistant secretary-general for economic affairs, an American assistant secretary-general for defense production, and an Italian assistant secretary-general for political affairs, as well as an international staff.

Through the North Atlantic Treaty fourteen states are cooperating to stiffen the defense of Western Europe against aggression. In doing so, however, they have run into fundamental problems for such an international organization, especially in realizing that military planning involves economic supports. As one commentator has written:

. . . except for the command functions vested in the military, no individual or agency of NATO up to the Council itself has any delegated power or authority. NATO is therefore not an administrative organ except in a very limited sense. It is rather a mechanism for formulating combined international plans; for obtaining agreement among the Treaty partners in support of these plans; and so far to only a limited extent for stimulating national action to carry out the agreed plans [3].

At Lisbon in February 1952 the Council achieved the consent of the contracting states to increase boldly their military forces ready for action and in reserve. Ten months later at its tenth session, however, the Council took a more conservative view on the need of increased numbers and stressed the quality of the forces. The drain of the Korean and Indo-Chinese wars upon the economies of the United States, the United Kingdom, and France forced retrenchment, and the immediate menace of the Soviet Union seemed to be removed to another area. Proposals by the Supreme Allied Commander in Europe for military construction were sliced in half by the Council. At its eleventh session in the spring of 1953 the Council urged the ratification of the European Defense Community.

The continuation of NATO as an effective military alliance must invariably face up to the task of closer economic coordination. Not only does its military strength depend upon a realization of the European Defense Community as a part of its program, but its work is inextricable from such organizations as the Organization of European Economic Cooperation and the European Payments Union, seeking to stimulate productivity and trade to improve the economic base for moderate, democratic governments while saddled with the burden of high national-defense expenditures. NATO is presently a single-minded agency with overriding military considerations, but its purposes parallel the Council of Europe for the integration of the Continent, and the mighty economic-military weight of the United States behind its operations pushes the sovereign states into closer cooperation through international organization [4].

In the Pacific area a new tripartite security pact, somewhat the same as the North Atlantic Treaty, went into effect among Australia, New Zealand, and the United States on 29 April 1952 [5]. It also established a Council, composed of the foreign ministers of the three states, which plans to meet annually to consider matters connected with the implementation of the treaty, and the Council has provided for permanent deputies to meet normally in Washington. The Australia–New Zealand–United States (ANZUS) Council has hardly begun its work, much less faced the larger problems that now confront the operation of NATO, but it has naturally begun with a Military Committee to consider plans for mutual defense and military assistance. Such secretarial services as may be required for the beginnings of this international organization are presently drawn from the U.S. Department of State and the Australian–New Zealand Embassies in Washington. In September 1953 the ANZUS Council met to review the work of its military representatives while it endorsed the view that under the present circumstances no question of the recognition of the Chinese Communist government or of the admission of its representatives to the United Nations should be entertained.

THE CARIBBEAN AND SOUTH PACIFIC COMMISSIONS

Apart from the two recent international organizations in the Atlantic and Pacific areas for mutual defense, the Caribbean and Pacific Commissions represent another young thrust of international cooperation through standing agencies. To the Trusteeship Council of the UN, created in the image of the League of Nations mandates system, the Charter added a strikingly original page for the benefit of dependent peoples. Indeed, Chapter XI of the UN Charter "constitutes the first general international instrument in history in which all states administering Non-Self-Governing Territories have agreed to be bound by a set of principles applying to all such territories." In their own colonies and dependencies, therefore, the members of the UN are obliged to advance the political, economic, social, and educational status of the native population, indeed, "to develop self-government." Regularly, moreover, states with dependencies are expected to transmit to the UN Secretary-General statistical information about territories under their legal dominion.

Such a concern for dependent peoples in the mid-twentieth century encouraged the formation of the Caribbean Commission in 1946 and the South Pacific Commission in 1947. France, the Netherlands, the United Kingdom, and the United States are each represented by a delegation of four in the Caribbean Commission to advise and consult on the economic-social problems of some fifteen dependencies. Significantly enough, there is a biennial West Indian Conference in which representatives from the territories themselves have an opportunity to discuss their problems with the Commission. A permanent secretariat at Trinidad gives further definition to this special type of international organization. Except for the addition of New Zealand and Australia and the size of each delegation being two rather than four, the South Pacific Commission, looking after another fifteen dependencies, closely resembles the Caribbean organization; it has established a permanent secretariat in Nouméa.

By means of conferences on such subjects as fisheries, timber resources, trade promotion, hurricane-warning systems, education, nutrition, and so forth, the interested governments have focused their attention on the needs of their dependencies in these regions, have profited from an exchange of views and experiences, and have moved in the direction of binding agreements to carry out the recommendations of the commissions. The technical-assistance program of the UN and the specialized agencies have been tapped for aid in health, agriculture, communications, and education, thus enforcing the gains of dependent peoples through the multilateral cooperation which only an international organization can bring to dependent governments [6].

INTERNATIONAL ORGANIZATION IN RETROSPECT
AND PROSPECT

What of the future of international organization? Does the dazzling increase in the number of organizations presage a spectacular epoch of world government? World government is a concept quite different from international organization. International organization derives from the collaboration of nation-states upon some common problems and the complete exclusion of a very large number of political, economic, and social matters of "domestic jurisdiction" from international action. World government requires the *permanent* yielding of substantial political power by the states of the world to some universal organization [7]. Nothing in the UN Charter, in the statutes of the Organization of American States, the Arab League, and the Council of Europe, or in any of the specialized administrative organizations established by international agreement indicates such a disposition on the part of the nation-states, whether giants or dwarfs.

The basis of international organization rests solidly upon the treaty or interstate contract undertaken on the good faith of sovereigns. Since the latter half of the nineteenth century an increasing number of such treaties have shared three distinct movements in the direction of international organization: *first,* they have become multilateral, signed by many nations and sometimes open to the adherence of many more; *second,* they have been self-perpetuating documents established with permanence in mind and allowing both instant renewal and gradual modification of terms; *third,* they have provided for active institutions in the form of periodic congresses and permanent secretariats.

The nation-state historically owes its creation to force; occasionally a voluntary accession or separation of territory has varied the drastic theme of politics, and once or twice in a century, under the most propitious circumstances, a tiny, free federation has crossed the void like a single flash in a galaxy of stars. International organization does not purport to unite nations. It attempts to provide the maximum conveniences for states that are willing to work together on common problems [8]. Military security, economic improvement, and social rehabilitation affect the people of every nation. On some aspects of these problems their governments have agreed to consult and collaborate through one international organization or another. But this is a far cry from world government empowered to mobilize the resources of the earth under one political hand and capable of piercing the present political sheaths of state, nation, or tribe to reach the individual. To federate all nations in one government is always possible, but highly improbable; to fasten states by force to a single empire has a better historical chance of success, but may cost world wars of calamitous physical and moral devastation.

The remedy for many world-wide ills in the mid-twentieth century seems so obviously to be international organization that one may take its hard, patient, persevering history for granted. The North Atlantic Treaty Organization, the European Defense and Coal and Steel Communities, the colonial commissions, just to mention a few of the late-comers, slide into an ideological and organizational groove worn by decades of progress. Simple, sporadic consultations antedated today's permanent councils, and prim secretaries, correct to the last diplomatic protocol, created the international bureaucracy which holds together the growing international organization. None of these changes came easily or rapidly. The International Bureau of Telegraphic Administrations, first of the score of permanent international administrative agencies, is still less than one hundred years old; the first significant congress at The Hague to standardize the rules of warfare and generally promote the law of nations has barely fifty years behind it; both the League of Nations, which gave the world its first permanent council of political conciliation and collective security, and the Permanent Court of International Justice, sire of today's International Court of Justice, can muster only thirty-three or thirty-four anniversaries; and the first application of force by the UN to repel an aggression is so new, so untested by time, that the judgment of history must await the future.

A grievous error would be the supposition that the pyramid of international organizations necessarily soars to the perfect apex of peace. The list of agencies dedicated to the ways and means of resolving international problems, of course, has grown by leaps and bounds. The refreshing universality of participation by equal sovereigns in the mighty councils of the world and their far-reaching accord on economic-social issues rightly embolden the faintest heart. On the other hand, the world moves at a snail's pace to eradicate the deep-seated passions of war. The greatest battles of history, unfortunately, have been fought between the richest nations, so that even the improvement of living standards by international organization bears no automatic augury of beating swords into plowshares. Rational men in the familiarity of their homes, the habitude of their community, and the security of their state touch the charged perimeter of violence every day. Between nations the fretful adjustments of territory, trade, and other tensions of power constantly jostle the keg of explosives.

What international organization offers is a way of channeling the egocentric drives of a sovereign state into world cooperation. The UN, the specialized agencies, the regional groups, and the hundred other guides of international collaboration provide the forums in which the states can raise and discuss their weighty problems, but it would be fatuous to ignore the fact that these organizations depend upon an ever-uneasy power relationship between states with vast areas, dense populations, fertile resources, high industrial productivity, or combinations of them. Such factors are dynamic; they are the stuff of international politics. International organizations may try to harness them, but their masters, the nation-states, have an unruly character and a wild spirit fit to break all traces.

As frequently observed, the UN cannot "solve" the contemporary tug of war between the United States and the Soviet Union. The precepts of international organization fashioned by national sovereignty and domestic jurisdiction easily allow a wide interpretation of obligations under the Charter. Crushing majority votes, moreover, in an international assembly where governments and not people are represented, have a mocking resemblance to the will of a democratic parliament. Mere membership in the League of Nations did not prevent Japan in 1931, Italy in 1935, and the Soviet Union in 1939 from taking the warpath. Should a state now feel that its vital national interest is not being served by the UN—as already is the case with the Union of South Africa with respect to South-West Africa, or the Latin-American states that failed to heed the resolution of the General Assembly on withdrawing diplomatic officers from Franco Spain, or the belated responses of the belligerent parties in the Israel-Arab dispute or the Kashmir dispute—then it will graciously skirt the recommendations of the international organization by legal detours or, worse, snub them entirely. As a last resort the nation may seize cudgels to gain its point, calculating that no force mobilized by the world community can successfully thwart its ambition. All the foregoing points apply with double vigor to the giant powers of the world today.

LAWMAKING THROUGH INTERNATIONAL ORGANIZATIONS

Nevertheless international organizations have certain advantages and sanctions with which all states must reckon. Foolhardy, indeed, would be the government which defied the Universal Postal Union and had to begin negotiating with scores of postal administrations for adequate mail service. Even the Soviet Union, which has practiced a forbidding isolation from the non-Communist world in a manner reminiscent of many past kingdoms of zealots, participated before the Second World War in international economic conferences; concluded treaties on patents, trade-marks, and copyrights; cooperated with the International Hydrographic Bureau, the Office for the Control of Liquor Traffic in Africa, and the Nansen International Office for Refugees; and acceded to the Baltic Geodetic Convention and the International Labor Organization as well as the Universal Postal Union. From 1946 to 1949 Russia dallied with the beneficent World Health Organization and still uses the technical facilities of the Universal Postal Union, International Telecommunication Union, and World Meteorological Organization. Despite the vituperation which the Communist government of China has lavished upon the UN, one of its chief points of political struggle has been to gain admission to it, not out of any magnanimous view of world society but for the international recognition which membership confers. Moreover, the possibility of sharing the relief and reconstruction funds, the technical competence, and the host of other services available through the UN and its specialized agencies draws the attention and respect of many nations. In a world where income is so egregiously unbalanced, international organizations can distribute eco-

nomic and social aid with less partiality than a rich, charitable state whose
government is naturally limited by the political temperatures of its executive, parliament, or other controlling interests.

Thus, before the regional associations or the UN resort to the punitive
sanctions proper to collective security, a number of gravitational pulls
within the system keep the roaming states within the orbit of international
organization. As the threat of reprisals by international collaboration
further limits the arbitrary conduct of governments, another step toward
an international legal order will have been taken.

The progress of making law for nations did not cease with the First
World War, although some of the old philosophical and academic systems
of "international law" suffered the blows of misfortune. As the nineteenth-
century active European community tried to apply its special international practices to eastern nations with different cultures, these practices were inevitably transformed. And the singular Christian, liberal
culture of Europe itself suffered the brutal attacks of state totalitarianism,
thereby wounding the traditional international relationships [9]. The
Hague Peace Conferences, which today seem to be rather quaint but un-
real, only reflected a contemporary attitude on what nations ought to do,
not a final, immutable code. No one can predict in either national law or international law how new technologies and revised social attitudes will affect future legal judgments. With adequate international agencies the
habits, opinions, and demands of states can be recorded, adjusted, har-
monized, and made acceptable as the legal norm. That is the paramount
mission of international organization.

Norms of International Behavior. The need for norms of international
behavior is manifest. As modern communications reduce time and space,
drawing every government and people into daily association and daily
competition, the need for communal responsibility is more urgent. No
society can survive without some law; only beasts tolerate the law of the
jungle. The society of nation-states, primitive as it may be, appreciates
two norms for international behavior. (*a*) Some fundamental rules have
been formulated by immemorial *custom*. The treatment of ambassadors
varies little from state to state. The very suspicious Soviet Union claims
no more than twelve miles of sea from her coast line, and 88 per cent of
the merchant-shipping tonnage of the world is registered with states that
abide by the three- or four-mile limit [10]. (*b*) By definition a *treaty* creates rights and/or obligations for the subscribing states. Sometimes a treaty
grants rights or imposes obligations upon members of the community
other than the contracting parties. For instance, the Hay-Pauncefote
Treaty (1901) between Britain and the United States opened the Panama

Canal on equal terms to all nations; the Versailles Treaty (1919) both created and imposed international obligations upon the Free City of Danzig; the provisions of great, multilateral treaties are likely to be accepted as the law for all nations, and both the League of Nations Covenant and the UN Charter have provisions which require nonmember states to act in accordance with their principles [11].

The clarification and codification of customary international law has been a long-standing object of international conferences, but in the main the resolutions, rules, and regulations of international organizations today serve to prepare, develop, and amplify the interstate compacts so fundamental to a mature legal order. The UN and its organs, for instance, are engaged in the strengthening of international law by the process of investigation, formulation, resolution, and opinion. The UN International Law Commission, to cite one agency, was established by resolution of the General Assembly on 21 November 1947 to promote the progressive development of international law and its eventual codification. The commission has been working on arbitral procedure; nationality, including statelessness, as a legal problem; the regimes of the territorial and high seas; and the law of treaties [12]. After painstaking inquiry and discussion, the fifteen eminent men of the commission may prepare a number of draft articles or an entire draft convention. Such draft articles do not bind states legally—as do fixed customs, treaties, or the decisions of international courts—but they serve as clarifications of the existing law or as pronouncements by qualified jurists as to a rational and desirable development of international law. In this form they have a good chance of finding their way into the reasoning of judicial decisions by courts or into the articles of a convention properly ratified by states.

The Economic and Social Council or the specialized agencies of the UN, to illustrate further the development of international law through international organization, are constantly occupied with studies of the needs of the world community. Such studies may bring forth declarations highly indicative of international opinion or may lead to concrete recommendations by an international organization to states. Most significantly, however, this work can—and frequently does—initiate international conventions aimed at placing legal obligations upon governments. Finally, the rule-making power of international agencies suggests the ability of an international organization to fill out a basic convention without requiring the specific consent of each contracting state for decisions taken under the general purposes of the treaty. In some instances (*e.g.*, the Universal Postal Union and the International Telecommunication Union), states are practically bound by rules made without their consent; in other cases (*e.g.*, the International Civil Aviation Organization and the World Health Organization), states are bound by rules of the organization unless they make an overt objection within a certain period.

In consequence of these activities of international organizations, one close student of international law has observed:

The specialized agencies related to the United Nations are thus developing the potentialities of international law both substantively and procedurally. With the gradual extension of international law to such fields as labor legislation, civil aviation, food and agriculture, currency stabilization, economic development, international trade, public health, human rights, dependent peoples, and other social, economic, and cultural problems, the scope of international law bids fair to become as broad as the recognized need for regulation of fields of human endeavor [13].

Day in and day out the actions taken in the councils and conferences of international organizations are spun into the ever-widening mesh of law. The individual filaments of this net of custom, treaty, and judicial decision are pliant and breakable, but the whole effect, strengthened by international agencies, is to tangle, slow down, and sometimes stop the blind flight of nations.

A New Legal Order. A competent legal order requires lawmaking, law-judging, and law-enforcing agencies. Traditional democracy has tried to separate these functions so as to minimize the excessive combinations of power which characterize tyranny. Whatever the mechanism, the study of the law is "the study of principles of order revealing themselves in uniformities of antecedents and consequents. When the uniformities are sufficiently constant to be the subject of prediction with reasonable certainty, we say that law exists [14]." The society of nations in a dragging, awkward, ponderous way seems capable of developing the institutions required for an articulate legal system, and throughout the history of international organization it has been constructing better and better devices for this purpose. The possibility that a blundering, merciless war might destroy such institutions, indeed, destroy the nation-state system itself, cannot be discounted. But optimism based upon a frank historical analysis does not seem completely out of place.

Legislation. The sheer increase of multilateral treaties and conventions, aided and abetted by the resolutions and regulations of international organizations, affects every facet of life, and it does crudely approximate "legislation" for a community which acknowledges no legal superior. Treaties are manifestations of international law: while they may obtain rights, they also may impose obligations upon states and, in any event, they are positive enactments open to the reasoned views and opinions of all men. Although international organizations do not legislate, as do national parliaments, they have developed regular sessions, copious agenda, divisions into specialized committees, plenary debates, permanent records, weighted voting, rules of procedure, and nonpolitical secretaries for administration. Such devices are excellent preparations for legislation. Limited, naturally, by the premise of national sovereignty and the lack of condign punishment for the bully, trespasser, or thief, international organization sets down the markers on the highroad to a law-abiding community.

Adjudication. For law judging in international cases some national courts have long and earnestly consulted the law of nations rather than the narrow terms of their own state's interest. By analyzing custom, treaty, and international opinion they have generally achieved a high standard of impartiality, building up thousands of instances of international law well-adjudicated and promptly executed by national authorities. The many arbitration panels, boards of inquiry, and mixed claims commissions, moreover, have eased the forbidding effects of sovereignty, thus facilitating conciliation and compromise. As early as 1831 the International Commission of the Rhine River was empowered to hear appeals from national courts; in 1907 four states established the Central American Court of Justice which carried on business for ten years. Under the aegis of the League of Nations and the UN, the International Court of Justice is a lasting tribute to the men who first recognized that a permanent tribunal constituted above state courts would be a necessary approach to a just international order. By its decisions and by its opinions given to the UN, the Court gives an authoritative interpretation of international law.

The movement toward the organization of international courts has not ceased [15]. Some Americans have constantly urged an international court for the Organization of American States; the European Convention on Human Rights, the European Coal and Steel Community, and the European Defense Community all anticipate a special adjudicating body. In the cautious quest to invoke the sanction of international law against the individual, as in the Nürnberg trials, one proposal after another for an international criminal court has thus far failed for lack of sponsorship. In 1951, the Committee on International Jurisdiction, appointed by the General Assembly in December 1950, brought forth a draft statute for an international criminal court [16], but the seventh session of the General Assembly late in 1952 sent the conservative document back to another committee for further examination. The difficulties of conferring jurisdiction upon an international court are formidable. Still held by the sensitive slings of sovereignty, the law-judging agencies will nevertheless diligently endeavor to fill, little by little, the crevasses of an international legal order.

Execution. The main reason why a halo of doubt circles the term "international law" is the lack of law-enforcing agencies. Without policemen and without a supernational brigade, the society of nations seems a sham, for all experience with political communities proves the necessity of some coercive agency to preserve the law by restraining and punishing offenders. One of the salient obstacles to the development of a police power for the community has been the doctrine that breaches of international law are torts, not crimes, that is, wrongs against particular states who must seek what redress they can, rather than a general menace to the community which should punish the crime itself.

Even without the hard hand of an international authority, the national officers regularly carry out legal judgments on international issues. Noteworthy, too, are the constitutions of such new states as the Philippines and Korea and such new governments as the Republic of Italy and the Bonn Federal Republic of Germany, which specify that international law is a binding, constituent part of their national law. Above all, however, the principle of collective security and the concentration of world opinion in the halls of international organization are steadily strengthening the idea of a community interest in international law and, therefore, a community police power.

The League of Nations flamboyantly declared that it would preserve the political independence and territorial integrity of all its members from external aggression and then went on to affirm that *any* war, whether immediately affecting members of the League or not, was a concern of the organization. Wishes often race ahead of deeds. Whatever selfish reasons dictated the plan for a Security Council in the UN, behind them was the concealed hope of strengthening the executive power of the new international organization. *Any* dispute or *any* situation which might lead to international friction may be investigated by the eleven-member Council, whose united might could easily enforce the rulings of international organization. Again the wish flies ahead of the deed, but whatever the UN action in Korea means to the foreign policies of the juggernaut states, it does involve and it does stand upon a principle of law enforcement. The Organization of American States offers collective security throughout two continents and pledges every member to use genuine coercion (short of war) if requested by two-thirds of the group, while the alliance under the North Atlantic Treaty extends a steel-ribbed umbrella over fourteen states and Western Germany. In truth, these compacts are primarily concerned with wanton military attacks, not the abiding principles of day-to-day justice among states. But the search for security is the essence of law. Collective security develops the idea of community responsibility and the public enforcement of law.

Furthermore, only a fragment of the sanctions of a society relies on overt force. Men obey their laws out of convenience, respect for tradition or opinion, a sense of duty, inertia, or habit. Fear of the police does restrain a potential culprit, but people ordinarily hew to the legal line for other reasons. So, too, international society has sanctions independent of a standing army; most customs, most treaties, and most rules of international agencies are fastidiously observed [17]. The multifaceted prism of international organization reflects a sharpening world opinion which can cogently express approval or disapproval of international actions. The policies of the nation-states, whether in the field of trade or finance, the treatment of colonial peoples, the nationalization of foreign concerns, labor, social welfare, or armaments, must be prepared to withstand the blasts of criticism carefully mounted upon international rostra. All this inclines governments to a sense of responsibility beyond the frontiers of the state and a mood to view the maintenance of international law as a public responsibility.

The history of international organization indicates a slow but reasonable way to a respectable world society. Screaming headlines of the latest catastrophe, the latest revolution, the latest aggression emphasize the unhappy plight of the twentieth century. That the world, lashed by so many misfortunes, manages to keep its head up and its feet forward is a wonder. But attention ought not to be diverted from the work of international organization, so courageously wrought, so intricately patterned, for here is a plan for universal progress and peace with justice in this time of troubles. Man in his tortured endeavors to bring law and order to his society is not beyond smashing such a design. Can the same intelligence which has learned to release the most fearful energies of the earth at one stroke continue in the patient pursuit of peace through international organization?

NOTES

1. Text of the North Atlantic Treaty was reprinted separately in *The North Atlantic Treaty,* U.S. Department of State Publication 3464, 1949. See also *North Atlantic Treaty,* Report of the Senate Committee on Foreign Relations, 81st Cong., 1st sess., 1949.

2. The development and significance of the North Atlantic Treaty with descriptions of its organization are in *NATO,* U.S. Department of State Publication 4630, 1952.

3. C. M. Stafford, "NATO's Growing Pains," *Foreign Affairs,* Vol. 31, No. 1 (October 1952), p. 96.

4. For other comments on NATO, see M. Salvin, "The North Atlantic Pact," *International Conciliation,* No. 451 (May 1949), New York, Carnegie Endowment; W. H. Draper, Jr., United States special representative in Europe, *Report to President Truman,* Paris, 22 August 1952; and W. A. Macintosh. "The Fissure in NATO," *Foreign Affairs,* Vol. 31, No. 2 (January 1953), pp. 268–279.

5. For text of treaty, see *Documents on American Foreign Relations,* Boston, World Peace Foundation, 1951, Chap. V. The communiqué of the ANZUS Council meeting in 1953 was published in

The New York Times, Sept. 11, 1953.

6. For the work of the Caribbean Commission, see Caribbean Commission, *Monthly Information Bulletin* and *Reports,* Port of Spain, Trinidad. See also A. B. Fox, *Freedom and Welfare in the Caribbean,* New York, Harcourt, Brace, 1949. For the South Pacific Commission, see South Pacific Commission, *Bulletin* (quarterly), and *Report* (annual), Wellington, N.Z.

7. The literature on world government and its various approaches and problems is quite extensive. See G. J. Mangone, *The Idea and Practice of World Government,* New York, Columbia University Press, 1951, which contains an extensive bibliography. In particular, see C. Meyer, *Peace or Anarchy,* Boston, Little, Brown, 1947, and C. Brinton, *From Many One,* Cambridge, Mass., Harvard University Press, 1948. For diagrams of peace plans, see E. Wynner and G. Lloyd, *Searchlight on Peace Plans,* New York, Dutton, 1944, and S. J. Hemleben, *Plans for World Peace through Six Centuries,* Chicago, University of Chicago Press, 1943.

8. For an incisive study of international organization along "functional" lines, see W. Levi, *Fundamentals of World Organization,* Minneapolis, Minn., University of Minnesota Press, 1950.

9. See H. A. Smith, *The Crisis in the Law of Nations,* London, Stevens and Sons, 1947, for a brief, penetrating analysis of changes in the traditional law of nations.

10. S. W. Boggs, "National Claims in Adjacent Seas," *Geographical Review,* Vol. 41 (April 1951), pp. 185–209.

11. H. Kelsen, *Principles of International Law,* New York, Rinehart, 1952, has an especially good chapter on this subject, "The Creation (Sources) of International Law," pp. 303–397.

12. See United Nations, *Report of the International Law Commission,* Doc. A/2163, 1952, covering work of its fourth session, 4 June–8 August 1952.

13. H. W. Briggs, "New Dimensions in International Law," *American Political Science Review,* Vol. 46, No. 3 (September 1952), p. 693.

14. B. N. Cardozo, *The Growth of Law,* New Haven, Conn., Yale University Press, 1924, Lecture II.

15. See M. O. Hudson, *International Tribunals,* New York, Carnegie Endowment, and Washington, Brookings, 1944, for a general survey.

16. United Nations, *Report of the Committee on International Criminal Jurisdiction,* Doc. A/2136, 1952, on its session held from 1 to 31 August 1951.

17. For the ubiquity and application of international law, see such works as L. Oppenheim, *International Law,* 6th ed., ed. by H. Lauterpacht, London, Longmans, 1944 and 1947, 2 vols.; C. C. Hyde, *International Law Chiefly as Interpreted and Applied by the United States,* 2d ed., Boston, Little, Brown, 1945, 3 vols.; G. H. Hackworth, *Digest of International Law,* Washington, Government Printing Office, 1940–1944, 8 vols.; C. G. Fenwick, *International Law,* 3d ed., New York, Appleton-Century-Crofts, 1948; and H. W. Briggs, *The Law of Nations,* rev. ed., New York, Appleton-Century-Crofts, 1952.

I. *The North Atlantic Treaty* (Washington, 4 April 1949)

The Parties to this Treaty reaffirm their faith in the purposes and principles of the Charter of the United Nations and their desire to live in peace with all peoples and all governments.

They are determined to safeguard the freedom, common heritage and civilization of their peoples, founded on the principles of democracy, individual liberty and the rule of law.

They seek to promote stability and well-being in the North Atlantic area.

They are resolved to unite their efforts for collective defense and for the preservation of peace and security.

They therefore agree to this North Atlantic Treaty:

ARTICLE 1

The Parties undertake, as set forth in the Charter of the United Nations, to settle any international disputes in which they may be involved by peaceful means in such a manner that international peace and security, and justice, are not endangered, and to refrain in their international relations from the threat or use of force in any manner inconsistent with the purposes of the United Nations.

ARTICLE 2

The Parties will contribute toward the further development of peaceful and friendly international relations by strengthening their free institutions, by bringing about a better understanding of the principles upon which these institutions are founded, and by promoting conditions of stability and well-being. They will seek to eliminate conflict in their international economic policies and will encourage economic collaboration between any or all of them.

ARTICLE 3

In order more effectively to achieve the objectives of this Treaty, the Parties, separately and jointly, by means of continuous and effective self-help and mutual aid, will maintain and develop their individual and collective capacity to resist armed attack.

ARTICLE 4

The Parties will consult together whenever, in the opinion of any of them, the territorial integrity, political independence or security of any of the Parties is threatened.

ARTICLE 5

The Parties agree that an armed attack against one or more of them in Europe or North America shall be considered an attack against them all; and consequently they agree that, if such an armed attack occurs, each of them, in exercise of the right of individual or collective self-defense recognized by Article 51 of the Charter of the United Nations, will assist the Party or Parties so attacked by taking forthwith, individually and in concert with the other Parties, such action as it deems necessary, including the use of armed force, to restore and maintain the security of the North Atlantic area.

Any such armed attack and all measures taken as a result thereof shall immediately be reported to the Security Council. Such measures shall be terminated when the Security Council has taken the measures necessary to restore and maintain international peace and security.

ARTICLE 6

For the purpose of Article 5 an armed attack on one or more of the Parties is deemed to include an armed attack on the territory of any of the Parties in Europe or North America, on the Algerian departments of France, on the occupation forces of any Party in Europe, on the islands under the jurisdiction of any Party in the North Atlantic area north of the Tropic of Cancer, or on the vessels or aircraft in this area of any of the Parties.

ARTICLE 7

This Treaty does not affect, and shall not be interpreted as affecting, in any way the rights and obligations under the Charter of the Parties which are members of the United Nations, or the primary responsibility of the Security Council for the maintenance of international peace and security.

ARTICLE 8

Each Party declares that none of the international agreements now in force between it and any other of the Parties or any third state is in conflict with the provisions of this Treaty, and undertakes not to enter into any international engagement in conflict with this Treaty.

ARTICLE 9

The Parties hereby establish a council, on which each of them shall be represented, to consider matters concerning the implementation of this Treaty. The council shall be so organized as to be able to meet promptly at any time. The council shall set up such subsidiary bodies as may be necessary; in particular it shall establish immediately a defense committee which shall recommend measures for the implementation of Articles 3 and 5.

ARTICLE 10

The Parties may, by unanimous agreement, invite any other European state in a position to further the principles of this Treaty and to contribute to the security of the North Atlantic area to accede to this Treaty. Any state so invited may become a party to the Treaty by depositing its instrument of accession with the Government of the United States of America. The Government of the United States of America will inform each of the Parties of the deposit of each such instrument of accession.

Articles 11 to 14 deal with provisions for ratification, reviewing, denunciation, and deposit of the Treaty.

II. *The North Atlantic Treaty Organization*

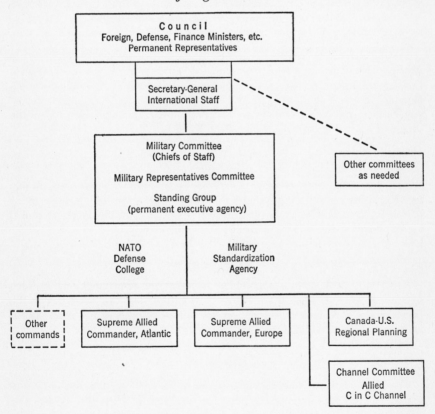

III. *Recent Conventions Concluded Under the Auspices of the United Nations But Excluding Others Drawn up under the Auspices of the Specialized Agencies*

1. Convention Relating to the Status of Refugees, signed at Geneva, 28 July 1951.

2. First Protocol of Rectifications and Modifications to the Texts of the Schedules to the General Agreement on Tariffs and Trade, signed at Geneva, 27 October 1951.

3. International Convention to Facilitate the Crossing of Frontiers for Passengers and Baggage Carried by Rail, signed at Geneva, 10 January 1952.

4. Convention on the Declaration of Death of Missing Persons, entered into force 24 January 1952.

5. Agreement on the Importation of Educational, Scientific, and Cultural Materials, entered into force 21 May 1952.

6. Convention on Political Status of Women, open to signature at conclusion of seventh session of General Assembly, 1953.

7. Convention on the International Right of (News) Correction, open to signature at the conclusion of the seventh session of General Assembly, 1953.

8. Protocol for Limiting and Regulating the Cultivation of the Poppy Plant, open to signature at New York, 23 June 1953.

The number of international agreements for which the Secretary-General of the United Nations exercises depositary functions has risen to 104, not including agreements concluded under the auspices of the League of Nations for which the Secretary-General exercises depositary functions.

Between 14 December 1946 and 30 June 1953 the number of treaties and international agreements registered or filed and recorded with the UN, including subsequent actions regarding these treaties, was 4,312. In the single year ending 30 June 1953, 579 treaties and international agreements were registered or filed and recorded by nineteen governments, 307 by five specialized agencies, and 175 *ex officio* by the Secretariat. (Information drawn from United Nations, General Assembly, *Annual Report of the Secretary-General on the Work of the Organization, 1 July 1952–30 June 1953*, 1953.)

IV. *Hypothetical International Legislation via International Organization*

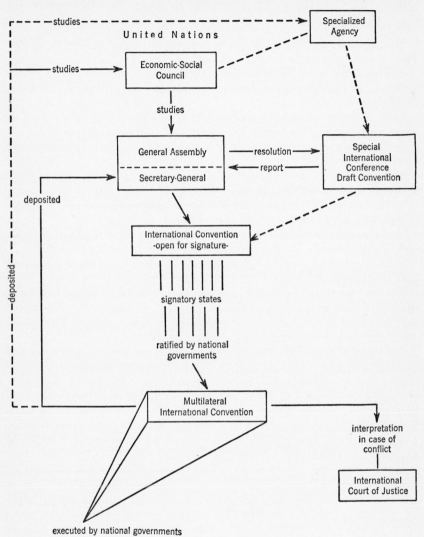

Index

311

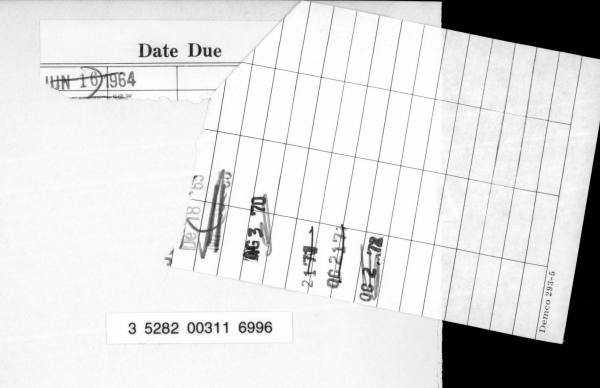